# Speaking of Indigenous Politics

# INDIGENOUS AMERICAS

ROBERT WARRIOR, SERIES EDITOR

Chadwick Allen, *Trans-Indigenous: Methodologies for Global Native Literary Studies*

Raymond D. Austin, *Navajo Courts and Navajo Common Law: A Tradition of Tribal Self-Governance*

Lisa Brooks, *The Common Pot: The Recovery of Native Space in the Northeast*

Kevin Bruyneel, *The Third Space of Sovereignty: The Postcolonial Politics of U.S.–Indigenous Relations*

Glen Sean Coulthard, *Red Skin, White Masks: Rejecting the Colonial Politics of Recognition*

James H. Cox, *The Red Land to the South: American Indian Writers and Indigenous Mexico*

Brendan Hokowhitu and Vijay Devadas, *The Fourth Eye: Māori Media in Aotearoa New Zealand*

Daniel Heath Justice, *Our Fire Survives the Storm: A Cherokee Literary History*

J. Kēhaulani Kauanui, *Speaking of Indigenous Politics: Conversations with Activists, Scholars, and Tribal Leaders*

Thomas King, *The Truth About Stories: A Native Narrative*

Scott Richard Lyons, *X-Marks: Native Signatures of Assent*

Aileen Moreton-Robinson, *The White Possessive: Property, Power, and Indigenous Sovereignty*

Jean M. O'Brien, *Firsting and Lasting: Writing Indians out of Existence in New England*

Shiri Pasternak, *Grounded Authority: The Algonquins of Barriere Lake against the State*

Steven Salaita, *Inter/Nationalism: Decolonizing Native America and Palestine*

Leanne Betasamosake Simpson, *As We Have Always Done: Indigenous Freedom through Radical Resistance*

Paul Chaat Smith, *Everything You Know about Indians Is Wrong*

Lisa Tatonetti, *The Queerness of Native American Literature*

Gerald Vizenor, *Bear Island: The War at Sugar Point*

Robert Warrior, *The People and the Word: Reading Native Nonfiction*

Robert A. Williams Jr., *Like a Loaded Weapon: The Rehnquist Court, Indian Rights, and the Legal History of Racism in America*

# SPEAKING OF
# INDIGENOUS POLITICS

## CONVERSATIONS WITH ACTIVISTS, SCHOLARS, AND TRIBAL LEADERS

J. Kēhaulani Kauanui

Foreword by Robert Warrior

**INDIGENOUS AMERICAS**

University of Minnesota Press

MINNEAPOLIS | LONDON

The interview with Jean M. O'Brien was previously published as "Settler Logics and Writing Indians Out of Existence: A Conversation between J. Kēhaulani Kauanui and Jean M. O'Brien," special issue on settler colonialism for *Politica & Società*, Michele Spanò, guest editor (June 2012): 259–78. The interview with Patrick Wolfe was previously published as "Settler Colonialism Then and Now: A Conversation between J. Kēhaulani Kauanui and Patrick Wolfe," special issue on settler colonialism for *Politica & Società*, Michele Spanò, guest editor (June 2012): 235–58. Reprinted with permission.

Published by the University of Minnesota Press
111 Third Avenue South, Suite 290
Minneapolis, MN 55401-2520
http://www.upress.umn.edu

ISBN 978-1-5179-0477-7 (hc)
ISBN 978-1-5179-0478-4 (pb)
A Cataloging-in-Publication record for this book is available from the Library of Congress.

Printed in the United States of America on acid-free paper

The University of Minnesota is an equal-opportunity educator and employer.

22 21 20 19 18     10 9 8 7 6 5 4 3 2 1

*In memory of Gale Courey Toensing (1946–2018), a Connecticut-based journalist of Palestinian and Lebanese descent who was an outstanding staff reporter for* Indian Country Today. *Her friendship and significant work covering Indigenous issues in Native North America were instructive and continue to inspire me.*

# CONTENTS

# FOREWORD

## Robert Warrior

Though you won't hear it said directly in the interviews collected here from J. Kēhaulani Kauanui's radio show *Indigenous Politics: From Native New England and Beyond*, one way to read this book is as an Indigenous subversion of one of the basic tools of settler-colonial intervention, scholarship, and even entertainment. From police and military interrogation to social and behavioral scientific research to sensationalistic journalistic or travelogues, interviewing—too often of rude and invasive imposition—is central to the exercise of the power of whiteness over Native peoples and the places they inhabit.

Kauanui fights back against those centuries of imposition by showing that a recorded conversation around prepared questions can break its own mold to become something else. She's far from the first Indigenous interviewer to use the form in this way, but the conversations collected here are especially successful at demonstrating that it's possible to achieve the kind of scholarly and intellectual subversion of which Indigenous thinkers so often speak.

Kauanui harnessed that subversive energy at a particularly opportune moment, just as international Indigenous politics was coming to a critical juncture with the adoption, in 2007, of the United Nations Declaration of the Rights of Indigenous Peoples. The emergence of global Indigenous studies as a field became possible due to, among other things, the development of the Native American and Indigenous Studies Association, for which Kauanui and I served on the founding steering committee, acting council, and elected council from 2005 to 2012. Kauanui's radio show is an invaluable chronicle of that crucial period in the intellectual and political life of the Indigenous world. Among her guests are many of the leading figures in global Indigenous studies, including Aileen Moreton-Robinson, Steven Salaita, and Margo Tamez, among many others.

The interviews from *Indigenous Politics: From Native New England and Beyond* remain lively reading, though not just because of a happy coincidence of timing. I want to suggest three factors that imbue them with energy that makes them compelling years later. First, Kauanui clearly becomes masterful at the art of the broadcast interview over the life of her show. Along with her interview of me in this book, I've been an interviewee many times for a broad range of radio and television shows, and I can say with some authority that being a good interviewer requires much more than being a raconteur with a quality recording deck and a good Rolodex. Amid the deeply informed questions and sometimes playful back-and-forth in the interviews in this volume, what we can't see is Kauanui looking ahead at the next question and the next segment, getting ready for a news break or a station identification, and checking sound levels all while keeping an eye on the clock and making notes about any glitches that can be fixed through editing.

Those things we can't see are part of the magic of radio, its artifice. The fact that in this case the host is also the producer, director, and sound engineer rolled into one behind this aural veil makes that artifice even more impressive. (Another part of the artifice is that the guests sound like they might be sitting in a quiet studio with the host when in fact they are almost always joining the conversation by phone and could very well be wearing pajamas or some other form of loungewear, which is why I love doing radio—but I digress.) The art of the interview, especially for a solo host/producer like Kauanui, is wrapped up in keeping up with the technical aspects while managing simultaneously to keep a high-level conversation moving along seamlessly. Even though the interviews published here come from the radio, they carry with them on the page the cool vibe of the easy (natural) but revealing conversation that one associates with *Playboy*, *Rolling Stone*, and, of course, *Interview*.

The second factor that gives these interviews such long-lasting impact is the high level of knowledge about so many different places and fields of scholarship Kauanui brings to them. Listening to Kauanui having a detailed conversation with Aileen Moreton-Robinson, for instance, about the military intervention by Australian armed forces that was happening in Aboriginal communities in the Northern Territories in Australia in 2007 is much more meaningful than a lecture or prepared talk on the topic. It matters, in other words, that the host of the show knows enough about what is happening halfway around the world to be able to create a meaningful context for dialogue. The same is true for interviews that focus on South America, Palestine, or Florida.

Factor three has to do with the way Kauanui manages to highlight local and regional Indigenous communities in the midst of a global agenda, which leads us back to the idea of subversion that I started with. The name of the show, *Indigenous Politics: From Native New England and Beyond*, is, in fact, a statement of an ethical imperative that provides a fundamental grounding to the show even as it also embraces a global agenda. At the beginning of each show, Kauanui reminded listeners that she was speaking from the homelands of the Wangunk people, and she returned often to stories and people from the region. In this, the show is itself a lesson in how to practice recognizing the fundamental truth that every inch of the Americas is Indigenous territory.

What I loved about the show and what I appreciate about these interviews today is how they provide us as listeners and readers with a guide to how to act on the Indigenous ethical imperative of starting where you are. That imperative can seem daunting, especially when you are starting out. In the end, though, the way to build success will involve some version of what you see happening in these interviews: You have to get into conversations with people about what's happening in their communities. To do that, you are going to have to do some reading and some preparation to learn something about the people you are trying to be in conversation with. That reading and preparation might very well require you to develop some expertise you don't already have.

Let me end by pointing out the very first thing that this Indigenous ethical imperative is going to demand, which is this: regardless of whom in the Indigenous world you are talking to and where you are hoping to make an impact, the first thing you should do is take a good look around and figure out where you are. Whether or not that sounds simple or complicated, do yourself a favor and read these interviews for a great example of how to start from where you are.

# INTRODUCTION
## Indigenous Politics from Native New England and Beyond

The state of Native and Indigenous political resurgence and resistance in this twenty-first century moment is exciting and has much to teach the rest of the world. We can see this in the ongoing #NoDAPL struggle to stop the Dakota Access Pipeline. The Standing Rock Sioux Tribe who led this effort is guided by the principle of "Mni wiconi": "Water is life." We have also witnessed a fierce stance in the battle over the Thirty Meter Telescope at Mauna a Wākea on Hawai'i Island, a $1.4 billion project for an eighteen-story observatory on the summit that Kanaka Maoli (Native Hawaiians) consider sacred. Calling out to "Ku Kia'i Mauna," Kanaka Maoli protectors have taken up the struggle to guard the mountain. Both are cases of Indigenous resistance to extractive economies, rampant capitalism, and militarized violence and involve thousands of Indigenous individuals and diverse allies lending their support and solidarity. And in December 2017, Trump announced he would reduce the size of Bears Ears National Monument in southern Utah—a site sacred to Indigenous peoples in the region—in order to open it up for mining. Leading the resistance, the Bears Ears Inter-Tribal Coalition—launched by the Hopi Tribe, Navajo Nation, Ute Mountain Ute Tribe, Pueblo of Zuni, and the Ute Indian Tribe—has amassed the support of thirty tribal nations with ancestral, historical, and contemporary ties to the Bears Ears region committed to protecting the site and advancing their own Bears Ears conservation proposal. While these struggles eventually gained some mainstream media attention, most Indigenous peoples' activism is too often invisible to the dominant, settler-colonial society. This underscores the importance of independent media in making visible the diverse struggles and forms of resistance.

In February 2007, I launched a public-affairs radio show called *Indigenous Politics: From Native New England and Beyond* at WESU, a radio station affiliated with Wesleyan University, where I teach.[1] The use of "Native New England and Beyond" in the subtitle of the program was a political decision, part of my commitment to support the struggles of Indigenous peoples of the region as well as to cover those issues in relation to global Indigenous struggles "beyond." I featured interviews with nearly two hundred Indigenous officials, political leaders, activists, scholars, cultural workers, and artists about a range of topics documenting Native resistance to settler colonialism. The thirty interviews included here are just a slice of the vast audio archive.[2] One of the aims of *Indigenous Politics* was to address the politics of erasure. Notably, the conversations the radio show produced were themselves a political act against that ongoing violence and the logic of elimination endemic to settler colonialism.

Patrick Wolfe contrasts settler colonialism with franchise colonialism—through comparative work focused on Australia, Israel-Palestine, and the United States—showing how the former is premised on the logic of elimination of Indigenous peoples.[3] As Wolfe theorized, and as he discussed in his interview included here, because settler colonialism "destroys to replace," it is "inherently eliminatory but not invariably genocidal."[4] He was careful to point out that there are cases of genocide without settler colonialism and that, in the context of settler colonialism, "elimination refers to more than the summary liquidation of Indigenous peoples, though it includes that."[5] Hence, he suggested that structural genocide avoids the question of degree and enables an understanding of the relationships between spatial removal, mass killings, and biocultural assimilation. In other words, the logic of elimination of the Native is also about the elimination of the Native *as Native*. Because settler colonialism is a land-centered project entailing permanent settlement, Wolfe says, "settler colonizers come to stay: invasion is a structure not an event."[6] As a result, settler colonialism cannot be relegated to the past; it is an ongoing process. Importantly, indigeneity is a counterpart analytic to settler colonialism, and indigeneity itself is enduring; hence the operative logic of settler colonialism may be to "eliminate the Native," but Indigenous peoples exist, resist, and persist. Moreover, settler colonialism is a structure that endures indigeneity, even as it holds out against it.[7]

Wesleyan University, and its listener-supported radio station WESU, are located in Middletown, Connecticut. The Indigenous place-name is Mattabesset, and the Indigenous people of the land are the Wangunk, part of the Algonquin cultural-linguistic group. Although regarded as largely "extinct" prior to the American Revolution, Wangunks continue to live into the twenty-first century. This is a little-known history—one submerged within a landscape overdetermined by settler colonialism. The history of erasure of this place and its original inhabitants is common not just in Middletown but throughout the Northeast. When I first moved to Connecticut from California in 2000, I wanted to find out who the people of the land in the place we call Middletown are. I called the city council and asked, but was told there were none, and my asking was not taken kindly to.[8] Others I asked mentioned the Mashantucket Pequots and the Mohegans—the only two federally recognized tribes in Connecticut, both better known in some part due to their casinos, Foxwoods and the Mohegan Sun, respectively.

It wasn't long before I caught wind of the anti-Indian initiatives emanating from officials in the state, including then–Attorney General Richard Blumenthal (now a U.S. senator) and then–U.S. Senator Christopher Dodd. The tribes' wealth had visibly stirred non-Native (predominantly white) resentment by those I call the "twenty-first-century Indian haters." During that same period in the early 2000s, some even held town hall meetings to confer on "the Indian problem," namely, the possibility of new Indian casinos of the three tribal nations—the Schaghticoke, Eastern Pequots, and the Golden Hill Paugussetts— that were petitioning for federal recognition at the time.

One way I made a few inroads within that climate was through the anchoring of the radio program. To my knowledge, it was the only Native-issues show produced in New England at the time.[9] However, I didn't come at it with a journalistic approach, but out of a responsibility to the Indigenous peoples of the region where I reside (as someone not of that place) and in an effort to engage in the work of a public intellectual. The show was explicitly pro-sovereignty and in solidarity with Indigenous people(s). My aim was to connect my ongoing academic work to my political activism to the public realm to address what I see as major social concerns. The program aimed to reach multiple audiences about serious political and cultural issues. I designed it to provide a platform for the general public to think carefully about a range of Indigenous politics that shape everyday life in "Native New England and beyond" in an accessible language that was also analytically rigorous. This was my own version of "digital humanities," engaging the public in critical conversations. As such, the show became an experiment in civic education by, in part, unpacking legal issues for a lay audience.

The program included episodes on Indigenous activism in various parts of Canada, Latin America (including Mexico, Chile, Bolivia, and Peru), Palestine, Hawai'i, Australia, and Aotearoa (New Zealand). I focused on themes such as land desecration, treaty rights, political status, and cultural revitalization. I aimed to bring American Indian and other Indigenous voices to the airways by providing crucial commentary rooted in the scholarly research and activism of Native peoples and our allies.

The air dates of the program—from 2007 to 2013—spanned many critical developments in the Indigenous world globally. An international academic meeting held at the University of Oklahoma in April 2007 led to the establishment of the Native American and Indigenous Studies Association the following year, which I helped found as part of a six-person steering committee. On September 13, 2007, the UN General Assembly passed the Declaration on the Rights of Indigenous Peoples, despite opposition from the United States, Canada, Australia, and New Zealand. Other exciting developments during the years the show aired include the launching of the U.S. Campaign for the Academic and Cultural Boycott of Israel, which is part of the Boycott, Divestment, Sanctions movement called for by Palestine civil society to put nonviolent pressure on Israel until it complies with international law. That same year, we saw Bolivia write provisions for Indigenous peoples into its state constitution through a narrow but major referendum. The year 2011 saw the founding of the Māori Party, a New Zealand political party with Hone Harawira initially at the helm. And in 2012 we saw the formation of Idle No More, an ongoing grassroots movement among the First Nations, Métis, and Inuit peoples along with non-Indigenous supporters challenging Canadian state power. These are just a few important developments that occurred during the program's airing.

For readers (and past listeners) asking what the value of publishing these interviews is now, after the show has ended, I suggest that they can still teach us about the politics of settler colonialism and Indigenous resistance. In relation to Native and Indigenous studies alone, the interviews provide a window into an entire field in an accessible form from some high-profile scholars. They also serve to document a period of history in terms of regional and global Indigenous resistance. But besides offering a rich archive of these myriad developments, because the struggles facing Indigenous peoples have not changed in structural terms, but have intensified in many ways—especially with the onslaught of neoliberal policies—most of these interviews offer crucial genealogical contexts for so many ongoing political cases.

Most immediately, in the U.S. context, the show sought to address the general public's profound and pervasive ignorance and denial regarding the legal rights of Indigenous peoples, especially since they are often treated as racial minorities rather than sovereigns. For example, the conflation of race and indigeneity is one issue American Indians face in confronting challenges to their distinct legal status that presume their rights are based on "racial privileges" rather than political formations as nations. In *American Indian Politics and the American Political System,* David E. Wilkins (Lumbee) and Heidi Kiiwetinepinesiik Stark (Turtle Mountain Ojibwe) outline four realities that set American Indians apart from racial minorities in the United States.[10] First, American Indians were the original inhabitants of what is now considered the United States. Second, this preexistence necessitated the negotiation of political compacts, treaties, and alliances with European nations and the United States. Third, as recognized sovereigns, Indian peoples are subject to the Federal Trust Doctrine, which is supposed to be a unique legal relationship with the U.S. federal government that entails protection. Finally, stemming from the trust relationship, the United States asserts plenary power over tribal nations, which is exclusive and preemptive. The latter issue is the most difficult due to the ways in which the U.S. judiciary has interpreted the Commerce Clause of the U.S. Constitution to mean full and total power over tribal nations. The Commerce Clause gives Congress the power to "regulate commerce with foreign nations, and among the several states, and with the Indian tribes."[11] In other words, the U.S. government will not allow any state or foreign nation to interfere in commerce with tribal nations, since the government reserves the right to interact in a nation-to-nation capacity.

Historical recognition for state-recognized tribes from the original thirteen colonies is different from that of the "treaty tribes" in the western states or the Pueblo Indians because of their earlier incorporation into the U.S. nation-state. Furthermore, the contemporary backlash against casino development throughout the United States continues to be instrumental in the opposition to federal recognition. It appears that most non-Native residents and U.S. citizens have a difficult time uncoupling the question of tribal economic development, which is about the political economy of a nation, and the issue of social justice in honoring the U.S. trust doctrine.

The Indian Gaming Regulatory Act of 1988—a U.S. federal law passed to regulate the conduct of gaming on Indian lands—served as a catalyst for renewed political opposition to Native sovereignty movements throughout the United States. This took the form of "reverse racism" arguments to challenge laws recognizing Native rights to sovereignty and self-determination. As such, the identification of Indigenous peoples as both "special interest groups" and "racial minorities" is used to undermine the unique status of Indigenous peoples under U.S. federal law and international law. This changing political terrain creates the need for multiple interventions on different fronts when challenging the logic and workings of settler colonialism and how the logic of capital functions in relation to settler colonialism. Here we see the distinct ways capitalism acts in these different contexts—whether through the gaming industry or the commodification of land—both tied to state economics. This is all the more complicated because non-Native communities can be affected by Indian gaming establishments in both positive and negative ways. Also, there is growing resentment among some Americans who see Indian gaming rights as an unfair advantage based on race privileges. This climate grossly affected Connecticut tribes, an issue featured on the program.

The show also closely tracked the long-drawn-out federal recognition case of the Schaghticoke Tribal Nation (and intervention by the Connecticut state government) and the protracted battle over federal recognition in Hawai'i concerning Native Hawaiians. Briefly examining them here together gets at the heart of what my show aimed to do—to educate listeners about the distinctions regarding Indigenous politics as they differ from region to region and are often determined by their own settler-colonial historical specificities.

In the Connecticut case, the conflation of federal recognition with the specter of Indian casinos indicates that most non-tribal residents in these states refuse to uncouple questions of tribal economic development—that is, tribal nations' political economies—and the social justice issues of honoring the U.S. trust doctrine. This is yet another reason why independent community radio is so crucial to the democracy project and self-determination struggles. The problem with mainstream coverage of the Indigenous sovereignty struggle in Connecticut is that the media venues and individual journalists have aligned with the state instead of conducting investigative research and reporting on the issues they cover. In Connecticut, citizens' rights groups have bolstered the hostile response by state officials, who have implicated the federal process for tribes across the entire United States as they intervene to change policy more broadly through their extralegal meddling.

While tribes can secure federal recognition via judicial ruling and congressional legislation, the most common path in the last three decades has been through the Department of the Interior. From 1978 to 2015 (the regulations were revised after that under the Washburn administration at the Bureau of Indian Affairs), tribes seeking federal recognition were required to satisfy seven criteria according to the Office of Federal Acknowledgment of the Bureau of Indian Affairs (BIA), including one requirement that they prove they have maintained political authority or influence on a "substantially continuous basis from historical times until the present," and another that they be externally viewed as a tribe on a continuous basis since 1900.[12] The criteria have changed slightly since then,[13] but essentially tribes are still expected to show that they have survived every government policy and doctrine designed to destroy them—markers of settler-colonial violence and its attendant structural genocide—as distinct, collective entities.

Nowhere was (and still is) this more apparent than in Connecticut, where the state government set new legal precedents in cases involving the Schaghticoke Tribal Nation.[14] As journalist Gale Courey Toensing reported extensively for *Indian Country Today* throughout that period, State Attorney General Richard Blumenthal, with support from Senators Chris Dodd and Joe Lieberman, interfered in the BIA's decision. In these cases, we saw the misuse of the conception of tribes as racial minorities—and in a way that fueled ignorance and hatred. My show featured the political leader of the Schaghticokes, Chief Richard Velky, twice at different stages of the tribe's struggle. Despite the fact that the tribe had painstakingly followed the process and achieved recognition on their thirty-thousand-page petition's merits, political opponents launched a public-relations campaign accusing the tribe of politically manipulating the process to gain federal recognition. Then they launched their own secret campaign to politically manipulate the process to reverse that decision. In 2005, under pressure and illegal lobbying that violated a court order, the BIA reversed its federal acknowledgment of the Schaghticoke in 2004 (the BIA also did the same thing that same year with the Eastern Pequots, who had received a positive acknowledgment decision in 2002).

The state defended its actions by saying it speaks for the non-Native residents of Connecticut. It is also bolstered by "citizens' rights" groups such as Town Action to Save Kent (TASK) and the Connecticut Alliance against Casino Expansion, both of which hired one of the most powerful lobbying firms in the world, Barbour, Griffith and Rogers, to try to stop regional tribes from securing federal recognition. TASK argued that the Schaghticoke Tribal Nation's impending recognition was a threat to the "traditions" that "took settlers more than three hundred years to build" and that their ability to "preserve them for generations to come" was at risk. Thus, TASK positioned the Schaghticoke as the "colonizers" and reversed the usual position regarding whose traditions have been attacked by settler colonialism.

The Schaghticoke appealed their case in the federal court in January 2006 and followed up with a motion for summary judgment for their claim that their loss of federal status resulted from unlawful political influence by powerful politicians and a White House–connected lobbyist, who violated federal laws, agency regulations, congressional ethics rules, and court orders to have the BIA decision reversed. But, in his fifty-four-page ruling, the judge opined that pressure on agency officials did not amount to undue political influence on the agency process.

The state of Connecticut's current stance marked a 180-degree shift compared to earlier cases of federal recognition. In 1983, Connecticut and federal representatives recognized the Mashantucket Pequot's tribal status via the Mashantucket Pequot Indian Land Claims Settlement Act. Arguably, the political terrain was quite different at the time, given that the tribe had not yet gained the wealth and power for which it is notable today and was not then a major contender. In any case, the state benefits financially from the Foxwoods Resort Casino owned by the Mashantucket Pequots, as it does from the revenue (25 percent) brought in by the Mohegan tribal nation's gaming establishment.

This contrast reveals the differences and overlaps at work in confronting present-day conditions of settler colonialism in the United States, in which a state may take a different stance depending on what it may gain financially. This means that some states may support a Native nation's quest for federal recognition, while others remain strongly opposed. But it also indicates a different political climate overall, given the political and economic power among the Mashantucket Pequot and the Mohegan tribal nations (at least prior to the financial crisis of 2007–8)—presumably as a result of casino revenues that have state budget implications as well as political lobbying within and beyond the state.

Unlike the cases in Connecticut, from 2000 to 2012 the government of Hawai'i pushed a federally driven bill in favor of Native Hawaiian federal recognition known as the "Akaka Bill," named after then–U.S. Senator Daniel Akaka. The legislative proposal aimed to reconstitute a Native Hawaiian governing entity under U.S. federal law. The bill, officially named the Native Hawaiian Reorganization Act, stalled in the Senate due to Republican opposition and has been defeated each session since 2000, with neoconservatives in the Senate condemning it as a proposal for "race-based government." The proposal was hotly contested and repeatedly reintroduced until 2012, when it finally seemed to die. However, those driving the legislation found an alternative route through the executive branch by appealing to the Department of the Interior to craft a new administrative rule to recognize a "Native Hawaiian governing entity" that would have the political status comparable to Native American tribal nations without having to meet the same criteria they are subject to.[15]

In the Hawaiian context, federal recognition would allow for nothing more than a Hawaiian nation as a domestic and dependent entity under the full and exclusive plenary power of the federal government. Most immediately, it would set up a process for the termination of Hawaiian land claims in exchange for that recognition. And if past versions of the Akaka Bill are any indication, this form of federal recognition would mean a degraded version of the tribal nation model, since past proposals specified that Hawai'i state law would apply in both civil and criminal application, and there was no land designated for the projected Native Hawaiian governing entity (NHGE). At stake here is the obliteration of unadjudicated claims to the former Crown and Government Lands of the Hawaiian Kingdom, which amount to 1.8 million acres. These lands are currently held in trust by the state, which leases them out to select corporate entities. The U.S. government would then have its federally reorganized NHGE empowered to negotiate a cash settlement in exchange for forfeiting land title, which is why many Hawaiian activists oppose federal recognition in favor of full independence under international law. One of the factors fueling this problem is that the government wants to clear the way for U.S. military expansion on substantial part of the lands, and the state wants to sell the rest.

In February 2009 the U.S. Supreme Court heard a major case on Hawaiian land issues, *State of Hawaii v. Office of Hawaiian Affairs, et al.,* which addressed whether or not the state has the authority to sell, exchange, or transfer these same lands. Included in this volume is my interview with one of the original plaintiffs in the case, Jonathan Kamakawiwo'ole Osorio, who fought the state's attempt to sell. This land base constitutes 29 percent of the total land area of what is now known as the State of Hawai'i, and almost all the land claimed by the state as "public lands." These lands were claimed by the U.S. government when it unilaterally annexed the Hawaiian Islands through a joint resolution by the U.S. Congress in 1898, after they had been "ceded" by the Republic of Hawaii, which had established itself a year after the armed and unlawful overthrow of the Hawaiian monarchy under Queen Liliuokalani in 1893. These are the same lands mentioned in a 1993 joint resolution "To acknowledge the 100th anniversary of the January 17, 1893 overthrow of the Kingdom of Hawaii," in which Congress acknowledged and apologized for the United States' role. Specifically, the apology affirmed that "the indigenous Hawaiian people never directly relinquished their claims to their inherent sovereignty as a people or over their national lands to the United States, either through their monarchy or through a plebiscite or referendum."

Prior to the state government's appeal to the U.S. Supreme Court, the state supreme court ruled unanimously, based on the 1993 joint resolution, that the state should keep the land trust intact until Native Hawaiian claims to these lands are settled, and it prohibited the state from selling or otherwise disposing of the properties to private parties. What looms in the background of all of this is the question of a political settlement with Native Hawaiians about the status of and title to these lands and the potential to restore Hawaiian nationhood. What kind of nation would it be? An independent nation-state, or a domestic dependent nation under U.S. federal policy?

I understood my radio show to be playing a critical role in bringing these contested histories into the public sphere. As the dominant culture continues to marginalize Native issues, so too does the academy see them as "niche." This double discount needs urgent attention as the detrimental state policies against Indigenous peoples arguably constitute a new wave of twenty-first-century attempts at genocide. In other words, the politics of settler colonialism and their ramifications continue to deal hard blows to Native nations, despite the UN's adoption of the Declaration on the Rights of Indigenous Peoples.

The ongoing relevancy of the interviews included here also point to the high stakes involved. For example, the two interviews with Margo Tamez—cofounder of the Lipan Apache Women Defense—provide a crucial genealogy for the contemporary politics of the U.S.–Mexico border wall. The interviews detail her and her mother's legal battle with the Department of Defense and the Department of Homeland Security (DHS) to prevent the Texas–Mexico border wall from cutting through Indigenous lands in El Calaboz ranchería in South Texas. These interviews take on added significance when situated in relation to candidate Trump's calls to "build the wall." On January 25, 2017, just days after his inauguration, President Trump signed two executive orders related to immigration and border security.[16] The orders are related, as one concerns the active deportation of people who are in the country illegally, while the other focuses on his plans to build a wall along the U.S.–Mexico border. Related to this development, DHS announced on August 1, 2017, that it will use its authority to bypass environmental laws and other regulations to "ensure the expeditious construction of barriers and roads" near the U.S.–Mexico border south of San Diego.[17] The waiver focuses on fifteen miles of contiguous land stretching eastward from the Pacific Ocean and enables the avoidance of the legal requirement to complete an environmental impact study before building on public lands.[18] DHS says it has "the authority to waive all legal requirements" that its secretary deems necessary "to deter illegal crossings in areas of high illegal entry into the United States." The waiver is pursuant to authority granted to the DHS secretary by Congress and covers a variety of environmental, natural resource, and land-management laws.[19] This development has broad implications for Indigenous peoples across the country. Tamez recently explained to me that this "no-constitution zone" prevails because neither Bush nor Obama repealed section 102 of the Secure

Fence Act, which she addressed in her two interviews included here.[20] Hence we see the significance of this volume in providing critical genealogies to ongoing obstacles to Native self-determination and Indigenous peoples' efforts to challenge the states that dominate them.

In another example, the interviews included here with Steven Salaita and Omar Barghouti on the Boycott, Divestment, Sanctions (BDS) campaign provide a foundation for comprehending Israel as a settler-colonial state and for understanding the legal and social challenges to BDS and Palestinian activism today by both the Israeli and U.S. governments. In my interview with Salaita, besides discussing the ethics of BDS and its resonance with conditions in Native America (a comparison addressed in his book *The Holy Land in Transit: Colonialism and the Quest for Canaan*), including a comparative analysis of colonialism in the New World and the Holy Land, exploring the ways in which settler societies transform theological narratives into national histories to justify their occupation of foreign land. As part of the backlash against BDS and Palestinian advocacy, Salaita gained a heightened public profile after writing a series of editorials in the wake of the backlash against the resolution for academic boycott of Israel passed by the American Studies Association. Increased surveillance has greatly affected his livelihood, and in 2014 the University of Illinois withdrew or "de-hired" Salaita from a professorial post in the American Indian Studies Program after the university's board of trustees' attention was drawn to his tweets on the Israeli military's onslaught in Gaza.[21] The following year, the Illinois legislature unanimously passed a bill that prevents the state's pension fund from investing in companies that boycott Israel.[22] This was the first anti-BDS law passed in the country, and governments across the United States have passed comparable legislation since then. [23] At the time of this writing there is a bill before the U.S. Congress, the Israel Anti-Boycott Act (H.R. 1697/S. 720). The radio archive and interviews included here offer vital, prescient insight into these developments.

In the case of the interview with Omar Barghouti, it is important to note that he is a cofounder of the Palestinian Campaign for the Academic and Cultural Boycott of Israel, founded in 2004, as well as cofounder of the broader BDS movement and call issued in 2005. He is arguably one of the best-known spokespersons about the issue and has gained notoriety for his indefatigable activism. As a result, he has also endured repeated attacks by the Israeli state, including repression, attempts to undermine his residency, and travel bans to prevent his international advocacy and hinder his work. In March 2017, Israeli tax authorities invaded his home and detained and interrogated him on unfounded tax fraud charges.[24] Again, the significance of Barghouti's interview, like so many others from *Indigenous Politics* radio, is in offering a foundation for understanding the current moment and beyond.

From Palestine to Aotearoa, the interviews included here offer a platform for critical voices—highlighting Indigenous agency and resurgence—in their immediate context through a global approach to addressing the ongoing nature of settler-colonial domination and Indigenous resistance. These conversations about the past and future, then, enable public engagement that can lead to mobilization and broad-based solidarity. This book is meant to provide both context for contemporary Indigenous resurgence and inspiration for its continuance.

## Individuals Included on the Program

Ali Abunimah
Tupac Enrique Acosta (Nahuatl-Xicano)
Czarina Aggabao Thelen
Julian Aguon (Chamorro)
Christina Akanoa
Z 'Aki (Kanaka Maoli)
Ahmad Amara
S. James Anaya (Purepecha and Chiricahua Apache)
Chris Andersen (Métis)
Michael Anderson (Nyoongar Ghurradjong Murri Ghillar)
Mikki Anganstata (Eastern Cherokee)
Tim Aqukkasuk Argetsinger (Iñupiaq)
José Aylwin
Jessie Little Doe Baird (Mashpee Wampanoag)
Omar Barghouti
Joanne Barker (Delaware Tribe of Indians)
Giovanni Batz (K'iche' Maya)
Shanadeen Begay (Diné)
Nicholas F. Bellantoni
Clayson Benally (Diné)
Jeneda Benally (Diné)
Sherna Berger Gluck
Ned Blackhawk (Te-Moak Tribe of Western Shoshone)
Eva Blake (Assonet Wampanoag)*[25]
Victoria Bomberry (Muscogee)
Alexis Bonogofsky
Jesse Bowman Bruchac (St Francis/Sokoki band of the Abenaki)
Steve Brady (Northern Cheyenne Tribe)
James BrownEagle (Elem Pomo Tribe)
Lisa Brooks (Abenaki)
Kathleen A. Brown-Pérez (Brothertown Indian Nation)
Margaret Bruchac (Abenaki)
Luis E. Cárcamo-Huechante (Mapuche)

Andrea Carmen (Yacqui)
Tony Castanha (Jibaro)
'Iokepa Casumbal-Salazar (Kanaka Maoli)
Jessica Cattelino
Clarence Kukauakahi Ching (Kanaka Maoli)
Marty Cobenais (Red Lake Ojibwe)
Radmilla Cody (Diné)
Betsy Conway*
David Cornsilk (Cherokee Nation)
Glen Coulthard (Yellowknives Dene First Nation)*
Sarah Croucher
Sarah Deer (Muscogee [Creek] Nation)
Philip J. Deloria (Dakota descent)
Paul DeMain (Oneida)*
Jennifer Denetdale (Diné)
Amy Den Ouden
Judy Dow (Abenaki)
Sir Edward Taikahurei Durie (Ngati Kauwhata)
Bruce Duthu (Houma)
Tom Dye
Angelique EagleWoman (Sisseton-Wahpeton Dakota Oyate)
Walter Echo-Hawk (Pawnee)
John EchoHawk (Pawnee)*
Jorge Estevez (Taino)
Alicia Ivonne Estrada
Farrett (Cree)
Stephanie Morning Fire Mugford Fielding (Mohegan)
Maurice Fox (Mashpee Wampanoag)*
Katherine Fuchs
Nancy Gallagher
Ruth Garby Torres (Schaghticoke Tribal Nation)
Tiokasin Ghosthorse (Cheyenne River Lakota)
Mishuana Goeman (Tonawanda Band of Seneca)*
Tonya Gonnella Frichner (Onondaga Nation, Snipe clan)
Wendy Gonyea (Onandaga)
J. Noelani Goodyear-Kaʻōpua (Kanaka Maoli)*
Corrina Gould (Karkin and Chochenyo Ohone)
Rae Gould (Nipmuc)*
Shane Greene
Hone Harawira (Ngāti Hau, Ngāti Wai, Ngāti Hine,
    Te Aupōuri, Ngāpuhi, and Ngāti Whātua)
Joy Harjo (Mvskoke)

Suzan Shown Harjo (Cheyenne and Hodulgee Muscogee)
Kimberly Hatcher-White (Mashantucket Pequot)
Stanley Heller
Mose Herne (Akwesasne Mohawk)
Susana Hito
Santi Hitorangi (Maʻohi)
James T. Jackson* (Mashantucket Pequot)
Moonanum James (Aquinnah Wampanoag)
Hannibal B. Johnson
Tēvita Ō. Kaʻili (Tongan)
Kamuela Kalaʻi (Kanaka Maoli)
Kaʻanohi Kaleikini (Kanaka Maoli)
John Kane (Mohawk)*
Philomena Kebec (Bad River Band of Lake Superior Chippewa)
Taylor Keen (Cherokee Nation)
Rashid Khalidi
Jackson T. King Jr.*
Suzanne Koepplinger
Annette Kolodny
Mike Krebs (Blackfoot descent)*
Jennifer Kreisberg (Tuscarora)
Winona LaDuke (Anishinaabe)
Richard Anguksuar LaFortune (Yupʻik),
Maria LaHood
Gloria Larocque (Sturgeon Lake Cree Nation)
Kent Lebsock (Lakota descent)
Erica Lee (Cree)
Stacy Leeds (Cherokee Nation)
Randolph Lewis
José Antonio Lucero
James Luna (Luiseño, La Jolla band of Mission Indians)
Andy Mager
Kaʻiulani Mahuka (Kanaka Maoli)
Lynn Malerba (Mohegan)
Daniel Mandell*
Wilma Mankiller (Cherokee)*
Desireé Reneé Martinez (Gabrieliño)
Jose R. Matus (Yaqui)
Malinda Maynor Lowry (Lumbee)
Kevin A. McBride
Steven Paul McSloy*
Marianela Medrano-Marra (Taino)*

Rigoberta Menchú Tum (Quiche-Mayan)*
Robert J. Miller (Eastern Shawnee Tribe of Oklahoma)
Sherri L. Mitchell (Penobscot)
Cindi Moar Alvitre (Tongva)
Rosa Moiwend
Richard Monette (Turtle Mountain Band of Chippewa)
Tristan Moone (Diné)
Aileen Moreton-Robinson (Quandamooka)
Alyssa Mt. Pleasant (Tuscorora)
Kaimana Namihira (Kanaka Maoli)
Steven Newcomb (Shawnee/Lenape)
Vivian Newdick
Jean M. O'Brien (White Earth Ojibwe)
Dana Olwan
Paco de Onís
Jonathan Kay Kamakawiwo'ole Osorio (Kanaka Maoli)
Karla Palma (Mapuche)*
Pamela Palmater (Mi'kmaq)
Lorrin Pang
Violet Parrish (Kashi Pomo)
Vivian Parrish Wilder (Kashi Pomo)
Sherman Paul (Maliseet)
Andre Perez (Kanaka Maoli)
Ramona Nosapocket Peters (Mashpee Wampanoag)
Victoria Phillips
Alexandra Pierce (Seneca)
Kealoha Pisciotta (Kanaka Maoli)
Robert Odawi Porter (Seneca)*
Rick Pouliot (Megantiquois Abenaki)
Evan Pritchard (Mi'kmaq descendant)
Mazin Qumsiyeh
Renya Ramirez (Winnebago Tribe of Nebraska)
Jonathan Ramones (Mi'kmaq)
Madeleine Redfern (Inuit)
Debbie Reese (Nambe Pueblo)
Trudie Lamb Richmond (Schaghticoke)
Janet Marie Rogers (Mohawk)
Judy Rohrer
Loriene Roy (Minnesota Chippewa)
L. Mixashawn Rozie (Mahicanu)
Keanu Sai (Kanaka Maoli)*
Katoa Sailusi

Steven Salaita
Dean Saranillio
Katherine Saunders
Brandon J. Sazue Sr. (Crow Creek Sioux Tribe)
Binayak Sen
Charles Norman Shay (Penobscot Nation)
Moana Sinclair (Ngati Rangatahi, Kauwhata, Raukawa, and Maniapoto)
Niigaanwewidam James Sinclair (Anishinaabe, St. Peter's/Little Peguis)
Sonia Smallacombe (Maramanindji)
Paul Chaat Smith (Comanche)
Alex Soto (Tohono O'odham Nation)
Loren Spears (Narragansett)
Circe Sturm (Mississippi Choctaw descendant)
Annette Sykes (Te Arawa)
Margo Tamez (Ndé Konitsaaiigokiyaa'en)
Wendy Giddens Teeter
Ty Kāwika Tengan (Kanaka Maoli)
Gale Courey Toensing
Rebecca Tsosie (Yaqui)*
Dale Turner (Temagami First Nation)
Marilyn Vann (Cherokee Nation)
Valerie Nana Ture Varges (Taino)
Chief Richard Velky (Schaghticoke)
Herman Wainggai
Harry B. Wallace (Unkechaug)
Wanbli (Sioux Valley Dakota descendant)
Robert Warrior (Osage Nation)
Brian Baguck Wescott (Koyukon and Yup'ik)
Charles Whalen (Oglala Lakota)
Philip Whiteman (Northern Cheyenne Tribe)
Deborah White Plume (Oglala Lakota)
Violet Wilder (Kashi Pomo)
David E. Wilkins (Lumbee)*
Alexandra Wilson (Opaskwayak Cree Nation)
Patrick Wolfe
Cedric Woods (Lumbee)
Kristen Wyman (Natick Nipmuc)
Jessica Yee (Mohawk)
Michael Yellow Bird (Sahnish/Arikara and Hidatsa Nations)*
William S. YellowRobe Jr. (Assiniboine Tribe of the Assiniboine and
    Sioux Tribes of the Fort Peck Indian Reservation)
Melissa Tantaquidgeon Zobel (Mohegan)

## Notes

1. Notably, WESU is the second-oldest student-run college radio station in the United States. It is unique in that it also allows community members who are not affiliated with the university to produce and host programs. See www.wesufm.org for more information.

2. The archive can be accessed at www.indigenouspolitics.com.

3. Patrick Wolfe, "Settler Colonialism and the Elimination of the Native," *Journal of Genocide Research* 8, no. 4 (December 2006): 387–409.

4. Ibid., 387.

5. Ibid., 390.

6. Ibid., 388. Wolfe's earlier work advanced the same analysis: "The colonizers come to stay—invasion is a structure not an event." See *Settler Colonialism and the Transformation of Anthropology* (London: Continuum International, 1998), 2. Wolfe's first book provided a history of settler colonialism in Australia through a history of anthropology that explores the links between metropolitan anthropological theory and local colonial politics from the nineteenth century up to the late twentieth century, settler colonialism, and the ideological and sexual regimes that characterize it. The work is an incisive analysis of the politics of anthropological knowledge given its production through the historical dispossession and continuing oppression of Indigenous peoples.

7. J. Kēhaulani Kauanui, "'A Structure, Not an Event': Settler Colonialism and Enduring Indigeneity," *Lateral* 5, no. 1 (Spring 2016), http://csalateral.org/wp/issue/5-1/forum-alt-humanities-settler-colonialism-enduring-indigeneity-kauanui/#fnref-351-4.

8. The radio program eventually served as one of the catalysts for my teaching a service-learning course in the fall of 2015, "Decolonizing Indigenous Middletown: Native Histories of the Wangunk Indian People." The course engaged the field of settler-colonial studies and critical Indigenous studies, along with Native American history and historiography addressing southern New England. Taking up a decolonizing methodological approach, the class focused on the sparsely documented history of the Wangunk, with students conducting primary research through the seventeenth-century archives of the Middlesex Historical Society and eventually launching a Wikipedia entry about the Wangunk.

9. Further south, in New York City, there was and still is Tiokasin Ghosthorse's program *First Voices Indigenous Radio* on WBAI.

10. David E. Wilkins and Heidi Kiiwetinepinesiik Stark, *American Indian Politics and the American Political System,* 4th ed. (Lanham, Md.: Rowman & Littlefield, 2017), 33–37.

11. Ibid., 37.

12. The criteria until 2015 were: "1. a statement of facts establishing that the tribe has been identified as an Indian entity by reliable external sources on a substantially continuous basis since 1900; 2. evidence that it has maintained a continuous community; 3. evidence that it has maintained political authority or influence on a substantially continuous basis from historical times until the present; 4. a copy of its governing document, or if it does not have one, a statement describing its membership criteria and governing procedures; 5. a list of all current members, who as a whole must descend from

a historic tribe or tribes that amalgamated; 6. evidence that it consists mainly of people who are not already federally recognized; and 7. a statement that it is not the subject of congressional legislation that has terminated or forbidden the federal trust relationship." Bureau of Indian Affairs, "Revisions to Regulations on Federal Acknowledgment of Indian Tribes (25 CFR 83 or Part 83)," June 29, 2015, https://www.bia.gov/WhoWeAre/AS-IA/ORM/83revise/index.htm.

13. In 2014, the same summer that DOI officials held public meetings in Hawai'i on the Advanced Notice of Proposed Rule Making, another set of public meetings was held on the federal regulations for tribal acknowledgment. As a result, the regulations on federal acknowledgment were revised in 2015 (https://www.doi.gov/hawaiian/reorg). See Bureau of Indian Affairs, "Revisions to Regulations on Federal Acknowledgment of Indian Tribes (25 CFR 83 or Part 83)," June 29, 2015, https://www.bia.gov/WhoWeAre/AS-IA/ORM/83revise/index.htm.

14. This also affected the Eastern Pequot Tribal Nation in Connecticut, but it did not result in a legal battle afterward.

15. U.S. Department of the Interior press release, "Considers Procedures to Reestablish a Government-to-Government Relationship with the Native Hawaiian Community," June 18. 2014, http://www.doi.gov/news/pressreleases/interior-considers-procedures-to-reestablish-a-government-to-government-relationship-with-the-native-hawaiian-community.cfm.

16. President Donald Trump, "Executive Order: Border Security and Immigration Enforcement Improvements," The White House, January 25, 2017, https://www.whitehouse.gov/the-press-office/2017/01/25/executive-order-border-security-and-immigration-enforcement-improvements; Bill Chappell et al., "'A Nation without Borders Is Not a Nation': Trump Moves Forward with U.S.–Mexico Wall," *National Public Radio*, January 25, 2017, http://www.npr.org/sections/thetwo-way/2017/01/25/511565740/trump-expected-to-order-building-of-u-s-mexico-wall-wednesday.

17. Colin Dwyer, "Homeland Security to Waive Environmental Rules on Border Wall Projects," National Public Radio, August 1, 2017, http://www.npr.org/sections/thetwo-way/2017/08/01/540892890/homeland-security-to-waive-environmental-rules-on-border-wall-projects?sc=17&f=1003&utm_source=iosnewsapp&utm_medium=Email&utm_campaign=app.

18. Ibid.

19. Department of Homeland Security press release, "DHS Issues Waiver to Expedite Border Construction Projects in San Diego Area," August 1, 2017, https://www.dhs.gov/news/2017/08/01/dhs-issues-waiver-expedite-border-construction-projects-san-diego-area.

20. As a now permanent fixture of the state, in conjunction with the authority being imposed by federal agencies, the Secure Fence Act threatens federally recognized tribes, including those located far from the border, as evidenced in the logic already applied in the Standing Rock case.

21. For an overview of the legal case, see Center for Constitutional Rights, "Professor Steven Salaita," February 9, 2015, https://ccrjustice.org/professor-steven-salaita.

22. Eugene Kantorovich, "Illinois Passes Historic Anti-BDS Bill, as Congress Mulls Similar Moves," *Washington Post*, May 18, 2015, https://www.washingtonpost.com/news/

volokh-conspiracy/wp/2015/05/18/illinois-passes-historic-anti-bds-bill-as-congress
-mulls-similar-moves/?utm_term=.9b986cbbb97b.

23. "Anti-BDS Legislation Updates: Illinois, Florida, Colorado, Arizona (Up-
dated)," Palestine Legal, March 24, 2016, http://palestinelegal.org/news/2016/3/24/
antibds-leg-update-co-fl-il.

24. Amnesty International, "Israeli Government Must Cease Intimidation of Human
Rights Defenders, Protect Them from Attacks," April 12, 2016, https://www.amnestyusa
.org/press-releases/israeli-government-must-cease-intimidation-of-human-rights
-defenders-protect-them-from-attacks/; "Israeli Attacks on Omar Barghouti Part of
Ongoing Attempt to Silence and Criminalize Growing BDS Movement," Samidoun:
Palestine Prisoner Solidarity Network, March 22, 2017, http://samidoun.net/2017/03/
israeli-attacks-on-omar-barghouti-part-of-ongoing-attempt-to-silence-and-criminalize
-growing-bds-movement/.

25. An asterisk following the name indicates an occasion when a talk by that individual was aired, rather than an interview.

# JESSIE LITTLE DOE BAIRD ON REVIVING THE WAMPANOAG LANGUAGE

In 2009, a year before she was awarded the MacArthur Fellowship, I had the privilege of interviewing the indefatigable Jessie Little Doe Baird, cofounder of the Wôpanâak Language Reclamation Project. This is an intertribal effort that began in 1993, between the Mashpee, Aquinnah, Assonet, Herring Pond, and Chappaquiddick Wampanoag. The aim of the project is to reclaim Wôpanâak as a spoken language after there had been no speakers of the language for six generations. Little Doe is a citizen of the Mashpee Wampanoag Tribe and Wampanoag Women's Medicine Society. She lives in Mashpee, Massachusetts, and teaches Wôpanâak in Aquinnah and Mashpee. Little Doe received her master of science in linguistics from MIT in 2000. She has completed a layperson's grammar of the language as well as a curriculum for teaching and is currently working toward the completion of a dictionary and expansion of the curriculum. She has also assisted in rebuilding the Pequot language and teaching at Mashantucket, Connecticut. She also serves as the vice-chair of the Mashpee Wampanoag Indian Tribal Council. Her work on language revitalization is featured in a documentary film by Anne Makepeace, *We Still Live Here—Âs Nutayuneân* (2011), which had its broadcast premiere on the PBS series *Independent Lens* in November 2011.

This interview took place on April 4, 2009.

**J. Kēhaulani Kauanui:** I want to ask if you could start off by telling more about your background and what led to the birth of the Wôpanâak Language Reclamation Project.

**Jessie Little Doe Baird:** Well, my background. I am a Mashpee Wampanoag woman, born and raised in the community, and I think that really the language chose me rather than me choosing it. We have a prophecy around language, leaving our home and returning to our home and, I think that the work that we are doing right now, all of us together, is really fulfillment of a part of that prophecy.

**JKK:** When you say that it chose you rather than you choosing it, could you say a little bit more about that, and how you came to it or how you felt that it chose you?

**JLDB:** I guess I'm just talking about the fact that when there is prophecy, when there's knowledge from outside of us, it generally knows what's best and what people need and when they need it. I think when work needs to be done, people are asked to pitch in, and sometimes people are ready and have the time and energy to pitch in, and in those times I think our best and most hopeful work gets done. I think that's what's happening now in my community, and it involves me as well as others behind me.

**JKK:** And this began in 1993, when you were called to do this work, right?

**JLDB:** Yes.

**JKK:** How long had it been that the language lay dormant or left home, so to speak?

**JLDB:** As near as I can count, for six generations there were no speakers. And there weren't any until this seventh generation, so roughly 150 years.

**JKK:** Can you tell our listeners more about how this is a result of the joint collaborative effort among the Mashpee, Aquinnah, and Assonet Wampanoag communities?

**JLDB:** Well, originally, when the project started, I contacted an elder here— one of the few elders that I had any information about or any background relationship with—and by "here" I mean Aquinnah. I contacted Miss Helen, who has since deceased. She was well respected in this community, and has been in her community, and that's really important for people here, so I asked her if she thought that there were any ways in which we could start to have a dialogue about bringing language home. She was completely receptive to that and said that she had been thinking about it for a long time and thought that we should get together and meet to discuss the possibilities and the implications of the prophecy and whether or not this was the time. So we met initially, and then we started to organize monthly meetings, which the Mashpee and Aquinnah would trade off hosting. Eventually, the Assonet Band of Wampanoag—which is not a historic tribe, but a Wampanoag community— joined the project in, I think, 1994. Last year, we had the Chappaquiddick people and the Herring Pond people join the project, so now there are actually five communities participating.

**JKK:** Are you the instructor for all five communities, traveling from place to place?

**JLDB:** Not always. I've had some students in my class for eight years now and some of those students have taught classes at various times, so I don't have to teach all of the classes. During our Emerging Camp Beach Summer there are plenty of other facilitators to help with instruction.

**JKK:** Now, in terms of the language itself; I understand that it's one of more than three dozen languages classified as belonging to the Algonquian language family. Could you speak to that, in terms of the context of the language and how you came to do the early translation work that relied on the Eliot Bible in the Massachusett language?

**JLDB:** The language is one in nearly forty languages in a family called the Algonquian family, and so they are sister languages in the same way that Portuguese, Spanish, Italian, French, all of those are sisters in the Romance family. Wampanoag is just one of those languages with at least two dialects—the mainland dialect and an island's dialect. We don't call it Massachusetts; that's a designation that's given to the language by non-Native folks. We do call the language Wampanoag, because it's a language spoken by the Wampanoag Nation.

There were originally sixty-nine tribes in the nation, so the language is, as you said, just one of over three dozen languages in the family, and the Eliot Bible is but one of lots of documents—in fact, Wampanoag people were the first Amerindian people to use an alphabetic writing system to codify their language. There are many Native-written documents so we use all of those documents, not just the Bible specifically. I'm actually working on a body of research right now to display something I suspect, to prove that Eliot didn't actually do the translation of the Bible, but more supervised it, and it was done by Native speakers.

**JKK:** And this was when there were several—six or seven—Natives that were selected, and he supervised them and they were at the Indian college at Harvard?

**JLDB:** I don't think that that was the case. I don't think that he was really trying to rely on those students to do the translation. I know that he initially worked with one of his protégés by the name of John Sassamon, who got himself into trouble and turned up dead. Then he started working with another informant by the name of Joel Neesum, and I don't have the evidence that Joel Neesum was ever a student at the Indian college [Harvard Indian College], but I do know that he did some translation work with Joel Hiacombs. I doubt that even six or seven people could have completed the work, because there was a point in time when John Eliot wrote to his benefactors and basically said, "Okay, well, I think I was too ambitious trying to translate a whole Bible. Both of my informants have died, so maybe I'll just do some selective religious tracts and we'll just have to go with those."

Some eight months later, we have a whole Bible, and he said too that some of the Indians about the country laughed at him because his grammar was not very good. If you look at his attempt at the book of Genesis, in 1655, and then you look at the book of Genesis in the finished whole Bible, in 1663, there are significant differences. I think that when he says in his memoirs that he decided to try to teach some Wampanoag people about English grammar he found that they're all "genius." I think what he did was he farmed the work out among lots of people, probably a lot of the converts that were coming from all around Wampanoag country—from Cape Ann and Gloucester to the Cape and Islands—who were converging anywhere in the area of Massachusetts, which is a place-name north of Boston. I think there was a large body of people that did the work.

**JKK:** So this is another one of those epic cases where one singular European man gets the credit for the labor of a larger collective?

**JLDB:** Well, I do honestly think that he worked really hard. And I honestly think that he supervised this work and collected it, but because of the fact that there are places in that Bible where English idioms are used, clearly the person translating the idiom didn't understand what it meant, so they translated it literally and it came out really hilarious.

**JKK:** Could you give an example of that?

**JLDB:** If somebody says they were sitting around "chewing the cud," we all know what that means; that means having a casual conversation. If somebody translates that as "and then they all began to chew on the insides of their cheeks," these are the types of things that get translated when people don't understand what the idiom is. An English translator would not do that, because they would understand the idiom, so there are these sorts of problems.

And then there are also other issues. There are times when a particular translator picks a verb that talks about something that is possible within the realm of Wampanoag philosophy but not possible within the realm of Christianity, so a Christian translator wouldn't select that particular verb. For example, there's this very common stem—nup, NUP, nup—and it means "to die." Of course, you see that all over the Bible, because people are dying left and right. In one instance, there is an idiom that says "and he gave up the ghost." We all know that when somebody says "and he gave up the ghost," they mean, "and he died." In this particular case, at least in two instances in the Bible, this translator does not say "he died." He doesn't say "wânah nupuw," "he died," and he also doesn't say "wânah 'makuw wunahshânut8ah," "and he gave away his spirit," or anything like that. What he says is, "wânah âhqapuw," and that's amazing because if you pulled apart the morphemes of the verb stem *âhqapuw* is a verb meaning "to cease to exist in any form." So he didn't die, he ceased to exist in any form. In Christianity, that's not a possibility; you are going to die, and you're either going to go to the boogey man or you're going to go onto some wonderful reward somewhere up in the sky. To choose "to cease to exist in any form" isn't an option in Christianity. So clearly, this translator is reading the story, saying oh no, no, no, the story doesn't really mean he died. The story means this: this guy decided he'd had it, period. He was not going to exist anymore in any form, spiritually or otherwise. Clearly, this is not something that a Christian translator would pick for a verb.

**JKK:** Your example really highlights the difference in epistemological frames.

Speaking of Christianity, you mentioned converts earlier on, helping Eliot doing some of that translation work. In terms of the primary reason for the development of an alphabet, was it the goal then for missionaries arriving from England in the early 1600s to convert the language into written script in order to convert the Wampanoag to Christianity?

**JLDB:** I can say this. If I feel led to convert people, and I arrive at a place where there are literally tens of thousands of people speaking a particular language, I imagine I've got two choices. I've either got to teach those tens of thousands of people to speak whatever language all the material is in, or I need to get the material converted into their language. So, it just makes common sense if you have to use this written material that it has to be understandable across a wide number of people.

**JKK:** And so there is the first Christian Bible published in (British) North America in 1663?

**JLDB:** Well, the first complete one. There were some texts and the Old Testament prior to that. There's the book of Psalms and the Psalter, and there are some other religious documents that had been translated.

**JKK:** You mentioned earlier, too, that the language was used to record other documents that were non-religious. I wanted to ask you, in terms of personal letters, wills, or deeds—what constitutes the corpus of the material that you're able to go to now, and also how long was the language in use? I read that Wampanoag rivaled English literacy during the eighteenth century. What is the breaking point for the language going away after having been so successfully taken in written form among the communities?

**JLDB:** The language itself actually has the largest corpus of Native written documents on the continent. We're talking about everything from something called the logic primer—which is a document that teaches us about rhetoric and debate—to personal letters of complaint, personal letters of apology, personal wills, deeds that are recorded in proxy of land transactions that took place a hundred years earlier, personal marginalia along the edges of Bibles. There are documents occasionally turning up, still, and there are probably lots more out there yet to be surveyed. That's the body material besides the Bible that's being used. It's not a simple question as to what happened; a lot of things happened. One thing that happened prior to the advent of even codifying the language using an alphabetic writing system—most people aren't aware that in the Wampanoag nation, from 1616 to 1619, approximately forty thousand people died before the *Mayflower* even landed here, from yellow fever that was brought by a previous trading ship. That in itself wiped out lots of elders and lots of children all the way to Narragansett Bay, which is the critical group for any language: your elders and your babies.

So disease was happening, and then there was also warfare—there was also King Phillip's War. Then there was economics. Then there was forced citizenship, which is a whole separate topic that not too many people are aware of—it was sort of like an Indian Reorganization Act that the state of Massachusetts conducted in 1742. After that, at one period of time, the only place with any virgin hardwood left in the region was Mashpee and Aquinnah, and those were also the only two places left with any Native governments and Native populations still in place. The wood was needed for fuel; there was no kerosene, there was no oil, people weren't using coal, and so there was a movement to force U.S. citizenship on both of these communities, even though the communities voted against it. By 1869 both Mashpee and Aquinnah had U.S. citizenship forced upon them, and what that did was it took all of the lands in common from the tribes and it separated the land—sixty acres for every person eighteen years or older—and then eight months later everybody got a tax bill. If you couldn't pay the tax, and somebody else could pay the tax, they could then cart the wood off.

All of this push started in the 1820s, and by 1833, when things were really reaching a boiling point, we read about William Apess, a Pequot preacher, coming here from western Massachusetts to see what was going on. He actually encouraged Mashpee to take their territory back, but one of the complaints at the time was that there was a white minister by the name Phineas Fish who was being paid $500 a year by the Williams Fund at Harvard College to preach the gospel to the Indians. One of the complaints was that he speaks English, we don't even speak English, and he was taking over our meetinghouse. I think a lot of things happened, but long story short, let's say by 1900 there were very few speakers left, if any. Along with citizenship [issues] that we can read in the hearing transcripts of these meetings, there was a push for Wampanoag to start educating the children and having schools in English.

**JKK:** The push for assimilation, that process between 1742 and 1883, sounds like the IRA [Indian Reorganization Act] and the General Allotment Act rolled into one.

**JLDB:** If you look at it, I mean, even the formation of Harvard College. I think that there were two things going on. I'm not a historian by any means, but I know my people, and I know my people's history in Mashpee, and I know how they feel about their history now. Just looking back, I can clearly see that if I were an investor and I wanted to reap the benefits of the resources here in New England, one of the things I might do is try to fund a missionary effort. There were actually people that really felt like they were called by God to save a people from themselves, whether that was good, bad, or otherwise. Investors, like the New England Company, looked at this and said, "Okay, well, the easiest way for us to appropriate some of these resources is to get the people there thinking more like us, and to get them involved in the capital economy." One of the ways to do that is to let them be converted, so they supported the mission effort and supported the building of an Indian college to assimilate people so that there would be less fighting, less strife, and so that their workers wouldn't leave and their investors would be willing to send more money over.

**JKK:** These are the large dynamics of the colonial process that you're talking about.

**JLDB:** Yes. I also think that a lot of people had to eat and pay their bills. Clearly, looking at some of these documents—like, I was looking at one by Josiah Cotton the other day—by putting themselves out to be more knowledgeable about the language than they are, they become more useful to the colony.

There were problems with the translation, but some of the other problems were with cultural limitations. There were all these terms in this language that can mean "sister," so I was looking at a term for "sister," "my sister," "your sister," that's fine. It does mean "sister," but it only means "sister" if it's said by a male. "Brother" says that it means "my sister." If a sister says it, it means "my brother."

**JKK:** So it's very context-specific.

**JLDB:** It just means "sibling of the opposite sex," depending on the speaker. So there are these translation problems with the documents as well.

**JKK:** Now, when you were working at the beginning of the project to get things started, were you influenced by other, related efforts? Did you look at other models for language revitalization efforts elsewhere?

**JLDB:** No, I didn't have the first clue about language revitalization. In fact, none of us knew that this had never happened before, that there had been a language that was reclaimed. We just knew that there were lots of American Indian languages, we knew that a lot of them weren't spoken anymore; we didn't know that there were none that weren't spoken that were then being spoken again. We just didn't know, and we were just trying to look at the possibility of welcoming language home if people were ready to do that. Then we discovered that we were going to definitely need an Algonquian linguist, and then we realized we couldn't afford one and that someone was going to have to go off to school.

**JKK:** And that someone was you.

**JLDB:** Yes. And you know, I don't think we realized that that someone would be me either. I know I certainly didn't. But that's just the way it turned out.

**JKK:** What's the central aim of the language reclamation project, in terms of the relationship between the language and the nation?

**JLDB:** Well, I think that depends on who you ask. The people in the community are so varied, so there can never be any single answer, really, for your people. You get lots of different answers. For me, my aim is to bring the language back to a place where it's the principal means of expression in the community. For other folks, they might say the same thing, they might say, "I'd like to be able to present myself in my language when I die." For other people, it might be that they're Wampanoag and they've been away from home and they want to better understand their history and their philosophy and their culture by looking at language. A lot of people will go away from home, and a lot of times, lately, it's through no fault of their own; parents raise them wherever, and while they're members of the community it's hard to really get hold on what that means. I think people miss out on a huge piece of what it is to be that, without having come up in that community. Learning about language and learning about the semantics of each item really gives us a window for the people that are born and raised here. This is why we do the things the way we do them.

Language answers that question: "Oh, this is where that came from. This is the philosophy and that makes perfect sense." And for people that haven't had the privilege of having been raised home, it gives them a better understanding of their own people and the motivations of their own people and the processes that take place within the community. All of those things are reflected in language. There are still practices that happen at burial ceremonies and nobody understood why, and now when we look at language we can clearly see why we do certain things at burial ceremonies, and language gives us those answers. But I think the answers to why are varied. I do know our next step: our next goal in the project is to get our immersion school opened.

**JKK:** Yes.

**JLDB:** Right now, we're working on getting the master apprenticeship program going better so we can grow more Native speakers and get some fluent speakers on board with teaching.

**JKK:** I want to ask more about that, but first I want to go back to this question of philosophy. You're talking about language acquisition giving your people insight into the traditional worldview and Indigenous knowledge. In terms of returning to fluency, you've mentioned to me that you're raising your toddler to speak Wampanoag as a first language, right? Please tell us more about that process, in terms of raising somebody as one of the first Native-born speakers, so to speak.

**JLDB:** It's really hard. It's really hard. I mean, it's not a whole lot of fun sometimes, because it's gotten to the point—which is good—where she will correct you and she challenges your skill at every minute because she's asking you to explain things. She's four and a half now, so her concepts are becoming more complicated and her abstract thought process is becoming more honed, so she's asking me to explain things. They're topics and subjects that really press you to further your own level of speaking ability in order to communicate back to her properly, so it's a real challenge. It is rewarding, but it doesn't mean that May will be a teacher. It doesn't mean anything really. It means that it's one small thing that helps to welcome language home, because she could decide not to be involved in the work at all as an adult—and that would be her choice and I would still love and respect her either way—but it is a challenge. It means that, come the fall, we need to make some hard decisions about her schooling and what's going to happen, and jut how to keep her speaking when there won't be anyone else at school speaking if she goes to public schools.

**JKK:** So having to ensure that she has access to a community of speakers?

**JLDB:** Yeah, and she won't at school. She just won't because they don't exist.

**JKK:** Right. Now, in terms of the immersion school, would you speak more to that as a project? I also want to ask you what the project's successes are to date, since you started the language revitalization project.

**JLDB:** Well, the goal right now is to secure some funding to get some speakers, from novice speakers to more intermediate or advanced speakers, in the hopes that once that's complete we're ready to hit the ground running with an immersion school. The immersion school is initially for preschool, kindergarten, first and second grade, but maybe expanding if we can get more teachers trained to add a grade every other year. That's the goal with the immersion school. One of my students—Nitana Hicks, who's a brilliant young woman—went to grad school and got her master of science and linguistics as well. She has now been accepted to one school and waiting for answers from others to get her PhD in education, so that we can get the school credentialed as well. That's the goal.

**JKK:** So now there are two credentialed Wampanoag linguists?

**JLDB:** Yes.

**JKK:** Excellent. And would you tell us about the dictionary project?

**JLDB:** The dictionary project started in 1996. I chuckle because I got a research fellowship and I just thought, "Well, I'll do something really useful with the year. I can make a dictionary, certainly you should be able to make a dictionary in a year." Well, you can't make a dictionary in a year.

It's been since 1996, so it has now been about thirteen years. There are things being worked on; there are approximately eleven thousand items in it today, which are basically verb stems and nouns, because the language is poly-synthetic, where you start with a piece that carries meaning and then you inflect that meaning by adding a system of prefixes, suffixes, and fixes to complete a phrase. Usually, one word in our language is really a whole sentence in English, so it gets pretty complicated.

Let's say something is black—if I wanted to say the bear is black and the road is black—black would be different, because the verbs come in pairs. Because the bear is considered animate and the road is considered inanimate, I would say, "mashq m8usuw," and the "m8usuw" means "he or she (singular) is black." "Mashq" is the bear. But if I said "the road is black," then I would say "may m8âyuw," with "may," meaning "the road," which is an inanimate noun, and "m8âyuw," meaning it (singular) is black. It's inanimate and it's black, so you would have "M8usuw" as opposed to "M8âyuw" for singular.

Most of the verbs work in this way. If I see something, "I see" is going to come out differently depending on whether what I'm seeing is animate or inanimate. So, really, the dictionary is about eleven thousand of these items with a citation for where the verb stems come from, where the nouns pull from, and the original sentence or paragraph where the word is found is retyped in its original orthographic system. Then, underneath that, it's retyped in the standardized orthographic system, because there was no regularized spelling for Wampanoag or English for the seventeenth and eighteenth centuries. You can find a word spelled twenty different ways, which is not helpful, so we standardized that and then underneath that there's an example of the word used in context, which is really important, because you don't want something to be ambiguous. If somebody wants to name their child Free you want the name "she is free" to mean "unrestricted" rather than "she is free" as in "anybody can have her." There are those sort of confusions that take place in English that you don't want to take place, and you have to have the items used in context. One of my colleagues, Norman Richards, who I met in what might have been my final year at graduate school, has been putting in a ton of work on that dictionary. He likes to do that, and I told him, "Knock yourself out," so that's the dictionary.

**JKK:** Such vast cultural differences. In terms of developing curriculum, could you speak a bit around the pedagogical styles you use and also the curriculum for adult learners versus children? Are you writing books for both speakers in terms of adult learners?

**JLDB:** Yes. One of the problems that I found was that we looked around to find curriculum for an Algonquian language, and it just really doesn't exist. There's no curriculum that you can pick up that covers an Algonquian language and that covers all parts of speech; there's no comprehensive curriculum that you can supplant that Algonquian language with, whichever one happens to be yours. That frame doesn't exist, so we've had to experiment with curriculum. Your students will usually tell you what's working and what's not working, so we have workbooks that are all recorded—in case people either can't read them—or, in a couple cases, we've had blind students, and we've had the books done in Braille as well as audio. We have workbooks, we have coloring books, we have story books, we have a general phrase book that's pretty popular that gets handed out during large events when people are home or gathering. We have some script materials done for some DVDs that we're hoping to develop, but we always have to get more folks to volunteer their time to get this stuff done. It's been difficult.

**JKK:** It sounds really exciting.

**JLDB:** We also have TPR curriculum—which stands for total physical response—so they're a set of classes where people don't get any written material at all, they just watch and they hear and they say. I really like that, in combination with the NEST [Newborn Enhanced Support Team] system that Hawaiians have going. A group of us went to Hawai'i two years ago to look at the various types of curriculum, and the school system, and Pūnana Leo [private, nonprofit preschools run by families, in which the Hawaiian language is the language of instruction and administration], and we got some ideas for curriculum style that way, but it's constantly being adjusted.

**JKK:** So you tailor it for the specific needs of the nation.

**JLDB:** Yes, and people will tell you, you know, "This works really well for me, I like this, let's do this again?" or "This really doesn't do anything for me, can we change this, can we change that?" To build a decent curriculum is to listen to folks and respond, and that seems to work out.

**JKK:** Now, in terms of the human labor you need to do that work. It's my understanding that the language reclamation project receives no government funding, neither tribal nor federal, state or local. Is that right?

**JLDB:** Yes, pretty much. This year my community has actually given me some money to teach some classes, which is great, but no, we don't receive any funding for all of us. It really is just doing what needs to be done to take care of the community, and I think that there has to be a balance; we do definitely have to pay our bills, and that's the real world we live in. On the other hand, as Indigenous nations, when we talk about self-determination and sovereignty, it sounds great and it sounds really sexy and romantic and all of that, but you need to walk the walk. You need to take care of your own business and get things done and not really whine about why something can't get done—just get in there and do it—and if you're not sure how to do it, then mess it up. And if you mess it up, at least the next time you'll know what not to do, so you've learned something and just keep working. That's been my philosophy.

**JKK:** Besides the tireless work of your volunteers—those who are financially generous or able—in terms of individuals that are committed to your mission, what kinds of materials would financial support go toward?

**JLDB:** Probably just the stuff we've been doing, which is workbooks, camp material, children's books, subject books, and things for immersion camp. I definitely am going to try to get some funding from the National Park Service this year. I'm putting out a request for proposals to work on traditional place-names. I found a document that has roughly four thousand traditional place-names in it, and I'm going to start working on this ethnohistory map project to overlay maps from the 1600s to today, to account for all of the historic boundaries, start to place the place-names on the map, fix the spelling, translate them, and see what they can tell us about the region and about activities and history. So I'm going to try and get some money from the federal government for that this year.

**JKK:** It sounds like an incredible project.

**JLDB:** Yes, it'll be a lot of fun, and hopefully we'll get some money to work on that this year. We just missed the Administration for Native Americans grant application, but my council had actually just voted to establish an official language department with the Mashpee Tribal Council, and I've been pushing for that for sixteen years, so I'm really glad that finally happened this month. That'll give me some more teeth to go after funding. It's hard to get funding for a language department if the department doesn't exist.

**JKK:** That's also part of new tribal leadership at Mashpee, right?

**JLDB:** I think so. Most of the people who are actually in the leadership are—or have been—students of the project, so that's definitely helpful.

**JKK:** That's great. As we're wrapping up, I want to ask if you'd speak to something that I read, something you said in an interview. You've mentioned that bringing back the language is the tribe's sacred privilege and right.

**JLDB:** I think I probably said it's a privilege and a responsibility. I think the point that I was probably making was that everything we have in the world has a balance, and the balance is a lot of times a privilege and a responsibility. We talk about the privileges that we have, and in our teachings the privileges are only there if we keep the responsibility to those privileges. So, while we can say that language is a privilege, there's also a responsibility that goes with it.

The language is our privilege because it helps us communicate with the rest of creation; but, on the other hand, our responsibility to language is to use it, to keep it changing, because language has to change in order to be vital. When people stop using it, it stops changing, and it stops being vital, so that's what I'm talking about.

**JKK:** Beautiful. Would you be willing to tell us about the lullaby that your husband did?

**JLDB:** Yes. It's a song that he sings to May; he sings to the baby. It's a grieving song as well, meaning "Please don't be sad; today is a new day, and all things are going to be good."

**JKK:** And that's your husband, Jason Baird.

**JLDB:** Yes. He sings beautifully, and I can't carry a tune with a forklift. I'm glad somebody in this house can.

**JKK:** I want to invite you to leave us with anything that you want us to consider.

**JLDB:** I would like people to consider that if they want to look at history, to understand the motivations and reasons and "whys" and the "what for" of history, that they consider learning about a people's language before they start to study that culture. I know that a lot of historians are doing this and have, indeed, in southern New England. But sometimes I think they rest a bit too much on the fact that there's not a lot of Native written material. The Native written material that is there is good. And there are places where people definitely have something to say about their conditions as Indian people, and about their feelings around attempted assimilation and their feeling about their connectedness to the land.

I think that I, as a human being, would be seen as preposterous if I set out to study, say, the country of China and to write a history of the country of China, if someone asked me, "Do you know the language?" and I said, "No." "Do you read the language?" "No." "Do you know anything of the language?" "No, but I'm still going to make a history of those people and their place in history." People would see how ridiculous that is, but when we talk about American Indian history, people find that it is acceptable not to study these languages. I think that is not acceptable.

# OMAR BARGHOUTI ON THE ETHICS OF BOYCOTT, DIVESTMENT, AND SANCTIONS

My interview with Omar Barghouti was featured in the first part of a two-part series (which also included Steven Salaita, whose interview is included later in this volume) exploring Palestinian self-determination as a question of Indigenous sovereignty and the politics of Israeli occupation and settler colonialism with a specific focus on the Boycott, Divestment, Sanctions movement. Barghouti is a founding committee member of the Palestinian Campaign for the Academic and Cultural Boycott of Israel and cofounder of the Boycott, Divestment, Sanctions movement. He is the author of *Boycott, Divestment, Sanctions: The Global Struggle for Palestinian Rights* (2011). Here he answers frequently asked questions such as Why "single out" Israel? Doesn't an academic boycott create more barriers at a time when we should be building bridges? What does the boycott entail? How does this relate to issues of academic freedom? How can we productively critique Israel and Zionism and stand firm against all forms of anti-Semitism?

This interview took place on May 5, 2009.

**J. Kēhaulani Kauanui:** I want to start by asking you about your personal background in relation the question of Palestine, and also how you became involved in the Palestinian Campaign for the Academic and Cultural Boycott of Israel [PACBI].

**Omar Barghouti:** As a Palestinian son of refugees, as most Palestinians are, I had no choice but to be involved in the question of Palestine. The core of the question of Palestine is the question of refugees and our right to return. By coincidence, I got married to a Palestinian citizen of Israel, and through an arduous and long, long process I finally attained permanent residence in Israel a while back. Since then I've been living in this country as a permanent resident, not a citizen. Chances are I will not become a citizen, because I am not Jewish and my wife is not Jewish and this is part of the apartheid reality we live through.

All these issues put together—status as a refugee, the apartheid reality, the occupation, and so on—forces many of us to get involved. It's not a choice that you consciously make; you just have to resist this oppression in order to attain any sense of freedom and dignity.

This was the main motive for me to join the Palestinian Campaign for the Academic and Cultural Boycott of Israel, after seeing how the academic community, the so-called international community, world governments, the United Nations, and so on have failed us miserably for six decades. They have failed to hold Israel to account for international law and have failed to protect our basic fundamental human rights, including our right to self-determination. That pushed us to appeal to people of conscience and to civil society around the world to act, to carry the moral burden, so to speak, as they did during the anti-apartheid movement in South Africa. So that's the basic motive behind PACBI.

**JKK:** I see. You use the word "apartheid." Could you speak to the use of that category? In the United States, many who are resistant to the boycott and indeed resistant to the Boycott, Divestment, Sanctions [BDS] campaign targeting Israel are very resistant to acknowledge that there is a system of apartheid in place.

**OB:** Sure. Even some well-meaning people say, "Well, Israel is not identical to South Africa, so how can it be apartheid?" That's a misunderstanding of apartheid, it's a misunderstanding of international law. Apartheid is a generalized crime. It's not South African patented, it's not something that was created only in South Africa. It's true that South Africa gave it its name, and that's how it became famous—like how the Palestinians gave the name *intifada* to the world, but you have many *intifadas* around the world.

The UN conventions on the crime of apartheid have specific criteria. If these criteria apply to a specific situation of racial discrimination that is persistent, that is prevalent, that is lasting, then they define that situation as an apartheid situation. If anybody had done retrospective research on the U.S. South, they would have found out that it absolutely was an apartheid situation because there were two sets of laws—one applying to a certain set of people with a specific identity, and another applying to the people with a different identity—and that's what apartheid is.

In Israel, unlike what many people think, it's not just a problem of occupying Palestinian territories, which is the most obvious part that everybody acknowledges, including the U.S. government. The basic question about Israel is that it has ethnically cleansed most of the Palestinian people—now, the majority of Palestinians are refugees—and refuses to let them back simply because they are not Jewish. Pure and simple. Any Jew around the world can go to Israel and attain citizenship and nationality on the spot. Palestinians, the indigenous people of Palestine, the Palestinians who were expelled and who were ethnically cleansed from their land, cannot go back home as international law stipulates. They cannot go back home, simply because they're not Jewish. That's one aspect that's extremely important in our specific Israeli apartheid reality. Other than the denial of UN-sanctioned refugee rights, inside the country itself there are twenty-plus laws that institutionally discriminate between Jews and non-Jews among citizens of Israel. The Jewish citizens are considered nationals and are entitled to the rights of nationals. Palestinians, the indigenous people of the land who are citizens of Israel, are not nationals, they're just citizens, and they're not entitled to the rights that nationals are entitled to.

There's a two-tier legal system that discriminates across the board in every important domain of life, from education, to health, to land ownership, to jobs, to every major aspect of life. So the fact that Palestinian citizens of Israel can vote, unlike South African Blacks, who could not vote, is minimal. It's symbolic, that's the difference, but it's a meaningless difference. The basic reality of apartheid is across the board, in every vital domain of life.

**JKK:** Given this reality that you're talking about, in terms of its touching every major aspect of life, how then are we to respond to the claim that Israel is a democracy? You know, the saying that Israel is the only democracy in the Middle East . . .

**OB:** You cannot reconcile democracy with apartheid. South Africa was a democracy for whites and an apartheid for Blacks. Israel is certainly a democracy for Jewish Israelis and it's an apartheid for Palestinians. And again, if a democracy does not include all the citizens and if the state is not defined as a state with all its citizens, it's not really a democracy. That's a real far-fetched definition of democracy that does not conform to any of the standard definitions. In Israel, the Palestinians are simply disenfranchised from most of the decision-making processes in the state. It's not a real democracy when you have institutionalized racial discrimination.

**JKK:** I wanted to know if you could discuss the linkages you see. You've acknowledged that Palestinians are an indigenous people, and there's definitely a paucity of understanding of Palestinians as indigenous. Could you speak to question of ethnic cleansing, indigeneity, and also the linkages to genocide?

**OB:** Yes, the Palestinian people are such a mix. I also joke about it, and I say we must be the least pure people on Earth because we are such a mix of every occupying power that came, generation after generation, and we're proud of it. We're proud of being such a mix of so-called races and ethnicities and nationalities and so on, but that's the Palestinian people, and this is the people that existed on this land for many, many, many generations. White settler-colonists came mainly from Europe and colonized the state, just like North America, Australia, New Zealand, Canada, and so on were colonized. There were so many indigenous Palestinians, predominantly Arabs, that in order to establish this white colony, you had to get rid of them. The basic tenet of the Zionist ideology is "a land without a people to a people without a land." The problem is that Palestine did have a people.

It's a self-fulfilling prophecy; in order to make this a reality, they had to ethnically cleanse between 700,000 and 900,000 Palestinians in 1947 and 1948, creating the massive refugee population outside the borders of current Israel and destroying their villages in order to prevent their return. This is a very important part that people forget. Destroying the villages continued many, many years after the refugees were ethnically cleansed in order to create a new reality, whereby the refugees had nowhere to go back to. So, even if they went through the borders clandestinely somehow, they wouldn't find any place to go back to and they would be caught and expelled again or killed. We did not see the same level of genocide that Native Americans did in North America or Aborigines did in Australia, for example, but that was a different era, when white settlers could get away with mass genocide without any accountability.

Israel came a bit too late for that. It was created in 1948, and you already had a United Nations, you already had a certain international system in which, to a large extent, coming after the Holocaust, it was completely unacceptable for mass genocide to occur. So Israel and Zionists opted for what was the second-best choice from their perspective: ethnic cleansing. Get rid of the population. Kill a few, terrorize them, kick them out, and bulldoze their homes. And since then, Israel has been continuing this process of ethnic cleansing and very slow genocide. We cannot compare the genocide that happened in North America. Even the recent massacre in Gaza, for example. It's really an act of genocide, what they've been doing in Gaza—not just war against Gaza, but the year and a half of siege prior to that aggression which starved people almost to the verge of death. It's a very slow death. It's not a massive death as happened in the Holocaust or as happened in North American genocide of the Indigenous population, but this is an act of genocide.

**JKK:** Thank you for explaining that. That's really helpful in understanding the situation. Within the U.S. Campaign for the Academic and Cultural Boycott of Israel, I've heard the term "scholasticide" used to describe Israeli assaults in Gaza that have targeted institutions of education. Did that term originate with the Palestinian campaign?

**OB:** No, actually, it did not come out of PACBI. I think one of the Palestinian academics in Britain, Dr. Karma Nabulsi, was the first to coin that term, but I'm not 100 percent sure. In any case, it's a term we certainly endorse. Israel's war against Palestinian education is decades old. It did not start with destroying buildings in the Islamic university in Gaza or with destroying tens of schools—partially or fully—including some UN-run schools in Gaza. That was the latest chapter of Israel's war against Palestinian education, but that war started long ago.

Ever since the ethnic cleansing of 1948, which we call the *nakba* (catastrophe), ever since the existence of the state of Israel on top of the ruined Palestinian society, they've targeted our institutions for education, especially high education. They've prevented any possibility of establishing higher education until Palestinians established universities despite the occupation, despite all the restrictions. And ever since Palestinian universities were established under occupation, in the '70s, '80s, and so on, Israel did its best to prevent them from developing. During the First Intifada, for example, in 1987, until 1993, Israel closed all Palestinian universities, some of them for four consecutive years. Imagine a university closed for four consecutive years. It closed all schools and it banned alternative education, so as a little kid, if you were caught with books in your hands, you would go to jail, and you would be tortured. Every child had to hide their books under their clothes, because if an army patroller was passing by and they noticed the books, they would be in real trouble for carrying them. This was a reality that is undeniable, that is extremely well documented by many reliable sources.

Closing schools and universities for years on end was intended to make Palestinians a less-educated people, a people who cannot ask for their rights, a people who cannot realize their aspirations. It was what Professor Sara Roy of Harvard University calls de-development. This policy of de-developing Palestinian society and Palestinian reality is an ongoing Israeli policy, from 1948 to the present. The massacre and acts of genocide in Gaza, the destruction of so many schools and academic institutions in Gaza is just a chapter in a long book. It's the most massive, the most criminal chapter in a long record of Israel's targeting of Palestinian education.

**JKK:** In terms of the Palestinian Campaign for the Academic and Cultural Boycott of Israel, could you please speak to the origins of that initiative and your role?

**OB:** Sure. PACBI was established in 2004. It has issued its call for academic and cultural boycott of all Israeli institutions since then. In July of 2005, a year after the International Court of Justice had ruled against Israel's wall built on occupied territories as illegal, that general Boycott, Divestment, Sanctions campaign was launched. PACBI called specifically for boycotting academic and cultural institutions, generating a lot of criticism, a lot of debate, a lot of controversy: Why start with the academy? Aren't they your natural allies? Aren't academics and cultural figures the most progressive? So on and so forth.

All the myths put out by the so-called Zionist class—the academy in Israel and cultural institutions in Israel—are in fact no different than general Israeli society. They're as racist, they're as supporting of racial discrimination, of occupation, of apartheid. Academic institutions have never taken a position, for example, to end occupation. Never, ever. No academic institution or union in Israel has ever taken a stand against occupation, let alone for ending the apartheid reality within Israel itself or for the refugee's right of return. So, even the simplest, most basic, black-and-white issue of ending the occupation has been off the agenda for Israeli academic institutions and individuals, and this applies to cultural institutions as well.

Second, academic and cultural institutions play an extremely important role as an organic part of the military-security complex in Israel. They play an extremely important part not just in perpetuating occupation through research, studies, justification, and so on, but they also act as an ambassador for Israel, giving Israel this deceptive image of an enlightened, Western democracy that does not have any problem except some disputes with its neighbors. This false image has been created meticulously over decades, mainly by academics and artists from Israel and academics' and artists' institutions.

Now, we do not call for boycotting artists, writers, and academics, but we do call for boycotting their institutions, and that's an important difference. It's not a blanket boycott; it's an institutional boycott. It always was. We never called for boycotting individuals. We don't believe in boycotting individuals, for the simple reason that that would involve some form of McCarthyism—we'd have a political test and decide who's the good artist, who's the good academic, and who's not. We oppose this on principle, and we oppose it on pragmatic grounds as well. We're in no position to have a political test to decide who's a good Israeli and who's a bad Israeli. We don't believe in that. This happened during the South African anti-apartheid struggle, but much later on, by the UN. The UN did have a political test to decide who was a good South African, who was not a good South African. We're not there, and we are certainly, as a campaign, not interested in being that thought police to decide who's a good person and who's not.

With institutions, it's 100 percent complicity. There is no academic or cultural institution in Israel that has ever stood out as calling for the ending of occupation or for ending any form of Israeli oppression against the Palestinians. They don't recognize our rights. They play a major part in our oppression, and they must be boycotted.

**JKK:** Would you speak to the conditions for the boycott in terms of compelling Israel to abide by certain precepts of international law? What are the key issues of compliance?

**OB:** Yeah, what's the endgame? People always ask us: Do you want to destroy Israel? Do you want a one-state solution? What exactly do you want?

In fact, the BDS campaign, which PACBI is a key part of, is not a political-solution-based campaign, it's a *rights-based* campaign. In other words, we focus on three fundamental, basic rights that are recognized by international law. Those are the most basic rights, without which there can never be a just peace and, therefore, there can never be a durable or sustainable peace. Those rights are, first, the right to live in freedom without occupation—without colonization in the West Bank in Gaza, including in Jerusalem. The second right is the right to live free from racial discrimination inside Israel. In others words, the Palestinian citizens of Israel deserve full individual and collective equality. The third is the right of return for our refugees. According to UN Resolution 194, they have a right to their homes of origin and to reparations. This is basic. Every refugee in the world has a right to go home; that's basic in international law. Palestinians have been denied that just for being non-Jewish. This has to end.

**JKK:** Any thoughts you want to leave us with?

**OB:** Yes. I think our nonviolent civil form of resistance had a lot of potential, as its South African predecessor did, in turning the tables against Israel and the hegemonic powers that support Israel, including the EU and the U.S. government. I think it's the responsibility of people of conscience to fight back, to resist this hegemony, and to show solidarity among ourselves from the Indigenous peoples of North America to the Palestinians to people fighting for justice and for ending of oppression everywhere in the world. We stand together in one fight against injustice, against this oppression.

# LISA BROOKS ON THE RECOVERY OF NATIVE SPACE IN THE NORTHEAST

Lisa Brooks (Abenaki) was a guest on the show in 2009 to discuss her new book, *The Common Pot: The Recovery of Native Space in the Northeast*, which focuses on the role of writing as a tool of social reconstruction and land reclamation. In it she documents and analyzes the ways in which Native leaders—including Samson Occom, Joseph Brant, Hendrick Aupaumut, and William Apess—adopted writing as a tool to assert their rights and reclaim land. At the time, Brooks was an assistant professor of history and literature and of folklore and mythology at Harvard University, where she was promoted to associate professor before taking up a position at Amherst College in 2012. Among her other projects, she coauthored the collaborative volume *Reasoning Together: The Native Critics Collective* (2008) and served on the editorial board of *Studies in American Indian Literatures*, on the council of the Native American and Indigenous Studies Association, and on the advisory board of Gedakina, a nonprofit organization focused on Indigenous cultural revitalization, educational outreach, and community wellness in northern New England. Her newest book, *Our Beloved Kin: A New History of King Philip's War*, was published in 2018.

This interview took place on September 8, 2009.

**J. Kēhaulani Kauanui:** I want say how incredibly rich I found your book [*The Common Pot*] to be, and that I learned an awful lot from it. It's really important that people all over read it, but particularly those like myself who are not from this land, but living in the Northeast. I'm really happy to include an exploration of this book, especially given the subtitle of my show: "From Native New England and Beyond."

**Lisa Brooks:** Right, right. Thank you. And thank you for doing the show and helping us to tell our stories.

**JKK:** Yes. I find that this book is a major contribution. I really see it as a way that you've reconsidered the historical record and reframed it—and I'll ask you some questions about that. You've really provided an important genealogy written in the appropriate cultural framework to understand what's going on right now today, whether it be state domination of tribal nations or intertribal rivalries, and you're bringing about an understanding of how Indigenous peoples responded to that colonial encroachment. I want to start by asking you if you would talk some about your personal background, and how you came to study the early writings of Native Americans in the Northeast.

**LB:** Sure. It's a long story, so I'll try to give a brief version of it. I think there are so many places where I could begin the story, but one of the places where the book came about was back when I was in my early twenties, when I was an undergraduate working in the tribal office of the Abenaki Nation. One of the reasons I was working there is because I, as a young person, like a lot of young people, was trying to find out and understand more of where I and my family fit into the larger Abenaki network. I was trying to connect a lot of the stories that my dad and grandpa told me to other people's stories, and also trying to give back in a way.

I had grown up outside of northern New England, where my family's originally from—where my dad and his granddad were from—so it was really important to me to reconnect. Especially since the early nineties were a time of real strong resistance in the Abenaki Nation, I was really fortunate to get my education during those times, when people where fighting very hard for sovereignty and for land rights and land reclamation. That's where I got a lot of my education and training in history, working on those land-rights cases and aboriginal rights cases and having teachers like Chief Homer St. Francis and the tribal judge Michael Delaney, elders like Bob Wells and Doris Minckler. And especially, for me, it was really doing a lot of work and sitting up late over coffee with the Lampman family—especially Louise Lampman Larivee and her brother Lenny Lampman—trading stories back and forth and being taught how important it was to understand how the oral history, the written documents, and land-based knowledge are combined. And then, learning how you translate that to non-Native people, how you explain that, how you fight to protect the land by doing that kind of diplomacy. It's not an easy thing, and it's a tightrope that a lot of Native leaders walk all the time.

I was a student then, and I'm a student now. I don't think I will ever be in the position of a leader where I'd be able to do the kind of diplomacy that those folks did, but I sure learned a lot from being there with them. And I'm still learning a lot today. Basically, it's a long way of saying that at that time, I was totally immersed in a lot of these documents and in the stories themselves. Then, years later, when I decided to go to graduate school, I was really shocked when I took my first classes—and they were classes on early New England literature and a class in American nature writing—and I was shocked that there was nothing by Native people or about Native people in those classes. Because to me that was central; for me, when I was learning the history of New England, our struggles were the main story, right? It was shocking to me that none of it was there.

My dad had always said that there's a reason why American history starts with the Pilgrims and then goes immediately to the Revolution. He said it was because of the 150 years in between, where we had the upper hand, where Native people had the upper hand, and there was a way that was hidden. Sure enough, that's what I found when I went to graduate school, and when I talked to the professors about it I was even more shocked to learn that from their point of view, there was nothing out there that they could teach, that the material just wasn't there. They assumed that there were no writings by Native people that would really fit in, and this shocked me even more, because a couple of other Abenaki people—authors Cheryl Savageau and Joseph Bruchac—had introduced me into the networks of Native writers through Wordcraft Circle, and I knew that there were hundreds and thousands of Native writers out there living today. So the idea that mainstream professors of, say, literature and history didn't know the wealth of material that was out there, that motivated me to get out there and show how much there was, and also prove the people wrong who said there wasn't anything out there, that there were no writings.

When I set about to do the research on it, I was amazed at just how much there was. It was like I knew there was a good amount of material out there, but once I started doing the research and archives I found that there was enough to fill ten books easily, and that was just restricting myself to the Northeast. It was just amazing how much writing is out there by Native people. And, of course, what you have to realize is that Native people weren't writing poetry and short fiction. They were using writing as a tool that would help them to take back their lands and to reconstruct their communities. They were saying, How could we make this useful to our communities? So that was a really important thing that I learned while I was doing my research.

**JKK:** Right. Now, I'll come back around in terms of how that early writing technology's been regarded, but I want to ask first if you could tell us more about the title of your book and the metaphor of the common pot?

**LB:** Sure. I think it's a metaphor that a lot of Native people will automatically understand, on both a basic and a more complicated level. It was interesting to me because it was really when I was immersed in a lot of the writings by Native people that the title came to me, and I knew right away that that had to be the title because I kept finding these writings by Native leaders and treaty literature, as well, where this metaphor was used. It was used in so many different ways, but it all meant the same thing. Whether somebody was talking about the dish with one spoon, in reference to a large network of Native nations who are in alliance, or talking about the village as a dish that needed to be protected, or, later on, there was a petition from the Stockbridge Mohicans where they talked about how they had to cut up their dish into pieces. There's one by the Mohegans like that, and then there's another one by Stockbridge later on. And then, of course, in the language there are all these metaphors for land, where the land is like a dish. You see this in both Algonquin writings and in Iroquois writings, which to me seemed really important. It's in the Great Law as well, this metaphor, the common pot. It's difficult to talk about in short because it means so many things, and in some ways it's a metaphor for the land as a bowl that contains everything.

You've heard, in European history, about how people once thought the world was flat, and then had this grand discovery that it actually was round. Well, for Native people the world was always round, but if you can imagine it being a bowl where whatever you put in is there. It's not like if you put something into the bowl, you can then take it out later on. You've got to deal with it. Whatever's in the bowl, you have to deal with.

It also means that everything is in the bowl together, so that everything that you do within the bowl impacts something else. So, sort of like this idea of a web; if you pull on the spider's web, it affects every other part of the web. Well, a bowl is like that, and in some ways it really fits well with how ecologists understand the way the world works now. I think in a lot of ways, people were thinking in ways that really mesh with ecology now, and ecologists are just coming on to this idea.

**JKK:** So, a holistic approach that talks about that interdependency in terms of, say, an ecosystem.

**LB:** Exactly. Yes, and in addition to understanding people and everything that's in the world as part of that ecosystem, in our languages, a lot of the things in the world that would be objects in English are actually very much alive and acting on us, and we're acting on them. It's also about all those social networks, right, that everything we do impacts everything else. Part of the metaphor is that the bowl is a shared space, and that it's a space where we have to keep balance. If a bowl has too much on one side, it could lean over and everything makes a mess. You need to keep that balance, and the way that people in the Northeast believed that that balance could be kept was by making sure everything was distributed evenly. So, one of the roles of leaders in Native networks was to ensure that resources within the community were distributed equally among the community, but also that they were giving out resources to other folks in the network, and that they were coming back.

War often resulted when people failed to achieve that goal, and I think what a lot of people assume is that Native people were living in some kind of perfect harmony or something like that, before the colonists came. Of course, we know that's not true. I mean, harmony was the ideal goal, and we had a lot of strategies in place to try to maintain that goal and achieve that goal, but just like any other human beings on Earth, we also failed in doing that. A lot of the stories that we have come out of learning from those failures.

**JKK:** Well, and you do talk in the book about balance always being the aim, and sometimes the way that that romanticization takes place today—for example, when people romanticize Native cultures in a precolonial era—is to assume, say, there is no violence when, in fact, violent retribution is in some cases actually a part of achieving balance once somebody's overstepped, so to speak, right?

**LB:** Yes, that's right.

**JKK:** I want to go back to that concept of Native space, because one of the things you mentioned when you were talking about balance is living on the land together. In your focus on Native writings during the eighteenth and nineteenth centuries, you examine the centrality of land, community, and the shared space of sustenance among relations. I wonder if you could talk more about how you worked with the concept of Native space. I also want to acknowledge the subtitle of your book, "The Recovery of Native Space in the Northeast," and ask you to speak to that.

**LB:** Sure. In some ways, using the phrase "Native space" was a way to talk about this place before it was called "New England," and also that this place continues to be Native space even after "New England" is imposed upon it. I think a lot of people, again, when they look at the Northeast, they assume that it's almost as if New England has always been here, like this has always been destined to be New England. There's that sort of underlying current in a lot of the scholarship I see, and one of the things I wanted to do was to acknowledge this place as Native territory both before and after colonization. One of the ways I tried to do that in the book, and hopefully succeeded at somewhat, was to dislocate the reader and put them in what for many people would be an unfamiliar territory, in many ways mirroring how the colonists would have come into this place. They didn't come into it as a known territory of New England; they came into it as it being Indian Country.

The idea of Native space focused on the networks of riverways that Native people traveled and the networks of relations—the networks of kinship that connected people in this space. The riverways were really our highways, and even a lot of the place-names of villages and other gathering places, you can really only understand the place-names if you're in a canoe on the river. They're not names from an outside place, they're names from within the river, they're about navigating the riverways, about navigating and getting to these places that are named often in relation to the riverways themselves. Oftentimes people don't understand how these rivers connected Native people almost all the way across the continent. It's really phenomenal, when you look at a map of the Northeast just with the riverways, it's an incredible thing to see, and also to un-derstand the networks of kinship that connected people, because so often when we see Native people in American history or literature we only see individuals or we just see "Indians" as a mass. I really wanted to get to the people as parts of families, and as parts of communities, and turn the way that we often look at New England history around. Whereas historians of New England always know the Mathers—the individuals of New England history on the English side—very few people understand who the individuals or families are on the Native side. That's a lot of how I oriented my research, too, was looking up family names and things like that, to try to find the writings of particular Native peo-ple. I don't know if that completely gives the sense of what I mean by "Native space," but I guess it gives a little bit of a snapshot, anyway.

**JKK:** Certainly. Well, and as you say, you are locating individuals within that—how they are enmeshed with their own social and familial networks and then beyond their own Native nation. Speaking of orientation, you mention the strategy of dislocating the unfamiliar reader from the get-go, and I want to look at that a little bit with you. Your book includes pictures of many maps, and very different kinds of maps, and I wonder if you could talk about how they func-tion and how your strategic placing of them assists in reframing the historical landscape of the region. You really give us a new picture of Native space before and after colonization, and in the transitional period. I also wonder about something very provocative that you say at the beginning, where you state: "The map and the book are the same thing." Can you speak to both of those?

**LB:** Sure. So the maps, I love. The maps were one of my favorite parts of doing the book. They actually just came about, originally, as a tool for me because I found that once I was enmeshed in the writings and in a lot of the land-based research that I was doing, none of the maps that I had worked to help me understand where all these places were. I found myself taking an old road map and redrawing things and putting sticky notes on it, and then, one day—I was just a graduate student and I was at Cornell—I said, "I need a new map. I need a map that just has the riverways." Luckily, Cornell had a map department in the library, so I went there and told the map specialist, look, this is what I need. And, of course, there is no such map, so she actually helped me at that time to make a really rudimentary map of the riverways just in New England using GIS. And the funny thing was that at the time, we couldn't put Canada on there because the systems for Canada and the U.S. were completely separate. Then, even later on, when we went to make a map for the book, we found we had to use two separate programs. We always talked about those borders separating us, and that was a great example; we had to work really hard to get the rivers in Canada and the rivers in the U.S. to match.

**JKK:** Isn't that something? And that's GIS as in Geographic Information Systems.

**LB:** Right. It's a computer-based program that we were using, which was really the only route to doing this, and that allowed me to create maps that would have as the base the riverways and the mountain ranges and the lakes and ponds that were really instrumental to Native people in terms of understanding their own territories. I was really happy that we were able to create maps for the book. I had a research assistant, a former student named Jenny Davis, who really had a fantastic grasp of Native geographies. She worked closely with me in creating those maps and using GIS, and it was an exciting thing for both of us to work on.

In the book, they really function as guides. I feel like it would be almost impossible to understand the chapters without using the maps as reference. My hope is that readers use the maps and constantly go back and forth, because there are a lot of Native place-names in the chapters and I don't often note what the colonial names are of those places, so it's important to be able to go back and forth with the maps. Really, what the maps do is remind and relocate the reader in that Native space and in the Native places, because the writers that I'm working didn't understand, say, "New Hampshire" as a place. They didn't understand the Connecticut River in the way the colonists did, they under-stand Kwinitekw as this central trade route that had lots of Native villages on it, that people traveled through and that connected people all over the country. They understood that area—it's interesting, because they understood that area as being central, whereas today we think of the Connecticut River as the boundary between Vermont and New Hampshire. Native people never would have seen the Connecticut River as a boundary; instead, the mountains are more boundaries, which sort of makes sense when you think about it geographically.

I wanted people to understand these places had names—and still have names—that precede the colonial cities and the colonial states and the colonial boundaries. It was really important to me to take away the maps of the states, because I think a lot of misunderstanding happens when we assume that places existed during those times, when they really didn't.

**JKK:** It's interesting that you've turned the map on its head. I mean, often we think of maps as being a tool for colonization because it abstracts the land, yet you're decolonizing this cartographic approach. I want to use that as a segue to talk about this binary between oral and literate cultures, and I wonder if you could tell our listeners a bit more about that. To me, when you say "the map and the book are the same thing," it really challenges that; and this goes to one of the central arguments of your book, where you suggest that Native individuals learning Western literacy were not corrupted by forms of writing introduced by the European colonizers, but instead that they were using these skills they acquired to compose petitions and political speeches. I wonder if you could speak to that, to writing as a tool of resistance rather than merely being cast as what you call a "coercive colonial enterprise," and challenging that notion.

**LB:** That, for me, was one of the most exciting things to work on, because when I was in graduate school I was again shocked to discover that many literary scholars sort of assumed that once Native people took up writing it was somehow a corrupting influence. They assumed that it would make them abandon their oral forms, and also that an oral story recorded by an anthropologist was somehow a purer form of Native American literature than, say, one of the Pequot author William Apess's very strong political treatises.

I just wouldn't accept that argument. I found more and more that it was rooted in European and European-American anthropologists' ideas about purity, about what's a pure culture and what's a corrupted culture. One of the things that I found in looking at the early writings is that, although there are plenty of Native people that have adopted that point of view, many of the early writers did not see writing that way at all. Instead, they saw writing as a complement. In fact, I was also pushed into looking at some of the earlier forms of writing—such as wampum and birch-bark scrolls and even the Mayan codices. There have been many Native authors, including Craig Womack, Leslie Marmon Silko, and Louise Erdrich, who have talked about this, that in indigenous languages and indigenous practices, this graphic way of writing—with petroglyphs, or with the codices or birch-bark scrolls or wampum—it's the same thing as writing in script.

In fact, our word for "book" in the Abenaki language, *awikhigan*, evolved from the words for "birch-bark writing." That word encompasses all sorts of writing—from letters to maps to what many people would see as artistic representation—but they are all part of the same thing, and they are all tools for marking, writing, drawing, for communicating. And they could be tools for remembering as well, for remembering histories, for remembering stories.

For Native people, writing came to be used in the same way that wampum was used or that birch-bark scrolls were used or, in the case of Mesoamerica, that the codices were used. In many ways, writing has always been complementary to oral tradition, and in practice it has, too. Today we are often using writings that were put down by the people who came before us to recover language or to recover traditional stories, and if we use them in that way then they are really important tools for maintaining and recovering oral tradition.

**JKK:** Well, if we could dwell for moment on the wampum. You refer to wampum as an example, in terms of the relationship between that and the written word, to take down that binary, that wampum, along with birch bark, can be a tool for communicating. For those unfamiliar with the way wampum was worked into early treaties, as written word, could you just explain that a bit more? When you get into these examples of different conflicts that you go into in the different chapters, wampum plays a really central role.

**LB:** Yes. We could probably do a whole hour on wampum and, again, that's something I feel like I'm a student in, but let me give it a try.

Again, there's this perception that wampum was sort of like money—and that's the way that the English perceived it and adopted it in their own colonial networks—but for Native people, wampum was a vehicle for so much more. One of the things that wampum did was "bind words to deeds." I think that's a quote from Arthur Parker, the Seneca scholar. Wampum was used in councils, in treaties, in marriages, and what it would do is if you said words with wampum, it would bind you to those words. So it wasn't seen as something that was just symbolic either; wampum itself is seen to have a power, much like writing, that could be used either for destruction or creation. It could either be used to create relationships or it could be used to destroy relationships. It's something that you have to be really careful with, and you don't want to put wampum with your words unless you really are serious and mean to stand by them.

One of the really interesting things, in regards to writing, is that one of the authors whose writings I talk about in the book—Hendrick Aupaumut, who was a Mohican sachem and who was very instrumental in playing a mediating role in the 1780s and '90s—talked about that if a message was relayed without wampum, or writing, it was disregarded. So it was thought to not have real weight. I think that's really important, because it's showing writing fulfilling that role of wampum, but not replacing wampum. They were both in use at the same time; and, in fact, during that time, say when you see the United States sending a message to Native nations, they would often send their message with wampum, because they understood the importance of that. In the same ways, Hendrick Aupaumut was sometimes asked by other nations to send a message and to record it in writing to bring to those nations, because they were both serving the function of binding those words to deeds and of recording the words in earnest. So both continued to play a really important role.

**JKK:** I'm so glad you've laid that out too, because even in contemporary comedy and cartoons on television, the joke about wampum is that money gets linked to the stereotypes of "casino Indians"—without any acknowledgment about the symbolic and in some ways ritualistic importance of wampum. I recall in your book that you talk about it also as a valued conduit for rebalancing, as a material.

**LB:** Yes. Especially in times of real conflict, wampum was high in demand because it was used in important ceremonies where the emotions that cause violence would be appeased. These were long ceremonies that we're lucky enough to have, in some case, recorded by Native speakers, not as anthropologists or informants but as important records of political council. These ceremonies went on for days, and they had to happen before any political agreements could happen. And you had to have wampum in order to do this, in order for people to clear their minds of the things that would cause violence and conflict between them. Again, wampum wasn't just symbolic here, but it was thought to be a really important material that would help cause this transformation. It's part of many, many nations' very old stories about how to appease conflict.

**JKK:** You have a chapter on Joseph Brant and Aupaumut as they were in conflict due to competing visions of the common pot, "Two Paths to Peace." I found that really enriching, also, because in what little I've read in terms of different individual Native leaders, Joseph Brant gets talked about, but I had never heard of Aupaumut before reading your book.

**LB:** Yes, Joseph Brant's really famous. I was surprised too, because I felt so much of a pull to looking at Aupaumut that I've been surprised in that past couple of years to learn that so many people have not heard of him. He was such an important and often controversial figure, much like Joseph Brant was during that time. For me, the conflict between Aupaumut and Brant was fascinating, because here you had two Native leaders—one a Mohican leader, one a Mohawk leader—both of whose communities had been ravaged by the Revolutionary War, even though they served on different sides. Neither of them made out well, and in the aftermath of that—they were both young captains in that war—both of them went to try to forge a peace between the nations to the west and the Ohio Valley—that entire region—and the United States. They both had different visions of how that was to be done, and I felt like I learned so much by putting those two side by side. You know, there's plenty of books out there on Joseph Brant or that deal with Joseph Brant, and then there's some book chapters and articles that deal with Hendrick Aupaumut, but seeing the two of them together, I learned so much.

One of the really important things about their story and that chapter is—just ask your readers, how many of them have heard of the United Indian Nations? I always ask that question to folks, and I hadn't heard of it before I started doing this research, and so few Americans know about it. It's one of the most important confederations in our history, whether we're Native people or we're Americans, it's really something that we need to know about and that I think should be taught in schools. There was this incredible confederation of Native nations in, again, the Ohio Valley region—but by that region I'm talking about a *huge* area, all the way from New York out into Illinois, probably, and south to Cherokee territory. There were Cherokees and Creeks that had representatives that went into the United Indian Nations. At one time in American and Canadian and Native history, there was a real possibility that there would be an entire country that would be called the United Indian Nations that would consist of this confederation of Native nations, that would be to the west and north of the United States—and again, let's remind ourselves that the United States didn't exist to the west of the territories at that time—and that would be south of British Canada.

Both Joseph Brant and Hendrick Aupaumut were involved in an agreement between these nations and the United States. The story is really compelling, and almost heartbreaking, in some ways, because it came so close. For reasons it would take me too long to get into, in the end the negotiations unfortunately collapsed. But it was probably two decades where Native leaders were working with each other and counciling with each other for months on end every summer, to figure out what to do in the wake of the American Revolution and how they were going to survive. This sort of metaphor of the common pot and, in their words, the dish with one spoon was an important way of them thinking about themselves as a confederation.

**JKK:** And what's so important, what I learned from that chapter, is how none of what we see as the U.S. empire's expansion was inevitable.

**LB:** Right! That's right.

**JKK:** Now, speaking about the American Revolution, I wanted to ask you about your chapter on William Apess, the Pequot author. You give an account of his writing on the Mashpee Woodland Revolt, where you argue that Native people not only used writing to resist but that they also used the political rhetoric of American independence to assert their own Indigenous claims. Can you tell us about that revolt, how they worked with that rhetoric and writing as a tool for resistance?

**LB:** Sure, absolutely. That chapter is really important because it takes place long after the American Revolution, during the 1830s, when a lot of people tend to believe that all of the Indians had already "vanished" from New England. It's important to see that Native people, including the Mashpee Wampanoags, were seeing themselves as still continuing and as reclaiming their land, that again, like you said, it's not like the existence of the U.S. is an assumed thing. It's not like the eradication of Native peoples is an assumed thing; it goes in cycles, and Native people in the 1830s were also reclaiming their lands and reclaiming their communities as sovereign nations, and the Mashpee Revolt is a great example.

Just to give a quick summary, during the Mashpee Revolt, the Mashpees reasserted their right as a community to their land base, and especially to their resources on that land base. They were one of the only places in Massachusetts that was still forested, and it was largely due to the fact that they were still practicing indigenous forest management techniques. As you can imagine, their neighbors were coveting their woods. With William Apess's help, and in council together, they created this fantastic declaration that was much like the United States' Declaration of Independence, saying that they reclaimed and claimed the rights, the resources, and the self-control of their communities, the self-government of their community. One of the things they did to publicize their cause was that William Apess and the Mashpees wrote many times in newspapers, and spoke to the Massachusetts Senate, and talked about their struggle in comparison to the American struggle against the British. This was a great move because the Americans, at the time, were really celebrating their own separate identity from the British and so the last thing they would want to have done to them is to be compared to the British tyrants, and this is exactly what the Mashpees did. For example, in the *Barnstable Journal* they compared their revolt to the Revolution, saying, "We unloaded two wagons of wood in place of English ships of tea." They have a great quote where they say, "And now, good people of Massachusetts, when your fathers dare to unfurl the banners of freedom amidst the hostile fleets and armies of Great Britain, it was then that Mashpee furnished them with some of her bravest men to fight your battles, yes by the side of your fathers, they fought and bled and now their blood cries to you from the ground to restore that liberty so unjustly taken from us by their sons."

So the Mashpees had sent many men to fight on behalf of the Americans and the Revolution—side by side, as brothers—and so they're then asking, as neighbors, as the people of Massachusetts, where the Revolution started, why they then are not fulfilling their commitment as brothers to respect the rights of these people who have fought and died beside them and on their behalf? So it's a *very* powerful statement and a powerful strategy, and it worked.

**JKK:** Pointing out that hypocrisy.

**LB:** Yes, absolutely. Absolutely. And pointing out the uneven power relations too. Yeah, I mean, we went and helped you, why are you now not helping us?

**JKK:** I want to make sure to ask you about the chapter that you wrote that focuses on the Mohegan land case, which was a legal battle that spanned nearly a century. I wonder if you might speak to that and the role of Samson Occom, and also how writing played an instrumental role in that conflict, as well as women's resistance, which you also point out.

**LB:** Yes. That chapter, I think, in some ways for me started with Samson Occom. He was one of the writers who I saw too many literary critics focusing on as somebody who was somehow a victim, who had been corrupted by writing and Christianity, and when you look at Samson Occom's life as a whole, rather than focusing on, say, his time, his association with Eleazar Wheelock; if you don't focus on, say, his Christianity, you see an incredibly rich and complex leader. One of the things that bothered me is that people tended to focus on two texts of Occom's: his one published sermon, which is understandable, because as literary folks we often want to look at the things that people have actually published, and I get that, but the other thing that people focused on was something that was called his autobiography but wasn't an autobiography; it was simply a fragment of a letter that he wrote. A lot of literary scholars focused on it because it fit this European form, and one of the things that I wanted to do with this chapter is feature some of Occom's other writings, specifically his petitions and letters that were more political in nature and that showed his efforts as a Mohegan leader on behalf of the Mohegan people to restore land rights and to restore territory that had been illegally taken from them by the Connecticut colonists.

One of the things that I discovered in looking at his papers was that that fragment of writing, called his autobiography, was actually written as a result of the Mohegan land case. This was really interesting because he was so involved in the Mohegan land case that some of his mentor's—Eleazar Wheelock's—benefactors wanted to withdraw support for Occom because he was so political. He was so much of an activist on behalf of his people, and he had to write this little snippet of an autobiography to dispel the rumors that were circulating about him. Some people even were putting rumors around as if he wasn't even Mohegan, as if he was some white guy pretending to be the Mohegan preacher. So, he actually talks about genealogy, he had to lay down how he was born, and who he was born to, and where he was born, and that he was actually a "savage" originally. And he had to write this in order to prove himself to outsiders. But it was not an autobiography in the sense of Samson Occom decided at the end of his life to write down his life story.

**JKK:** Right.

**LB:** So that frames that document—that everybody uses, that even got published in anthologies of American literature—in a different way. And I think Samson Occom becomes a much more interesting person when we're looking at his petitions where he's arguing as a spokesperson for the Mohegans on behalf of the community to people like William Johnson, to the king of England, and where he's actually making an effort to bring two factions who have been fighting for generations together and to make them a whole. He uses that language, and one of his life's goals was to get Mohegans to see each other as one family, to ameliorate some the common conflicts that had divided them and [to show that] they were really colonial conflicts that were tearing them apart. For me, that was one of the most important things to look at. I think one of the things that I learned when I was young, working in the tribal office, is that the worst thing that can happen to any community is to be divided by these colonial conflicts and these land cases that don't turn out so well.

**JKK:** That's right.

**LB:** And that a lot of times those conflicts create fissures, create breaks in the community that we cannot seem to find any way to heal.

So, one of the things I wanted to look at in this book is how did other leaders deal with that? How did they heal the community from those terrible, terrible divisions that had torn people apart? And what tools did they use—what Indigenous tools did they use and what non-Indigenous tools did they use to be able to do that? I knew that I'd never be a person who could actually do that work, but there were other people out there who have those skills, so if I could at least understand how people did it in the past, I figured it could work as a resource for those people who have the diplomatic skills to be able to do that, that maybe we could learn something from the leaders that came before us.

**JKK:** Absolutely. And when you say that Occom was striving to have people become a whole again, that reminds me of your discussion of decolonization, where you really take up that fuller meaning of decolonization as the process of striving to become whole again.

**LB:** Yes.

**JKK:** I want to acknowledge that your book is a really important contribution that also is exemplary in its use of decolonizing methodologies. In conclusion, I want to invite you to leave us with anything that you'd like us to consider.

**LB:** I guess I can go back to what you just mentioned with Ngũgĩ wa Thiong'o's theories of decolonization. One of the ideas that he speaks about that really resonated with me is the idea of rememberment, and that memory is a way for us to put ourselves back together. Part of the reason why I wrote the book was the hope that New Englanders in general—not just Native people but non-Native people as well—that perhaps the book could help serve as a tool for that process of rememberment. Because I don't think that any of us can heal, and I don't think that the land itself can heal, unless we do the really hard work that William Apess asked us to do 150 years ago or more: to confront the history of this place, to confront all of our ancestors rolled in it, and really, to confront the hard parts of history that too many of our ancestors worked too hard to forget. And that maybe we weren't ready to hear William Apess until now.

My hope is that this is the time to really listen to his plea. He talked about colonial violence as a cancer that would spread out of control and devour us all, and I think, in many ways, that's an illness that we are still suffering from, in our treatment of each other and in our treatment of the land and in the way we understand each other or don't understand each other. I think that's my biggest hope, that this is a book that can help New Englanders confront that history and to see this land in a whole different way.

# KATHLEEN A. BROWN-PÉREZ ON TRIBAL LEGITIMACY IN THE FACE OF TERMINATION

When I interviewed Kathleen A. Brown-Pérez (Brothertown Indian Nation) she was chair of her tribe's Federal Acknowledgment Committee and liaison to the Bureau of Indian Affairs' Office of Federal Acknowledgment. On August 17, 2009, the Bureau of Indian Affairs (BIA) issued a "proposed finding against acknowledgment" of the Brothertown Indian Nation because, according to the office, "the petitioner does not meet five of the seven mandatory criteria for federal acknowledgment." These criteria, which were in effect from 1978 to 2015, were part of the U.S. federal procedures for "Establishing That an American Indian Group Exists as an Indian Tribe" and determining whether any petitioning group is an Indian tribe within the meaning of federal law. The BIA's finding that the tribe was terminated by an 1839 act of Congress is the most controversial, because one of the seven criteria is that Congress must not have terminated the petitioning tribe. The Brothertown Indian Nation was formed in 1785 by members of various eastern coastal nations—Mohegan, Pequot, Narragansett, Montauk, Niantic and Tunxis—who moved to Oneida territory in upstate New York, where the Oneida Indian Nation had set aside land for them. The Brothertown was formalized in 1785 and later moved to Wisconsin, where a majority of members still live. Brown-Pérez is an assistant professor in the Commonwealth College at the University of Massachusetts Amherst. She has a BA in political science from Augustana College (Illinois) and a JD and an MBA (with a concentration in discrimination law) from the University of Iowa. For three decades she has worked with her tribe on their quest for federal acknowledgment. She currently practices federal Indian law in a pro bono role for her tribe and serves as liaison to the BIA and a research consultant.

This interview took place on October 27, 2009.

**J. Kēhaulani Kauanui:** I'm glad to have you on the show, and especially to talk about this really important case and the rich history of the Brothertown Indian

Nation and the struggle that the tribe is up against with regard to the Bureau of Indian Affairs' decision for the Office of Federal Acknowledgment [OFA]. I want to start by asking if you would give some historical background and some basic facts about the tribe: Where is the tribal nation based, and how many members are there and how did the tribe become formalized?

**Kathleen A. Brown-Pérez:** Well, it really starts with the Great Awakening of 1740, which will take us back a few years. It was during that Great Awakening in the colony of Connecticut that my tenth great-grandfather, a man by the name Samson Occom, discovered Christianity, you might say—or it discovered him. He was a Mohegan Indian and he was very interested in how to read the Bible because of the Great Awakening. He wanted to learn how to read and write English, so at about the age of twenty, in 1743, he had his mother approach a man by the name of Reverend Eleazar Wheelock to learn a little bit about the English language, as well as Latin, French, Greek, and mathematics—and Eleazar agreed to teach him. Samson was under the instruction of Reverend Wheelock for about four years, and he was pretty much forced to stop studying at that time because he had bad eyesight and he couldn't read as well, so he stopped his instruction. He actually became a schoolmaster of the Montauk Indians of Long Island, where he stayed for several years. Over time, he realized what was really necessary in New England was a school specifically for Indian youth, and Eleazar Wheelock helped him found this school.

In about 1760 they had the idea of sending Samson over to England to preach. By this time he was an ordained Presbyterian minister and, of course, he was Mohegan, so he spoke the Mohegan language as well. He also spoke Oneida and English, so he went over to England and, as you can imagine, he was almost like a carnival show attraction. It's not that he was the first Indian in England, but he was very different: he dressed like an Englishman, he spoke like an Englishman, and he was a minister. He spent about two and a half years there raising funds, and these funds were supposed to go for an Indian school. He raised about 12,000 pounds, which was a record sum for a colonial charity—I believe it comes to about $1.9 million in 2009 dollars. He raised all this money, and he entrusted it to Eleazar Wheelock to found an Indian school. And what was actually founded was Dartmouth College, which—it's not that they did not have any Indian youth there in the beginning, but it really was not a school for Indian youth.

**JKK:** The hidden history of the Ivy Leagues, right?

**KBP:** Yes, exactly. What happened as a result of that was that my grandfather became very disheartened by what was happening in New England. He tried so hard to follow the rules and be "a good Indian," to do what was expected of him, and he thought it would help his tribe and other Indian people. Instead, like I said, he became very disheartened; he thought that he had done what he could and it wasn't good enough for the English people in the colonies, so he had an idea of bringing together what we tend to term the "Christian remnants" of various tribes in New England. That would include his tribe, the Mohegan, his mother's tribe, the Pequot, the Narragansett, the Montauk that he had schooled in Long Island, and the Niantic tribe as well.

He brought them all together thinking that he would form sort of a Christian Indian tribe, because all of the members at that point would have been Christian. The Oneida that he had missioned to several years earlier offered him some land in upstate New York, so he accepted that land. Unfortunately, right about that time the American Revolution took place, and it took place right through Oneida country. Those of us who had already moved up to upstate New York from New England and Long Island were actually forced down into Massachusetts, in the area of Stockbridge, and lived with the Stockbridge Indians—who were also a Christian Indian tribe—throughout the Revolution.

After the Revolution we all, including the Stockbridge, moved back up to upstate New York, and we continued to live there for many years. The New England tribes moved up there, and we lived there from about 1785 until about the late 1820s. At that point in time, we realized that we had not moved far enough away from the non-Indian settlers and everyone was moving in on top of us, so we started looking for land elsewhere, and Wisconsin was actually the state that we ended up in and it's where we are today. We have land that was previously owned by the Menominee Indians right on the eastern side of Lake Winnipeg. It's a beautiful area, and we are still there and that's obviously where we are trying to continue to survive to this day.

**JKK:** Right. Now, you used the term "remnants"—the Christian "remnant" tribes. These would be people who survived King Philip's War and united together, regrouped?

**KBP:** Yes. It's important that you know that we make a point of distinction that the Mohegan, Pequot, Narragansett, and Montauk tribes still exist today. It was only a few of the members of these tribes that left them and joined with the Brothertown Indians. I think that, for the most part, it was heavily Mohegan, but the Mohegan tribe still exists in Connecticut, as does the Pequot, and the Narragansett are still in Rhode Island. So it definitely was not a confederacy of all of these tribes' governments joining together; it was just a few people leaving.

**JKK:** And also you mentioned the shift in Wisconsin coinciding in the late 1820s, is that right? Now, that's also coinciding with the context of Indian removal. Would you speak to that just a bit?

**KBP:** I can. The BIA wants me to make sure that I never say that we were removed: we moved. We sold our land in upstate New York, we were very involved with the state legislature, and we asked for their assistance as well as the U.S. government's approval to sell the land that the Oneida had given us. We received money for it, we purchased land in New York, and the leftover money was put into a trust fund. But like you said, this did coincide with the Indian Removal Act, which was passed by the infamous President Jackson, so—

**JKK:** In 1830, right?

**KBP:** We were very aware of that as a tribe, and we thought that we were in control of our destiny. We definitely had that illusion, because the BIA keeps saying they did not remove us, but that we moved to Wisconsin. What actually happened after we moved there was that within a year, the federal government thought that perhaps we should be removed further west, and they thought of the Kansas area. Some of our tribal members did move to Kansas, and many of them died. The few that made it back up to Wisconsin said, please do whatever it takes to not be removed to Kansas, because we will die there. And so we did become very involved in our own survival at that point. We wanted to make sure that we could stay in Wisconsin, so my ancestors had the idea to petition Congress for U.S. citizenship as well as allotment of our tribal lands, because we thought that they could not remove U.S. citizens.

**JKK:** Interesting. So they're really trying to negotiate with these colonial structures to protect their people.

**KBP:** Yes, exactly. And they still did everything as a tribe. We had tribal leaders, we certainly knew our history, we knew that we were not part of the dominant culture, but we were trying to negotiate the rules the dominant culture had set up and do what we could to survive. Because we knew they were not going away.

**JKK:** Now the Brothertown Indians did become U.S. citizens at that time—this is in the early 1830s?

**KBP:** Actually, what happened was that the first time we petitioned Congress for citizenship, Congress said absolutely not, American Indians couldn't be citizens. It took a second petition, which they did approve, and on March 3, 1839. We became the first American Indians to receive U.S. citizenship. Our land was also allotted at that time, so I consider that to be a bit of a precursor to the Allotment Act, which of course was very, very devastating for all Indian people.

**JKK:** I see. And we know the General Allotment Act was passed in 1887, so we are talking several decades prior. Now, in terms of where the tribe is now, you said the east side of Lake Winnebago.

**KBP:** We no longer have a reservation, unfortunately. It was about twenty-five thousand acres originally, and the land was allotted and, very much like what followed with the General Allotment Act, we pretty quickly lost a lot of our land to tax foreclosures and swindling. So, now as a tribe we actually own only one acre of that original reservation. Therefore, we're trying desperately. We have a fund, and we save up our money, and we ask for donations, and we are attempting to purchase more land. Obviously, it's a very slow process if we don't have a lot of money.

As for tribal members, we have almost four thousand tribal members right now, about half of whom live in Wisconsin. The other half are spread out around the United States, mostly in the Midwest, but throughout the United States—and actually the world: we also have members who live in China.

**JKK:** You said at the beginning that the BIA really does not want you to say the tribe was ever removed or relocated. Could you explain why? What are the politics of that?

**KBP:** It's sort of the difference between us being a victim—victimized by the federal government—versus us taking control, and we always did try to take control. The truth of the matter is, though, we were very aware of what was going on in this country. We had some amazing leaders in our tribe, and they knew what was going on. They did try to sort of navigate that stormy sea of colonialism, and so it appeared that we were making decisions. But the truth of the matter was we were still trying to operate within that colonial system. We made a lot of decisions we would not have otherwise made. Certainly, we did not ask to become U.S. citizens because we were no longer Indians—that was definitely not the case—but I think the BIA would like people to believe that.

**JKK:** That gets to some of the mythmaking in terms of the BIA. Was U.S. citizenship for the Brothertown Indian Nation in the early nineteenth century cited as a reason that the petition was rejected?

**KBP:** It was. It was cited as one of the reasons why our petition was rejected, and we were shocked. I mean, honestly, the entire proposed finding is very poorly written. It's very hard to dig through, and I know our history inside and out. I know the petition, our original petition. Though our original petition was submitted to the BIA in 1995, it sat and waited and waited and waited, and about ten years later we asked them what was going on with our petition and if could we submit some more documents, and they said we could submit more documents, so I actually sat down with our original petition and I rewrote a bit and organized it a little differently, and we submitted ten bankers boxes full of supporting documentation in 2005. And we submitted more materials in 2008.

I know the Brothertown documentation inside and out, so the proposed finding should have been very clear to me. But it wasn't. I had a hard time following it. I believe that the proposed finding was written in a way to be intentionally misleading. It was anything but clear, even to me. I should have at least been able to follow it. What was especially frustrating was that the proposed finding is available for anyone to read. The confusing and misleading way in which it was written would lead many people to agree with the finding. This would put the general public and other Indian tribes on the side of the OFA.

The truth is that this type of writing—which I don't know what to call other than BS—I think it really is intended to brainwash the general public, but I'm not going to allow that to happen. I want to make sure that everyone gets the truth and becomes aware of exactly what the OFA is like. I no longer consider this quest to be just about my tribe. Having seen how horribly they demean us in this document, I decided this is actually about all American Indian people, and if they can do this to us, they can do it to anyone.

**JKK:** Right. Now, you said that the petition was submitted in 1995 and you had to register an intent to submit a petition, which was much earlier, right? This has been going on for three decades?

**KBP:** It has. We sent in our original letter, where we expressed intent to send a petition, in 1980, so this has been going on for about thirty years. There was concern from the very beginning that the BIA would interpret our U.S. citizenship to be a termination from Congress. Because of the way that the regulations are written, because it is an administrative agency that is determining which tribes are really tribes; they may not undo an act of Congress. So, if Congress terminated you, the BIA may not "un-terminate" you. So that was a concern, definitely, from the very beginning.

One of the things that we did was request a determination from the solicitor's office—the solicitor is the attorney for the Bureau of Indian Affairs—and we received a letter back stating that we had not been terminated by Congress, and that was why we continued to work on our petition for so many years. This was a letter that came out of Minneapolis, the Twin Cities regional BIA office, and then there was a follow-up memo sometime later. It was really that 1993 memo that made it very clear that we could continue with our petition for federal acknowledgment and that there was really no reason to think at that point that Congress had terminated us. Of course, when we look at the act in which Congress gave us citizenship, there is no language about termination at all, unlike what happened to the Menominee and Klamath and other tribes in the fifties and sixties.

Congress did not have a clear intent to terminate our tribe in 1839 when we got citizenship, and that was what the solicitor's office made very clear in 1993. We spent a couple more years getting everything put together, and in 1995 sent off our petition, and then waited, and waited, and waited for fourteen years. And it breaks my heart when I think of all of the tribal elders who died in the fourteen years and weren't able to see this come to fruition. They wasted fourteen years of our lives. And when I think of how many years I've been dealing with this personally . . . I can remember in the summer of 1980, I was fourteen years old, and my mother took me up to Wisconsin—I grew up in northern Illinois—because there was going to be a tribal meeting. At that point the BIA had decided that we were no longer a tribe, and we needed to fix that. So, here I was, fourteen years old, the bored kid in the back of the room, not really wanting to be there, but I remember how passionate everybody was at that initial meeting.

And then, many years pass and it's 1995 and I'm in law school. I was at my great-uncle Cy Welch's house in Madison, Wisconsin, and he said, "You know, we just sent this petition to the federal government. I want you to have this copy of it, you're going to need it." And I thought, "Please, God, don't let me ever need this." And sure enough, many years pass—Uncle Cy passed away a couple years ago—and sure enough in 2005 we sent more supporting documentation and kept sending material and researching. I can't even tell you how much money and time we spent researching and sending all of this material to the BIA. Had they—in 1980, when we sent in our letter of intent to petition, or in 1995, when we sent the original petition—had they just said "Congress terminated you," we would have gone to Congress. But they wasted years and years of our lives and, honestly, the interesting thing is that I actually think that they have made a legal error in determining that Congress had terminated us. So we are going through the regular administrative appeals process, we're exhausting our administrative appeals before we even think of doing anything with Congress, but I really think they simply made a mistake.

**JKK:** In terms of interpreting that 1993 memorandum?

**KBP:** Exactly, and in the lack of weight they're giving their own solicitor's opinion. That's sort of shocking. It wasn't like our own attorneys told us that we had not been terminated by Congress; their attorney told us Congress had not terminated us, and it's sort of a shocking revelation, really.

**JKK:** Now, for those who may be unfamiliar with this process overall, one of the things that I want to make sure that people are aware of is that it is not in the U.S. federal government's interest to federally recognize a tribal nation.

**KBP:** Correct.

**JKK:** The last thing the federal government—or any of the fifty states—wants is to have another sovereign entity within their boundaries. The politics of gaining federal recognition are many-fold, and tribes historically have been able to secure federal recognition through the judiciary, through the legislative branch, and then also through the executive branch of government—that is, through the administrative process under the BIA.

Now Kathleen, you've used the word *termination* several times, and I want to ask you about the criteria for federal acknowledgment: the seven criteria that the OFA uses. If you could first back up and tell us why, why wasn't the Brothertown Indian Nation federally acknowledged in the first place? And what is the history of treat-making, or is that just something that people use to cite to try and destabilize a petition? Could you speak to that history, and then eventually work us up to these seven criteria?

**KBP:** Well, the Brothertown Indian Nation was federally recognized for a very long time. Federal recognition is a government-to-government relationship with the federal government. And it is more or less unilateral: the decision of whether that relationship exists is unilateral, and the federal government is the only party that gets a say in whether this relationship exists. If your tribe has this relationship with the federal government, you are eligible for Indian Health Services and various educational funding. You're eligible to have a reservation, and you're a much more sovereign nation. The U.S. government, as a sovereign nation, recognizes you.

If your tribe does not have that government-to-government relationship, you don't have any of these so-called "benefits," and I always put that in quotation marks because we all know that it's not quite like what the general public thinks it is. We don't receive a monthly check from the government. We do pay taxes, you know. It's not quite like what a lot of people think it is.

But there's a certain amount of legitimacy that comes from that government-to-government relationship. And, unfortunately, the federal government has actually convinced federally acknowledged tribes [of that], so members of those tribes do not respect those of us that come from tribes that aren't federally acknowledged, and so there really is a tiered system of, well, is your tribe federally acknowledged or not? You know, people will always ask that. And we were acknowledged, like I said, for a very long time—certainly, according to the federal government, up until 1839, and we did have treaties as well with the federal government. The year 1839 was when we became U.S. citizens. They're even saying in the proposed finding that we were definitely federally acknowledged as late as 1855.

Now, interestingly enough, I told you we had this meeting back in the summer of 1980 because we were no longer federally acknowledged. It was in the late 1970s that members of our tribe started receiving rejection letters from the regional BIA office in Ashland, Wisconsin, saying we're not going to give you money for school anymore. But the federal government is saying they really don't have a good explanation for why we continued to receive funding. We didn't have a reservation and all of that in the 1970s, but it was really about that time that the Congress started cleaning house a little bit and started thinking about who else can we get rid of, because they had already gone through this official termination era in the 1950s and '60s. The Menominee are probably the classic example out of Wisconsin of a big tribe that was terminated, and once they were terminated their reservation was allotted and the whole bit.

That formal termination process did not happen to most tribes. For most tribes, the BIA just decided, we're not going to federally acknowledge you anymore. All of those tribes are eligible for the petition process due to federal regulations. If a tribe was actually terminated by Congress, then they can only become un-terminated—this is probably the best word—through an act of Congress. We considered ourselves federally acknowledged up through the late 1970s, and when I was kid I never thought about whether my tribe was federally acknowledged or not; the conversation never came up. And then we decided, well, you know, we do need to start in on this process of getting federally acknowledged.

It was a lot of work, but at least we had something written down. Congress had recently passed these federal regulations with seven criteria that a tribe must prove in order to become federally acknowledged. It was really easy in the beginning, for the early tribes whose petitions were looked at—they were just a few pages long, maybe twenty pages long. It took a few months. Originally, when the regulations were passed, the BIA estimated that it would take about four months to review a petition, and that did happen in the very beginning, but not for more than a few tribes I believe. And then the process became years long, and then decades, and so that's how we're sort of thirty years into this process. But it never occurred to us—certainly after we got that memo from the solicitor's office—that we should have been going through Congress. But we did work on trying to prove these seven criteria, and if you'd like I can go through those quickly.

**JKK:** And again, to clarify, this is part of the federal regulations?

**KBP:** Yes. These are the regulations that were passed in the late 1970s by Congress. The first criterion that we are suppose to prove is that external observers have identified the petitioners as an American Indian entity on a substantially continuous basis since 1900. So that's the first one: very vague, there's a lot of debate on how do you even prove this; external observers include anthropologists, historians, people outside the tribe see us as a tribe. The year is 1900. Well, because in looking at our petition the BIA determined that we had unambiguous previous federal acknowledgment, they changed the year 1900. They replaced it with 1839. So, they actually made that criterion harder for us. They decided that, well, we certainly federally acknowledged you in 1839, so that's the year we're going to use. From that starting point, we can see that we federally acknowledged you up through 1855, so then we were supposed to provide documentation between the years of 1855 and 1981.

**JKK:** So they switched the rules on you, violating their own federal criteria for federal acknowledgment.

**KBP:** There's actually a little caveat in those federal regulations that says that they can change those years on you. Of course, we didn't know this when we submitted the evidence, because we did not know they were going to determine that we had unambiguous previous federal acknowledgment and change the year. We had no idea we had to go back to 1839, so we submitted no evidence between the year 1839 and 1900, because we didn't know we had to.

**JKK:** And that's what you had to prove, that you were a historical Indian tribe— not just any old group of people who get together and call themselves an Indian tribe, right?

**KBP:** Correct. So we're supposed to go back many years, but had we known what the years were going to be, we certainly would have submitted different evidence. And we're now in the process of gathering this evidence from 1839 to 1855.

Okay, so that's the first criterion. The second one requires that a dominant portion of the petitioning group has comprised a distinct community since historical times. So, in our case, because they've determined that we were for-mally reorganized at that meeting that I was at in the summer of 1980, they've determined that we really only have to prove that we have been a distinct com-munity since 1980.

So in this case you'd think they've made it a little easier: only since 1980. But then they go in and they look at what we've done since 1980 and, you know, we have powwows and picnics and get-togethers. . . . Most of us really know what's going on in Wisconsin, and yet they kept raising the bar and raising the bar, that our powwows weren't quite good enough and there seemed to be some people there that weren't that interested in being there. Really, it's a very subjec-tive criterion, so they're able to come in and visit us in Wisconsin and decide that we really don't appear to be a distinct community.

Now, one of the ways that they were trying to show that we had not proven these criteria was that last fall they had an anthropologist from the OFA visit us during homecoming or powwow weekend. I guess I was being very naive in that it didn't occur to me that we were guilty until proven innocent, because she wasn't looking for evidence of community: she was looking for evidence that we were not a community. She was looking for anything that could be held against us. I know that now in retrospect, and it sort of shocked me.

**JKK:** So, a bad-faith effort there.

**KBP:** Oh, absolutely. And the sad thing about this particular anthropologist is that if you're thinking, oh, someone from the dominant culture who's colo-nizing Indians, she was actually a Narragansett Indian, and that is one of our historic tribes. Most of us descend from Narragansett Indians, but she was so intent on proving that the Brothertown Indians were not really a tribe. [For example,] she went so far as to, in doing interviews with individual tribal members, that when she interviewed me, she tape-recorded it, and never cited a single thing I said in the entire proposed finding.

**JKK:** Is that right?

**KBP:** She interviewed one of my mother's cousins, who is a "full blooded Indian." He's half Brothertown, he's half Mdewakanton Sioux, he is a dark man. She looked at him and said, "So, when you were growing up, did you know you were Indian?" And we knew it was downhill from there. I mean, we knew we were in trouble. She did not tape-record the interview with my second cousin. She did ask him a very demeaning question, but she'd already made up her mind at that point. I'm still not sure exactly what the OFA is going to look for in proving community.

Criterion three requires that a petitioning group has maintained political influence over its members as an autonomous entity since historical times. And, again, they changed the phrase "historical times" to be the year 1839, and it really has to do with governance or political influence, and whether we had tribal leaders. They don't like the fact that, for many years, we never called our leader a chief. "Chief" is a French word. We never used that. Most of us descend from Uncas (from the Mohegans)—he wasn't really a chief either.

The fourth criterion requires that the members descend from a historical Indian tribe. They actually determined that we don't even meet that criterion. They determined that only 51 percent of our members that were on the tribal role we submitted in 2005 had demonstrated descent from an individual known to be a member of the historical Brothertown Indian Tribe of Wisconsin. Now, the interesting thing about that is that they're saying we didn't really exist as a tribe until we were in Wisconsin, and that's not true. So that was an interesting interpretation.

**JKK:** So no acknowledgment of that migration between New York, Massachusetts, and the survival that it took to band together, to stay . . .

**KBP:** No recognition of that at all, and I found many spelling errors of names that their genealogists had written up for this particular criterion. But I thought it was interesting that their genealogist had used Ancestry.com, which is really not accurate at all—the sort of website that people use to share genealogy information. Those aren't birth and death certificates. This is just people saying, this is who my grandmother was. It's not exactly scientific.

Okay, so the next criterion—actually, I'm sorry, I've actually only been going through the five that we did not meet. The final one that we did not meet requires that my tribe not be subject to congressional legislation that terminated or forbade our federal relationship. Of course, they said that we had failed that one.

The only criteria that we actually met—there was one criterion that requires us to submit a copy of our governing document. We did that, and they apparently didn't have a problem with our governing document. There's also a criterion that says that none of our members belong to other tribes, and we did meet that criterion as well. But we met the two that pretty much anyone would meet. I think the Boy Scouts would meet those two criteria. But the other five, we did not.

**JKK:** So, in saying that Brothertown Indian Nation did not meet five of the seven mandatory criteria for federal acknowledgment, they basically denied the petition at large.

**KBP:** Oh, absolutely. And, you know, the truth is, they could have looked at everything we submitted, they could have looked at the criterion that required that we not be terminated by Congress at any point in time and said we're going to stop the review right here. They didn't do that. Instead, they did a review of the petition, and slaughtered us so that they've made it very, very hard to go to Congress and ask to be un-terminated, because the waters have sort of been poisoned. It was a gratuitous analysis. It was absolutely unnecessary.

After the OFA determined that the Brothertown had been terminated by Congress, its analysis should have stopped. There was no reason to consider the other six criteria. The regulations require that a tribe submit evidence proving all seven criteria. Failure to prove even a single criterion must result in the tribe's failure. Once the OFA determined Congress had terminated the Brothertown, there was no reason to review the other six criteria. It was not just a waste of time and taxpayer dollars, however. The OFA went above and beyond to ensure that the Brothertown did not deserve federal acknowledgment. It put on public record, for anyone to read, its detailed analysis of how we had failed to prove five criteria. I don't know how this cannot impact the support of members of Congress when we approach them to pass an act reversing our termination. They should have stopped right then. But they chose not to.

**JKK:** Can you give an example in terms of that gratuitous nature of the document?

**KBP:** Honestly, the whole thing. It's really hard to pick out one thing. They nitpicked through every sentence, every newspaper article we submitted. We would submit various articles from some of our historic tribes as well, or references to them, because I know that I have Narragansett grandparents and Pequot and Mohegan. We submitted articles certainly referencing them because we still have a connection to those tribes, and they discounted those entirely and were wondering why we had included them at all. They had issues with the fact that we had trouble coming up with proof that we had a governing body in the 1940s. Well, a lot of our tribal members were in the war, and they didn't seem to really care or acknowledge the fact that many of our men were in Europe fighting.

So, there was not really a lot of common sense used, in my opinion, in analyzing this document, but I think the thing that bothers me most is to read it.

And I didn't see it so much as a personal attack, I saw it as an attack on Indian sovereignty. I saw it as an attack on all Indian people. I consider us a historic tribe—we've existed since 1785, and everything we've done has been written down, including those times we went to the New York State Legislature and to Congress. We are *very* documented.

Many thought we had this easy, because we did have it written down, but because the process is so subjective they were still able to take us through the wringer on this, and they did. One of the things I've decided is that the Brothertown Indian Nation has played nice long enough. We followed the rules for centuries, and we continue to exist as a tribe, but it really hasn't gotten us any brownie points with the federal government.

I've been contacted by wonderful people such as Linda Locklear from the Lumbee Tribe, who is a federal Indian law attorney working to get Lumbee *un*terminated by Congress, and we have a great deal of support. What I want to make sure is that what really comes out of this, it may not be federal acknowledgment for my tribe, but what I want to see is a change in the process, and that's actually what I'm working on now.

**JKK:** Excellent. And now you, as well as the Brothertown Tribal Council chairman, will be traveling to DC this month in October for different meetings around your appeal, is that right?

**KBP:** That's correct. We are allowed to ask for technical assistance. We're also allowed to request a formal meeting with the OFA with this team of three that reviewed our petition, which includes an anthropologist, a genealogist, and a historian. We're allowed to ask them exactly why they made various decisions that they made, so that we can respond. We're also in the comment period, which goes until I believe February 22, 2010, during which time any interested and informed party may send a comment to the OFA, either in support of the office's determination or against it.

So this really is supposed to be a very public process. It has not always been in the past; it's been sort of secretive, I thought. But I plan on being very vocal about what's really going on so if people want to support us and they want to support Indian sovereignty against this colonizing government, they can do that. I think it's important for all of us.

**JKK:** Right. Absolutely. I want to back up on one other thing to clarify. What was issued in August 2009 was the proposed finding, and you've just mentioned the 180-day comment period. That is, that they are supposed to take notice of any outside opinions before a final determination.

**KBP:** Correct.

**JKK:** Okay. So there is still a window period where this could be turned around.

**KBP:** There is. Now, the interesting thing about this comment period is that, as an attorney, I would call it a legal fallacy in a way, because it gives us this impression that there's almost an appeal process, because people can submit their comments and we're supposed to see them, and the OFA is, of course, supposed to see them, and then OFA makes the final determination. The truth is, any additional information that we receive, or any comments that the OFA receives—it's not really an appeals process, because there isn't another layer. We are "appealing" to the exact same people who already decided that we did not meet five of seven criteria. They're not going to change their mind. I mean, I really don't see this happening, and so I consider us in this process of exhausting our administrative remedies so that we can say we did it. We really are doing what we can, but we are very mindful of the fact that they are probably not going to change their minds, and our next step is then going to be to appeal to Congress.

**JKK:** Yes, I see.

**KBP:** We're looking at many decades ahead of us still, I believe.

**JKK:** But the fight and struggle continues.

**KBP:** Absolutely.

**JKK:** And the other thing I just want to point out for those who may be new to this whole topic of federal recognition is that those seven criteria that tribes have to meet—the people in the tribal nations have to prove survival of existence in the exact same areas the U.S. federal government has been in the business of destroying for these centuries.

**KBP:** Yes, this is twenty-first-century smallpox. It really is. This is trying to define Indians out of existence. And it makes me think of that saying from World War II: first they came for the Catholics and I didn't speak up because I wasn't Catholic, and by the time they came for me there was no one left to speak up. And, to me, that's exactly what we're dealing with here, because when you think of who came up with these criteria and who can really meet them—I mean, I think there are tribes that are currently federally acknowledged that if they were asked to meet these seven criteria, they could not, they could not provide the evidence. And nobody knows we were federally acknowledged until the late 1970s, and then one day we were not, and nobody knows. No tribe knows whether they're going to be next. And it's a scary process.

**JKK:** I mentioned the ways that tribes can get federal recognition through the courts, the legislature, or the administrative process through the BIA. But what I didn't note is that many tribes have secured federal recognition through the Indian Reorganization Act of 1934 and other means prior to the late twentieth century; there were other ways, right, but then it was very limited.

**KBP:** It was a very ad hoc process, really, until recent years when tribes started insisting on some sort of process. Like I said, the criteria are so subjective that just trying to meet them is really awful, and maybe we should go back to the ad hoc process—who knows. But there has to be something better than what exists currently.

**JKK:** And this also suggests that not much changed under the Obama administration.

**KBP:** No, sadly, it doesn't appear that anything at this point has changed. I don't think President Obama is really aware of the violence against Indigenous people in this country. And that violence, of course, includes structural and cultural violence. The Indian wars and the scalping of Indians may have stopped, but this process continues, and they really are trying to define us out of existence. I mean, a classic example is that the federal government invented that one-quarter blood quantum rule.

And that doesn't exist for any other so-called "minority" in this country. If you say you are African American or Hispanic American, nobody questions that, nobody asks you what your blood quantum is. If you say you are an American Indian, they ask you what tribe you are, they ask you if your tribe is federally acknowledged, and how much Indian blood you have. And, you know, I grew up hearing this, really being colonized in my own brain to think, well, that's the way it is. Our blood matters. And then I realized who was making the rules, and it is violence and it is continuing.

**JKK:** And that is really particular to, as you say, Indigenous peoples. I should just note that the U.S. federal government defines Native Hawaiian using a 50 percent blood quantum rule, which was developed in 1920 and is still used against the Kanaka Maoli people.

**KBP:** Did the Native Hawaiian people get a vote on that?

**JKK:** No, absolutely not, that's part of a congressional law, the Hawaiian Homes Commission Act of 1920. And it goes against our own principles of how we genealogically define ourselves and each other.

**KBP:** Absolutely.

**JKK:** And, as you're pointing out, this is all in the service of dispossessing Indigenous nations.

**KBP:** Exactly, it is. And things really have not gotten better. I am hopeful that Barack Obama and his administration will change this, but I think that it's going to take some of the Brothertown and some of our supporters being very vocal about how horrible this process is.

**JKK:** Yes. Now, in concluding our interview I want to invite you to leave with any lasting thoughts that we might consider about this case.

**KBP:** Thank you, Kēhaulani. One of the things that we would like to make everyone aware of is how broken the federal acknowledgment process is. This isn't just about the Brothertown Indian Nation. This is about all of us. And it's about the federal government trying to tell us exactly who we are, and it's time for us to stop that. And that's going to include support from federally acknowledged tribes in particular who are going to have the guts to stand up and say, okay, maybe we have the status, but it is a broken process and this is not what our ancestors were looking for. So that's really all we want to come from this: somehow fixing what's broken, because in the year 2009 we shouldn't be dealing with this still.

# MARGARET BRUCHAC ON ERASURE AND THE UNINTENDED CONSEQUENCES OF REPATRIATION LEGISLATION

Margaret (Marge) Bruchac (Abenaki) is a scholar whose research focuses on the historical erasure and cultural recovery of Indigenous peoples in the Connecticut River Valley. She discusses the "unintended consequences" of the Native American Graves Protection and Repatriation Act of 1990 (NAGPRA) and the ways in which the language of erasure has been encoded into archaeological practices and state recognition, federal recognition, and federal law in ways that make northeastern Indians appear to have vanished, or to have been disconnected from their own ancestral past. Among Indigenous peoples in the United States, NAGPRA is considered landmark legislation that works to restore respect to ancestors whose remains have long been considered the property of non-Native others, since the legislation was grounded in recognition that alienation of human remains and items of cultural patrimony violated Native religious traditions and common-law rights to protect the dead. However, Bruchac's critical work in this area asks, How does this important legislation deal with the cultural differences and distinctive histories that mark the nation's hundreds of Native societies? Given the varied survival strategies of Native people, does the law accommodate groups whose legal status may differ significantly? What kinds of evidence should be accepted in repatriation decisions? Bruchac is an assistant professor of anthropology at the University of Pennsylvania and coordinator of the Native American and Indigenous Studies Initiative at Penn. From 2008 to 2012 she was an assistant professor of anthropology and coordinator of Native American and Indigenous studies at the University of Connecticut. Two years after this interview, the Department of the Interior announced a new rule implementing NAGPRA by adding procedures for the disposition of culturally unidentifiable Native American human remains in the possession or control of museums or federal agencies. This rule also amends sections related to the purpose and applicability of the regulations, definitions, inventories of human remains and related funerary objects, civil penalties, and limitations and remedies.

This interview took place on January 29, 2008.

**J. Kēhaulani Kauanui:** I understand that your doctoral thesis is titled "Historical Erasure and Cultural Recovery: Indigenous People in the Connecticut River Valley." In it, you explore the resonance of the "vanishing Indian" paradigm in historical, museological, and anthropological interpretations of Native American Indian peoples, including Agawam, Nonotuck, Pocumtuck, Sokoki, and Woronoco in the middle Connecticut River Valley of western Massachusetts. Please tell us more about this research, and explain what you mean by "historical erasure" in this context, and how it relates to the activities of local historians and collectors.

**Marge Bruchac:** The interesting thing about the middle Connecticut River Valley is that it's one of the regions on the North American continent where Native people are believed to have entirely vanished. If you read historical treatises from the nineteenth century, if you read even the list of federally recognized tribes today, it may look as though it's an empty space. But what I found when I was doing research into these collections is that that sense of emptiness, that sense of vanishing, was a direct artifact of the collecting process, and of the process of constructing histories that caused Native people to seem to have disappeared when in fact they were very much present, and very much connected to other tribes throughout the region.

When I went to do my doctoral research at the University of Massachusetts, I was stunned by the fact that there were more dead Indians in the anthropology collections than there were living Indians on campus. And that was an ethical problem as well as just a logistical problem. I was concerned about the fact that the museum and the institution seemed to have been rather slow in complying with NAGPRA. In fact, what was happening is not that the college was slow in complying but that because there were no federally recognized tribes directly associated with the vast majority of the individuals in the collections; they were classified under the NAGPRA process as "culturally unidentifiable." And that in itself is a powerful form of historical erasure.

**JKK:** Seeing as how that erasure is a product of the collecting process itself, please tell us more about the collectors at the time and how they were pulling these materials into their collections. And what was going on with living American Indian communities right in their midst?

**MB:** In the mid-nineteenth century, and right up really until about the mid-twentieth century, it was very difficult for Native people in New England to be considered as visible. The "vanishing Indian" paradigm was a very popular literary trope; the notion of salvage archaeology and salvage anthropology drove those disciplines in such a way that collectors were not particularly interested in living Native communities. They were interested in living Native communities out West when the Western Indian Wars were going on, but in the East there was this unfortunate perception that somehow colonial settlement had just washed over the region and spread westward and left nothing behind in its wake.

I didn't do research on the individuals in the collections themselves; the research I did was on the collectors who did the excavating. What I started to discover is that when you track the social networks of men like Harris Hawthorne Wilder of Smith College, Edward Hitchcock Jr. of Amherst College, and George Sheldon of the Pocumtuck Valley Memorial Association you find that they were part of a network of regional collectors who, in a sense, were conspiring to exhibit the dead as the most real and visible Indians, and they were truly not interested in ethnography or folklore or the political status of living Indians. They considered them to be immaterial to their studies. This collecting process was taking place during the emergence of anthropometric and craniometric studies that postulated the notion that white Euro-Americans were more civilized and more intelligent than Native American Indians. And so, even the focus and the fetishization of Native remains was based in this idea that the *bones* were valuable objects of study but the *people* were of very little or no interest.

I was concerned about seeing these ancestors repatriated; I was concerned about seeing them returned to their communities of origin, and there was a perception that there was little information available about those communities of origin. So my research project became a combined track into the colonial documents to see what information did exist, into eighteenth-century removals and displacements and diaspora of Native peoples, because there was a large-scale movement of Native people out of this region into surrounding areas.

By looking at the collecting process, what I discovered is that in the nineteenth century, Native people frequently were present in this valley, and they were often in direct communication with and contact with the collectors. It's fascinating to see how they were literally written out of the history.

In the twentieth century, many of the direct descendants of those Native people who were visible during the nineteenth century actually came to these colleges and museums and made their presence known—and this is in the early twentieth century, before the advent of Native American studies. People came and said, "Here's who we are, here's what our connections are," and their histories were sort of pushed aside because they weren't considered "real Indians"; they were considered either degenerates or remnants or mixed-bloods or in some way disconnected and immaterial to the scientific study of real Indians. This idea of what was "real" and what was "false" was constructed by the collectors.

**JKK:** So the collectors themselves had face-to-face contact with living Indian people at the time, and yet they wrote those encounters and those relationships out of the historical record?

**MB:** A good example of that is that Harris Hawthorne Wilder and Inez Wilder of Smith College went into Native communities during the first decades of the twentieth century to look for examples for craniometric study, to search for skulls of prominent individuals. And in one instance they actually did their excavations in the Royal Burying Ground at Narragansett territory in Charlestown, Rhode Island. They walked down the rows of marked graves of the Ninigret family to try to find individuals they were seeking, and these collectors had no compunctions whatsoever about going into marked gravesites from the historic era, as well as more ancient gravesites from the pre-European contact era.

There were also many instances I uncovered in the collectors' records where they would open a gravesite, for example, and find a family buried together—several people, and children, and dogs and sometimes there were funerary objects, sometimes there were not—and again, they had no compunctions about taking all these people and things apart and scattering them based on the nature of their scientific studies. So, what would happen is that skulls might go to one collector, pelvic bones might go to another, funerary objects might go to someone else, the red ochre that was buried with these people would be dust, and brushed away just like it was dust.

The level of disconnection and disturbance went far beyond just the scientific collecting process, it also went into the way in which these people were categorized and stacked in collections so that it became very, very difficult to figure out how to piece all of this back together. And when I started this research project, a number of people cautioned me that it would be virtually impossible to determine precisely where these remains came from or precisely who they were related to. What I found was the exact opposite, because the collectors' records were, in most cases, quite extensive and quite detailed about precisely where they had been digging, and many dig sites in the valley were so popular that collectors from all over New England came to dig them. So people from the Peabody Museum at Harvard, the Peabody Museum at Yale, Warren K. Morehead, collectors from all of these prominent institutions found the Connecticut River Valley to be a very prime collecting place and, as a result, individuals from the same gravesite were often scattered into different collections throughout the region.

**JKK:** So even in the collectors' search for what they considered to be the authentic Indian, which was "the dead Indian," there's still this issue of disconnection, dismemberment, and destruction?

**MB:** Right. And the other part of it too is the construction of information, because the idea that dead Indians were real, and that dead Indians were natural resources, became part of the construction of physical anthropology as a science.

**JKK:** Yes, and so you also have the different systems of classification of knowledge at work there. When you originally started working on your project, was it originally your intention to study these collectors? How did you come to settle on looking at them?

**MB:** This was honestly not my intention. When I went to graduate school, my intention was to continue the work that I do as an historian and as a folklorist and a storyteller, and what I was most interested in was how oral traditions connect people to the landscape. And it was when I discovered the collections of dead ancestors that were still literally trapped in the museums, I thought: "What has happened here? Why are these people still here?" And I started to feel, in a sense, that I had actually been drawn to do that work specifically to help untangle that process. So, for example, until I started working closely with the University of Massachusetts Amherst, there had been very little cooperation with Smith College and Amherst College, and those institutions had done much of the original digging. There had been some repatriation work already accomplished by the Pocumtuck Valley Memorial Association, but they thought the job there was essentially done. One of the things that I did in 2003 was to convince the institutions to form a five-college repatriation committee, and that committee now shares all information on these sites and these collections and whatever is known about the collecting processes, and it shares the consulting work as well. So that way there are no more hidden collections. There are no more secret places where items might be resting on a professor's shelf or hidden in someone's file cabinet. Because one of the problems I discovered with the NAGPRA legislation is that it does not require institutions to cooperate with each other. And so, as a result, any institution can construct whatever line of cultural affiliation it chooses, based on who they consult with, and based on what their assumptions are about their collections. I found during the process that, for example, the Springfield Science Museum had done excavating in some of the same sites but had refused to consult with Abenaki and Nipmuc people about repatriating these remains.

**JKK:** So in that process, where some parts were separated from other remains, say one institution wanted to try and put together the remains of one particular person, does that mean that someone might withhold their collection and not let the other institution know that they have part of the same individual?

**MB:** Right. And sometimes it's not a conscious withholding. Often it's the case where one institution might have the remains, and another might have the field notes, and another might have access to published articles based on those remains and field notes that might not be explicit. And that's why what I called for, midway through this process, was a regional approach to dealing with the "culturally unaffiliated" or so-called "unidentifiable." Because the other problem is that the NAGPRA legislation, which was intended to be a process of repair and restoration, also in itself became a process of disconnection, because by creating a category called "culturally unidentifiable and unaffiliated" it created the impression that these were primarily ancient remains with no provenience whatsoever, when in fact the remains of non-federally-recognized tribes are in that category and, in many cases, are quite well documented.

So, one of the things I've been arguing for with the changes in legislation coming along is that we need a category that says "historically identifiable" or "historically unidentifiable," "documented" or "undocumented," "known" or "unknown," because the concept of who has rights to their ancestors . . . I mean, it gets absurd after a while when you think about it, because the U.S. government didn't exist at the time that many of these ancestors were interred. And the notion of federal recognition didn't exist when many of these collectors were doing their work. So to use these modern categories to divide these people sometimes creates more disconnection than it does connection and repair. And so that's why the other thing I feel is so urgent and necessary is cooperation and collaboration on a number of different levels.

**JKK:** Right. Not just a legal issue, but an ethical imperative.

**MB:** I think museums should be held to the highest standards of documentation in releasing information about these collections. And, unfortunately, that requires work. That requires work that many museums don't have the funds to do, don't have the staff to do, and might not even have the knowledge or inclination to do. In fact, there's a funny aspect to this; there were several points where other Native people misunderstood what I was doing. Because I used the term "research," and because I am the repatriation research liaison for the five colleges, there were actually Native people who assumed that meant I somehow directed or participated in biological research, or physical research, or some kind of intrusive research into the bones themselves. I don't even go into the rooms where the ancestors are stored. All of my work is archival work on the collectors, and it's amazing how much information you really can draw out when you do that work.

So, for instance, I wrote a little position piece at one point called "Wilder's Hands," and I was trying to understand how Harris Hawthorne Wilder could justify putting his hands into other people's graves. How he could go into a marked gravesite and not think about these people as living beings. And so what I tried to find—through their writings, through their photographs, through their collections—was what kind of philosophical ideas, what kind of emotional connections these collectors felt. I found writings by George Sheldon, for example, who was ferociously determined to not allow Native people to have any kind of continued existence, and, in part, it's because his vision of the Pocumtuck Valley Memorial Association was based on the idea that the Indians had been driven out of the valley so that it could be a bastion of civilization. And even the possibility of interacting with living Native people—who, by the way, I discovered had actually been sitting beside him in

the church in 1837—he could not speak of. In his entire two-volume history
of Deerfield, he devoted a single line to these Indian visitors and he gave them
no names, no agency, nothing. But yet, if you look at the records of Dr. Steven
Williams, who encountered these same Indians in 1837, he said: "They come
to town frequently and people are constantly going to them for treatment of
their illnesses," because among them was the Indian doctor Louis Watso, who
was very effective and very involved with Native people and other people all
through this valley.

There are two quotes from my research into the archives that really, for
me, sum up the philosophy of these collectors. One is from Harris Hawthorne
Wilder writing to Clark Wissler in 1917, where he writes: "I have just finished
the preparation of a beautiful aboriginal skeleton of local origins, a young
woman of Pocumtuck's between Deerfield and Greenfield. I removed the entire
grave, earth and all and no bone has been disturbed from its original position."

Patricia Erikson, who found this quote for me, noted that, in fact, *every*
bone was disturbed. This was an incredible level of disturbance, but what
Wilder was focused on was this fetishized attachment to this woman's remains
in a way that ignored her personhood, ignored her nationhood, ignored her
actual connection to her home community and just turned her into this object
of adoration. There is another quote that, for me, really sums up the focus of
these collectors—and I have to note here that, during the most intense part of
the collecting era in the Connecticut River Valley, there was also a great deal
of discourse about sending missionaries to the western Indians, and many of
these colleges were involved in that missionary movement. In 1904, Edward
Hitchcock Jr. of Amherst College wrote to Harris Hawthorne Wilder: "My dear
Wilder, I thank you for the invitation, but we have a big missionary person here
on Saturday and I must be looking after the work of the perishing living savages rather than to look after the craniae of the dead ones. But perhaps we can do
something in the way of exchange, for if you can get a veritable skull or other
bones, I have several hundred stone implements which I can swap."

Now, I should say, much to their credit, that Amherst College and Smith
College have both been very forthcoming in supporting this collaborative research and in supporting the formation of the five-college committee. And it's
really quite heartening to have institutions that really are willing to step up and
understand the ethical dimensions and the level of work that really needs to be
done. They have been incredibly supportive of this research.

So, I uncovered a lot of really rich stories about these interactions and these
individuals, and it became so sad after a point. Here are these families who are
on Earth, families who are interred in a place that their people have been for
thousands and thousands of years, and they are resting only a few miles from
that spot, but at this moment in time they cannot go home until all of the legal
hurdles in NAGPRA are jumped in the appropriate sequence. So, there are

actually moments when I realize that, during the mid-twentieth century, some of the collaborations that local institutions in Massachusetts developed with the state historic preservation officer, with the Massachusetts Commission on Indian Affairs, and with local tribes, some of those collaborations formed a really good model for how to do ethical repatriation. And some of those collaborations have been delayed by the NAGPRA process, which requires an entirely different model of consulting and reporting and repatriating.

**JKK:** I want to ask you more about this issue of the hurdles of NAGPRA. For tribal peoples who are still present on the land, they might be able to prove cultural affiliation. What about those that might not be as visible? I live in Middletown, Connecticut (the indigenous homeland of the Wangunk people)—how might Wangunk remains be re-interred or repatriated?

**MB:** You know, that's a really excellent question and I can tell you what I know from the middle Connecticut River Valley. I know very little about the Wongunk people or Wangunk people. But what we do know is that during that eighteenth-century era of relocation, many of the smaller tribes—the Pocumtuck from Deerfield, the Nonotuck from Northampton, the Podunk from around Hartford—shifted and folded in with surrounding tribes. In some cases, in Connecticut for example, some of those surrounding tribes are federally recognized. So the Mohegan and Pequot might have information, the Schaghticoke—who are not recognized—might have information, the Paugussett might have information. In the middle to upper Connecticut River Valley, we need to be consulting with the Nipmuc, the Hassanamisco and the Chaubunagungamaug Nipmuc; we also need to be consulting with the Missisquoi Abenaki and the Pennacook Abenaki.

And part of what is problematic in NAGPRA is that it pays very little attention to the historical connections among different tribal groups, and a great deal of attention to the modern political connections. So, I think that every regional consulting process needs to be very very attuned to that, to which tribes can historically be traced to those sites and those individuals or those regions over time, and how are they connected. So, for instance, one of the oddities of NAGPRA is that people often assume that the legislation does not allow institutions to repatriate to non-federally-recognized tribes, and that's simply not true. There have been, I think, roughly on the order of twenty to thirty direct repatriations to unrecognized tribes, and often with the full consent of surrounding recognized tribes.

A great example is Vermont and New Hampshire. It's understood, and it's also been widely practiced, that any remains found in Vermont and New Hampshire are Abenaki. There is no question, at this point, as far as I know, there have been no claims by other tribes, and there's no reason for other tribes to claim remains from that area. So the Peabody Harvard Museum has done some repatriations, the Peabody Museum at Andover Academy has also done some, and, of course, there have been repatriations from Franklin Pierce College in New Hampshire and others. As I say, a lot of the problem is in the discourse around ownership and power, a lot of the problem is in the definitions of affiliation and history and tribe, and in many cases we have contemporary definitions that have very little grounding in common sense and a great deal of grounding in particular political entitlements. And when you think about it, the whole idea of federal recognition is a shifting category, because tribes that are not recognized now may be recognized ten years down the road, or twenty years down the road.

**JKK:** In terms of collaboration, what role do Native oral traditions play in these histories and their erasure and/or enduring presence?

**MB:** Oral traditions are an essential part of the consulting process, and again, we need to consider the oral traditions of many different tribes. So, for instance, many archaeologists are reluctant to even consider oral traditions in part because there's this assumption that an oral tradition is a story or a bit of folklore, but in fact, many of these stories that Native people share are linked to particular places on the landscape, particular moments in time, to geological events, and often there's a great deal of information contained in oral traditions that might not be obvious at first hearing.

A great example is in the Connecticut River Valley. One of the oldest oral traditions I'm aware of is a story that's linked to the shaping of the Pocumtuck range, of the hill that's called the Pemawatchuwatunck, "the long hill," and of the people who call themselves the Amiskwôlowôkoiak, meaning "the people of the beaver-tail hill." And there is a Pocumtuck oral tradition about a giant beaver coming down the river and creating a great hollow by digging out the land, and it fills up with water and he builds a dam, and then the beaver is killed and the dam is opened and the water drains out; and this story is a metaphor for the creation of a glacial lake that, ironically, is now called glacial "Lake Hitchcock." It's named for President Hitchcock of Amherst College. But that glacial lake formed in such a way that, as the water flowed back and as the glaciers moved, over the resistant rock, it left one of the hills in the shape of a reclining beaver. And so, it's not just an anthropomorphic version of a hill that looks like a beaver; it's an oral tradition that contains within it the knowledge of how this region was shaped, in a form that's recognizable to generations of Native people.

Now, that particular oral tradition survived among Abenaki people in the north—Abenaki people around Missisquoi, around Odanak, and around other mission villages in the north who had moved, who became "Abenaki" as they moved out of this valley. And that's one of the ironies here, is that tribal names shift over time based on how observers are identifying those people. Many of the Native people that we call "St. Francis Abenaki" today are themselves an amalgam of Pennacook, Pequawket, Cowasuck, sometimes Missisquoi, often Pocumtuck and Agawam and Sokoki and even Woronoco people who during the late 1600s and 1700s moved north to join their allies as the English were pushing them around in central New England. And so, when you trace those oral traditions, and when you trace where they survive and the detail with which they survive, that often can be a clue about who those people are and where they come from.

**JKK:** So this issue is bound to these histories in order to repair and restore. I really like that you're thinking about this so expansively in terms of countering what you've called, in other contexts, the unintended consequences of NAG-PRA. Can you speak more to some of the ways that the language of erasure has been encoded in the law and/or in archaeological practices?

**MB:** There's actually a fairly easy way to answer that, in that the NAGPRA legislation itself lists a broad category of material that can be used as evidence for cultural affiliation. And, in working with the University of Massachusetts Repatriation Committee, we sat down and decided to actually compile the evidence that we had on hand. The archaeological, biological, ethnohistorical, linguistic, geopolitical, geographical, genealogical—we put all of it together, and what we found is that it corresponded very well, ironically, to the original assessment of the collectors themselves. The collectors said, these people that we're excavating are Nonotuck, Pocumtuck, Sokoki, and when the evidence is weighed it points to not only those same original tribes, but it also points quite directly to Abenaki and, in some cases, Nipmuc affiliations. So, interestingly enough, the process of actually doing the on-the-ground research with Native oral traditions, with interviews with tribes, with looking at the existing material, does create a very clear line of evidence.

But, I think what happens is that in the consulting process, many museums and institutions cut to the chase. And they cut to the chase because NAGPRA is an inordinately expensive process. It takes time and effort to consult, it takes a great deal of attention and interest that many museums simply don't have the expertise or the money for, and we also found, unfortunately, that when you apply for a NAGPRA grant, the grants are far more likely to go to institutions that are consulting with recognized tribes. And so it's very difficult to get funding for consulting with non-federally-recognized tribes, which is another inequity in the process.

**JKK:** Say that institutions get researchers on board—not to do the biological research, but to do the painstaking process of archival research, oral tradition, looking at collectors' materials—and are able to make the affiliation connection. What would the next step be?

**MB:** I think the next step is probably the most delicate and diplomatic one, and it's sometimes the most difficult for museums to do. And that's the step of coming to some kind of consensus: among federally recognized tribes that have expressed an interest in the collections; among non-federally-recognized tribes if they are seen to be culturally affiliated; among the institutions that may or may not share collections; and even sometimes among the members of those institutions themselves, because there still is a great deal of resistance to repatriation in some corners. There are still many archaeologists who have made their careers on studying Native remains, there are still many institutions that have large collections of Native artifacts that they are reluctant to part with. That process is so delicate and needs to be so diplomatic. It also requires academics and collectors to think differently about the notion of ownership, because so much of American and Euro-American science is built on the concept that it is appropriate and right and just and even good for researchers to own the remains and the personal possessions of other people for the purpose of academic study; that is somehow seen as a universal good that will serve humanity as a whole. But for Indigenous people, that is a universal wrong that is incredibly hurtful and painful and destructive of personal possessions, of personal privacy, of personhood.

It's so hard sometimes to explain how painful it is to even consider the fact that one's ancestors and ancestral remains and possessions could be owned by or touched by or held by someone else who is not connected to that person. In many of our tribes, we believe that it can cause great damage to people who are walking around in this moment in time if the ancestors are disturbed. And we often, many of us have often also expressed that concern to the people who are in these institutions, saying that we are concerned on your behalf as well.

This entire problem is a difficult one, but legislation is not the *best* and the *only* answer to the problem. I don't know if you've followed any of the controversy around the new NAGPRA regs right now, but I'm so dismayed at responses of groups like the Society for American Archaeology. They have just put out really histrionic papers, saying this will destroy the database of material and information that we've founded our entire discipline on. And I think that response doesn't even begin to consider the human dimension of the excavation of someone else's remains.

**JKK:** Yes, that also links to academics and museum officials who are resistant to these legislative revisions because they are crying out for more research on these remains as an excuse to hang on to the so-called culturally unidentifiable Native remains. In terms of the legislative revisions that are currently pending on NAGPRA, do you think that they might better provide for the repatriation of remains currently categorized as culturally unaffiliated and unidentifiable? And what are the regional issues—to get back to one of your main points— around getting institutions to work together to do these repairs, rather than just doing secret deals behind the scenes to sort out their collections into affiliated and unaffiliated piles regardless of the actual evidence?

**MB:** I hope that the new revisions will help, but I remain skeptical, because the language is so problematic. Historical erasure is so profoundly embedded in the way we describe other people and the way we categorize people, and the fact that NAGPRA has a "culturally unidentifiable" category in itself is a problem that will continue to haunt us as long as we rely on this legislation. I truly believe that if there was a way to change the legislation itself, so that it used commonsense definitions of tribe and of relationship and of affiliation, and commonsense definitions of federally recognized and non-federally recognized, then we would all be speaking the same language. Because what I've seen is, some institutions use the confusing language of NAGPRA as a way to work around the legislation and construct it to mean what they choose it to mean.

**JKK:** Why isn't there more of a drive or more of a moral outcry to investigate the activities of collectors both public and private?

**MB:** I think that has everything to do with the notion of property and everything to do with the notion of science. People are hesitant about repatriation in part because they don't want to part with things, but I think people are also hesitant about repatriation and about investigating the collectors who've created the collections because they think that that's already been done, there's nothing to be found. There's a Euro-American conception that knowledge somehow builds upon itself; it's almost like a social evolution of knowledge, the assumption that the knowledge we have now is appropriate and right because it is built on everything that came beforehand, and this is often how academic knowledge tends to construct itself. But that's not necessarily an Indigenous perception, and it's also not necessarily good historiography, because if we go back and look at how the collectors constructed their collections, it's very easy to find places where they jumped to conclusions, and made assumptions, and recombined things. I also have an odd perspective on this because my father was a taxidermist, and so I know what's involved in the process of literally reconstructing the dead, of trying to put life back into something that is no longer living, and there are not only technical details, but there are also procedural details where you create an illusion of the past by the way you construct something that is in your hands in the present. I think historians do it, I think taxidermists do it, I think storytellers do it, and I think many archaeologists do it; it's the nature of their work. And so, part of the resistance is not just ethical, but it's also procedural. People may be reluctant to challenge their mentors or their teachers or their professors or the people who preceded them in their profession.

**JKK:** And given the persistent narratives of the "vanishing Indian" in this region in particular, in Native New England, how might we think about issues of historical erasure related to repatriation issues and how they continue to haunt contemporary visibility?

**MB:** I think we run the risk of focusing on the dead too much. When I started to do this work I was certain that it was good work and necessary work, but I've reached the point where what I don't want to do is create a new body of data that will result in more research on the dead. And that's a very fine line, because I've created a very dense body of data about these particular individuals, but it was all created as part of the goal to get them re-interred and not to make them continue to be research subjects. And I think that's a danger that we all face in doing repatriation. I think it's a national danger that NAGPRA has not necessarily dealt with, because there are now databases like these around the country with vast amounts of information circulating about the Native dead that in many communities is best left unsaid and best left untouched. And so, what I hope to do is to try to figure out, how do we move beyond NAGPRA? How do we find an ethical resolution to this horrific problem and move beyond that so that we are focusing on living communities, but in the way that they want to be focused upon? So that it's not all research directed from the outside, it's not all focused on, "Do they meet this specific criteria for federal recognition?" But it's work focused on, "How do these communities see themselves? What are their own knowledge systems? What remarkably unique and wonderful bits of information do they have about their families and their histories and the places they have lived in for millennia, and how do they choose to share those histories with the rest of us?" That's where I feel our efforts should be placed, because as long as the process of constructing history and constructing the past is in the hands of non-Native interlocutors who are focused on erasing Indians, I don't know if we're going to get anything close to the truth. But the truth seems to be that whether or not we are federally recognized, we know each other, we know who we are and where we come from, and we know this land, and this land knows us, and the ancestors know us. And it's an unfortunate twist of history that many of us are not federally recognized, but that fact should never be a barrier between our own past and us.

There was a legislative case tried in Vermont some years ago that concluded that the Vermont Abenaki had ceased to exist due to the "weight of history," and yet when the BIA considered our federal recognition petition, they concluded that we indeed had continue to exist up until 1905, and that we existed from 1970 to the present, but somehow we had vanished for a sixty-five-year time period—coincidentally, a sixty-five-year time period within which Abenaki children were being removed from families by social service agencies, within which the eugenics project was operating, within which, you know, vigilantes were chasing people down, within which families were scattering into upstate New York and upstate New Hampshire and Vermont and ceasing to identify as Abenaki, intermarrying with other people so they could hide their children and their families. You take that moment in time when people had to, if not go underground, hide in plain sight just to survive, and then for someone on the outside to have the arrogance to say, "You therefore ceased to exist"? It's equivalent to saying that the Jewish people ceased to exist because of the Holocaust. And I think until we can change that paradigm, until we can really understand what survival is and that survival is adaptation to the modern era, survival is whatever it takes to maintain your community and maintain your traditions: that should be a standard for recognition, not whether or not you're in a particular document at a particular moment in time.

**JKK:** Hear, hear!

**MB:** In some ways I feel that this research has brought me full circle, because I grew up in the lower Adirondacks, in another region where Native people are believed to have vanished, and even though I knew my grandfather was Native, it was something that we didn't talk about. And I had no idea as a child how that kind of erasure came to be, how it came to affect my own family, how it came to affect the region I grew up in. And when I realized that this story is not unique to the Connecticut River Valley, that it's also the story of where I come from, it's the story of where many Native people come from, and in some ways I feel that the best thing I can do, and the best sort of revenge I have to counter this erasure, is to work in cultural recovery, to find those stories that were hidden away, to restore those pieces that were broken, to put back together what was disconnected and to somehow, from here forward, make it a more coherent and inclusive and Indigenous story. And that's the work I try to do.

# JESSICA CATTELINO ON INDIAN GAMING, RENEWED SELF-GOVERNANCE, AND ECONOMIC STRENGTH

Jessica Cattelino offered an interview about her new book, *High Stakes: Florida Seminole Gaming and Sovereignty* (2008), a stellar work that documents how economic strength through casino development also enabled renewed political self-governance for the tribe that has transformed decades of U.S. federal control. As her research shows, this dramatic shift from poverty to relative economic security has created substantial benefits for tribal citizens, including employment, universal health insurance, and social services. At the same time, this growth has brought new dilemmas to reservation communities and prompted outside accusations that Seminoles are sacrificing their culture by embracing capitalism. Cattelino's book challenges those charges, showing how Seminoles use gaming revenue to enact their sovereignty, in part, through relations of interdependency with others. Cattelino earned her PhD at New York University in 2004. She is an associate professor of anthropology at the University of California Los Angeles. She has been an assistant professor at the University of Chicago; a member in the School of Social Science at the Institute for Advanced Study in Princeton, New Jersey; and a Weatherhead Fellow at the School of American Research, now the School for Advanced Research, in Santa Fe, New Mexico. It was there in 2003 that we first met, while we were both in-residence fellows. Her current research project explores citizenship and territoriality in the Florida Everglades, with a focus on the Seminole Big Cyprus Reservation and the nearby agricultural town of Clewiston.

This interview took place on October 13, 2009.

**J. Kēhaulani Kauanui:** I wanted to ask if you would start by telling us a bit about your personal background and how you came to this project.

**Jessica Cattelino:** Well, it was a long way from growing up as a white farm kid in northern Wisconsin to doing research in South Florida on Seminole gaming. No doubt part of this was because, when I was growing up, treaty rights in the form of hunting and fishing were big issues in Wisconsin. But, more generally, I came to anthropology as an anthropologist of the United States, with the conviction that we have a lot to learn about the ways that economy, culture, and small-p politics come together in everyday life. And when I was in graduate school in the 1990s, tribal gaming was hitting the news, especially in the Northeast, with Mashantucket Pequots and Mohegans in Connecticut opening lucrative casinos near big media markets like New York and Boston.

I thought that the debates about casinos lacked a deep understanding of what gaming looked like in practice in reservation life and how it raised big questions that would be of concern to a broad public, and there was no better place to look into this than in Seminole Country in South Florida.

**JKK:** Would you tell us some of the brief history of Seminole gaming and the landmark court case that opened up gaming across Indian Country?

**JC:** Absolutely. Seminoles were the first tribe to start Indian gaming back in 1979, when they opened a high-stakes bingo hall, really a modest operation, on their urban Hollywood Reservation. Seminoles have six reservations that are scattered across the swamps and the suburbs of South Florida, and at the time they were facing endemic poverty on those reservations. The important thing to note is that gaming, when Seminoles started it, was not a federal grant or a federal program that somehow allowed them to start gaming. Rather, they were part of a larger trend in Indian Country of looking around and seeing how tribes could engage in self-determination, could undertake economic and political activities to look out for their own people on their own terms. And Seminoles decided that gaming was part of a larger set of activities that they could run and operate, that they could run on their own reservations. And so they just did it, and didn't ask anybody: didn't ask the federal government, didn't ask the state, decided this was within their sphere of authority.

The state of Florida balked at this and said, you know, that this was not legal. And this led to a big case: *Seminole Tribe of Florida v. Butterworth,* which went up into the federal courts. And eventually the courts ruled in favor of the tribe, saying that states could not regulate on-reservation economic activities as long as those activities were not illegal in the larger state. Bingo wasn't illegal—churches were running bingo games—and so the Seminole tribe could proceed to set up its own jackpots, its hours of operation, and other regulations and run its bingo hall. This then opened the floodgates for other tribes to start exploring gaming as a revenue generator, although it wasn't until 1987 that the Supreme Court weighed in and made tribes more confident across the country that they could do this.

This wasn't the end of the story, though. The courts ruled in favor of the tribe, but after that later Supreme Court case the states grew anxious about regulating tribal gaming, and that led to the big federal law that regulates gaming, the Indian Gaming Regulatory Act, in 1988. What's important to remember here is that the Indian Gaming Regulatory Act wasn't what started gaming, wasn't what allowed gaming on reservations. Gaming is based in the tribe's authority to run their own reservation's economic activities, and the law came later to regulate those activities.

**JKK:** And just to clarify, these sort of historical moments and these periods: you've got the first case going up in 1979, the Supreme Court ruling in 1987, and then it's in 1988 that you get the federal law, right?

**JC:** Exactly.

**JKK:** And that was under the Reagan administration.

**JC:** Right. Well, and it's a fairly quick turnaround to respond to the Supreme Court case, where the states really wanted Congress to give them some direction on what their role was in Indian gaming.

**JKK:** Could you give more background, perhaps "Indian Gaming Regulatory Act 101," just so that people get the nuts and bolts of what that federal law did? As you say, it did not authorize gaming—it regulates gaming.

**JC:** Exactly. I should start by saying that it's a complicated law, and I'm not a legal scholar, so I would encourage those who are especially interested to turn to a legal analysis, but I can give you a rough outline.

The Indian Gaming Regulatory Act divided games into a set of classes, and it said how different kinds of games could be regulated on Indian reservations. The first class was traditional games, and Indian tribes can do those however they want; there's no outside regulation there. The second class, Class II gaming, are games like bingo, some forms of poker, and lottery; if they're legal in the surrounding state, so in this case in Florida, the Seminole tribe—or any tribe—can operate those games on their reservation, can regulate them, can set up their own businesses without the states being involved. And that's in fact how Seminoles made their gaming empire; they did it on Class II games like bingo and lottery, including video bingo and video lottery.

Now, there's a third class, and this is where gaming often makes the news. It's called Class III games, and this was the grand compromise of the Indian Gaming Regulatory Act. These are the most lucrative games, like slot machines and blackjack, games of chance. And IGRA, the law, said that although generally tribes as nations have relationships with the federal government, in order to operate these most lucrative games the tribes have to negotiate a good-faith agreement with the state they're in. These agreements are usually called compacts, and you see them in the news all the time, negotiating the terms of compacts. Each side has to get something in these compacts. And this was a big compromise, because the tribes had to agree to negotiate with states, and the states had to negotiate in good faith and give the tribes something in order to operate those big games.

In Florida right now, this is the hot issue. After decades, the Seminole tribe is closer than ever to a compact with the state of Florida, and they're negotiating that right now. Now, I've been talking about law here, but it's probably helpful to give a sense just of what's happened with Indian gaming since 1979. Gaming has really reshaped the economies on a lot of Native American reservations. It's also reshaped non-Indian perceptions of who Indigenous people are. In 2008, according to federal figures, gaming revenues from tribal gaming were almost $27 billion. This was a massive expansion in a very short period of time. It's important to note that not all tribes have casinos—in fact, the minority of them do—and that how much those casinos make varies dramatically, largely dependent on your geography. If you're near a big urban center or a tourist destination or a major highway, you're more likely to make money on your casinos. If your reservation is in the middle of a rural area, it might be a little tent with a few slot machines inside, and nothing much more. So it ranges dramatically depending on a lot of factors.

**JKK:** Absolutely, and for those who might be familiar with the Connecticut situation that you referenced earlier with the Mashantucket Pequots and the Mohegans, the compact agreements for those two tribal nations with the state of Connecticut was that the state would get a quarter cut from the Class III gaming.

**JC:** Indeed, and one of the interesting developments of the expansion of tribal gaming is that states like Connecticut, which are facing huge budget deficits and are really trying to get themselves out of difficult budgetary situations, are increasingly turning to tribal governments for revenues from gaming as a way to fill the gaps in their own budgets. And so tribes are becoming more and more important to state economies across the nation.

**JKK:** Yes, and that definitely leads to something I want to ask you about later, what you're calling casino-era sovereignty, in terms of how tribal gaming really implicates tribal governance. Now, for those who might still be unfamiliar, I want to just lay out this groundwork with you first about how tribal gaming is distinct from commercial gaming. How are the Seminole tribe's gaming facilities different than Donald Trump's?

**JC:** This is vital to understanding what tribal gaming is. And too often those two, government gaming and commercial gaming, get conflated in people's understandings of what's at stake with tribal casinos.

Tribal gaming, by definition and by law, is run by a government. So, tribal gaming is more like a state lottery, say, than it is like Donald Trump's operation. Individual tribal citizens—an individual Seminole, for example—can't open up a casino. That would be illegal; only tribal governments can do this. So, commercial gaming is for profit, but tribal government gaming is for governments to raise revenues. And here it's important to remember that most tribes don't have the capacity to issue taxes, to gain money, say, property taxes, because their lands are federal lands. Tribal nations have long struggled with the question of how to raise revenues that are necessary to run their government operations, something that every government struggles with. You know, nationally in the United States we're debating right now over taxation and redistribution issues. So, in the case of the Seminole Tribe of Florida, gaming revenues from their seven casinos go directly to the democratically elected tribal council, the government. And that group of elected officials makes decisions, makes policies, over how that money will be distributed. Will it be used to invest in other economic activities, to give funds to each individual Seminole, to run cultural programs or social services? People may disagree or agree with those policies, but it's important to remember that those are government policies, not individual decisions. It's not like, you know, a casino owner of a commercial casino being able to decide how to use the money however he pleases.

And, although it might seem strange to run your government on gambling, it might be interesting to note that gambling long has been a governmental activity on this continent. The U.S. colonies raised revenues through lotteries, to a large extent actually. And today, states that are grappling with how to fill their budgetary holes often turn to lotteries as a way to do that. So American Indian tribal gaming is part of a larger, nationwide expansion of governmental gaming that began back in the 1960s when New Hampshire legalized its state lottery. The larger point that I'm trying to make here is that, not only for Indian tribes but also more generally, gaming can be part of a government economy, a national economy, and a way to raise revenues for governments.

**JKK:** Yes, and I'm interested, too, in why you think this point gets confused with non-Native individuals, and I think you've mentioned earlier that linkage between casino rights and tribal sovereignty is the key to looking at it. But I also remember from your book that you note that tribes that have gaming are often characterized in the media and in the citizenry at large as lawless, and yet the gaming industry seems so incredibly and intensively regulated. What do you think about these perceptions that flood the mainstream?

**JC:** Well, in the United States there's a fundamental question of how all of our governments are organized that needs to be brought to the center of any discussion of gaming. That is that gaming, again, is run by tribal governments, and that American Indian tribal nations are governments. I mean, that's the first and most basic fact that people must consider when they think about gaming.

You know, we're used to crossing state borders and seeing that there are different laws on either side. Where do you buy your fireworks on the Fourth of July? Where do you buy alcohol with different taxes, or cheaper gasoline? Where do companies relocate because they can get tax breaks from certain states? We're used to the idea that different polities, different jurisdictions, have the authority to make different laws that will have effects on how they do business. Tribes are no different in that regard. They're a complicated part of our multifaceted governmental system in the United States. It's not that laws don't apply on Indian reservations. Rather, it's that a complicated mix of federal, sometimes state, and always tribal laws apply. This is true not only for gaming but also for areas like tribal water quality, zoning, and in myriad areas of laws. Indian gaming is quite regulated under the Indian Gaming Regulatory Act.

There was a federal agency set up to regulate tribal gaming, and it requires all tribes to issue ordinances, tribal gaming ordinances. There are layers and layers and layers of regulations here. It's complicated, and everyone gets frustrated by the complexity of understanding what laws apply on Indian reservations, but this is often a problem not of lawlessness but rather of excess law, of too many different kinds of law all coming together in a confusing and jumbled way.

**JKK:** I think it's important for both readers and listeners to note that while you do establish the legal facts and the historical facts, you actually do not take a position one way or another on the questions and controversies of Indian gaming in your book, right?

**JC:** Yes, that's generally true. I think, you know, there is an important place for policy analysis. People need to be talking about what's good and what's bad about Indian gaming, but I think that can blind us to other issues that are really important. In part, I respect the fact that tribes across the country have taken very different approaches to gaming. Some tribal nations choose not to pursue it at all; they see it as anathema to their cultural values. Others do. It's a mistake to extrapolate from just one case. I'm not trying to dodge the real questions; rather, I'm suggesting that focusing on whether gaming is positive or negative sometime leads us to ignore too many of the real questions that gaming raises.

**JKK:** And that leads me to really get to the method you undertook in this study. You tell this story of Seminole gaming through an ethnographic lens, that is, through your fieldwork in southern Florida with the tribe. You had tribal permission to conduct this research, right?

**JC:** Yes, I did.

**JKK:** Could you talk about what this approach entails, for those unfamiliar with the field of anthropology, and how it differs from, say, a statistical focus or simply a focus on law and policy as you've sort of already broached?

**JC:** Ethnographic research focuses on depth of understanding in a single community. It means, in my case, relocating to South Florida for a year and then for countless trips back and forth since then, trying to take a lot of time to understand what gaming means in everyday life. Most importantly, ethnography, this kind of intensive fieldwork, not only helps to get at answers but also helps you develop questions that you might not have anticipated at first. It took me months to develop all my questions, to keep my ear to the ground, to learn what questions are relevant here that I might not have thought of in a library or when reading other books. What are the questions that are really important to hear?

Now, I'm an outsider to Seminole tribe. I'm not Seminole, I'm not Native. And so I'm not claiming to tell this story from any Seminole point of view, but rather taking a closer look as is appropriate from an outside perspective. Gaming is not only understood by looking at economic indicators. Rather, gaming has both allowed and forced Seminoles to examine who they are, who they've been, who they want to be. And those are kinds of questions that are hard to get at through statistics or through policy analysis, and I think you can only get at them through ethnographic research.

**JKK:** Well, it is so beautifully written. You have such an incredible ethnographic eye, and as you've said, you try and get as close as you can, as close a look as is possible that is appropriate. This is a very compelling book with a lot of rich detail in terms of trying to sketch for the outside reader what is going on inside the tribal community, and, as you put it earlier, how they are grappling with who they are and who they want to be, and what they might become in light of this economic upsurge.

**JC:** And one of the funny things about ethnography is that it leads you in unexpected directions. So, for example, I thought I'd spend a lot of time in casinos, but it turned out I really didn't, because it wasn't where Seminoles were spending their time mostly, and it wasn't the most important place to understand. It was more important to go to birthday parties, or tribal council meetings, or school tours to understand what casinos meant. I didn't expect to be writing about things like housing, but people kept on bringing it up, and I took that cue, and said there's something important here that I need to follow up. And that's the kind of intuition that ethnography allows.

**JKK:** Well, could you give our readers a brief overview of the book and why you've organized it into the two sections, the first being economy and the second sovereignty?

**JC:** The goal of the book is to tell the story of Seminoles' complex efforts to maintain their political and also their culturally distinct values and ways of life under dramatically new economic conditions. I am trying to explore major issues raised by gaming that are of widespread importance to a broad readership.

As I mentioned before, Seminoles, through gaming, have been able but also have been forced to ask big questions. Things like, what kind of government is a good government? What's the balance between investing in collective activities and providing resources to individuals to spend however they want? What's the relationship between culture and money? How do you raise children under new economic conditions? These are questions that are being asked in our health-care debates, in debates over taxation, in households across the country.

Gaming has really brought those into relief, in ways that I explore. I do that in a range of chapters that cover everything from how culture and economy have been tied together in Seminole activities like alligator wrestling or wage labor; on how culture in the casino era has blossomed but also faced challenges like bureaucratization; on new forms of consumptions, such as what Seminoles are buying with the money; on economic diversification, such as how they are spending the money to pursue other kinds of economic activities, from agriculture to commercial real estate investment. And I look at sovereignty issues both by studying how Seminoles seek their control over their self-governance and also by seeing how Seminoles interact with other governments as they stake out their sovereign territory.

The book's main arguments are that, on the one hand, about money and economy, there's a widespread expectation in American popular culture and law that money interferes with culture. I don't think that's necessarily so, and I show how it's not. And then, secondly, that sovereignty is the most meaningful and powerful explanation for gaming and its effects, but sovereignty is complicated, and I explore the ways it is. Both of these—both economy and sovereignty—point to the significance of gaming, not just for law or money but for the ways that, in everyday life, politics and economic action are deeply intertwined, and that's what I hope to shed some light on with this book.

**JKK:** I think you certainly have. Now, I want to dwell on that question around culture in terms of how you really looked at how the Seminole people grapple with the question of cultural integrity. In your book you explain how many of the tribal members explicitly explained to you that casinos are their business, not their culture, and yet, as you've just said, there's this assumption by non-Indians that casinos are causing Indians to lose their culture. Could you say more about that sort of equation that your book really undoes? You really challenge that assumption, offering evidence that is very persuasive. And I wonder if you would speak to that, and also how that stereotype of the "rich Indian" might be playing into this.

**JC:** Absolutely. Well, back in the seventies, when Seminoles started casinos, there was widespread surprise on the part of outside observers, whether government officials or local media or academics, that it would be Seminoles who were considered to be so traditional, so tough—they're really proud of being un-conquered because they never signed a peace treaty with the United States—why would these Seminoles, so traditional, start gaming and embrace casino capitalism, which seemingly stood for all that was American?

Part of the explanation in the book is that it's precisely those values of independence, of political toughness, of cultural integrity, that spurred Seminoles to pursue gaming as a way to make money to look out for themselves. There is a widespread assumption that, well, I should say that one of the most common questions I get when I tell people that I work on tribal nation gaming is whether casinos lead Indians to cultural loss. And this question is based, in part, on an assumption about money and what it is and does in the world. And gaming, I think, raises big issues about the nature of money. Money is very often seen as corroding culture, as abstraction, as reducing the individual and collective differences and distinctions that make people who they are. There's a long-standing association in the United States of Indigenous peoples with poverty, and more specifically with the inability to use money. So money kind of stands for modern life, for all that's good and bad in modern life. That powerful image, then, makes it seem almost like an oxymoron or a contradiction in American life, that you can be wealthy and Indigenous, pursue money and be Indigenous at the same time.

Now, this is, I think, an impoverished, wrong view of both the diversity of Indigenous people's economic lives and also of what money is more generally. Seminoles use money in a variety of ways. They see money as necessary to operating cultural programs, to a kind of cultural renaissance that they're undertaking. And, to understand why that's so, we need to look a little bit into history. Seminoles will often say that they were self-sufficient and relatively wealthy until they became poor with the expansion of colonialism, with the population boom that came to South Florida and stripped them of their lands, with the economic space falling out from underneath them when settlers took over South Florida. A lot of Seminoles will associate poverty with colonialism, and will associate poverty with cultural loss, because when you don't have any money you're working three jobs, you have almost no control over your governmental activities. It's hard to sustain a cultural way of life that you value. So, this led me to ask the question, why do we so often associate poverty with culture and wealth with a lack of culture, or cultural loss, when in fact for many Seminoles—not all, there's disagreement on this for sure—but for many Seminoles, they would more associate poverty with cultural loss and regaining resources and control over resources with a cultural renaissance?

**JKK:** Thank you for laying that out, and telling us what you found in your study. I want to just go back and qualify something I said around the stereotype of the "rich Indian." In New England the way that stereotype operates is a way for non-Native people to assert that Indians aren't really Indians. So it actually gets used to discount a Native person's claim to being Indigenous, precisely because there's this dominant assumption that you cannot have your culture intact and still drive a really nice car that you got through casino income, right?

**JC:** That is an old and powerful assumption, and it's not only something that people, individuals, might think, but it's also been an assumption built into law and policy. And just one quick example of that: back in the 1950s, there was a policy, a federal policy, that's often called "termination," whereby the United States government sought to make Indian tribes no longer governmental entities, to dissolve them as tribal nations. And one of the criteria the federal government used to decide which tribes to dissolve was their economic capacity; if you had more resources you were more likely to formally and legally no longer be allowed to be called an Indian tribal nation. And that's a rather obscure example, but it's one that indicates a bright thread running through the last couple hundred years, which is that when Indians got wealth, their status as Indians was often called into question. And gaming is a new chapter in that story.

**JKK:** Yes. I want to come back to that question of cultural renaissance in a moment, but first I want to ask you something else. I notice that you refused, in the book, to divulge the amount of tribal members' per capita payments, and I'm wondering if you could explain why. And also some of the issues that arise when non-Indians expose those figures in hostile ways, which sort of also leads to another kind of question of how the tribe administers the funds. You talked earlier about the way the economic funding from the gaming institutions goes directly to the tribal council, so maybe you could sort of take us there in terms of what is the tribe doing with it.

**JC:** Well, the Seminole tribe has chosen to use a large portion of its casino revenues for governmental activities, especially for social services like housing, education, health care, and welfare more generally. It also has devoted casino monies to cultural programs, such as a wonderful museum that your listeners can go see on the Big Cypress Reservation, outside of Fort Lauderdale— language programs, cultural education, and the like. It also has invested in economic diversification, trying to go beyond gaming into agriculture, into just a wide range of activities, such as buying Hard Rock International, Hard Rock Cafes in forty-five countries around the world.

So, there have been a wide range of ways to spend the money. One of them, and the one that gets the most attention in local media, is the use of casino revenues to distribute money in per capita payments to each tribal citizen on a regular basis. This has been a controversial issue, within Indian communities and more broadly. I should start by saying that different tribes choose different ways of distributing casino money. Some don't distribute any of it in per capita payments but put it all into collective programs; others focus on individual payments. That's a decision that is made locally.

Outsiders often want to know how much Seminoles make in per capita payments. I've taken a cue from Seminoles. They don't publish the number; they don't make it public. Seminoles often take great offense when asked by strangers how much they make. It's an area of great resentment. We don't often ask each other how much money we make and exactly how we make it as individuals. So, instead, I want to ask other questions. Why do we want to know? Why do outsiders want to know that? What is it that we seek? Why not ask, instead, how much is spent on social services? On crime prevention? This raises big questions about what's a legitimate way to make a living, what's a legitimate way to distribute revenues by governments. And per capita payments have been a hot issue all around the country because of this.

**JKK:** Yes, indeed. Now, going back to your point about economic diversification, you suggest in your book that tribal economic power both undergirds and threatens tribal sovereignty. Could you explain the ways that economic diversification can pose a threat, and how the tribe is navigating those currents in this time?

**JC:** Well, you know, the economic integration is both an opportunity and a threat. You can't make money off of casinos without being economically entangled with larger communities. So Seminoles have become more reliant on a non-Seminole public as consumers in their casinos, as legislators. If you're going to, say, buy Hard Rock International, like Seminoles did, you're going to have to waive some of your sovereign rights to enter into contracts that your investors will approve of. And in order to do business overseas, for example. So, gaming has brought tribes into the realm of big business, Wall Street investing, international finance—not all tribes, but the ones with the most lucrative games. And this has led to tough discussions over how much do you keep your economy on your reservation, under your own regulations, and how much do you venture into broader economic waters and navigate all of the compromises to your sovereignty that that will require.

**JKK:** Now, you've just touched on the going global. Bringing it closer to home, you mentioned housing and listening carefully to the people that you met in the field site, people of the tribe, and you said that they kept talking about housing, so you followed your intellectual intuition and thought you better take a look at that. What is going on with housing in terms of what the tribe decided to do with some of those funds? What has helped bolster that cultural revitalization? You also just mentioned how difficult it can be when people are working multiple part-time jobs to really keep up, and it seems from your book that housing has been a way to really ground and stabilize the community in traditional and new ways.

**JC:** Well, some of the ways that casinos have changed life are more obvious. Individuals have more options how to live their lives because they have higher incomes—you see shiny new buildings. Seminoles now can work for the tribe in a range of jobs that was never available before. They can stay on the reservation to work; they can go to endless numbers of tribal activities. Everybody has dresser drawers filled with commemorative T-shirts from, you know, the Miss Seminole Princess Pageant, or the school awards, or the sporting tournaments on reservations. Those are easier to see, as is Seminoles' prominence in law, in politics at a local, state, and national level. So, those I had a better handle on.

But people, like you said, kept on talking about housing, or medicine, and this led me to look at the ways in which gaming has changed everyday social services on the reservations. Now, if you go on a Seminole reservation, the houses are changing. They're going from small, little Housing and Urban Development federal, little concrete block-structure houses, to houses that more closely resemble middle-class neighborhoods throughout South Florida. That itself is, of course, a consequence of gaming; the tribe has gone from having most of its housing funded by the federal government to having most of it funded by tribal money from casinos. But it's not just that there's more or nicer housing; it's what housing means to people that I want to focus on.

Housing was a key site of colonialism, you could say, on Seminole reservations. Seminole households had been run by women in matrilineal, clan-based families. Extended families had lived together in thatched-roof chickee houses dispersed across the landscape of South Florida. The federal government moved Seminoles into dense housing developments. They would only issue leases to male heads of households, and they would settle people in nuclear family units, rather than the extended families that people had lived in before. Suddenly, you weren't surrounded by people from the Panther clan like you, but you had your little nuclear family next to somebody else that you maybe didn't even know. Many, many Seminoles will talk about this as a period of great distress for cultural transmission, for living a way of life that people were used to. So, it's no coincidence that when Seminoles began to exercise their political self-determination and gather their economic resources from gaming, housing was one of the places they turned, and you're seeing a return to larger households with multiple generations dispersed more broadly across the landscape, and more and more houses are owned by women and accommodate a way of life that's more familiar. There's a housing shortage, so it's not all roses here, and there's controversies over who gets housing, but nonetheless, you're seeing a shift back to fighting for a way of life where it matters most in the less obvious places, like how your house is structured.

**JKK:** As we wrap up, I want to be sure that we have some time to talk about how you end your book with that chapter discussion on sovereign interdependencies. You spoke earlier, when you were talking about how you organized the book, about the question of sovereignty and how complicated sovereignty is when the tribe is, say, doing global investments, getting entangled with a lot of different forces that can implicate their expression of sovereignty and exercise of it. Can you share more as to how you theorize sovereign interdependencies?

**JC:** Absolutely. All too often, sovereignty is taken to be synonymous with autonomy. Insofar as you're autonomous, you're sovereign; insofar as you're dependent, you're not. Well, if this is our definition of sovereignty, it makes American Indian tribal nations, on the face of it, seem like failed sovereigns. But it also makes a lot of countries around the world not seem like sovereigns at all.

Very few polities are autonomous. Countries all over are dependent on others for economic aid, military protection, and political alliances. So, actually, what sovereignty is in the modern age is not so clear at all, for anyone. Seminoles have certainly had their sovereignty compromised by colonialism, but it's a mistake to see any time that they're entangled with other polities as going against their sovereignty, because part of sovereignty is being able to decide and assert your claim to political distinctiveness in relation to other governments, other peoples, and that can mean negotiating agreements, it can mean getting legally entangled.

You can't determine sovereignty solely based on autonomy. Instead, we need to assess whether relations among governments and peoples lead to the ability of communities like the Seminole Tribe of Florida to claim and realize their political distinctiveness on their own terms. And sometimes that leads us to look in unexpected places. American Indian tribes have much to teach us about globalization and world power today, far beyond the limits of any given reservation.

**JKK:** Yes! In conclusion, I want to invite you to leave us with anything you'd like us to consider.

**JC:** Well, I think the biggest thing is just to realize that, again, gaming isn't just about money, or about political loopholes or special rights, but rather, it's about big questions of fundamental importance, not only to Indigenous people but to your broader listening public. And that tribal nations like Seminoles are among the most creative places and peoples to be thinking about fundamental questions that are debated in the news and in the public everywhere, and if we pay attention to the creative ways that they're using their casino revenues, we have a lot to learn about issues far beyond what first hits us on the surface as being Indian gaming.

# DAVID CORNSILK ON FREEDMEN CITIZENSHIP RIGHTS AT CHEROKEE

As context for my overview with David Cornsilk (Cherokee Nation) and the question of African American slave descendants who are part of their nation, it should be noted that many enslaved black people accompanied the Cherokee when the U.S. federal government forcibly removed the tribe from their traditional homeland in what became North Carolina and Georgia in the 1830s. The Freedmen became full citizens of the Cherokee Nation after Emancipation, as part of the Treaty of 1866, between the Cherokee Nation and the United States, as documented in *Blood Politics: Race, Culture, and Identity in the Cherokee Nation of Oklahoma*, by Circe Sturm.

The Cherokee signed the 1866 treaty in defeat, after the Civil War, since they had fought for the Confederacy. The treaty committed that the slaves, who had been freed by tribal decree during the war, would be absorbed as citizens in the Cherokee Nation. However, by the late 1880s, during the allotment period, when the U.S. government opened up tribal lands in Oklahoma to white settlers, thus breaking its agreement with the tribes, Congress created a new census of the Five Civilized Tribes, of which the Cherokee are one, along with the Seminoles, the Chickasaws, the Choctaws, and the Muscogee. This new census was created by the Dawes Commission, named after the Dawes Allotment Act of 1887, and it is this same census that the Cherokee Nation would later use to determine the eligibility of Freedmen to become citizens of the tribe. Prior to this Dawes census, the previous census of the tribe had noted both the Native and the African ancestry of the Freedmen and counted those of mixed ancestry as Cherokee. However, under the new census, census takers reclassified those who looked black (or had known African ancestry) as Freedmen, without noting their Indian ancestry. Nonetheless, whether classified as Indians or Freedmen, they were considered citizens of the Cherokee Nation under the 1866 treaty.

Despite the guarantee of the Freedmen's citizenship rights through the 1866 treaty, by 1983 the Cherokee Nation had expelled many descendants of slaves by requiring them to show a degree of Indian blood through the Dawes Rolls.

Thus began a long legal battle by the Freedmen descendants and some Cherokee citizens to be re-enfranchised. By March 2006 the Cherokee Supreme Court reinstated them, but that ruling incited a special election within the Cherokee Nation on February 3, 2007, when 75 percent of the Cherokee voters cast their ballot in favor of an amendment limiting citizenship. The election specifically asked voters whether to amend the Cherokee Nation's constitution to limit citizenship to those who can trace their heritage to the "Cherokee by Blood" Rolls, part of the census known as the Dawes Rolls of 1906.

David Cornsilk is a recognized tribal genealogist, historian, and legal advocate and a civil rights activist. He joined the program for an interview on the recent vote in the Cherokee Nation that disenfranchised the Freedmen. Cornsilk self-identifies as a "by-blood citizen" of the Cherokee Nation and lives in Tulsa, Oklahoma. As he shared, he is the son of John and Tinsy Cornsilk and the father of J. W. and Elena Cornsilk, all of Tahlequah, Oklahoma. He received his early education in schools around Tahlequah, which is the hub of the Cherokee Nation, and spent some time in various states. He graduated from Northeastern State University with a bachelor's degree in biology. Cornsilk worked in education for a number of years and started a tribal newspaper called the *Cherokee Observer*, which has been an active publication since 1993, in addition to his longtime work as a legal advocate. He began working as a civil rights activist to protect the rights of Cherokee Freedmen in 1988, five years after their first unlawful expulsion. Cornsilk filed a lawsuit against the Cherokee Nation Tribal Council on behalf of Freedman descendant Lucy Allen in 2004. In March 2006 the Cherokee Supreme Court ruled that Freedmen have long-standing citizenship rights rooted in the Treaty of 1866 and recognized by the Cherokee Constitution. The Freedmen case remained in federal litigation and eventually went to the District Court of the District of Columbia with the Honorable Thomas Hogan presiding. The Freedmen case was finally decided on August 30, 2017. The ruling was in favor of the Freedmen descendants, who are now able to register as citizens of the Cherokee Nation.

This interview took place on March 12, 2007.

**J. Kēhaulani Kauanui:** The Cherokee Nation expelled many descendants of slaves in 1983 by requiring them to show a degree of Indian blood through the Dawes Rolls. What prompted that expulsion in 1983, given that the treaty provisions had been honored before that time since the 1866 treaty?

**David Cornsilk:** Well, in doing research on the activity that was taking place at that time, we found that there was a belief by the principal chief then, Ross Swimmer, who is currently serving in a trust position with the Bureau of Indian Affairs, that he believed there was a bloc vote of Freedmen who would vote against him in the upcoming chief's race. And in order to prevent them from voting, he required a certificate of Indian blood degree card that basically excluded them from enrollment.

**JKK:** So a very instrumental exclusion to keep himself in power?

**DC:** That's what we believe, yes.

**JKK:** I see. Now, recently Principal Chief of the Cherokee Nation Chad Smith has defended this recent vote from February 3, 2007, by arguing that it was simply a matter of self-determination, while some opponents of the ballot question argue that attempts to remove the Freedmen from the tribe were motivated by racism. Can you please tell us, what are these tensions between the assertions of self-determination to define the tribal citizenry and the racist legacy left by the Cherokee tradition of slaveholding?

**DC:** Well, the basic premise of tribal sovereignty is the authority to determine who you are, who constitutes the citizens of your nation. The problem that we face in this instance is that that determination is being made on a racial line. The rolls that were made of the Cherokees that we use to determine our citizenship were made in an era of rabid racism in the United States, 1902, and so the fact that persons of African ancestry were put on a separate roll in 1902 should not exclude them from citizenship today, and that's exactly what's happening. The Freedmen Roll is constituted of persons of African descent, most of them having some Cherokee blood, just the same as the "Cherokee by Blood" section, but their section was not recorded, because in the era in which that roll was made it was believed that African blood tainted you to a degree that your other blood didn't count.

**JKK:** Right, and that's one of the racist holdovers from the institution of slavery and the Jim Crow laws, right?

**DC:** And so what we're doing now is we're punishing descendants today for a racist act that happened against their ancestors a hundred years ago.

**JKK:** Right. What about tribal leaders who claim that the Freedmen don't have any Cherokee ancestry?

**DC:** Well there's only two possible answers to that statement. The first one is that they're ignorant of their own tribal history. Or they're lying. And I believe the latter.

**JKK:** And also, as I pointed out in my introduction, even for those who may not have Cherokee ancestry, the treaty still provides for them to be enfranchised in the Cherokee Nation, no?

**DC:** Exactly. The Cherokee Nation, whenever the first person was adopted into the tribe who had no Cherokee blood, stopped being just a tribe and became a nation. We became an ethnically plural nation, the Cherokee tribe being a part of that nation along with now the Delaware tribe, the Shawnee tribe, the Freedmen, some adopted whites, some adopted Creeks. We are an ethnically plural nation that is currently trying to remove the black members of our tribe.

**JKK:** I recall when we met back in the summer of 2004 at a conference organized by the descendants of Freedmen of the Five Civilized Tribes, with president Marilyn Vann as a key figure of this Oklahoma City–based organization. What impressed me there were the links being made between those who already had their rights as citizens, although few in number there in attendance, and those who are still fighting for their place in the Cherokee Nation. Can you tell us about the coalitions between so-called "by blood" citizens such as yourself and members of the Freedmen organization in terms of working toward social justice? Do many other Cherokee citizens accompany you in your support of the Freedmen's legal rights?

**DC:** Well, I think probably we would be if an educational campaign were out there. The principal chief sent out material that painted the Freedmen as newcomers, as persons who are trying to access services, benefits, only that they had no Indian blood. And I believe that given the proper amount of time and education, the Cherokee people would come to realize the folly of their actions and would stand beside the Freedmen. But there are a large number of—well, I don't want to say large—but there are a number of Cherokee citizens by blood who support the Freedmen. I think the vote indicates that, because for every person who voted there's approximately a hundred people who believe the same way that they believe.

**JKK:** Now, in terms of an educational campaign, what do you think it would take for people to really have to confront their own family histories as a part of a broader tribal history of this legacy of slavery?

**DC:** Well, I think that if each Cherokee citizen would do what I have done and look at their own family history, their own connections to the tribe, to slavery, to the descendants of the Freedmen who are connected to their own particular families, they would find exactly the same thing I have found. That just because the Freedmen can be looked at and identified phenotypically differently from us—they may have curly hair or African features—when you look at the paperwork, you find that the Freedmen are inextricably intertwined in the Cherokee Nation. What we have done, we have basically cut off an arm of our nation, and I believe that in so doing we face the possibility of a national hemorrhage, because once you start chopping pieces of yourself away, what part is next? Will we now see the thin-bloods questioned as to their rights? Are you really an Indian if you're $1/512$ degree of blood? Will we say to the Delawares, the Shawnees, "You're not really Cherokee Indians, so let's chop you out"? It's just a slippery slope and it's frightening.

**JKK:** It sounds like a literal disembodiment of the nation's citizenry in terms of cutting out family. Family expulsions.

**DC:** Well, and, is it really legitimate, I ask, that once made a citizen, someone could be unmade? That's the question I would ask. You know, the American Indians were made citizens of the United States in 1924. You know, of course, some were made citizens under particular legislation, the Cherokee being one, but could now the people of the United States say, "Well, you know, we don't particularly like these people, you know, we don't like their brown skin or their straight black hair, so let's do a petition and let's vote them out." And it's, really, it sets a bad precedent. It has shamed the Cherokee Nation. You know, our tribal culture is one of inclusion, and this has shown that we have an underlying racist view that has festered in our nation since the Civil War.

**JKK:** Are there any visions or discussions about the Freedmen who have been expelled? To create their own tribal entity and seek separate federal recognition?

**DC:** There has been some discussion of that, and the Treaty of 1866 makes some provision for self-governance for the Freedmen if the Cherokee people do what we've done, basically, exclude them from participation in our government. I am reluctant to embrace that, because I have a strong belief in the inclusive philosophy of our people, and I would hate to see, and I have hated to see, division in our nation. You know, there's strength in unity, and this has created so much disharmony and disunity in our nation. And I believe that in the end, the Freedmen will be citizens in the Cherokee Nation. I believe in justice and that justice will prevail.

**JKK:** I want to go back to something you said. You drew the analogy between the Freedmen being citizens and the Delaware. What about the Delaware? What's parallel about that given that so many Delaware want to break away in terms of having their own recognized nation outside of Cherokee?

**DC:** Well, one thing that has exposed a hypocrisy in our tribal government is that they have used the 1866 treaty to enslave the Delawares, while using opposing language saying the 1866 treaty is not valid in reference to the Freedmen.

**JKK:** I see, so a total contradiction.

**DC:** A very total contradiction.

**JKK:** What about the family, the very profound way that you put it around chopping pieces of oneself away? It would seem, then, that if people really looked seriously at their family histories they would find that the Freedmen that they seek to exclude are their own kin, that is, that they trace to the same forebears.

**DC:** That is true, and I just did some research on a very prominent Cherokee family. I won't state their name, because I don't know if they would want me to, but I found that their ancestor, who appears on the Dawes Roll, was the patriarch of a very large, prominent, and very wealthy formerly slaveholding family, and the Dawes Commission in 1902 was asking him if he was familiar with this one particular woman who was of "Negro descent" and was listed on the Freedmen Roll. And he said, "Yes, that is my colored cousin." And they said, "Are you familiar with her death?" And he said, "Yes, she passed away right here in my home."

And then they said, "Where was she buried?" "She was buried in our family cemetery." Now that tells you that there was a very strong tie between that Freedman individual and that particular Cherokee family. And that is how the Cherokees viewed their former slaves, family members after the Civil War and prior to Oklahoma statehood. It was the influx of southern, white racists into Oklahoma after statehood that forced the Cherokees to adopt a very rabid form of racism that was imported. It was not indigenous to our people. You know, the first law passed in the state of Oklahoma was segregation of railcars.

**JKK:** You filed the lawsuit against the Cherokee Nation in 2004 on behalf of Freedmen descendant Lucy Allen. Can you tell us more about the specific circumstances of that lawsuit?

**DC:** Well, Lucy Allen came to me in 2004. She's an elderly Cherokee woman of Freedmen descent, and she was hurt. She had been denied access to her civil rights in the Cherokee Nation, as had all of the Freedmen since 1983, and whenever she asked me "What can we do?," well, I believe strongly in tribal self-determination, that being the right to live under our own laws and have our own court. And so I said, "Let's take it to court; let's take it to tribal court." I trusted that our tribal court would look at the issue fairly and justly and come to a just conclusion. And so we did. And the basic argument that we made was that the 1976 constitution was inclusive of all the citizens of the Cherokee Nation. It said if you have an ancestor on the Dawes Roll that you were in. If you don't, you're not it. And Lucy Allen, both of her parents appear on the Dawes Roll as Freedmen. She also had Cherokee blood that was not recorded by the Dawes Commission, because her family was of African descent. So we made our argument, and it was really kind of funny. I'm not a lawyer. I'm just an average guy who loves law, and the argument that I made got some snickers but it was basically that if you go to a hamburger stand and you order the deluxe cheeseburger, then you get everything that comes on the deluxe cheeseburger. If you don't want onions on it, you have to say "no onions." And when the Cherokees reorganized in 1976 they said, "We want one Cherokee Nation to go," and they didn't say "hold the Freedmen." And so, we got all the citizens, and rightly so.

**JKK:** Now, from '76 to '83 it wasn't an issue. So, what did it take in all those years? From 1983, when you said Ross Swimmer perpetuated that exclusion, and then your lawsuit on behalf of Lucy Allen comes in 2004, what happened in the interim years?

**DC:** Well there were some minor skirmishes. Well, I don't want to say minor. They were major, they just were moving us forward in this battle. In 1983, Reverend Roger H. Nero—he was an original enrollee on the Dawes Roll—filed suit because he was not permitted to vote. And that went to the federal court and the Tenth Circuit Court in Denver, and that court ruled that the Cherokee Nation had its own court, and therefore his argument was an internal matter of the tribe and should go to tribal court.

He subsequently passed away, and was not able to complete that process. And so then, in 1988, I began a campaign trying to get the officials of the Cherokee Nation to reverse what had happened to the Freedmen. I wrote a letter to the Chief Mankiller, and she responded in the press by saying the Freedmen have no Indian blood and therefore should not be members of the tribe. And so I realized that this was not going to be solved politically, it would have to be determined by the courts. And so that's when I filed a case for a woman named Bernice Riggs, who also had Cherokee blood, and the final ruling of the court was that she had Cherokee blood, but because her ancestors were on the Freedmen Roll she was excluded from enrollment. They applied the *Martinez v. Santa Clara Pueblo* doctrine that says the tribe has the right to determine its own citizenship.

**JKK:** Right, the 1978 U.S. Supreme Court ruling.

**DC:** But it was a misapplication because, previous to that, the tribal court had already ruled that the council did not have the authority to add requirements to constitutional provisions. They had previously added a residency require-ment to the office of the principal chief, and the tribal court struck it down as unconstitutional, because it was extra-constitutional. And that's what happened in the Lucy Allen case: the blood requirement was struck down because it was extra-constitutional.

And the court reversed itself in the Allen case, saying that because the provision was extra-constitutional Lucy Allen and all the Freedmen should be members of the tribe. And what's interesting is in the reversal: one of the judges, who had been a judge in the Riggs case, reversed himself and wrote a special concurrence stating why he had reversed himself and why he had been convinced that the Freedmen were citizens of the nation.

**JKK:** Wow, that is remarkable.

**DC:** It is very remarkable, and shows that given the right information, the right conclusion can be reached.

**JKK:** Now, in wrapping up, I want to ask you, I want to go back to something you said about the principal chief of the Cherokee Nation, Chad Smith, painting the Freedmen as newcomers. Now, advocates of expelling the Freedmen call it a matter of "safeguarding" tribal resources, which news reports have said include a $350 million annual budget from federal and tribal revenue, and Cherokee share of the gaming industry that for U.S. tribes overall takes in over $22 billion a year. The grassroots campaign for expulsion has given heavy play to warnings that keeping Freedmen in the Cherokee Nation would encourage thousands more to sign up. Now, news reports say that since the ruling last March 2006, more than two thousand Freedmen descendants had enrolled in citizens of the tribe. Was that spike in enrollment what prompted this recent ballot initiative?

**DC:** I believe that the potential for new voters is what prompted this petition. It's not a matter of protecting tribal resources, because the Cherokee Nation goes on in hundreds of communities around Oklahoma and around the United States begging for Cherokees to enroll. Our tribal enrollment increases by a thousand citizens every month, and that's phenomenal. That's not just births, those are Cherokees whose great-great-grandma moved away, and suddenly they decide to come back. So it's not about protecting tribal resources from new citizens, it's about protecting Chad Smith's ability to get reelected in the June election. He is afraid of the Freedmen vote, just the same as Ross Swimmer was, because he has been so virulently racist against them, and so he wanted them excluded. His supporters on the council attempted to get a special election several times and were defeated, and when they were finally able to get it on the June ballot, well that wasn't good enough, because that still allowed the Freedmen to vote in the June 2007 election for the principal chief. And so he wanted them excluded ahead of time.

**JKK:** I see. Very similar to the 1983 situation.

**DC:** Identical.

**JKK:** I understand the court challenges by Freedmen descendants seeking to stop the election were denied, but that a federal judge left open the possibility that the case could be refiled if the Cherokees voted to lift their membership rights. What do you think is the next step, legally, given this recent vote?

**DC:** Well, I'm not going to address that, because the attorneys right now are in conference trying to determine what their next step is, and I really don't want to jeopardize the information that I have in my head that they have shared with me.

**JKK:** Fair enough.

**DC:** Because we don't want the other side to know what's going to happen until it happens. But I do believe that the federal court will take action, and I believe that the Bureau of Indian Affairs will also be required, although reluctant, to take action.

**JKK:** Would you like to leave us with any last thoughts on this issue that we can take with us and meditate on?

**DC:** Well, I think the most important thing for the average American citizen to keep in mind is that the Cherokee Nation draws down approximately $300 million in tax money from their pockets. And they are using that money to fund an election to discriminate against their own citizens, and I think it would be incumbent upon every U.S. citizen to approach their representative and ask them, "Is this an appropriate use of my tax money?"

# SARAH DEER ON NATIVE WOMEN AND SEXUAL VIOLENCE

## First Interview

Sarah Deer (Muscogee [Creek] Nation) gave two interviews on the program, presented back-to-back here. She was the lead writer of an April 24, 2007, report issued by Amnesty International USA titled "Maze of Injustice: The Failure to Protect Indigenous Women from Sexual Violence in the USA." In it, Amnesty International cited U.S. Justice Department figures which indicate that American Indian and Alaska Native women are two and one-half times more likely to be raped or sexually assaulted than women overall in the United States, and that more than one in three Native women experience rape in their lifetime. The report also details how that neglect is exacerbated by structural barriers such as jurisdictional questions and chronic underfunding of law enforcement and Indian health services.

At the time of the first interview, Deer was employed as victim advocacy legal specialist for the Tribal Law and Policy Institute in St. Paul, Minnesota, and was an online instructor of tribal legal studies at UCLA Extension. Formerly, she had been a lecturer in law at UCLA Law School and had worked as a grant program specialist at the U.S. Department of Justice in the Office on Violence Against Women in Washington, D.C. She received her JD, with tribal lawyer certificate, from the University of Kansas School of Law and her BA in women's studies and philosophy from the University of Kansas. While a law student, Deer was employed as assistant director of Douglas County Rape Victims Survivor Service Incorporated. She serves on advisory boards for numerous anti-violence organizations and projects, including the American Bar Association's Commission on Domestic Violence and the National Alliance to End Sexual Violence. She is the coauthor of several textbooks, including *Structuring Sovereignty: Constitutions of Native Nations* (2014), *Introduction to Tribal Legal Studies* (2010), *Tribal Criminal Law and Procedure* (2004), and *Sharing Our Stories of Survival: Native Women Surviving Violence* (2008). In 2014, Deer was awarded the MacArthur Fellowship for her tireless and important work. Since then she has returned to her alma mater, the University of Kansas, where she is professor of women's studies and public policy. Her most recent book is *The Beginning and End of Rape: Confronting Sexual Violence in Native America* (2015).

This interview took place on May 7, 2007.

**J. Kēhaulani Kauanui:** It's wonderful to be able to talk to a consultant who worked on this report, but also to learn more about your ongoing work in this area and the major pathbreaking work you're doing to bring together questions of safety and sovereignty. I'd like to ask you to begin, if you will, by offering us an overview of the ever-increasing epidemic of sexual violence committed against Native women and girls. Indigenous women researchers have shown that rape was once extremely rare in tribal communities. How is it, then, that Native women are suffering from sexual violence at such outrageous proportions?

**Sarah Deer:** Well, I think a number of factors come into play, but I think the most obvious one is that colonial projects that from the get-go—from literally Columbus on—have viewed Native women as less that human, as rape-able: people that are, you know, non-people; people that didn't matter; people that needed to be done away with. Part of that colonial project, Native women have consistently, over the last five hundred years, seen very high rates of rape. My colleague and coworker Bonnie Clairmont, who is a Ho-Chunk woman and a survivor, an advocate in her own right, in her capacity of doing advocacy work in Indian Country, many tribal languages don't even have a word for rape, because there wasn't a need for a word for rape prior to colonization. So, the words that are used to describe rape are new words that have become part of a language since colonization.

**JKK:** I think that's a really important point. Still, we have to deal with the reluctance of people to understand how colonialism is gendered and also sexualized.

**SD:** Right. You'll often see in the journals or the history of the European male perspective that they talked even about the land here as a woman, as if it was theirs for the taking. The Spanish missionaries would talk about the virgin land, and you know, the fertile land, and other kinds of very gendered terms when examining their "right" to the land and the Manifest Destiny, etc. So it has always been very gendered, and a lot of time, history doesn't really play that out. When you look at the scholarly history, many times the gendered analysis is left out.

**JKK:** Yes, and there's that notion of conquering virgin land in that colonial logic.

Now, I've read in the Amnesty International report that most of the perpetrators of rape against Native women are white Americans. Can you please explain this phenomenon and how it stems from colonialism, since we are living in a settler-colonial society? And why does the authority over most sexual assaults in Indian Country fall under the auspices of the federal government? Does this differ from other kinds of rapes in the United States? Who deals with rape—you know, why is the federal government playing a role here? And also, for those who might be asking, how does this issue of whether perpetrators are Native or not, what does it matter? What's the difference? How does it impact the issue of who handles the case and the distinct roles of the tribes and states and the federal government?

**SD:** Well, starting with the most recent legal problem that we have in Indian Country would be 1978. There was a Supreme Court decision called *Oliphant v. Suquamish Indian Tribe*, and essentially what that Supreme Court did was take away from tribal governments the ability to criminally prosecute a non-Indian: a person who is not enrolled in a federally recognized tribe cannot be brought before a tribal court and prosecuted. So, that has been a deep concern for tribal governments since 1978, and there have been a number of strategies that have tried to potentially address that and even get a congressional bill that would overturn that Supreme Court decision.

But, if you back up even further than that, in 1885 the Congress passed the Major Crimes Act, which included a number of felonies that the bill said now the federal government is going to step in and prosecute certain felonies that happen in Indian Country. Prior to that, even though there were definitely efforts to extinguish tribal governments and commit ethnic cleansing and genocide, there was still, believe it or not, kind of an understanding that tribes had their own judicial systems and could handle things in their own right.

What the Major Crimes Act then did was suggest that tribes were not capable of handling the jurisprudence of a crime such as rape. It's very paternalistic, the view that we have to turn to the Great White Father to come into our community and essentially say, "Okay, this rape was wrong and we're going to prosecute the offender and protect you as your guardians." And so the problem really began then, although there was certainly history behind that, that the actual legal deconstruction of tribal justice systems can be linked to the Major Crimes Act.

**JKK:** So, there's a cross-cutting effect: on the one hand, the federal government insists that it will prosecute and handle issues that constitute these major crimes, and rape is considered one of them, cross-cut with the fact that tribes are prohibited from prosecuting non-Natives, or non-citizens of their tribal nations?

**SD:** Well, that's a great question. For a while, for a few years there, tribes could only prosecute members of their own tribe. Congress did address that in the mid-nineties, and so the law now stands that as long as the defendant is enrolled in a federally recognized tribe, they can be prosecuted by the tribal government, but they don't have to be from the tribe.

**JKK**: And now, if the evidence shows that it's non-Natives—period—who are committing the majority of these acts of violence, how do we understand that? For those who might not be familiar with reservations, they might be thinking that reservations are where only American Indians are living. What is the sort of demographic scenario for these three sites that the study focused on—the Sioux Reservation, Alaska, and Oklahoma? What is the connection between non-Natives and Natives in those sites that will help us understand the racial question of perpetration?

**SD**: Right. Well, largely these statistics are coming out of the Justice Department and they're based on victimization surveys. So the statistics about non-Indian offenders are not based in reported crimes. We're not going to tribal police departments and gathering this data; it's coming from anonymous telephone surveys that are conducted by the Census Bureau that call random samples of Americans, ask them for their race, if they've been the victim of a crime, and if so what was the race of the perpetrator. And that's where most of these numbers are coming from. The challenge is that these surveys don't ask the women where these crimes took place.

They're not differentiating between a crime that happened on a reservation and a crime that happened in the city.

There's a lot of dispute and debate about what these numbers really mean, and the ultimate goal that I have is that I think we need research designed and led by Native women in Indian Country to get the full picture of what's really happening, because certainly there are reservations that are very remote and that have very few non-Native people living there. But the other trend that we're seeing for Native women is in border towns, for towns just off the reservation where there may be bars where Native women may go. They're targeted there by a non-Native person who recognizes them—because she's a very vulnerable person who's probably not going to be believed anyway, and perpetrators target her because she's not somebody that's going to be believed or supported. So that's one issue.

The other issue that we found is there's been actually a lot of really detailed work done in Anchorage, around the *very* high rates of rape against Native women. And we see the same phenomenon there, in that they actually did a crime map of reported rapes in downtown Anchorage and were able to pinpoint that most of the rapes took place in a four-block radius, where it looked like—from what we know from the survivors that have been brave enough to speak—Native women are targeted when the bars close and offered rides.

And that is where we see the non-Native perpetrators really focusing in and finding victims that will not be believed or that will not report.

**JKK**: So, really, predatory situations here.

**SD**: Very predatory.

**JKK**: Sexualized racial profiling.

**SD**: Exactly.

**JKK**: And now, in terms of whether the perpetrators are Native, since the sexual assault on Indian reservations falls under the auspices of the federal government, how does that differ from most rapes in the United States?

**SD**: Well, you have a group of prosecutors and U.S. attorneys and assistant U.S. attorneys who went into that field, not because they wanted to prosecute everyday, interpersonal crime but because they wanted to do bank robberies and terrorism and white-collar crime and drug trafficking. And the federal judicial system has never really been set up to handle things like domestic violence or rape. So you have a group of career attorneys who may or may not have wanted to take on these kinds of crimes. And, in fact, we hear culturally within the Department of Justice, attorneys say, "Oh God, not one of these. That's not why I came here; I wanted to do bank robberies."

There's a culture—and I'm not saying every federal prosecutor falls under that, because there are certainly exceptions to it, but with the FBI and the U.S. Attorney's Office, they didn't go into those careers to deal with what they consider to be minor Indian issues. They want to do the big ones; they want to do the high-profile white-collar-crime cases. So there's a culture there of indifference, of Why do we care? And then, of course, there's the distance. You might be three hundred miles away from where the victim lives, and she doesn't have a telephone. So how do you keep her informed about what her case is looking like, and how do you keep her from feeling abandoned by the system? It's very difficult.

**JKK**: Or educating her about her political and legal rights, too, right? It sounds like a culture of indifference and a cowboy culture mentality.

**SD**: Definitely.

**JKK**: Now, in terms of the federal government playing a role. For those who are not familiar with the federal purview over Indian reservations, I just want to remind people that the federal government considers Indian reservations federal property. And they assert full rein on those lands. Aren't rapes generally dealt with by the state prosecutors?

**SD**: Yes. For any other parcel of land—with the exception of, say, national parks or something along those lines—rape falls under the purview of a state prosecutor, not a federal prosecutor. So, again, that's why people go into the federal U.S. Attorney's Office; they're not thinking they're going to be prosecuting crimes like rape; that's a state issue.

**JKK**: Now, regarding whether the perpetrators are Native or non-Native. Since the 1978 *Oliphant* case at the U.S. Supreme Court, if the tribes are not allowed to prosecute non-Natives, that means that what we're seeing here is the U.S. failing to protect Native women. This is part of the trust obligation of U.S. federal government, right? The federal government is supposed to protect tribes. And if they're not protecting Indigenous women from non-Natives committing acts of violence on their land, and the tribe is prohibited from prosecuting those non-Natives, that just seems to be a complete paradox. I mean, to me, that is an incredible example of the structural violence that Native women find themselves in, in terms of the barriers to seek justice. So, I just want to clarify, tribes cannot prosecute a non-Native who commits an act of rape against one of their tribal citizens on Native land.

**SD:** Correct.

**JKK:** You mentioned something else about the culture of the Department of Justice and issues around the sort of cultural roots of the criminal justice system in the United States. What about the current way that the criminal justice system stems from Anglo-American jurisprudence? How is this a limited model in terms of adequacy for addressing sexual assault against Native women?

**SD:** Well, from the roots in English common law, women have long suffered problems in getting justice in an Anglo-American, very patriarchal justice system. Even until the late seventies, there were still laws on the books at the state level that indicated that women usually lie about rape, that it's very difficult to prove a rape, that a woman who had a sexual background of perhaps having had sex before marriage or was not a virgin could not be seen as a victim under the eyes of the law. So, the Anglo-American judicial construct of rape has never been one that is victim-friendly. It is set up and designed to protect white, male property owners and their right to have sex with whom they want, and not to look at the world through the eyes of a victim.

What's happened is that many tribes, in an effort to develop their own judicial system and have some independence, have emulated that Anglo-American construct. You don't find that the tribal governments are necessarily doing anything very innovative around sexual violence, but are rather just replicating what they see at the state level, which is not necessarily the fault of the tribes. I mean, a lot of times these laws and these court systems were set up by outsiders from Washington, you know, coming from Washington, D.C., instead of the tribal courts system. But what they have then is just a mini version of what we have at the state and federal level, which has never even helped white women.

**JKK:** That's right. And you mentioned the laws in the books through the seventies. Didn't the majority of states still say there was no such thing as a husband raping the woman he's married to?

**SD:** I think all fifty states at this point have corrected that marital rape exemption to some extent. However, there are still states in which a crime of rape against a spouse, or ex-spouse, is a lesser felony than a rape against somebody whom you've not been married to. So, even though there's no exemption left, there's still the mentality that a woman who has married somebody is then forced to provide sexual pleasure to that man for the rest of her life.

**JKK**: And that gets right to the heart of marriage under a patriarchal system in which men consider women their property. Now, what about giving them an overview of the legal entanglements concerning jurisdiction over these cases and some of the distinct barriers to reporting the crimes? You mentioned earlier that the data was taken through some of these pools. What are the distinct barriers in reporting the crimes, and also undergoing forensic examinations? What are these barriers that Native women are facing? Can you give us some examples?

**SD**: Well, I think one of the saddest things we heard when we were doing our research with Amnesty is that in many communities, rape has become so common and such an everyday occurrence in the community that, in a sense, women—young women and teens and girls—don't know that it's wrong because it's happened to everyone that they know. It's happened to their mothers and their sisters and their friends and their aunties and their grandmothers, and nothing was ever done in those cases. So, at some level, there's no reporting, or there's very low reporting, because there almost is this acceptance that this is a rite of passage, that this is expected, that you will be raped in your lifetime, probably more than once. And therefore you find that that very visceral level of that immediate response is not "Oh, I need to call the police" or "I need to go to the doctor" but that this is what everyone told me to expect, this is what happens to Native women. That's one of the saddest things we heard.

Beyond that, if a woman does go forward and says, "I want to contact law enforcement" or "I want to contact health care," there's certainly a lot of barriers there. In Alaska it takes two or three days for the state troopers to arrive there by air. By that time, you've lost a lot of forensic evidence. And even in the lower forty-eight, where you don't have the problem with getting law enforcement there within the day, you go to the Indian Health Service and they don't have anyone on staff that understands how to perform a forensic exam to preserve evidence of the assault. So you lose. You know, juries today expect that. They want that rape kit; they want that DNA. And if you don't have it, then you're not, you know, very few prosecutors will actually go through with the case. So Indian Health Service has really dropped the ball here. They don't have a national protocol for forensic exams. For those few women that do come forward and say "I want this exam," it's not available in most parts of the country.

**JKK**: I see. And is that largely a financial issue that the government hasn't made a commitment to that as part of its trust obligations?

**SD:** I think that's a huge part of it. I think resources in Indian Country are always a factor. But, I think beyond that, Indian Health Service has not shown a lot of initiative in terms of providing training for their staff on how to perform these exams and how to work with the FBI to make sure the evidence is collected in a timely manner. There are Department of Justice guidelines that came out about two or three years ago that provide national guidance and protocol, and none of those, as far as I know, none of those guidelines have been implemented at the Indian Health Service.

**JKK:** Is that right? What kind of mechanism would force their hand there?

**SD:** About a year and a half ago, maybe two years ago now, the National Congress of American Indians developed a call for Indian Health Service to adopt the guidelines of the Justice Department in terms of the forensic exams, and they haven't done so yet. I don't know what it would take. Maybe bringing Congress in and providing a mandate, which hopefully would be also supplemented with the funding necessary to provide the training to those health-care officials. But most rapes nationwide are never reported—it's not just Native women.

Most women never report their rape to law enforcement, not just Native women. So not only do we need to provide that cushion for Indian Health Service and for the federal prosecutors to do their thing, and do it right, but we also need to make sure that all of those women who don't report—and that's their right and we should respect that—have support services that are run by and for Native women: culturally appropriate healing services that incorporate traditional beliefs and sisterhood. That has to be there, because we can't change the culture overnight, and there are women that are still not going to report, even if we make changes, because they don't trust the system. So we need to make sure that there are advocacy services, not just mental health services. A lot of times people want to say, "Oh, these women need therapy," but I think more so women need to be around their sisters and their communities who can help them think through these things and feel safe again, and that to me is where the bulk of the resources need to go.

**JKK:** Advocacy and support without pathologizing women.

**SD:** Right.

**JKK:** One of the things that I noticed online at Amnesty is that the report itself has some incredible data, and the writing is very clear and concise; it's a very compelling report. But also, there are some amazing photographs—snapshots—of changing that culture in terms of community. You get a sense of the geography, like the example of women in Alaska being an airplane away from any state trooper that's going to come in. There's a photo essay, and I also noticed there's a video with interviews of women who have stayed in their communities to help other women survivors. And it was also very moving to hear those interviews.

You mentioned the issue of culturally appropriate methods and working traditions into systematic approaches. You mentioned also, earlier, the issue of tribal governments replicating the dominant model that hasn't worked for anybody. How can we think about these issues in relation to the broader undertaking of decolonization? And given the numerous financial and legal limitations faced by the tribal court systems, what else needs to change in order for tribal governments to position themselves in a way that they need not rely on the federal or state system to prosecute these cases? What's going on with perpetrators within tribes, and also do we want to have a call for tribal governments to prosecute? What is the rub of tribes being dependent on the federal government in a certain way that's set up structurally?

**SD**: Well, I think each community needs to decide for itself what the appropriate response to rape should be in their community, and I would hope that women would be at the center of that discussion. I would hope that Native women in their own communities could set up community forums, or discussions, or healing lodges—or whatever is appropriate for that community—to bring people together and say, "No more, we're not going to tolerate this onslaught of sexual violence that has taken over our community. We're going to start to say no to that." And what that might look like in each individual community is going to differ; but I think that ultimately, holding men accountable, whether they be Native men or non-Native men, is critical to the future of our nation.

**JKK**: Yes.

**SD**: With this level of sexual violence in our communities, I really don't see how we can see a long future. Because without your women, where are your mothers? Where are your grandmothers? If you're devastated by the aftereffects of a sexual assault, how are you able to contribute to the culture, if you're so devastated and so hurt by what has happened that you're not able to contribute? That's why those support systems are so critical, to bring women back into the community.

In terms of holding men accountable, there are a number of different ideas that people have, and some of them are being implemented. They may not be obvious to an outsider, and it may not be within the tribal court system, but they are being held accountable culturally and spiritually. It's not necessarily appropriate for me, as a lawyer and a writer, to expose or write about some of those things, because it's not my story to tell, but I do hear of those things happening, of men being held accountable in a way that an Anglo-American legal system would never even be able to wrap its head around, things that happen spiritually that are appropriate in that particular community. So, I think giving women the power to speak and the power to engage at that level is the key to holding accountability.

**JKK**: So re-empowering women and also having a collective response of intolerance to this kind of violence in whatever cultural lines are most appropriate.

**SD**: Yes.

**JKK**: And that the solution I'm hearing you say really needs to be conceptualized by Native women, first and foremost, but that everybody is responsible, right?

**SD**: Absolutely. I mean, men definitely have a role to play here in holding their brothers accountable and their fathers accountable for their behavior, and as long as Native women are at the center of the analysis, there's a place for everyone at the table in terms of saying we want our community to be free of this sexual violence.

**JKK**: I've read some incredible articles that you've written in your professional practice and activism. It's clear that you've worked to decolonize rape law and are theorizing a Native feminist response that synthesizes both the need for safety and a pro-sovereignty approach. I'm hoping you could please delineate these issues. What would it mean to decolonize rape law? And what sorts of tribal protection orders are there for survivors of sexual assault?

**SD**: Well, I think first and foremost we need to be able to acknowledge and dissect the problems with Anglo-American rape law—the newer problems based in English common rape law—and articulate why this isn't going to work with our community. Because it seems that the first place tribal courts go is to say, "Well, how did the state do this, and how can we make our system look kind of like that?" And that's an assimilative kind of ideology, where if we have a court that looks like a state court then we'll be legitimate. So the first thing that has to happen is an analysis that that's not really working for us, or for even the non-Native community.

Once you establish that, then you have to rebuild, to determine what our rape law is going to look like. One of the mistakes that I see being made is to go to the other extreme, is to say, "Well, we're going to do peacemaking," or "We're going to do healing circles," or "We're going to talk it out," or "We're going to do mediation." I think that is just as dangerous, frankly. And that gets me into a little bit of trouble with some people who are trying to theorize a non-adversarial approach.

I think rape, in and of itself, is an adversarial crime. And it's a political crime against women. And I think you have to respond to it at some level in an adversarial way, whether that be in a courtroom or in a sweat lodge or in a ceremony. There has to be some level of "This is wrong," not "We're going to talk it out" or "He had a rough childhood" or "There was alcohol involved so we don't really know what he meant to do," but really saying, "No, this behavior is not acceptable." And as long as the legal response includes that, I think we're going to see a vast improvement over the Anglo-American legal system.

**JKK**: So, combining that zero-tolerance policy within an Indigenous framework that is culturally appropriate.

**SD**: Yes.

**JKK**: And not turning to Anglo-American jurisprudence for the solutions.

**SD**: Right.

**JKK**: I've heard you speak in public about how, since the federal government asserts jurisdiction over major crimes, including rape, a lot of tribal nations have relinquished their right to engage in concurrent jurisdiction over sex crimes when there is a Native perpetrator. I wonder, are you seeing any kind of combination, any kind of best practices or examples within tribal nations that are asserting concurrent jurisdiction over sex crimes? Those that are responding to them through traditional solutions that are not just about "talking it out" but who do condemn it and try and restore right relations within that community context?

**SD**: Sure. I don't hear enough about it, but it is happening. I know that there's certainly communities that are moving this direction that aren't necessarily advertising that fact to the outside world. What I have heard is that there are tribes that have enacted banishment laws to remove perpetrators from their communities. Zero tolerance is one example: we're not going to allow sexual violence in our community, and if you commit it you are no longer welcome here. Another that has been very common throughout the century is to not allow people that have a background of sexual violence to hold leadership positions in the community. They're banned from running for office or from serving in any kind of capacity as a leader, whether that be as a spiritual leader or a political leader. Their history of perpetration against women and children is constantly acknowledged, such that that particular individual can't engage at the leadership level. I don't think that's enough, personally. I think that's a start, but I think that more needs to be done in terms of saying that this type of behavior cannot continue.

**JKK**: Right. And in the urban context, you're in St. Paul, Minnesota. Are you working with Native women in that area?

**SD**: I've lived here for about a year and a half, and I used to travel a lot, so I haven't really set up my homestead here in terms of working with Native women. But St. Paul and Minneapolis have a long history of Native women's activism, and I'm slowly starting to learn who the players are, and I have met some of the women who have been working in this area for many, many years.

One of the issues that recently arose with a community of women that I was talking to is the issue of trafficking of Native women into the Twin Cities, prostituting women from the reservations. What we're hearing anecdotally is that there is a drug issue on a reservation. Say if a woman has a meth habit and she's unable to pay her debt; her meth dealer will bring her to the Twin Cities, put her on the street, and tell her to pay that debt off with her body. That's one of the little-known issues that we're trying to learn more about and raise awareness about. It's not just the Twin Cities. It's happening in other communities around the nation as well.

**JKK**: Thank you for bringing that to our attention. I had no idea about that. I don't know why I should be surprised, but that's chilling to hear.

I remember right before the Amnesty International USA report was released, the BBC in England did an exposé on the U.S.'s failure to protect Indigenous women from sexual violence. I wanted to ask you if you could speak sort of to the international attention, and what you think the ripple effect will be for this report. What can we anticipate, or what should we activate around, in terms of bringing this issue to the attention for the entire American populace?

**SD**: One of the things that I've mentioned is that the report is groundbreaking on many levels, but for Native women it's really not something new. We knew this; we already knew most of the information that's in the report. So, it really was an effort to bring in our non-Native allies to the work and to raise awareness about the plight of Native women in the United States.

I think the reason it's receiving so much attention abroad, at least from what I can tell, is again because the United States is held up as this bastion of freedom and democracy, and we have to model ourselves after the freedom that the USA provides. It's shocking to people who don't know what happens on reservations what it's like for a Native woman to be a sexual assault victim in the United States. So there's that level of raising awareness around non-Natives.

I think, in particular, what I'm actually interested in is just solid resources. If people in Western Europe are moved by the story, help us. Send us money. I know that's not the only answer, but what happened out of the NPR—National Public Radio ran a piece last week about a shelter in South Dakota that was ready to close its doors, and within a few days the NPR listeners had rallied around this shelter and had raised several thousand dollars to help keep those shelter doors open. And I do think that that's important. I think that if the government can't fund us, then we're going to have to find alternate ways to fund our programs, and so awareness like this report provides is one door that we can open to see more resources come in.

I have a lot to learn yet about the international human rights movement and how it can come into play. I've focused my work domestically, about what can happen internally within tribal nations and within the United States. But with Amnesty International coming in, there will be more dialogue about human rights analysis and about how that, in particular, might be one part of the solution to what we face on the reservations and in the villages.

## Second Interview

I was fortunate to be able to bring Sarah Deer back to the program in 2013, six years after our first conversation. What prompted my second invitation was the Violence Against Women Act, also referred to as VAWA. Deer is known for her testimony supporting the 2010 passage of the Tribal Law and Order Act and for her instrumental role in the reauthorization of VAWA, which was signed into law by President Obama on March 7, 2013. This interview was given prior to that passage, but soon after the Senate passed its version of the bill, on February 12, 2013, authorizing $659 million over five years for various programs targeting domestic violence, including new protections for LGBT and Native American victims of domestic violence and gives more attention to sexual assault prevention. One of the biggest obstacles to getting VAWA through Congress was a provision that grants new authority to tribal governments to prosecute domestic abusers. Currently, tribal courts have no authority over non-Natives who domestically abuse Native American women on tribal lands. The Senate VAWA bill included a provision granting tribal courts the authority to prosecute in those cases, but many House Republicans opposed the provision and argued that tribal courts would not uphold the constitutional rights of non-Natives charged with sexual violence.

This interview took place on February 22, 2013.


**J. Kēhaulani Kauanui:** I was just reviewing my audio archive and noticed that it was May 2007 when you were last on *Indigenous Politics*, and that's when you were speaking about the newly released report from Amnesty International USA titled "Maze of Injustice: The Failure to Protect Indigenous Women from Sexual Violence in the USA," which relates to this issue that I want to talk to you about today.

**Sarah Deer:** Yes.

**JKK:** I want to ask you if you could start by letting us know a bit about your background, personal and professional, and also how you came to do this work. And if you could speak at some point about the trajectory from that Amnesty International report to the recent Senate bill passage of the Violence Against Women Act.

**SD:** Sure. Well, I'm a citizen of the Muscogee Creek Nation of Oklahoma, and I was actually raised in Wichita, Kansas. I was raised as an urban Indian, and my identity really stemmed from the community there in Wichita. I began working as a rape crisis counselor back in 1993. I was twenty years old, and I did direct advocacy for Native women in Lawrence, Kansas, where I was a student. And most of the women that I worked with had some connection to Haskell Indian Nations University, so they were Native students or Native faculty. And some of them had been assaulted on campus, but many had been assaulted on their homelands and had come to Haskell to get an education, and the stress and the uncertainty of being in a new place sometimes led them to call the rape crisis line.

That really informed what I wanted to do with the rest of my life. I wanted to be part of helping Native women recover from sexual assault and build a life for themselves. I was led to go to law school. I thought at the time that I would prosecute sex crimes, and that was sort of my goal when I entered law school, but I went in a different direction and started thinking more about policy and how federal law really impedes the ability of Native women to find justice. So, I ended up going into more of a policy direction with my work, and I'm a law professor now, but that's a relatively new development in my life. And when I began teaching, what was important to me was that I would be able to continue to research, write, and advocate for Native women, and fortunately, I'm in a place where I can do that.

**JKK:** Right, excellent. I want to acknowledge that you've just recently been named chair of a U.S. Department of Justice Federal Advisory Committee designed to develop a protocol for responding to sexual assault in tribal communities. Could you speak to your new role and how you are working with the Obama administration on these issues?

**SD:** Sure. I was asked by Eric Holder to chair this committee, and we are tasked with trying to untangle the web of jurisdiction for Native women living in Indian Country. And what that means is that, unlike any other place in the United States, Native women have to navigate a system that involves at least three separate federal agencies in order to find justice for rape. We have the Department of Health and Human Services, which houses the Indian Health Service. We have the Department of the Interior, which houses tribal police as well as some tribal prosecutors. And then we have the Department of Justice, with the FBI and the U.S. Attorney's Offices.

When those three agencies don't work together, what happens is that Native women who report a sexual assault are left basically to bring the pieces of their lives back together on their own. So the task force that I'm chairing is designed to try to ensure a constant stream of communication among and between those federal agencies, so that they're being consistent. One of the things that I've heard and that advocates have told me is those three federal agencies sometimes even issue conflicting policies. The task force is designed to try to sort that out and make sure all the federal agencies are working from one set of protocols. It's going to be an interesting couple of years as we try to do that.

**JKK:** I'll get back to that, because I want to get into some of those contradictions and issues around jurisdiction and coordination and the interface with the federal government. Just for a quick summary of what happened with the

Senate passage of the Violence Against Women Act on February 12. This was a 78-to-22 vote in the Senate?

**SD:** Yes.

**JKK:** Could you give us a sense of the history of the law? It's my understanding that it passed in 1994 and that 2012 was the first time it was not authorized.

**SD:** The Violence Against Women Act, as you said, was passed originally in 1994 as a strong bipartisan piece of legislation. In fact, it was called the Biden-Hatch Bill, if you can believe that, and Hatch has since abandoned the Violence Against Women Act for reasons I'll talk about. What happens is that the act needs to be reauthorized every five years, and that is to keep the budget available, the line item to actually appropriate money for this bill. So the five-year reauthorization has been a constant, and we have now a situation where the law has expired, because it expired back in 2011. If the VAWA is not reauthorized, then none of the funding programs are stable. In other words, Congress could decide not to fund all the programs available under VAWA.

What has happened is that each time the act is reauthorized, Congress checks in with the experts, the people who are working directly with victims across the United States, and asks what is missing. What pieces of this problem are still prevalent because of some sort of legal issue? And can we address that in Congress? In 2012 they identified three key categories of women in the United States who still can't find justice on a regular basis. Those include LGBT women and trans men, and immigrant women who do not have a documented status in the United States, and Native American women, because of the jurisdictional tangles at the tribal level. So when the Senate drafted the 2012 reauthorization, they included special provisions that would address these gaps, and because these three categories of women are politically problematic for Republicans, they actually put a stop to the bill. It did pass the Senate in April 2012, with a vote of sixty-eight in favor, but the House never brought the issue to a vote. And the reason was largely based in these concerns about special provisions for these women, that again, the Republican Party is not known to embrace these three categories of women. So they refused to put it to a vote at the end of the year.

**JKK:** I see. Now, as I understand it, the Senate bill that passed on February 12, 2013, does have provisions for services for women without regard for sexual orientation or immigrant status, right? So that made it in this time. And then there is the question around jurisdiction and authority for crimes committed against American Indian women on reservation.

**SD:** Yes, all three of those categories are included in the current 2013 Senate bill, which passed on February 12.

**JKK:** So then the question will be what happens when it gets to the Republican-led House?

**SD:** Correct.

**JKK:** And will they block it again?

**SD:** Right.

**JKK:** I see. Now, we know that lesbian, gay, bisexual, and trans—as a grouping—and American Indian women are not mutually exclusive categories, but I want to zone in and ask you to speak to this question of jurisdiction and authority for crimes committed on reservations around issues of governance and sovereignty. Some might know about reservations, but some people might not realize that reservations are part of Indian Country, which is a different legal terrain. The way that I think about this legislation is that it crosses the intersection between civil rights, including equal protection under the law, and sovereignty rights, the right to tribal authority to pursue these cases. Could you unpack some of this?

**SD:** The problem right now for tribal governments—and it's important to note that tribal governments preexist the United States Constitution by, you know, ten or eleven thousand years, depending on your perspective—the problem has been that in the last century both the Supreme Court and the federal government have started to impose restrictions on the kinds of things tribal governments can do. There are law review articles full of the various restrictions that Congress has imposed on tribes, but the one that's most relevant for the Violence Against Women Act discussion actually comes from the U.S. Supreme Court. In 1978 the U.S. Supreme Court issued a ruling that basically said that tribes cannot prosecute non-Indians. Prior to that time, tribal governments had been exercising criminal jurisdiction over anyone who came into their community and committed crime. There were other kinds of restrictions put on the tribe, but by and large, tribes had the authority and exercised the authority against anyone, regardless of who they were, what color their skin was, what race they were. The Supreme Court put a stop to that, and until Congress issues a correction to that decision, tribes have their hands tied if the perpetrator of a crime is non-Indian. There's nothing that the tribe can do; they have to depend on either the federal government or the state government to prosecute that crime, and many times they just don't.

If we're going to restore jurisdiction to the tribal governments, which is what we're trying to do with the Violence Against Women Act, one of the concerns that's been raised is whether defendants in these tribal courts will be given the rights that they are allowed in federal and state courts. It's interesting that that's the question being raised by the Republicans, because right now, tribal people are prosecuted by tribal governments, and no one seems to be concerned about their civil rights. The concern is when we want to prosecute non-Indians. All of a sudden the Republicans have become these civil libertarians who are concerned about the abuse of power, which is sort of ironic. But that's really what the objection is: Can we trust tribal governments to ensure that people are given due process in tribal courts? And that's what we're up against.

**JKK:** Well, when I was saying it's at the intersection of civil rights and sovereignty rights, I meant the civil rights for Native women.

**SD:** Oh, well, obviously that's not even part of the discussion for many of the Republicans. Their focus has been solely on the perpetrators.

**JKK:** And now, how does that 1978 ruling at the U.S. Supreme Court interface with or draw on the Major Crimes Act?

**SD:** Well, the Major Crimes Act was the first piece of federal legislation that allowed or imposed federal authority in Indian Country. And that's why, in many reservations, the crime is actually investigated by the FBI. And the FBI is really not in the business of looking at violent, interpersonal crime—they're trying to take on, you know, Enron and terrorists and drug traffickers. So, Indian Country is the only place where the Federal Bureau of Investigation would be coming in and actually investigating a crime that happened, which would include rape.

I outlined some specific types of crimes that the federal government would have authority over, and they're really the felonies, any violent crime where the punishment would be a year or more incarceration. But what happened when that law was passed is even though it didn't divest tribal governments of their inherent authority to prosecute crimes, the federal government sent a message to tribal governments for about one hundred years that they have exclusive authority, that they are the only ones that can prosecute murder, rape, kidnapping, sex abuse, and the tribes are divested of the jurisdiction. That actually isn't what the legislation says. In the last thirty years or so, tribes have started to prosecute crimes like homicide and rape, so they share that power, the concurrent authority that the tribe can prosecute a crime and the federal government can prosecute a crime. But after 1978 only the federal government can prosecute a crime committed by a non-Indian.

**JKK:** And now, is it any non-Indian, or could it even be an Indian who's not enrolled on the reservation where the crime is committed?

**SD:** It's interesting. There was some back-and-forth between Congress and the Court, starting in the 1990s, but as of a few years ago the Court clarified that tribes do have criminal jurisdiction over any Indian; they don't have to be from that reservation. The circuits are a little split on the question of whether the person has to be enrolled somewhere. Typically, what we tell prosecutors when we train them on this issue is that the person should be recognized as an Indian by their community. Even if they're not enrolled, the federal government may still have the jurisdiction in that case.

**JKK:** So if it really is about any non-Indians or any Indians, this really is a racial distinction then, isn't it? Not just a governmental or Indigenous distinction.

**SD:** It is. And it's a very frustrating distinction as well. For instance, my spouse is non-Indian. If we were to travel together to the Navajo reservation, I could commit a crime there and be penalized by the tribe and prosecuted by the tribe, and my husband, who would commit the same crime, would be immune from tribal prosecution. And the interesting thing is that neither one of us is Navajo. Politically, we don't have any connection with that tribe, but I could be prosecuted and he couldn't, and that presents some really interesting questions when it comes to whether tribes are a racial classification or a political entity.

**JKK:** Right. And it also shows the contradictions inherent in the settler-colonial world that we live in, because now you've got Indigenous women not only have to appeal to federal protection, which often seems to be a contradiction in terms, but also do so on the basis of racial equality, which has often been used in the past to undercut tribal sovereignty.

**SD:** Exactly.

**JKK:** Speaking to the settler-colonial question. I wanted to know if you could speak to the colonial roots of sexual violence committed against Indigenous women. I'm thinking about the Republican backlash against these categories—against immigrant women, against LGBT subjects, and against American Indian women—and I don't want to frame those as though they're all mutually exclusive. But you can see this question of homophobia, biphobia, transphobia, xenophobia as coming from a nativist perspective—that is, a white settler sort of backlash—and yet it's the colonial roots of sexual violence that are operating in the first place.

**SD:** Absolutely. When you talk to tribal elders, and you talk to people that are really well versed in the tribal traditional law, rape was so rare that in some languages there wasn't even a word to describe that kind of crime, because they didn't need it. The tribal governments have been dealing with women's equality and with homophobia as being contrary to tribal traditions, so it's interesting that the Republican opposition is to three categories of women that have been impacted the most by colonial rule.

**JKK:** That's right. Also, just speaking to the American Indian women in this equation, due to the fact that these crimes are committed in vast dispropor-tional skew in terms of non-Indian men, there seems to be a predatory nature to these crimes. I think of rape and all forms of sexual violence as predatory, but what do we make of the fact that so much of this is being perpetrated by non-Native men against Native women?

**SD**: I'm really glad you asked that. One of the challenges that we've had in addressing the jurisdictional problem is a seeming inability to accept the statistical data that's been consistently coming out since the mid-1990s. And that data is telling us that most Native women who are raped are raped by a non-Indian. That data comes from victimization surveys, unlike data collected from reported crimes. So this is really what's going on, and the data has been consistent for over fifteen years.

It's really unusual in American criminology to see interracial sexual assault statistics, and some of that has to do with gentrification and where people live and who they are around, but most crime in America is intraracial. So a perpetrator is more likely to attack someone of his own race. The only exception to that is Native women, and Native women—almost 80 percent, anywhere between 60 and 80 percent of Native women—report that their perpetrator was non-Indian. That's outrageous when you compare it to the interracial statistics for all other groups. So, something is going on. Something is either giving these perpetrators permission to target Native women or there's something about Native women that attracts perpetrators. And that piece of the puzzle is going to be critical if we're going to move this legislation forward in the House.

**JKK**: As I mentioned earlier, the complications of even relying on federal law have been the problem in many ways in the past. I know that you've done a lot of work on restorative justice, and I wanted to ask if you could speak from the Native feminist critiques that you've lodged regarding the legal remedies, but also that you've theorized the limits to restorative justice. And what I'm getting at here is that many times I'm trying to look outside the state, outside of the settler-colonial state, for the source of the remedy. And there have been critiques from radical women of color, for example, around the Violence Against Women Act by talking about some of those frameworks and their limitations. In closing, I want to ask if you would speak to some of those feminist critiques, but also what you have found to be sort of some of the limits of restorative justice in relation to the particularity of Native women's issues having to do with these jurisdictional quandaries.

**SD**: Absolutely. The federal criminal justice system is not going to be the savior of Native women. In fact, the federal criminal justice system is largely responsible for the high rates of crime in Indian Country. So, when I go to Congress seeking the remedy in the Violence Against Women Act, part of my underlying goal is that we need the federal government out of our business. We need the federal government to not police our communities, because they don't do it well and they end up harming and throwing away a great number of our men.

So the Violence Against Women Act does, in other contexts, present some real quandaries for radical feminists of color, because it reinforces or celebrates the criminal justice response to crime. We have to be very cautious of what the Violence Against Women Act does.

The piece that I'm most interested in actually would, in the long term, get the federal government out of the business of prosecuting crime in Indian Country and put it back in the hands of tribal officials of the sovereign governments that exist in the United States. And what does that mean? Let's say the federal government got completely out of the business of policing Indian Country tomorrow—that's not going to happen, but let's assume that for a moment. What would tribes be able to do with some of these very violent offenders, men who are serial rapists or molested a hundred or so children in some of the boarding schools—BIA employees, in some cases, in the 1980s? What would the tribe do if there was no other entity taking action? That's a difficult question, because a lot of our ability to govern ourselves has been damaged over the course of the last couple hundred years. And, in addition, a lot of these crimes would not have been committed prior to the colonial intrusion into our lives.

We're left to wonder, how can a tribe respond to something like a violent— I should clarify that all rape is violent, whether there is physical force, or coercion, or a drug- or alcohol-induced sexual assault—what can the tribe do? And we're really struggling with this question. We don't want to replicate the system that has been imposed on us, because it hasn't worked well. The challenge is, how do we hold people accountable under tribal law, or tribal tradition, without replicating Western law and order? The thing that concerns me when we talk about responding to sexual assault using traditional tribal law is that there's a tendency to want to implement a sort of mediation answer. I think Robert Yazzie, who is a Navajo Nation chief justice, called it a "horizontal justice" instead of vertical justice. The thing that concerns me about that is: are we really prioritizing safety? Because many of the people who commit these kinds of crimes are master manipulators. And whether the system is a Western law-and-order system or it's a traditional mediation-based horizontal system, they will use that system to torment victims. So, as we begin to rebuild a tribal response to sexual assault, we have to be really mindful of that, and safety has to be a priority. If a woman is not safe, either emotionally or physically, it's going to be difficult for her to participate in this system that's going to hold her perpetrator accountable. As we start to revisit how tribes will do this and how tribes can do this—and many tribes are—we have to prioritize safety.

**JKK:** I agree. Thank you so much for laying that out, I really appreciate it. Any closing thoughts?

**SD:** I'm really hopeful. I'm hopeful that the tribal provisions in the Violence Against Women Act will pass the House sometime this spring, and the reason

I'm hopeful is because I think more and more Native women are speaking out, and our stories are being heard. And that's really critical. We have to educate Congress so that they understand the issues, and ultimately the long-range vision for this whole process is that tribal communities will have full control over how crimes like this are treated in tribal communities. And it, unfortunately, has to happen piecemeal, has to happen one Congress at a time. But I'm committed to it because I believe that tribal governments can respond to these crimes on their own terms, and I think Native women are going to lead that effort. So that keeps me hopeful.

# PHILIP J. DELORIA ON GENEALOGIES OF ACTIVISM AND SCHOLARSHIP

Philip J. Deloria (Dakota) is the Carroll Smith-Rosenberg Collegiate Professor of American Culture and History at the University of Michigan. I had met him over the years before our interview, mainly in Native studies contexts. Our discussion occurred during his visit to Wesleyan University, where he delivered a public lecture, "Crossing the (Indian) Color Line." The day after his lecture, we sat down in my office for this interview to discuss his personal and professional trajectory as a scholar; the political and intellectual legacy of his late father, Vine Deloria Jr.; the relationships between activism, politics, scholarship, and Native American studies; cultural politics and decolonization; and his utopian political dreams. Deloria is the author of *Playing Indian* (1999), which won a Gustavus Myers Outstanding Book Award for the study of Bigotry and Human Rights in North America, and *Indians in Unexpected Places* (2004), the 2006 winner of the John C. Ewers Award of the Western History Association. Among other honors, he was awarded a National Endowment for the Humanities Fellowship in 1999. Deloria is a former associate dean of undergraduate education at the University of Michigan's College of Letters, Science, and the Arts and past director of the Program in American Culture and the Native American studies program. He has served as president of the American Studies Association, as a council member of the Organization of American Historians, and as a trustee of the Smithsonian National Museum of the American Indian.

This interview took place on March 24, 2009.

**J. Kēhaulani Kauanui:** I want to start by asking you if you would speak to some of your personal history in terms of how you came to be a scholar.

**Philip J. Deloria:** First of all, thanks for having me on the show. Well, my journey has a lot of twists and turns in it. As you know, my dad was Vine Deloria Jr., so I grew up in a household thinking about Native studies. Thinking about Native issues was omnipresent in a house with lots of different people coming through and lots of conversations going on, but for me in high school I was basically a band nerd. I played the trombone, and my undergraduate major in college was music education, and I was a middle school music teacher, so I kind of turned away about as far from that upbringing as one could imagine. But, after a couple years of teaching music I realized that I could do it for thirty years and I would do the same thing over and over again, more or less, and it was just not feeling very comfortable to me. And I went back and I did a master's degree in broadcast journalism.

**JKK:** Interesting. I did not know that journalism was part of your background.

**PD:** Well, I did that because I was playing music. I was playing in a band and I got roped into working on music videos in Denver in the early eighties, and so I was the guy carrying cable for the cameraman and the guy making smoke out of coffee grounds, you know, underneath the stage. I got really into it, and this was the high moment of music video in a lot of ways, and I really just wanted to learn how to use the equipment, so I went back and I did a master's degree in journalism. At the very end of that program you had to do either a professional project or a thesis, and I wanted to make a documentary. I had a friend who worked at Ampex, and we borrowed a brand-new camera—one of the early digital cameras—and I decided to do a project on Sioux land claims in the Black Hills, which were playing out right at that moment in the late eighties around the Bradley Bill and the efforts there. And I started going up with my dad, actually, so I kind of reconnected with my dad around this project, and sometimes I took a camera with me and sometimes I didn't, and I produced this documentary, which was not particularly great if I look back at it in retrospect, but for me it was a real growth experience and it took me right from where I'd been—which was music and video editing—and took me back into history and thinking about Native studies.

I applied for graduate programs. I couldn't think of what else to do. I ended up at Yale in American studies, and I think I ended up there largely because I could say I had this degree in broadcasting and journalism and it had some kind of relation to American studies. And while I was there I had to think hard about who I wanted to be as a scholar and how I wanted to position myself, and I don't mean that in a cynical way—"positioning"—but just what I was interested in and what I wanted to think about. And I should say when I went into graduate school at Yale, I was a totally different person than the person I am today. I was very, very shy, and I'm still pretty shy, but not as much as I used to be, and I had no sense of confidence at all, so I didn't speak my first semester of graduate school. I was literally silent for almost every class except the moments when you had to do a presentation, and I was terrified about that.

So, over the course of my time at Yale, what I ended up exploring was basically all the places that my father had not been, which were few. I had been interested in religion and religious studies, but he was there, and he was all over law and policy, and he was a fine historian, so I didn't feel that comfortable just doing the straight-ahead history. This being the late eighties and early nineties, the place where I ended up was cultural studies and cultural history.

I stake my claim around trying to do a kind of theoretical form of American studies. But I wasn't even thinking necessarily about Native studies, even at the point where I was writing my dissertation. My first dissertation idea had to do with Western identity in small towns, and I was interested in football games and rotary clubs and things like that. And my adviser said, "This doesn't seem like a very good dissertation to me," which was kind of a blessing, and then I found myself sitting in class—it was Bill Cronon's class, and he was lecturing on this group called the Woodcraft Indians. He put up this picture of all these little kids, these boys, dressed up in these Indian costumes roaming around in the woods, and at the same moment he did this, the person sitting next to me, Gunther Pack, a fine scholar, said, "Hey, have you ever heard of this group called The Improved Order of Red Men?" And I said, wow, I have, because in Empire, Colorado, there's this lodge, "the improved order of red men," and for whatever reason I had stopped there one time driving through the mountains. So, my first book, *Playing Indian,* just exploded in my head in about the next thirty seconds, and it was an amazing and wonderful experience, and I have to say that I've never had anything else like it. All of a sudden I thought, Boston Tea Party, these fraternal orders, these Boy Scouts and Campfire Girls who dress up like Indians. I had moved to New Haven from Boulder, Colorado, which was the center for all things New Age, so there were all these New Age people dressing up like Indians, and it literally exploded in my head: What is this about? What is this about when white people dress up like Indians, and what does it mean? And over the course of the next week, basically, the structure of the dissertation and later the book kind of fell into place. So it was kind of amazing, actually.

**JKK:** *Playing Indian* is such an important book, and certainly historians and American studies scholars and Native American studies, and other scholars in a variety of different fields, know this book well. For our general audience, could you tell us what you did find? What is going on with white people in particular, and other non-Natives, playing Indian?

**PD:** In the book, I made this large argument and I broke it down into two halves. Basically, in the first half I argued that people around the American Revolution had created an idea about Indians and then appropriated, and not just appropriated—had performed that identity. The performance, for me, was a really key part of this. The dressing up and acting like Indians was really important, and they had done so in order to claim a sort of aboriginal right to the continent. It's not just the Boston Tea Party; there are many, many incidents in which colonists dress up like Indians. They did this in order to stop being British and start becoming American, start being one with the continent. And in order to do it, they had taken older European rituals, which involved dressing up like something else—men dressing like women for example. They had taken those older structures and had put Indians into that, and so they had performed this Indian identity as a way of being not British. And thus, the argument really is that the foundations of thinking about American identities and claims to American identity really rest on this moment where people dress up like Indians.

In the first half of the book I kind of played that out and asked, "Well, what happens after the Revolution, when there's no longer a need for revolution and Indian dressing-up has been such a good identity for revolting?" Well, it turns out that all the rebellions in the early republic have something to do with also dressing up like Indians. And then later people actually find a way to contain this rebellious content through these paternal orders, which allow them a kind of separate political identity.

In the second half of the book I ask the same question about Americans' encounters with modernity—what does it mean to be modern? And part of what it meant to be modern was to lay claim to something that was considered primitive. So you have groups like the Campfire Girls and the Boy Scouts pretending to be primitive in order to gain this access to something that was original and authentic and true and then that, I argued in the rest of the book, sort of played out through the rest of the twentieth century.

**JKK:** Incredible. It's such an important work, I really see that text as giving us the genealogy of American nativism in terms of how colonialism manifests itself racially, and one of the things that blew my mind when I first moved here was driving up to Route 2, the Mohawk Trail, and seeing that Mohawk Park, where there is a park, put up by the new order of improved red men. They have this statue in honor of the so-called guy dying Mohawk and then all the different plates of all the different orders. So there's even the Maui tribe, number 442, and all this sort of thing, so it's certainly persistent. In terms of the question of modernity, and laying claim to something primitive, could you speak to *Indians in Unexpected Places,* your second book?

**PD:** Right. So this second book started off as a collection of essays, and the essays were inspired by an encounter I had with my grandfather. My grandfather had these memories of himself as an athlete. And these were very, very striking for him, and they made me think a lot about his generation of people at the turn of the twentieth century and how he seems to have effortlessly engaged questions of modernity in ways that we don't do today.

Right, today the lines between modern and primitive are ideological constructs, not necessarily things that describe anybody, but at that moment it

seemed to me that there were a number of Indian people who were able to engage all the things that gave white Americans an anxiety about being modern.
And I started to think about an archive; I thought about this at first in terms
of teaching a class. I started to collect an archive of Indian people who were
doing interesting things that caught people by surprise. I became very interested in Indian opera singers and Indian athletes, and Indian pole sitters and
roller-skating champions, and I became very taken with thinking about Buffalo
Bill's Wild West Show and the ways that it allowed Native people to travel, not
only around the country but around the world. I had a number of epiphany
moments in this, but one was reading an account from one of the Chicago
papers, in 1893, the same time Frederick Jackson Turner was making arguments about the marriage of the frontier and American character in Chicago,
and it was this report of two Native people who had left Buffalo Bill's show in
Europe, made their way across most of Europe, down into Australia, and were
being repatriated because they had been basically living this street party life in
one of the Australian cities. They were coming back to the United States, and
the question was, well, who had to pay for all of this? And the issue of who pays
for it seemed so trivial in relation to the thing that was happening in my head,
which was that this is pretty amazing. These are cosmopolitan Indian explor-
ers who are certainly not without effort but without the sort of anxiety that we
attach to—oh, you know, Indians couldn't possibly be modern, because they
live on reservations, they're so far away. So I started to think harder then about
what expectations non-Indians had of Indian people. They didn't participate in
market economies, they lived on these distant reservations, they were locked
back in some other kind of time, they didn't know how to use technology—you
know, all of these things were expectations. And then I started thinking about
how it would have been to live within those expectations.

**JKK:** Confining.

**PD:** Yes, very, very confining, yet there's all these Native people who really didn't
seem to think much about those expectations at all; they simply went out and
did things.

I became very interested in thinking about athletes who traveled a lot and
who played a lot of different sports at different levels and different kinds, Native
Olympians from the early twentieth century and Native college football players and baseball players and things like this. I ended up coming up with this
argument that was based on Jim Thorpe, so I would ask audiences, How many
Native athletes can you name? And, you know, everybody would raise their
hand—well, okay, not everybody, but many people would raise their hand—
and very eagerly say, Jim Thorpe. Jim Thorpe! And I said, great, that's great,
name another one. And periodically, someone would be able to say Billy Mills,
and then I'd say, okay, name another one, and you know, once in a rare, rare

moment some crazy old baseball fan would say Charles Albert Bender, Chief Bender, pitcher for the Philadelphia Athletics in the early twentieth century, and that was it. That was it.

I ended up developing the argument that we really fix on the anomaly, and that Jim Thorpe was anomalous. Once we name that anomaly, we can consolidate our expectations: Indians aren't athletes, because there's only one that I can name. What I then set out to do was to show a wide range of Native people engaged in a wide range of things. And each of the chapters—on sports, on music, on buying and driving cars, on participating in the Wild West Show, and later on Hollywood films—help to build a cohort of Indian people. I kept waiting to find a *community* of Indian people; I kept waiting to go to Southern California and find that they were having dinner parties together, and I didn't quite find that. I think with more time I might have, but I ended up making the argument that, in fact, Native people had deeply engaged in modernity and had been influential in forming American modernity—not by virtue of being primitives in opposition to modernity, but of being people who were engaged with all the practices of the modern—who did so under the rubric of primitivism, but who were quintessentially modern in so many ways. And, also, that they did so not as a self-conscious and active political resistance, but that their actions had some significant political content. And if we look back at that content today, it is quite meaningful.

**JKK:** Jumping to another project, do you mind speaking to the photo that you chose for the cover of *Indians in Unexpected Places*?

**PD:** It's a beautiful piece of art by Arthur Amiotte. He did a whole wonderful series of these things; they're kind of collages and they're quite wonderful, and I'm grateful that he allowed me to use that image. He basically used a ledger book art style, and what he's drawn is four or five Native people sitting in a car, and on the side of it he has Buffalo Bill's Wild West, which is actually a clip from a larger collage. He has beautiful ones in dresses, and a lot of the times what he does is he just puts strategic phrases in kind of a boarding-school-trained cursive. I think "Those white people sure were jealous of our cars" is the phrase he has on that image. It's a gorgeous image. and it captures a sense of the unexpectedness of Indian people doing these things.

**JKK:** And that gets at those questions of authenticity; questions of identity, identification, and cultural difference. One of the things that I really appreciate about your work is that it blows the lid off those expectations and what people see as an oxymoron, that the only real Native can't be modern, and just that entrapment in terms of it that still guides land claims issues and sovereignty politics today, in terms of Natives having to perform a certain kind of cultural continuity in order to make legal claims. Your work has profound implications for that kind of entrapment. You mentioned a little earlier people engaging in modernity by playing primitive, in terms of non-Natives, and you mentioned Campfire Girls. I wonder if you might speak to the family legacies around your aunt Ella Deloria in relation to those kinds of social formations?

**PD:** Right. So one of the things that I gesture to in *Playing Indian*—when I started thinking about the Campfire Girls, I'd always knew there had been this odd history in our family around Campfire Girls and Boy Scouts. My grandmother's family was very good friends with Dan Beard, who was one of the founders of the Scouts, and they always had pictures of them with Dan Beard wearing these scouting hats and his costume and all this stuff, and what I quickly realized in conversations with my dad and other members of my family was that my grandmother's family—my father's mother's family—had been really, really interested in Campfire Girls. My great-grandmother on that side had been on the national board of the Campfire Girls, and she lived outside of New York City and ran this incredibly successful Campfire Girls group.

I hadn't really paid that much attention to the Campfire Girls thing in *Playing Indian*, at least in terms of my own family, but my grandmother's family was very interested in Campfire Girls, and one of the things that they did was they sought out real Native people to help them learn the Indian ways of campfire; campfire was based entirely on this whole hierarchy of Indian things. You'd be a princess, and you would perform five hundred different tasks and you would get little badges and you would put them on your Indian dress. So, my great-grandmother found this Indian woman who turned out to be Ella Deloria, my great-aunt, in New York City, where she was working for Franz Boas at Columbia University, and brought her up to work with the Campfire Girls. She would teach them songs and dances and lead a campfire, and then she would go back to New York. This was part of the way that Ella made a living and survived at the time, but it allowed the connection of our two families. My grandmother met my grandfather through Ella, who introduced the two of them.

Ella died in 1971, when I was eleven, so I have memories of her, but not a tremendous number. I think my memories of my dad in the sixties have less to do with he and Ella engaged in intellectual conversation—or even he and his father engaged in that—and much more about him finding himself as the director of the National Congress of American Indians and finding that he had to jump in very quickly and become part of a political lobbying apparatus—which, you know, had had a certain number of problems. Part of the reason why he was elected was a power struggle. He showed up at the conference and people thought, "Well, there's a young guy we could toss in there. Maybe he won't do too much damage, and maybe we could even push him around a little bit." So he kind of emerged out of this meeting in Sheraton, Wyoming, as the director, and basically what he did was he went to Washington and he was gone for nine months. He slept on the couch in the office and he worked incredibly hard, I think both to bring himself up to speed on some of these policy issues and try to bring the tribes together and rebuild that functioning organization.

I remember him being gone a very long time and then coming back for not very long, and then going back to D.C. again. There was a period there, a couple of years, where he was on the road a lot, and I think what he was doing there was something akin to what my grandfather had done; my grandfather had done a big survey of all the different missions in the Episcopal Church, which had him driving all over the country in the fifties looking at different places. I think what my dad did at that point was an incredible crash course on the diversity of the issues and peoples across Native North America. He's a very, very smart guy and a very, very quick learner—very savvy politically—and it turned out that that job was really the job for him, in some ways. Before that job he was doing scholarships for the Indian scholarships services. One of the interesting legacies I would love to pursue at some point is to track down the people who he wrote scholarships for and see where those people went and what they did, but that's another story.

In any case, I don't think he was thinking of himself as a political activist or political theorist, or anything like that, and I think one of the big payoffs and lessons for us all is when we sit down and look back at the legacy of Vine Deloria Jr. and say, "This is the towering figure in American Indian intellectual thought." If we jump back to 1964, he didn't see himself in those terms at all, and I don't think he had any ambitions to that, and it shows the way that life is unpredictable.

So, after he became very cosmopolitan—he loved to go to NYC and he loved the Lion's Head bar and hanging out with all the writers. There's a wonderful little piece of writing that I did where he talks about his memories of being at the Lion's Head, hanging out with poets and writers and cracking jokes, and part of this witty, sophisticated literati kind of circle. He was remaking himself as a person in that moment, and then I think he sat down at his typewriter and he cranked out *Custer Died for Your Sins.* I remember him writing some of these books—we lived in a succession of houses, so he had a succession of offices, in that particular case in the late sixties.

**JKK:** Where was this?

**PD:** In Colorado, in Denver. My brother and I shared a room, and his office was right behind us, and I would hear his typewriter all night long, making typewriter sounds. He wrote that book, and that came out of his experiences with the National Congress of American Indians, but of course it catapulted everything for him, and I think for a lot of other people that followed. Then, that became a fairly regular kind of thing. I would hear him typing all night long, book after book after book, and I think he, at that moment, was coming into himself as an intellectual. You can really see the differences between *Custer*

*Died for Your Sins*, which has this very funny, sharp sense of humor—but it's very smart and it's very well informed and it still reads well today—and when he moved to *Behind the Trail of Broken Treaties,* you can see a much more scholarly, much more intellectual person who's concerned with making the same political arguments. Then, in his couple of books with Cliff Lytle, you can see him emerging as an academic; and then in books like—well, I skipped over *God Is Red,* but in *God Is Red* and *The Metaphysics of Modern Existence* you can see him engaging this question of philosophy and spirituality and religion that has concerned him, which he came back to at the end of his life.

So, you can see him, in the course of the late sixties to the late seventies, really developing as an intellectual in interesting ways. He made his turn into the academy, and he became a really skilled teacher, a senior faculty member at Colorado. He always said that he ought to be the one teaching the survey, and he taught the survey a lot, which is something that many academics just avoid teaching. I didn't know it at the time, and it's only in retrospect that I'm able to position myself as someone who was there, as he was coming into his intellectual own and producing this massive body of works. Of course, at the time I was just a teenage kid who didn't want anything to do with my parents—you know, I wanted to play music and to go down to Austin, Texas, and hang out with the redneck rock people. I have to say that my dad was the one who was able to let me do that, because he was hanging out with all those people too. I have these great memories of being backstage at Red Rocks Amphitheater and Jerry Jeff Walker concerts because my dad was so tied into this Austin music circle. So even with that sense, of music being something that was important to me, it was coming out of that family context.

I guess I would say my time in graduate school as a young faculty member is kind of analogous to what my dad did, but he kind of built that infrastructure on his own. It's not like he wasn't in contact with people like Clyde Warrior and folks in the sixties and John Echo-Hawk at Native American Rights Fund in the seventies. He was always in conversation with lots and lots of people, for sure, but I kind of did it the easy way, by going through classes and seminars and readings, and he did it more organically, on his own.

**JKK:** You mentioned at the beginning that Native issues were omnipresent in your household, in terms of seeing people stopping through, and obviously your father's labor in the policy world and political world. In terms of politics and activism, how do you think about those issues in relation to Native people and Native communities in relation to scholarship and Native American studies?

**PD:** Right. Well, that's a great question, and it's a question where the counterpoint between my dad and me is visible. One might ask, What kind of activist was he? Was he an activist who was on the barricades? Was he doing petitions?

Was he marching? No, he really wasn't doing any of that stuff; he was trying to provide the intellectual infrastructure through which people could then make arguments, and he was doing it very directly.

I remember when he started the Institute for Development of Indian Law series of treaties, these little brown-covered books which have been so valuable to so many people—the compilation of their treaties. I have a great personal memory of this, because he got them printed and my brother, my mom, my sister, and I collated every one of these volumes, and then he sent them off to the binder to save a couple hundred bucks on a few thousand books. We basically collated all those books

**JKK:** Team Deloria workshop!

**PD:** Exactly. Well, he paid us a nickel a copy for everything that we collated. We could collate twenty pages at a time, and then we had to do another twenty pages, and then the next twenty pages, and the next twenty pages. I have a series of those at home, which I value. So, anyone out there using those books, I may have collated some part of your book.

But that was very direct kind of intellectual activism, you know: "This is the stuff that we need to make the arguments, these are the things that when a legal trial comes up, we'll need this stuff available." That kind of activism that he was engaged in, it wasn't direct in the sense that he was out there doing, but it was direct intellectually—in the sense that he was out there producing. I think, for myself, I end up one step removed from that, but again, thinking hard about how we produce the intellectual arguments that are going to make changes in culture possible. So, if one of the central problems—and there's a lot of central problems—but if one of the central problems, for example, is that Native American people have to perform Indianness in order to have sovereignty taken seriously, in order to establish the sort of political status or the political framework that, say, my dad would have established—and not all people are in agreement with that—but in order to achieve that kind of recognition, you have to perform in the cultural realm. So, culture is always going to be the thing that supports politics.

Well, could we dream of a day when we didn't have to perform Indianness for someone in order to be taken seriously in your political argument? I can remember my dad saying, you know, where's that string tie, because that's this Indian look that I've got going, and I'm going to have to meet this donor or this guy who's maybe going to support this project, and I have to pretend to be more Indian for him. So he even was engaged with those sorts of issues.

**JKK:** In terms of self-representation?

**PD:** In terms of self-representation, so that fundamental dynamic that in order to make a political claim, you have to do a cultural performance. And does it always happen that way? No, but it does a lot, and it does a lot because non-Natives have expectations about what an Indian is and what an Indian does. If my work can make some sort of modest effort toward changing that—and I actually truly believe that scholarship has those types of effects over the long term and over broad space—then for me, that is a political contribution. It is one step removed from my dad, but I think it's also a really, really important kind of work to do; and again, it trickles down. It trickles down so slowly, but I know people have taken *Playing Indian*, for example, and they've used it at really strategic moments to say, "You know what, why do you want me to do this? Can't we just have a conversation? Can't we just engage the legal issues, please, without you asking me to wear a headdress?"

I think those things have a lot of content, and I think shifting culture is among the hardest things that we do. If there is the relationship between culture and politics that there is, changing culture is hard and long and slow labor. It's so slow that it oftentimes seems kind of pointless, and it actually seems like you're not doing very much. Well, I would recognize all the places where people are making amazing and fantastic contributions in the political realm, and I guess I would like to think that scholarship has a role in supporting that—in softening up the audiences so that they're receptive to the argument, and in making us self-conscious in the ways in which we're going to make our own arguments and the ways we're going to present ourselves.

**JKK:** In terms of your work in administrative leadership at Michigan, in American cultures and through American and Native American studies, how are you seeing the field of Native American studies here, as we sit in 2009? And the other part of that—we talked earlier about the ongoing question in Native American studies with the driving question of ties to community, and so I wonder if you might also speak to that.

**PD:** I think Native American studies is different from the other forms of ethnic studies that are out there, and it's different for all the reasons we've been talking about, because Native people have a particular kind of relationship to the U.S. nation-state. Because of that, Native studies is going to look different—all ethnic studies have different genealogies. I think it's important to think about how the genealogy of slavery and labor that comes out of African American studies is really different from the genealogy on conquest and colonialism and the ways in which we deal with these things intellectually and programmatically, and how they can end up being quite different and quite distinct.

So, Native American studies exists in relation to these other ethnic studies programs, and we have to think about how these things work. At Michigan we have four programs and a caucus: Native American studies, Asian Pacific American Islander studies, Latino/Latina studies, nascent Arab American studies, and African American caucus. That has been a great place to think about those kinds of relationships and how we want to make our scholarship useful, but it also makes clear the ways that Native studies is different and distinct because of the distinct status of Native people in relation to the U.S. nation-state. And that raises this question, again, about utility, about how useful our work is and in what ways is it useful. Is it useful, as I just suggested, in terms of making broad cultural shifts? Or is it useful in producing really concrete historical evidence that can be taken into court? Or is it useful in thinking about the ways in which we collectively imagine identities, or the way in which we separate out the question of identity from the question of subjectivity? So where are the places in which we can be most useful?

That raises the question that I think every Native scholar asks themselves: What's my tie to a community, what's the community that I serve, and to what extent does that community have claims on what I am able to say? That's a very problematic question: To what extent do I have an obligation to go in a certain direction and not in other directions? These are huge, huge, enormous questions, with people who've arranged their position; for example, James Riding In, who said, "Do you want to be accountable to a tribal council for your research? Think hard about that before we go down that road," as opposed to people who have defined community in a very broad sense—which is probably more of the side that I might fall on—as opposed to people who are really doing specific kinds of studies toward very specific kinds of aims and goals. It seems to me like there's a wide range of this, but that question becomes central to thinking about how we do Native studies, and it seems to be about this field: Are we going to allow a wide range of responses to that question, or are we going to be prescriptive and fractionalized and set up very, very narrow parameters for how that question is supposed to be answered?

I think over the past ten to fifteen years, what we've seen is both of those things. We've seen a number of people who've said we need to be big and broad and inclusive, and a number of people who've said no, we really need to be community-focused, particularistic, and very specific in our aims. And that's ranged from people who would make arguments about oral tradition as opposed to the archive, but it's also been people like Fred Hoxie—a kind of mainstream white scholar who supported Native scholars for a very, very long time and trained a number of people and have done an excellent job—who have said actually we need to return to thinking about communities and thinking about specificities.

So, it seems to me like this is a really fundamental question in Native American studies. I would actually counterpose it, in terms of thinking about the ways we've written this history. It's an older history that focused on U.S. policy, that one could call a kind of history of empire and colonialism in a very policy-driven level. So folks like Frances Paul Prucha, for example, produce these massive policy studies. These policy studies allowed one to synthesize

Native history—Native American history and Native American studies—in a certain sort of way, around those policies. We said this is the policy, and then it gets implemented in different places, and then the policy's the thing that brings together different tribal experiences. The turn to community studies has taken away that synthesis, because what it's done is it has recentered the action and the agency on Native people, rather than on U.S. policy makers, so that's absolutely what we should do.

That is the essence of the new Indian history, and part of any central definition of Native American studies is to center things on a Native perspective and to think through issues from that angle or vision. What it does do, though, is it robs us of a chance to think synthetically. It seems to be one of the things that has happened in this field of effort, to think, well, how would we return to a kind of broader sense of perspective, even while honoring distinctive experiences of communities? I think the fundamental way people have done that has been around decolonization arguments and decolonization theory. This is a way of imagining the monolithic-ness that came out of policy studies, but putting it in a tribal-specific context of thinking about how we decolonize.

For me, there is another kind of problem with that, which is, to decolonize what? What does that exactly mean? It really doesn't mean returning to 1492—although some people would say that. So if it doesn't mean that, and maybe it does, but if it doesn't mean that, then what exactly does it mean? What does it mean to throw off a certain kind of colonial thing. Is it to throw off your own internally colonized subjectivity? That seems to be a major, major difficulty, and I don't think it's possible—not for me, but maybe for some people it is. Does it mean throwing off certain kinds of older colonial practices which can be identified? I think it does. And in some ways for me, actually, it restores the importance of doing colonial and imperial history. To say, what exactly are the practices at what exact moment that we then want to undo? And what would it look like to undo them? So, in other words, for me moving away from the generalizing inclination of decolonizing and towards saying, specifically, what exactly are the institutions and what are the power relations here that we want to decolonize? And how is that going to work? That seems to me to be a really productive way in which Native studies can use the past, as well as use the present, to think again about returning to political terms and what matters and what's important.

**JKK:** And then it's not some kind of totalizing fantasy of trying to return to some purity, but becomes what scholar Lisa Lowe would call a sort of multidirectional assault on colonial practices.

**PD:** I think that's extremely well said, because the inclination of it that I resist is to have it turn into a fashion. Decolonize this, decolonize that, decolonize your diet, decolonize your mind; it's one of those words that if you say it long enough, it completely loses its meaning. That's always my fear with things like that. So, for me, having the specificity of the colonial practice to be undone would put something more solid in there. What I've been doing lately is thinking hard about returning to policy in that light, and thinking about the ways in which colonial policy is imperial policy in U.S. history, as well as the ways in which these things have been pried apart.

For me, the Northwest Ordinance—which is the quintessential piece in my mind of imperial structuring legislation in American history—goes hand in hand with the Land Ordinance of 1785, which parcels up the land and allows this imperial practice to happen. These things are absolutely central, so that points us in Native studies to return back to thinking about these policies, but hopefully thinking about them in a new light, because I look around, my graduate students and my colleagues, and I say, "Well, who's thinking about these things?" And it's very easy to not think so much about the Northwest Ordinance anymore, because who wants to? I'm not even sure I want to. But I think those things are actually turn out to be really, really important.

**JKK:** As we're wrapping up, I wanted to ask you about your sense of things right now, in terms of the U.S. political landscape and any climate change you want to discuss.

**PD:** I feel that we've suffered through eight years of a certain political formation—and it's not just the Bush years; in many ways this is the culmination of a lot of stuff. My wife has been a big Clinton supporter, but I have not been, because in many ways I saw a continuity straight across that presidency. So I think, like many people, I have hopes for thinking that this really does represent a changed political moment; and whether it'll actually play out that way, who know, but it seems to me that the possibilities are tremendous. They're tremendous not in the sense of, oh, there's a democratic administration, or oh, there's an Obama administration, or oh, there's a smart person in the White House who can actually put together a coherent sentence. I think those are part of the possibilities, but they're not really the whole possibilities. In fact, it seems to me that if we only imagine that part of the possibility, we're really doing ourselves a big disservice. The possibility is to imagine—and this is me as a cultural historian—and dream utopian dreams. I mean the possibilities to imagine a turn—a real turn—in the ways in which we see ourselves as Americans, and the ways in which we socialize ourselves in relation to the rest of the world, in relation to our internal diversities, and just in relation to the way in which we think about what's valuable and what matters.

So, it feels to me that this is our opportunity, and if we sit back and we just say, "Go Barack, do it, I'm supporting you all the way," we will fail. It seems to me like this is the moment when we have to write more, we have to say more, we have to exhort more, we have to try harder, to do things that will be viral, that will be viral in nature—and this is how culture works. Culture is transformed with every transmission, and it's produced with every transmission, and if we let the transmission part of culture stick with us, culture will change very slowly. If we make the change thing happen—the transformational things that happen when culture is produced—cultures have been known to change very quickly.

So that's the utopian dream of mine, and what I know is that it's in the forefront of my mind right now to think, What am I going to do? That's a question that is worth pondering, and I think it's worth pondering across the range of things we've been talking about. It's worth pondering in Native American studies and scholarship and the academy in general. It's funny, the way the academy produces a few public intellectuals and not any more than that, so it's like, are we going to rely on Stanley Fish to speak for us? Well, no we're not.

We've got to think more about how that is going to work. And is that me? I don't know, probably not. I don't feel that comfortable doing those kinds of things. It might be you, right? But it has got to be some of us, so we might think about that, in terms of the academy. We might think about that in terms of Native American studies as well, and then, I suppose, the utopian part would be to expand that out of my own little circle and into the world, writ large.

It's kind of overwhelming. The more I talk about it the more discouraging it seems, yet it seems like we all have some obligation to try. We elected the guy, you know, we said we wanted something different. We need to put up or shut up, and his inaugural was the start of saying, "Look, I'm going to hold you to it." And let's hope he really holds us to it, and let's hope we really respond.

# TONYA GONNELLA FRICHNER ON DEVELOPING THE UNITED NATIONS DECLARATION ON THE RIGHTS OF INDIGENOUS PEOPLES

Tonya Gonnella Frichner (1947–2015) was president and cofounder of the American Indian Law Alliance, a lawyer, and an activist whose academic and professional life was devoted to the pursuit of human rights for Indigenous peoples. She was part of the Snipe clan of the Onondaga Nation, part of the Haudenosaunee, also known as the Iroquois Confederacy. Frichner earned a bachelor's degree from St. John's University and a JD from the City of New York Law School at Queens College, where she was a member of the board of visitors. She sat on the board of directors and served as legal counsel to the Iroquois Nationals lacrosse team, international competitors at the World Cup level, representing the Haudenosaunee Confederacy.

In 1987, shortly after graduation from law school, she served as a delegate for, and was legal counsel to, the Haudenosaunee at the UN Subcommission on Human Rights Working Group on Indigenous Populations, in Geneva, Switzerland. From that time until her death, she was an active participant and legal—as well as diplomatic—counsel to Indigenous delegations in virtually all UN international forums affecting Indigenous peoples. She worked most closely with elders from the Haudenosaunee Confederacy, especially the Onondaga Nation, and with the Lakota Nation through the Teton Sioux Nation Treaty Council. Her work at the American Indian Law Alliance was known to be principled, effective, and transparent, thus facilitating collaborations with other Indigenous groups and nations, based on shared traditional values. She helped to establish the Permanent Forum on Indigenous Issues and was involved in drafting the UN Declaration on the Rights of Indigenous Peoples and the Organization of American States' proposed American Declaration on the Rights of Indigenous Peoples.

For her work with Indigenous peoples, Frichner received the Harriet Tubman Humanitarian Achievement Award, the Female Role Model of the Year (one of ten) of the Ms. Foundation for Women, the Thunderbird Indian of the

Year Award, the Ellis Island Medal of Honor, and the New York County Lawyers Association Award for outstanding public service, among many others. She also served on several boards, including the Seventh Generation Fund for Indigenous Peoples.

This interview took place on October 30, 2007.

**J. Kēhaulani Kauanui:** Given your rich history of achievement and contributions, can you tell us how you got involved in this important work, and what moved you to found the American Indian Law Alliance [AILA]?

**Tonya Gonnella Frichner:** Well, some years ago when I first came to New York, attending law school was a goal of mine, it just took me a while to get there. But with my family background and the emphasis on understanding the traditional ways of our peoples—I'm a citizen of the Onondaga Nation—moving into this arena was very comfortable and something that I readily understood, because our people have always taken the position that we have the nation-to-nation relationship with not only the United States but the rest of the nations of the world. With that jumping-off point, when I graduated from law school I was invited to attend a meeting in Geneva, Switzerland, at the United Nations as part of the Haudenosaunee delegation. And from there it was very clear to me that this is what I wanted to do, and I thought the best way to make that happen would be to create a nongovernmental organization and look to support from the United Nations, and we did receive credentials based on our ability to go in and out of that building. And those credentials came from the Economic and Social Council of the United Nation.

**JKK:** Yes, and that's what sets AILA apart from other NGOs, right, that consultative status with the United Nations?

**TGF:** Yes. There are other Indigenous NGOs with consultative status, but there aren't that many throughout the world. I would say there are probably less than thirty. And so we're very proud of that fact, but it wasn't something that came very quickly. We had to make the case and prove that we could do the work, and also that we had been doing the work that had to be established first. And then we went on from there. We got support from several people within the UN structure, which was very helpful, and here we are today.

**JKK:** That's wonderful, and quite inspiring.

**TGF:** Thank you.

**JKK:** Now, you mention that moving into that arena was very comfortable, and that you linked that to the way that you had been trained in terms of traditional ways within the Onondaga Nation, your nation. You also mention the Haudenosaunee Confederacy, which many of our listeners will know more popularly as the Iroquois Confederacy. Doesn't the Haudenosaunee Confederacy have a long history of appealing to the international family of nations?

**TGF:** Oh, we certainly do. If you don't mind, I'm going to bring the conversation to 1923, to one of our chiefs, the Cayuga chief whose title was Deskaheh, and that title still exists today. Deskaheh was very concerned about what the United States and Canada were doing in terms of the treaties that we had with them. They were violating those treaties, and he felt that we had more or less exhausted every place that we could go, legally, within the U.S. and Canada. And it was his idea, along with the support of the rest of the leaders, that he should meet with the Community of Nations in Geneva, Switzerland—and at that time they were referred to as the League of Nations. And he did bring our issues forward. Unfortunately, there were some nation-states that stopped his ability to make a formal presentation, but he worked behind the scenes and did quite a bit of lobbying. That's his legacy, which is an amazing legacy. And all these years later, here we are with a Declaration on the Rights of Indigenous Peoples.

**JKK:** That's beautiful. You mention that that is a chiefly title that is still in existence—Deskaheh—and that the legacy he left provides that genealogy that has now been realized. Thank you for sharing that. What role do you think tribal nations in North America have played in the development of this declaration, this momentous occasion?

**TGF:** Well, the role has been very, very strong, visible, and vocal. This negotiation, and the idea of having this declaration that acknowledges our rights, didn't start recently. This is something that did happen in 1977, when Indigenous peoples of the Western Hemisphere were invited by supportive NGOs to come to the UN and talk about issues that concerned us. The Haudenosaunee took that invitation very seriously, and we sent a delegation of about forty-four of our chiefs, clan mothers, face keepers, and others to attend this meeting. We brought a statement with us. That statement was called "A Basic Call to Consciousness," which was drafted by a wonderful scholar who we lost recently, John Mohawk. You can read that history in a book of that same title, *Basic Call to Consciousness,* and it tells about that wonderful history and the remarkable advances that our people made because of their vision.

In 1977 there were representatives of the Western Hemisphere—that was the focus of the meeting from North, Central, and South America. Now, because our regional experience in North America has been about treaties—we have 371 ratified treaties with the United States, not just the Haudenosaunee, but other Native nations within the U.S. So our leaders have always seen treaties as very sacrosanct. We made those agreements, we ratified them, and the United States Senate ratified them as well. So, to have them ignored or broken is quite stunning to our people. And one of the very first treaties that the United States made was with the Iroquois Confederacy, the Haudenosaunee.

**JKK:** Yes. I want to shift gears here a little bit. Can you explain how and why Indigenous peoples are collective polities, distinct from racial, ethnic, or linguist minorities under international law? When I do my radio program, usually I talk about the distinctions between Indians as nations and not racial minorities, drawing on the work of David Wilkins and other Native scholars. Under international law, how and why are Indigenous peoples distinct from minorities?

**TGF:** Well, minorities have a separate place within the UN structure. They also have their own body. And it was very clear that Indigenous peoples were not considered a part of that body. It has been an exclusionary relationship, just as our relationship with the United States at the very beginning was exclusionary. If you look at the U.S. Constitution, you see that language. It's very clear. "Indians not taxed." The only body that is allowed to have a relationship, whether it's trade or governmental, with Indian nations is the federal government, so we weren't seen as being part of the U.S.

Our relationships were on an ambassador level, they were government-to-government, nation-to-nation. That same relationship existed and exists in international law today. That is why our people felt that it was necessary to have a Declaration on the Rights of Indigenous Peoples, because we weren't included in that whole human rights discussion. From the beginning—from 1977 all the way through until just recently—governments were referring to us as "people" without an "s," as "populations," as "groups," and the only thing they left out was "gander of geese." But, we are peoples, with an "s," which means we are subject to the human rights of the world, of other human beings, just like everybody else. Our folks read the UN Universal Declaration, and we said, "Wait, hey, this applies to us as well." So we're going to bring forward our own document and make that a reality.

**JKK:** Yes. Now in making that a reality, how has AILA been an active participant in this decades-long process? Can you tell us more about some of the mechanics of that work, during which the draft declaration was negotiated? How did the negotiations come to get that "s" on the end of "peoples," for example?

**TGF:** Well, it was a long struggle, and we pushed it. Indigenous peoples globally just kept pushing it. Finally, after a bit of relenting on nations' parts, we got to that place just a few years ago, because it became clear that the declaration we had helped draft was going to move forward. It made it incredibly unique, and—I think I'm right on this—the first human rights instrument where the beneficiaries were directly involved in the negotiation process. So, much of that language came from our people. We drafted that language, and we sweated over it, and we fought over it.

In 1993 the Human Rights Commission began to move the declaration through the UN system. It had left the working group on Indigenous populations and our people said it was a minimum standard, and we struggled over it; we wanted stronger language. We struggled. That is the first declaration that I like to refer to.

When the declaration started to move through the process, it became one that just included states. But with our push, we were able to convince governments and the Human Rights Commission that we have to have direct participation in the negotiation. And we did. A working group on the declaration was established that was chaired by Ambassador Chavez of Peru. We went back to Geneva two or three times a year after 1993 to work with governments on this declaration. So you could imagine the emotional cost, the financial cost, and the cost to our communities in this process.

**JKK:** Yes, absolutely.

**TGF:** But we hung in there, and the declaration finally came out of that working group in 2005. That was the second version, which was the chairman's version of what we fought over. The chairman sent his version of it to the Human Rights Commission, and that became the new Human Rights Council. The council voted to adopt it—they didn't approve it by a consensus, but it was voted on by a majority, and we were delighted. That was the second version, and it took a great deal of work.

Imagine close to 500 million Indigenous people, including every continent in the world, coming to consensus—because that's how we work—saying "Alright, we will accept the chairman's text, but that's it." And that was a very difficult internal process, but we got to that point. But now we have a third version. Once the Human Rights Council approved the declaration and sent it to the General Assembly for immediate adoption, that's where we hit a wall. It was a very tough fight, because that is where our participation in the process stopped. Now it was just governments.

**JKK:** Now, just to clarify, the first draft was moved through the system by the Human Rights Commission in 1993?

**TGF:** It was actually the subcommission, and then the subcommission sent it to the Human Rights Commission, and that's where it stayed and was deliberated.

**JKK:** I see. And then it was the second version, which was put to the commission that then became the council in 2005. And the Human Rights Council voted on it in June 2006: is that right?

**TGF:** Yes, right.

**JKK:** Okay, and now I see from some of the work that AILA has done that there were some interventions made prior to that passage back before the Human Rights Council voted on it in 2006, but as I understand it, there was a priority given to moving it through so that it would go to the General Assembly's vote.

The third version going to the General Assembly is the modified version. Now, I understand that in 2007, just prior to the UN General Assembly's vote on this modified third draft of the declaration, Indigenous organizations were only given three days to respond to the changes in the draft.

**TGF:** Yes. The process was moving very quickly once governments decided to focus on it. The previous president of the UN General Assembly, Sheikha Haya Rashed Al Khalifa, used her good offices to move this process a little bit faster, because the commitment was to vote on this modified declaration before the end of the General Assembly session. And we made it right under the wire. The General Assembly had to go into session to formally vote on this declaration.

**JKK:** I see. I understand that there were nine changes made to the modified declaration and that AILA took a stand on three of these. Could you briefly tell us what these were and why they were seen as potentially harmful? And the importance of AILA to record its position even if it was clear that the three additions would probably not be changed in such a compressed timeline?

**TGF:** Right, exactly. I think that the two that will be most useful to discuss—and there are forty-six articles that make up the declaration—[are Articles 30 and 46]. Article number 30 refers to the militarization on our territories. The initial language talked about a "significant threat," which is a much higher standard than the language we have now, which is a "public interest." Now, having the military on Indigenous territories might not be something that would be extremely important to those of us in the U.S. and Canada, but it certainly is to our brothers and sisters in the South. It is to our brothers and sisters in Asia and in Africa, and we worked very hard to keep that language at a high level. But when you get to this point in the process, it's all about negotiation, and making and bending and horse-trading, if you will. What AILA wanted to do was make sure, for the record, that seven generations from now if one of our people said, "Was there any dispute about the language in Article 30?" they can at least find that we did object to it. There were several of us who showed our concern and put it into writing. And I will share with you that there were Indigenous people who didn't agree with us. But my responsibility is to the Onondaga Nation, and I knew that they would never go along with that language, and I cannot go back to my community and say, "Well, I let it go and I negotiated it out."

**JKK:** Right.

**TGF:** They would never, never accept that. And then, everybody's credibility is at stake.

**JKK:** Yes.

**TGF:** The other point was Article 46. This is where we had a great deal of conversation, and the discussion was about protecting the territorial integrity of nations versus the self-determination of Indigenous peoples. A great deal of discussion went into that. Now, what we agreed to—and I did not agree to it—was to apply the Vienna Declaration that came out in 1993, which spoke to the protection of the territorial integrity of states.

Now, why is that important? Well, the UN came to be right after World War II. What the nations of the world wanted to do was to put together a body that would look after the peace and safety of the world. And what came down the road was protecting the integrity of states, which means a state cannot invade or attack another state. That was going to be against international law, against the Charter of the United Nations, and if you're a member of the UN, you're subject to its laws—which is the UN Charter.

Seeing that that was protected has always been very important to governments, and we understand that. You don't want to be invaded, and there are certain things that have to be protected: borders, internal governments, et cetera. Just because a leader is a leader of a country and you think that leader is a dictator doesn't give you the right under international law to take that dictator out, unless you go to the UN and the Security Council and get a mandate or a resolution. This is quite important to governments.

We knew that that was going to happen, and our suggestion was to refer to the Declaration on Friendly Relations, which is about the relationship between states. So, governments put in the Declaration on Friendly Relations in Article 46, but the language mentions the integrity of states, as well as the political unity of states, and we've never had to deal with political unity language before so this is kind of new—how do we interpret it, how do we deal with it? They wanted not just a referral to the Declaration of Friendly Relations—which is a 1970 document—but they wanted specific language, and that's where our organization felt we can still move forward without having to lay it out. Because, let's say this declaration gets challenged by a tribunal along the way. If this gets brought to a tribunal, there needs to be some kind of legislative history, there needs to be some kind of information that those justices can look at. And we felt it was necessary to express that, that now states have brought in Indigenous peoples in a relationship that has always been just between states.

And this is new. This is very new. It wasn't something that our people wanted. And I would say pretty much the entire global caucus of the world didn't want that, but we had to reach some kind of an agreement, so there it is. So states' rights supersede Indigenous peoples' rights, and I guess the question is, after all of the wonderful language that we have in the declaration, will Article 46 supersede it? I don't know. I hope not.

**JKK:** I hope not either. That actually gets to the next question I wanted to ask you, which has exactly to do with that language in Article 46. That article says, in part, "Nothing in this declaration may be construed as authorizing or encouraging any action which would dismember or impair, totally or in part, the territorial integrity or political unity of sovereign and independent states." Now, that language seems to definitely give the balance of power over to the sovereign and independent states over and above Indigenous peoples.

There's also Article 3 of the declaration, which gets to the ambiguity of the overall declaration. Article 3 states: "Indigenous peoples have the right of self-determination. By virtue of that right, they freely determine their political status and freely pursue their economic, social, and cultural development." Now, given these two seemingly contradictory articles, how are we to understand what the right to self-determination means? And to what extent could the right to self-determination be realized by Indigenous peoples? What visions of autonomy do Indigenous peoples have that do not entail aspirations, say, to becoming nation-states?

**TGF:** Well, it's going to develop on a regional level. Let me just jump back to your question so that I answer that correctly. The protection and the duty to respect the territorial integrity and political unity of states is an international law that has been stated in that Declaration of Friendly Relations, as I stated earlier, and has only been imposed on states. These are the other states. The declaration doesn't have the authority or even the mandate to change that international legal framework. So, how is this going to play out? The Article 3 that you referred to, that was a huge sticking point, and something that governments did not want to support—specifically Canada, the United States, Australia, and New Zealand. That language comes directly out of the 1966 Covenants on Human Rights. It is not new language. It is, once again, language that our people believed applied to us as well.

**JKK:** Right, and that's the double standard then.

**TGF:** Yeah, so we're not asking for anything new. And that's why our people always say, well, this declaration is a minimum standard. It's not giving us any new rights.

Let's take it to the United States. What is going to happen? The United States voted against the declaration, unfortunately. And it said that it was a confusing document, et cetera. The U.S. has said, "We support the self-determination of Indigenous peoples," but internal self-determination, not external, not international. So, I guess the question is, if it's only internal, do the Covenants on Human Rights and the declaration apply to Native nations within the borders of the United States? We have to see how that's going to play out. I think the United States could take leadership on this, even though they voted against it, and begin to help us and work with us because this declaration is about one main thing, and that's partnership with governments.

**JKK:** I see, yes.

**TGF:** So this new partnership can bring us to another level.

**JKK:** How can we envision the most basic components for autonomy not disrupting the so-called territorial integrity of the nation-state? For example, one of the things that I like to think about is what this country would look like if the U.S. were to miraculously do just two major things. The first is if the U.S. actually honored and abided by all of the treaties signed between the U.S. government and Indigenous nations. And two, if the U.S. government federally recognized all tribal nations and entities who seek that model, which includes over two hundred tribal entities that have submitted their petitions and remain on the Bureau of Indian Affairs' waiting list. If we were to imagine just those two actions, how might we think about redefining what territorial integrity even means?

**TGF:** Well, let me share with you a statement from one of our leaders. I was asked to go to Onondaga a few years and try to explain this whole territorial integrity business, and when I began to explain it, one of our leaders at Onondaga said, "Well, what about our territorial integrity?" You know, bringing it to the reality of Native peoples here.

Article 26 of the declaration, and I hope I have the right number because I don't have it in front of me, refers to the protection of our treaties. It is in the declaration. Now, if we go back to the right to self-determination and apply Article 3 to those two-hundred-plus Native nations who are waiting for federal recognition, there shouldn't be a question.

**JKK:** I want to ask you, in conclusion, if you might leave us with some things to think about. Although the declaration is nonbinding on UN member states, that does not mean it won't have a positive effect. Could you leave us with some ideas as to how we might be able to mobilize around this declaration, which you've said is the minimum international standard for the international treatment of Indigenous peoples?

**TGF:** Well, if I may, I'd like to make a couple of suggestions. One is that I would encourage people to contact the State Department. If you're a citizen of the United States, the State Department is accountable to you; that's where your tax dollars are going. I would ask the State Department, because that was the department that was involved in the negotiations, and also states that it couldn't vote for the declaration. Ask them why. Why is it the United States does not support the human rights of Native Americans? We need to have that question answered, and we need to have it answered publicly.

Second, I would recommend that people in their query also state that the U.S. could take a leading role. That's why it's important for us to build relationships and partnerships, so that we support each other. It's just not about Native people. It's about all of us. It's about everyone in this country.

# HONE HARAWIRA ON MĀORI ACTIVISM AND SOVEREIGNTY

Hone Harawira has deep roots in the Tai Tokerau region of Aotearoa (a.k.a. New Zealand), with tribal links to Ngāpuhi Nui Tonu. He was an elected member of Parliament in New Zealand for Te Tai Tokerau. He is a member of the Finance and Expenditure Select Committee and the Privileges Committee. Harawira has had a long involvement in the fight for Māori rights as a member of Ngā Tamatoa, a 1970s activist group that led the fight for Māori-language education in the schools; as leader and spokesperson of the Waitangi Action Committee, which laid the foundation for legislative recognition of treaty rights; as a leader of He Taua, the group that ended years of student racism at Auckland University; leader of the Patu Squad, which opposed the 1981 Springbok Tour; as a founding member of the Kawariki, the far-north group responsible for maintaining pressure on the government to recognize Māori rights; and leader of the 2004 Foreshore and Seabed Hoki, the country's largest-ever demonstration and the event that launched the Māori Party. Harawira has served as manager of the Aupouri Ngati Kahu Te Rarawa Trust, manager of the Aupouri Māori Trust Board, manager of Te Reo Irirangi o Te Hiku o Te Ika, and CEO of Te Hiku Media. He has also had a strong hand in guiding numerous other organizations at the local and national level, many of which he founded and/or chaired. He joined me by telephone from his office in Wellington, from the New Zealand Parliament, known colloquially as "The Beehive."

This interview took place on August 24, 2010.

**J. Kēhaulani Kauanui:** Kia ora! I want to start by acknowledging that you've shown such an incredible lifelong commitment to Māori social, political, and economic development that is evident from all these decades of your work, and with that I'd to ask if you'd please tell us some about your familial and tribal background, and how you first became an activist.

**Hone Harawira:** Well, kia ora to everybody, greetings to everybody, my name is

Hone Pani Tamati Waka Nene Harawira, and Tamati Waka Nene was one of my ancestors who signed the Treaty of Waitangi back in 1840. He was of the tribe known as Ngāpuhi, the biggest single tribe in the whole of Aotearoa [New Zealand]. We have about 130,000 members, so I'm of that tribe.

I was born in the northern part of the North Island of New Zealand but raised in Auckland, which is the biggest city in New Zealand, so I had a very urban upbringing until I was about thirty, then moved home to the far north, where I now live with my wife and one of our grandchildren. All of our children have grown up and moved on in life. I first got involved in activist politics through my mum. I was still at school at the time, and my mum was always a very, very strong individual. Apparently she was like that even when she was at school. I've talked to some of her old schoolmates and others, and they said, "Oh, your mum was like that even when she was at Queen Victoria School." So she's been like that all of her life, and got involved just through the messages she used to bring home and the things she used to talk to us about. She never actively encouraged us to get involved in it, but just by listening to her and listening to others, it became quite clear that the issues that she was talking about, in terms of the treaty, in terms of our rights, that all of that was true. And so, it was really just a case of being brought up in that kind of atmosphere.

My father was an ordinary working man, he was a cab driver, and he was always the person at home looking after the family. He was a real gentleman, and my mother was the one who was very strongly involved in activism from the time I was a young fellow.

**JKK:** I see. And I want to just acknowledge too, I mean, certainly Hone you're so cherished and well known in Hawai'i and throughout the Pacific and beyond, but certainly also your mother, Titewhai, and you also mentioned your wife, Hilda. I want to acknowledge her too. It's incredible to hear how they've inspired you. Could you say a bit more in terms of Hilda's role in shaping your activism, and maybe segue to your work in the Māori activist group Ngā Tamatoa in the 1970s.

**HH:** Yes, there's a really strong political connection to my relationship with my wife, Hilda. I met her at an orientation evening for Māori students at Auckland University. And I was so taken by her that I couldn't see enough of her, and although my mother had raised us in the political activism sphere, it wasn't until I realized that Hilda was also already like that that I thought to myself, "Wow." So when she wanted to go to a Ngā Tamatoa meeting, it was very easy for me to just say, "Yeah let's go." So we went and I met people who I already knew from Ngā Tamatoa, but that was my first meeting at Ngā Tamatoa with Hilda, although I had been to Ngā Tamatoa meetings earlier with my mum.

But Hilda was also very, very steeped in political activism right from when she was at school. There's a story about how she gave a speech, a very strongly political Māori rights speech when she was still at school, to a visiting member of Parliament to Britain I think, and her name was Margaret Thatcher, who went on of course to become prime minister of Great Britain. So Hilda already had that political activism as well. It wasn't like she hooked up with me and thereby became an activist; she was already that way before she met me.

So the women in my life, probably the most influential women in my life—my mum and my wife—have always been very, very heavily politically involved in issues that have to do with Māori. I mentioned Ngā Tamatoa; Ngā Tamatoa is Māori for the "young warriors," and my mum was involved in that, as I say, when I was a schoolboy. And they were born out of their generation, after the war when there was a big urban drift into the cities, and a lot of the parents, a lot of the people at that time actually gave up the language, gave up a lot of their traditions and worked really, really hard so that the next generation coming though could have a good education.

And in that sacrifice, a lot of the young people who went away to university and learned about the world thought, "Hey, this world isn't that rosy at all," and started actively pushing for treaty-based issues, for land-based issues, for language issues, for all of those sorts of things. And that was the birthplace of Ngā Tamatoa, an educated understanding of what was happening to Māori. That is where Ngā Tamatoa came from, in 1970. I was still at school at the time, as was Hilda. We didn't know each other. We met at university, but my mum was involved with it way back then.

**JKK:** I see, and how long were you involved with Ngā Tamatoa, and how long did the group stay together?

**HH:** I guess Ngā Tamatoa's heyday would've been 1970 to probably about 1978. They were heavily involved in raising the people's consciousness to issues like treaty issues, land issues, language issues.

And at the time that they were raising them, not only were they looked down upon by white New Zealand, by Pākehā New Zealand, they also were very heavily frowned upon by the more conservative elements within Māoridom, which happen to be our leaders. A lot of our chiefs didn't like Ngā Tamatoa because they carried placards, they used loudhailers, they marched the streets. They did things which a lot of our people said, "That's not very Māori, that's not very traditional."

But, you know, if the aim of protest is to force people to think and to force people to act, then Ngā Tamatoa certainly did that. They were the forerunner of all of the things that have happened for Māori since 1970. That's my view. They were a national organization with very strong branches, one in Auckland and the other one down in Wellington, which is where our seat of government is, so there were two Ngā Tamatoa branches who were actively promoting Māori issues. So that was the heyday. They presented a petition to Parliament on the language. One thing about Ngā Tamatoa, the Auckland branch, hardly any of them could speak Māori at all. And then, on the other hand, there was one member, Tame Iti—world-famous guy—who, when he joined Ngā Tamatoa, could hardly speak any English! He could only speak Māori. Most of Ngā Tamatoa could only speak English. They were very well educated, very fiery, very passionate, and they were the ones who raised the issues of the treaty, land, and language and gave Māori people the sense that all is not well in our world, all is not well in Aotearoa—the land of the Long White Cloud. There are things that need to be fixed, and Ngā Tamatoa was saying we're going to fix them. So they challenged society, Pākehā society, and they challenged Māori society to get off its ass and do something about things. So it was very uncomfortable in those days.

At the time I was at a Māori boys boarding school, one of the elite boarding schools, kind of like Kamehameha Schools. And when I was going to these Ngā Tamatoa meetings, I went back to school and one of our teachers was putting down Ngā Tamatoa and trashing the things they were doing and so I stood up in class and said, "Do you know any of these people?" "No." "Have you ever been to any of their meetings?" "No." "Well, why on earth are you talking like that? I've been to these meetings and I know these people and I'd appreciate it if you'd just shut your mouth and never spoke like that about them again, unless of course you want to invite them to school to have a debate." Well, of course the teacher didn't like that one little bit, then mind you that's not the way you were supposed to talk at those schools either. I think I ended up getting caned for that little exercise, but still, Ngā Tamatoa were very much frowned upon, and they carried on. They were the ones who taught me, you know, if you are serious and if you truly believe you are right, don't give in, just keep going. You're going to cop shit from your own, and you're certainly going to cop shit from wider society, but keep fighting.

**JKK:** It reminds me of stories that veterans from the Black Panthers have told, where the fixation on radical politics undergirded all the work that they did even with the youth. I mean they started out providing free breakfasts for schoolchildren, and testing for sickle-cell anemia, as just a few examples.

**HH:** I went to a meeting of the International Indian Treaty Council in 1995, I think, and I ran into a lot of the old AIM guys, American Indian Movement guys, who were there from back in Wounded Knee, and they too were talking about all of those days. And back in those days, they were young, they were hot-blooded, they were very passionate, not so much about wanting to attack anyone or do that to anybody but just about raise the standards of their people and lift the hearts of their people, that sort of thing. And how mainstream society, through its control of the media, promoted them as gun-toting lawbreakers with murderous intent, all of that kind of thing.

And I guess pretty much the same with the guys back in the early days of the Protect Kahoʻolawe ʻOhana.

**JKK:** Yes, the Hawaiian struggle in the 1970 to get the U.S. Navy to stop using the island of Kahoʻolawe for bombing practice.

**HH:** Same sorts of thing. What they were doing was really just trying to show some care and respect for the land, but mainstream haole society did its best to paint them as rebellious and lawbreaking. So yes, Ngā Tamatoa is very much in that same vein, and very much in those times, if you know what I mean.

**JKK:** Yes.

**HH:** The world was changing, and Māori were riding that same wave.

**JKK:** That's right. Post-1968 there was global revolution really going on. You've mentioned the treaty and you've mentioned the land march, I want to just remind our listeners who may have heard part one of this two-part episode on Māori sovereignty issues that our last guest was Justice Eddie Durie, as well as Moana Sinclair, who discussed some about the Treaty of Waitangi.

Were you at the great Māori Land March to Wellington in 1975, and could you ground some of our listeners about that particular march in terms of protesting the loss of millions of acres of Māori land and breach of the treaty?

**HH:** I wasn't on the march. I was working at the time, and I didn't want to take any time off. But I followed it all the way through because my mum was on it. She was one of the organizers, and my brother was on it and one of my sisters was on it. So I kept tabs on it all the way through. I guess the great thing about the Māori Land March was to lift that statement from Ngā Tamatoa about land issues and raise it to a level that Ngā Tamatoa themselves just couldn't do. One of the women who became the focal point of the march, Dame Whina Cooper, she was an old battle ax, but she had been responsible for doing a whole lot of very positive things for Māori land and Māori women and Māori families. She led the land march to Wellington, and it lifted the whole issue of Māori land rights to a national stage, to the point where you could never again ignore it. This was 1975. And just by taking it right through the country and picking up on the passion of Māori people—and you know up until that point it had been pretty unclear as to just how Māori people did feel all around the country—but by binding together for the first time, I think, Māori realized that they might be able to have a collective say about issues, so that Māori Land March in 1975 was a landmark event in the history of this nation, actually. And I've seen the photos of Mum and my brother and all of my cousins carrying the flag and marching in to Wellington, you know, really really proud of them. But no, I worked right through that.

**JKK:** Well, related to the issue of Māori sovereignty, I wonder if you could please explain the principle of *tino rangatiratanga* for our general listening audience. I first met you in the mid-nineties when I was a graduate student in Māori studies at Auckland University, and that's one of the first Māori concepts I learned.

**HH:** Yes. You probably would have gotten a way better explanation of this from Judge Eddie Durie. I'm not a great academic, I'm not a great scholar; my history is as an activist. I don't have a degree, and I don't have an academic background. I know a lot of people put a lot of time into the study of the concept of *tino rangatiratanga* but, it was really an expression of the absolute authority that a chief could wield. So in very simple terms, *tino rangatiratanga* is absolute chiefdom or absolute sovereignty over lands and people.

Sir James Henare once told me—he's the person I actually considered to be the last paramount chief of my tribe of Ngāpuhi, he died quite some years ago—he said to me one day, while we were sitting outside the bus stop in a little town in the mid-north. When I asked him, "What is this *tino rangatiratanga* thing, what is this sovereignty that we are fighting for, us younger ones?" What did it mean to him? He'd been a colonel in the army and was a very well respected elder in Māori society. He said to me, "You know, boy"—it doesn't matter how old you are; I'm fifty-five now and some of my people still call me boy—he said, "You know, boy, you know you have sovereignty when you have the power of life and death over those around you."

Well, I almost fell over when he told me that. He said, "You may never ever exercise that power. And good leaders very rarely do, but to have that power is to have sovereignty." And what he was trying to say to me, I think, was that back in the day, *tino rangatiratanga* was a chief's ability to absolutely influence what was happening in his tribe and on his land, not necessarily by putting people to death or to grant life to individuals, but to say this is the way our people should be and this is where it is that we're going to be going. And a good leader, and one who lasted, was one who could hear what it was that his people were saying to him and take all of that *korero* [talk] and turn it into a vision that the tribe would go along with.

That level of sovereignty, that level of *tino rangatiratanga,* is no longer, in my view, as visible as it was when I talked to people like Sir James twenty, thirty years ago. But I understood what he was trying to tell me about how our people were. So that absolute sovereignty was the basis of what we believed to be our state before the coming of the white man, of the European, of the person we now call Pākehā.

**JKK:** Now, given that the Māori language version of the Treaty of Waitangi sets out to protect *tino rangatiratanga*, do you think it is the basis of good relations between Māori tribes and the British Crown, and the treaty itself as an enduring legal document?

**HH:** Well, I can tell you that the basis of relationship, not necessarily good, bad, or otherwise, but the basis of the relationship between Māori and the Crown is the treaty. The Treaty of Waitangi. We only have one in this country, and that treaty was signed on February 6 in 1840, and it said two things.

One, that the European would be granted the authority of governance, and that history tells us that governance was granted because Māori was sick of the way that European traders and whalers and settlers were behaving themselves, or misbehaving themselves, in the country, and there was a desperate need for some measure of control over those early settlers. So, Māori agreed to governance. But, in return, Māori were granted *tino rangatiratanga* over their lands, their forests, their fisheries, and the treasures that they held dear to them. Now, the only treaty that Māori signed was the Māori version, and in that one the governor asked us to grant unto him *kawanatanga,* which is just a form of governance, and allow us to retain our *tino rangatiratanga* which we understood to be our ability to exercise our chiefdom across our lands, et cetera.

I absolutely guarantee that if the governor at the time had asked Māori to give away their *tino rangatiratanga* they would have just said, "Thanks for the lunch, see you later," and gone home and prepared for war. And they didn't know that they were conned into giving away their sovereignty. And when government talks about it now and says, "Oh no, it was sovereignty." But in fact, the English version said one thing but the Māori version, that the Māori signed, certainly didn't.

**JKK:** So the Māori version says "absolute chieftanship"?

**HH:** The basis of the relationship is the treaty, and the fact that we were willing to cede governance, but to maintain our *tino rangatiratanga* over all of our land, our forests, our fisheries, and our treasures, and our people, protected under that treaty. And that is the basis for all government relations with Māori. Today that leads to some positive things and some negative things, and so it will be and so it should be, but we measure it against that original foundation, signed in 1840. And like I said, Tamati Waka Nene, my ancestor after whom I was named, he was one of the signatories.

**JKK:** Now, how did, I mean, I want to ask you about one of your parliamentary actions regarding a Treaty of Waitangi Commission, but first I want to ask you, how did you transition from a lifetime of activism to becoming a member of Parliament?

**HH:** In 2003 a tribe in the South Island took a case to court, saying they felt that they had rights to the foreshore and seabed in the area, and they wanted to put in a claim for it. When government caught wind of that they said, "Oh, hell no, this could ruin everything. They could get control of the foreshore and seabed and we'd lose control of that and all those minerals," et cetera. So the government moved to take complete control of the foreshore and seabed.

Now, that angered Māori up and down the country. You know, people were telling me that they wanted to go out and kill people; they wanted to burn down fisheries, buildings; they wanted to trash Department of Conservation vehicles. Things were getting quite nasty, and so it was decided to march to Wellington. Again, the same route as the great Māori Land March, and because I lived in the far north I was getting phone calls all day and all night to organize it, but all I could think of was, "No, no, no, there's things I want to do up here."

But it became clear that there needed to be a march and that that march needed to be national. And if it was going to be national, it was going to start in my territory, so I put my hand up and said, "Hell yes, I'll lead it." I contacted people all around the country, they agreed, we set up the structure within two weeks, and we were on the road. From when we left my area, fifteen, twenty days later we were in Wellington. Forty to fifty thousand people marched on Parliament. As a result of that, it became clear not only that Māori were angry toward government but also that Māori had said to themselves, "To hell with the Labour Party. We have given our all to Labour—that's the Democrats in the U.S.A.—and you treat us like this! We deserve better."

Well, when the march got to Wellington, they were passing out these cards saying "Join the Māori Party," and I was thinking, who's this crowd?

Anyway, two things became clear when I got home. One, that Māori right throughout the country, including up where I lived, wanted a Māori Party. And two, it was also clear that if there was going to be a person to lead the Māori Party in my area that it would be me, because, I think, of my years of activism, but particularly my leadership of that march to Wellington. So that's where I moved from activism into Parliament, on the back of a great tidal wave of Māori public rejection of what we call the foreshore and seabed theft.

**JKK:** Yes.

**HH:** So that's just how I segued into that.

**JKK:** Just to recap then, that was a New Zealand Parliamentary law that deemed that title to the foreshore and seabed was held entirely by the British Crown, and that's what Māori were rejecting and have rejected categorically. And that was passed in 2004, right?

**HH:** In 2004, yes. But not the British Crown. We call it the Crown, but that's because we are still part of the Commonwealth. When we say "the Crown" it is pretty much the same as government, because the Crown in New Zealand is represented by a figurehead, a governor-general, who acts absolutely according to the whim of the government. So the "Crown," assuming ownership means government, has assumed that ownership and essentially denied Māori the right to claim that foreshore and seabed back. That's what led to the march, and the march is what led to the Māori Party.

**JKK:** Right. And protesting that act, based on the principles of the treaty itself, right?

**HH:** Absolutely.

**JKK:** And so you came, so you are part of this new party, this has only been since 2004 that the party actually was founded?

**HH:** Yes, 2004. About twenty days after the march in Wellington, a special meeting was called in Auckland at the *marae* of one of our coleaders—the *marae* is a meeting place. And there was a few thousand people there and it was decided to launch a Māori Party, and that's where it came from.

**JKK:** Yes, and for those who are unfamiliar with New Zealand governance, you have a mixed-member Parliament, so it's totally different from the U.S. two-party system.

**HH:** Yes, we do. We used to have what the U.S. has, which is pretty much just a two-party state. We have Labour and National. Labour is like the Democrats, and National is like the Republicans, and it's always been them, one or the other. Now it's a mix whereby there's a number of Green candidates, there's now a number of Māori Party candidates, there are some other smaller groups who have one member in Parliament. But it's really about making governments of the day realize that the theory behind our form of government is that the party that gets the most seats must now negotiate with smaller parties to be able to govern and have the ability to make decisions which impact on the whole country. It's a better way of government, because it reduces the measure of arrogance that either of the two major parties have always had. They've always assumed that because they have the territory benches, they didn't have to listen to anybody after that for the next three years.

Now, that's no longer the case, and so the Māori Party, we have been able to get a review of the Foreshore and Seabed Act, which has recommended repeal—we are in the process of a repeal of that act right now; we have now recognition of the Māori flag; we have signed up to the Declaration of the Rights of Indigenous Peoples; we have launched a new social welfare strategy based on Māori principles; and we are just about to start down the road of a constitutional review of this country, because we don't have a constitution in this country. We have what is known as constitutional arrangements, where we have a piece of this act and a piece of that act, and something from the Privy Council in London, all the way back to the Magna Carta, but we don't have a constitution as such.

And we have launched the constitutional review, because we want to see the Treaty of Waitangi put in the constitution so it applies to all pieces of legislation in the country. So, those sorts of things, those things in particular could never have happened if it was just a Labour government or a National government, they are there because we have fought to have them taken up on behalf of Māori people, and, in our view, for the betterment of the whole country.

**JKK:** So, in six short years, those are some major accomplishments.

**HH:** Well, in pretty much only the last eighteen months, because our first three years in government, 2005 to 2008, we were just on the cross [minority party] benches, we weren't in government, and we got into government in December 2008. So, what, eighteen, twenty months we've been here. So all of that has happened in the last twenty months.

**JKK:** Right. You mentioned that New Zealand is now in support of the UN Declaration of the Rights of Indigenous Peoples. They just recently changed their position, because they had voted against it in 2007. Could you speak to that shift in the government's position?

**HH:** Yes, we were one of the horrible foursome: the U.S., Canada, Australia, and New Zealand. "CANZUS" they're known as, at a political and trade level: Canada, Australia, New Zealand, and the U.S. And I guess that's because those are the four countries which withhold lands which were very strongly claimed back by the Indigenous peoples of those lands. We opposed it for the same reasons the others did, because we have those kind of governments which are racist by nature, and pretty much anti-Indigenous development in policy and practice. And in all of those countries, without me having to go to the statistics books and statisticians to check, I could absolutely guarantee that the Indigenous people—we have a high child mortality rate, we are likely to be suspended or expelled from school more often than others, we are likely to suffer from high imprisonment rates, high unemployment, poor housing, and a high mortality rate overall. Now, that's our history in all of those four countries, and we are part and parcel of opposing—our government was part and parcel of opposing it for those reasons. Because those countries have gained their authority, have gained their strength, and their power, and their financial base to a large degree from the denial of those Indigenous rights, and New Zealand was part and parcel of that same strategy.

**JKK:** Yes.

**HH:** Now, New Zealand changed its mind for a couple of reasons. One, because we, the Māori Party, got into government and started pestering government over it. I don't think, though, that that probably would have been enough, except the United Nations released its human rights report at about the same time as the government came in in 2008, which didn't say too many nice things about the New Zealand government. When you're wanting to be a major player on the international stage, one thing you don't want to have is people pointing the bone at you over denial of human rights of this, that, and the other thing.

And so the New Zealand government, the national government, was persuaded by that report and by the insistence of the Māori Party to change its mind. And so we signed up to it, a few months ago I think it was.

**JKK:** Yes, it was I believe just in April or May. And I remember when that report came out, and didn't that report on human rights also condemn the Foreshore and Seabed Act?

**HH:** It did, it did. In fact, we'd had a UN special rep or two here in 2005. His name was Rodolfo Stavenhagen, who'd been specifically asked to consider coming here by a number of tribes who had gone to the United Nations to protest the way in which the Foreshore and Seabed Act had been put into place. And so he came, and one of his reports back to the Committee on the Elimination of Racial Discrimination, the CERD Committee of the United Nations, was to highly protest what had happened to Māori human rights under the Foreshore and Seabed Act. And so, that was part of the report and so government had that on its back, the new government, when they came into power, and it wasn't something that they particularly wanted to hear other nations hit them over the head with whenever they got to the United Nations or wanted the international world stage. It's hard to talk about, to be critical about, the human rights of others if they can turn around and say, "Well, look at you guys." You know, "You can't talk." So there was that pressure and there was the internal pressure as well from the Māori Party.

**JKK:** Right. Now, I'm thinking about family on my side that has ties to Hawai'i, and how important Foreshore and Seabed is to any people who are reliant on the ocean for their well-being and sustenance. For a primarily North American audience, would you just sort of describe what the stakes are in terms of Foreshore and Seabed?

**HH:** I guess the, well, government, when we asked for review, the independent review committee came back with a report, and one clause that sticks out to me from that independent report said the Foreshore and Seabed Act was the single largest land nationalization statute in the history of New Zealand. So, you know, we the people who have suffered from land grabs throughout our history had been whacked with the biggest single land grab by any government, at any time, in the history of this country. So, for us, there was that issue, you know, we already understand what land grabs are all about. Particularly, though, for us and for those tribes and sub-tribes and those families living close to the sea, the *takutai moana*, it became very clear that all of the historical relationship to those seas, to the way in which you could gather *kaimoana* [seafood], the way in which you were responsible for caring for those areas, the way in which you manage those areas, and you could put down a *rahui* [ban] to stop certain things from happening, to encourage the seafood to regrow, et cetera, et cetera.

All of those had, in one fell swoop, been taken away from us. So we'd become landlocked within our own country, and our country is a series of islands. I mean, it's not as dramatic as Hawai'i, where you've got mountains in the middle and valleys which run straight to the sea from the mountaintop to the sea, but exactly the same thing, where total denial of any Māori relationship to their foreshore and seabed had been initiated in that one simple piece of legislation. And Māori, like I say, they were angry. That anger let to the march, and that march led to the birth of the Māori Party, and the Māori Party led rise to my getting into Parliament, along with my colleagues.

**JKK:** And all of these developments in such a short span of time. It's really incredible to think about how empowering that must be on that end. You talked about the constitutional development and sort of how the New Zealand government at this stage does sort of a piecemeal approach. In terms of embedding the Treaty of Waitangi in a constitution, is that key, do you think, to more New Zealand government accountability? I mean, one of the things that I read about your recent actions is that you're drafting a bill to establish a Parliamentary commissioner for the Treaty of Waitangi. Could you speak to some of those developments and also the implications this could have for treaty settlements for different tribes?

**HH:** Yes, the Parliamentary committee for the treaty is because the way the treaty has currently been treated, which is it's included in some pieces of legislation and not included in others, and because it can't be included in legislation, it's in or it's out, it's brought in and it's thrown out. And it's not treated with the respect that it's due, hence the need for us to talk about establishing the office of a Parliamentary commissioner for the Treaty of Waitangi to advocate and promote respect for the treaty as the nation's founding document and constitutional blueprint. So, that's to try and develop a Parliamentary respect for the treaty, to educate people about its real importance to our society, and to lay down some pathways for its future. So that's what the Parliamentary commissioner aims to achieve. The constitutional review was even bigger, of course, because our aim is to lift the treaty out of the quagmire of legislative debate and lift it up to the constitution, so that after that, once safely ensconced in the constitution, we don't need to have the treaty in legislation at all, because of pieces of legislation will have to be guided by the treaty as one of its constitutional elements.

**JKK:** So, totally mandated.

**HH:** So the commissioner is about trying to provide respect and recognition of its status, and the constitutional drive is to lift it beyond legislation, to a point where it helps to guide the future of the nation.

**JKK:** Kia ora. I want to ask you, you mentioned social welfare and uplift of Māori as a collective. But before I switch gears as we are wrapping up the interview, I wanted to ask you, in terms of you rising to the ranks of a member of Parliament, what kind of reception have you had? I mean, I spent several months back in New Zealand in 2007 and noticed when you went to Australia to comment on the military intervention in the Northern Territory that you took a lot of heat from your own colleagues in Parliament, and I just wonder how they responded to you in these last few years, in terms of you again shifting from activism to being an elected representative?

**HH:** It actually took me quite some time to work it out myself. And I've finally come to realize that I am an activist first and foremost. I am a member of Parliament now but I am still an activist by heart, and an activist by nature. That's what led me to go to Australia; that's what led me to raise the issues that I do raise in the way that I do raise them. And I've also come to realize that while I have respect for my parliamentary colleagues, I can't allow them to determine what my mind-set will be. My mind-set is determined by my own history, my own understanding of our country, my understanding of the history of my people, the current status of my people, and the future that my people want for themselves and for their children. I am just a cog in that, but I am comfortable maintaining the tag of being an activist-politician.

**JKK:** Beautiful. Well, I've always found your outspoken truth-telling to be quite refreshing. None of the false niceties, just Hone Harawira telling it like it is, and always drawing it back to the ongoing unresolved issues of self-determination. What do the people want? What do you think are the most pressing issues facing Māori people today?

**HH:** There's a whole range of issues, and I try not to clutter my mind up with trying to achieve everything at once. The overriding issue remains our sovereignty, our ability to determine our future, to exercise our own authority, to establish our own relationships as guaranteed to us under the Declaration of the Rights of Indigenous Peoples. In my view, that is still the ultimate. In immediate terms, they are some very simple things. They are health, they are education, they are employment. I mean, if I was an Indigenous Australian, I'd be saying exactly the same thing; if I was a Kanaka Maoli I'd be saying the same thing; if I was a Native American I'd be saying the same thing; if I was from the First Nations of Canada, I'd be saying exactly the same thing, no doubt. Simply because our story is a common story, our fight is a common fight, and our future is a common future. And we will achieve our objectives by staying close to one another, by standing alongside one another, and by giving each other strength in the struggles that we all share, because it's an old thing but it's a true one. None of us are free until everyone is free. And I like to think that any success in North America is something that gives us heart; anything that we can do here in Aotearoa I hope will give heart to those Indigenous people in Hawai'i, in Tahiti, and in other places where our future is yet to be determined.

**JKK:** Kia ora. As we're wrapping up, are there any closing thoughts you'd like to leave us with?

**HH:** Yes, it's something I like to leave everybody with; it's something I've picked up from an old guy in jail. He was a Catholic priest in the Philippines. He was in jail because he'd opposed martial law back in the days of Ferdinand Marcos. And I got to meet this guy, and he was a really pleasant guy, in jail. I said, "How can you be happy? You could be dead tomorrow." He said something to me, which I'd never heard before. He said to me, "Happy are those who dream dreams, and are prepared to pay the price to make those dreams come true." Happy are those who dream dreams, and are prepared to pay the price to make those dreams come true. I mean, I think we all, as Indigenous people, dream the dream of sovereignty, and the price that we have to pay, all of us, if we do it all together and collectively, it isn't much. It's a bit of energy, it's a bit of support for one another, it's a commitment to principles that have kept us alive for thousands upon thousands of years and will keep us that way for thousands more, as long as we stay true to those principles.

# SUZAN SHOWN HARJO ON THE TWENTIETH ANNIVERSARY OF THE NATIVE AMERICAN GRAVES PROTECTION AND REPATRIATION ACT

In this interview, Suzan Shown Harjo (Cheyenne and Hodulgee Muscogee) critically assesses the status of the Native American Graves Protection and Repatriation Act (NAGPRA), passed on November 16, 1990, for this episode recognizing the twentieth anniversary of the law. NAGPRA requires museums and federal agencies to return specific Native American items—including human remains, funerary objects, sacred objects, and other items of cultural patrimony—to lineal descendants and culturally affiliated Indian tribes and Native Hawaiian organizations.

Harjo is a poet, writer, lecturer, curator, and policy advocate who has helped Native peoples protect sacred places and recover more than 1 million acres of land. Over the course of four decades she has developed key laws to promote and protect Native nations, sovereignty, children, arts, cultures, and languages, including the 1978 American Indian Religious Freedom Act, the 1989 National Museum of the American Indian Act, NAGPRA, and the 1996 Executive Order on Indian Sacred Sites. Executive director of the National Congress of American Indians and the NCAI Fund from 1984 to 1989, she has also served as special assistant for Indian legislation and liaison in the Carter administration and principal author of the 1979 President's Report to Congress on American Indian religious freedom. She also served on the Native American Policy Committee for Senator Barack Obama's presidential campaign and as an adviser to the Obama transition team in 2008 and 2009.

She is the president of the Morning Star Institute, a national Native rights organization founded in 1984 for Native peoples' traditional and cultural advocacy, arts promotion, and research. She has been at the forefront of ongoing legal challenges to the disparaging name of the Washington, D.C., football team.

Harjo has also served as curator of numerous Native art exhibits as well as the Native Writer's Series at the national museum of the American Indian. She has been the recipient of numerous honors including the first Vine Deloria Jr. Distinguished Indigenous Scholar award and back-to-back residency fellowships by the School of Advanced Research (SAR) in Santa Fe, where she was the 2004 Dobkin artist for poetry as well as a summer scholar. It was there that I met Harjo, while I was an in-residence fellow at SAR.

Harjo, a veteran broadcaster, was producer and drama and literature director for the Pacifica WBAI-FM radio show *Seeing Red* and also served as news director for the American Indian Press Association, in addition to being founding cochair of the Howard Simmons Fund for American Indian Journalists. She joined us on the phone from Albuquerque, New Mexico, where she was attending the annual meeting of the National Congress of American Indians.

This interview took place on November 16, 2010.

**J. Kēhaulani Kauanui:** I want to start by asking if you would share how you came to be involved in the issue of repatriation and developed the federal law, the Native American Graves Protection and Repatriation Act of 1990.

**Suzan Shown Harjo:** My mother and I visited the Museum of the American Indian in 1965 in New York City and saw things that really disturbed us and made us cringe and some things that were sacrilegious, some things that were ill-treated and shouldn't be on display, and some things that weren't treated at all, they were just disintegrating. And my mother was very, very upset and she just kept telling me, "This doesn't belong there, that doesn't belong there, you have to do something about this." And then she would tell me things that I already knew and then things that I didn't know about what we could do, how we could do this. And she was talking about what we would do once we got things in the right hands. But I didn't have the piece of how you do that, how it goes from museum or agency or school to the right hands, to the people. And who actually could handle this items—I knew I couldn't, my mother couldn't—we had to certainly turn them over to people who were able to receive them and who knew how to either dispose of them or to care for them.

So that was a lot to think about, and I sought out Vine Deloria Jr. because he was at the time our most prominent Native person. And he was executive director of the National Congress of American Indians, and I asked him how I would go about getting sacred things back and other important things that belonged to the people. And he said, "I have no idea, I don't know." He said, "But here's what I'll promise. I'll help you think about this, I'll just back you up in whatever you want to do on it." So, he really kept that promise, and my mother kept up her energy and really pushed on the Cheyenne side to get some things going, and Vine and my mother pushed on the Lakota and Cheyenne side. And two people—a Sundance priest, Pete Catches, and our Cheyenne Arrow-Keeper, James Medicine Elk—convened a meeting about this at Bare Butte at Holy Mountain in South Dakota in June of 1967.

They asked people—there were some ceremonies going on, various ceremonies there at Holy Mountain—and they asked people to stay afterward to talk about this issues of our people being prisoners of war in these museums and being displayed in museums and roadside attractions and in schools. I mean all over the place you'd see these billboards driving all over the country saying, "See the three-legged pig and two-headed dog and the Indian mummy." And those were so common and they had grotesque images of all those things. And it was a widespread problem that was right in your face. And that was one set of issues that we were called to do something about; another was sacred places protection—which we're still working on—and another was trying to find some museums and some non-Native people who would help us. We couldn't think of a single museum or federal agency or state entity that was doing it right. And that's how we came to also envision and plan for and strategize for the National Museum of the American Indian. And those two—repatriation, which we didn't call repatriation at the time, and our cultural center which we call the National Museum right in front of Congress so they would have to look us in the face as they were making policies about us—were totally tied together, and ultimately our work that began in 1967 became the federal law that we crafted in 1989. And that was the National Museum of the American Indian Act [NMAI Act] with the historic repatriation provision that pertained only to the Smithsonian and then eleven months later we achieved the national repatriation act [NAGPRA], which applied to all federal agencies and all repositories of any kind that had a federal nexus that were either federal or federally assisted.

But for me, it began with my mother. Well, I should say that after we got the NMAI Act with that repatriation agreement, a *Washington Post* reporter called my mother and she said, "Oh, you don't want to talk with me, you want to talk with my daughter. I don't use words like that, repatriation; my daughter uses words like that." And so she totally sidestepped the fact that she was my inspiration for doing this work, and she's the one who handed it off to me as a young adult who was among the responsible adult Native people who needed to do this work.

**JKK:** And was she still living at the time of the passage of the 1989 and 1990 federal acts?

**SSH:** Yes, she was.

**JKK:** That's beautiful that she got to see that in her lifetime.

**SSH:** Yes, and, she passed on in 2003, and my dad was still living until 2007 and so he also was able to see the National Museum of the American Indian on the mall and to see his name on one of the walls, their names on one of the walls.

**JKK:** You know, when you were telling the story of the displays alongside roadsides and whatnot, you used the phrase "prisoner of war," and I want to ask you to speak to that a little bit more, especially for those who maybe haven't even thought about the fact that it's Native remains that are held in these museums and in these side "freak shows." Could you speak to the legacy of this sort of collecting and exhibition and the aspect of dehumanization that goes along with it?

**SSH:** So, part of it is the cult of the Indian head. So the people who came here from Europe brought their practices of beheading and placing heads on stakes in visible places. That I know of, Native people at least in North America—who are now Native Americans, if you will—didn't behead. And we kept hearing in this period in the sixties, when were working very hard to try to figure out what to do about this whole set of issues, we kept hearing about people being beheaded. Every meeting that we would have, tribal leaders and religious leaders and practitioners would talk about how it was in their family or in their nation that the non-Native people would come here and cut off their heads and cut off their ancestors' heads and dug up the graves and removed heads and removed whole bodies and took the precious things that people were buried with.

And a lot of the people we were working with were military veterans. And they—including my dad, a World War II hero—a lot of the younger people were Vietnam vets or people who had served in the military during the Vietnam War era, and this was right in the thick of it in the mid-sixties and late sixties and so the prisoner-of-war term they used advisedly. They understood, some of them had been prisoners of war, they were the ones who introduced that term into our discourse. They said that these are our people that the Europeans hated and saw as a threat and wanted to show us as trophies after we were dead. And that was something that really resonated for all of us who came from nations and cultures that had endured massacres in our recent collective memory.

At Sand Creek, at the massacre of our Cheyenne and Arapaho and some Cayuga at Sand Creek in Colorado in 1864, the Colorado Volunteers, after murdering the people who were there in a peaceful peace camp—flying white flags, and it was a treaty peace camp—attacked at dawn, just mowed everyone down, and then mutilated them, stripped them of their body parts, cut fetuses out of pregnant women, paraded these, put genitalia over their saddle horns, made necklaces of fingers and ears and just hideous, hideous things and took them to Denver, went to an opera house, interrupted the performance and strung up these body parts across the stage.

And the Colorado Volunteers were given a standing ovation for murdering the "horrible Cheyennes." And the head of the Colorado Volunteers had said in a public meeting before Sand Creek that all the Cheyennes had to be killed because they were just vermin. And he was asked, this horrible man named John Chivington, who later as a coroner actually stole money from a corpse and so then lost his coroner job, he was asked, "Do you mean Cheyenne babies too, do they have to be killed?" And he said, "Yes, nits make lice."

And so this is the kind of thing that we have in our recent, recent memory. And everyone that we were hearing from, every place we would go, at Zuni Pueblo, in California meeting with California Native peoples, in the Northeast we would hear about these beheadings, and that the people were left without body parts and without their heads. And whenever we asked officialdom in Washington and elsewhere about that, in educational institutions, whenever we asked scholars or bureaucrats or public officials about this kind of thing, they would say, "Oh, that never happened. You're just dreaming."

And it wasn't until the late seventies and eighties that we began to uncover this history of the Indian Crania Study of the Army Surgeon General in the late 1800s, and the fact that the Army Medical Museum and the Smithsonian Museum—as it was called then—were advertising in the *Rocky Mountain News* and elsewhere for the ordinary citizen to go out and harvest Indian skulls. We were able to find the evidence including evidence from the Indian Crania Study in the form of reports in the national anthropological archives saying such things as "I waited until the cover of darkness till the grieving family left the gravesite and exhumed the body and decapitated the head which is transmitted forthwith."

And these really grisly tales, the army officer report upon the murder of Mangas Coloradus, the Apaches' leader who had been written about in the literature as having a huge head, a giant head. And I think possibly he was murdered for it. The army officer report says, "As soon as the shot body fell to the ground I immediately decapitated the head, weighed the brains, measured the skull and found though the skull were smaller, the brains were larger than that of Daniel Webster." That's a heck of a lot of information for an army officer in a Western outpost to have at the fore as the shot body fell to the ground.

So eventually we found the evidence to back up or validate some or most of what we knew from oral history about beheadings and grave-robbing and other things that went on, the mutilation of people. This harvesting, or collecting, really has heinous origins—no matter what tributary you trace backward to try to find the headwaters, you still are confronted with some nightmare or some Native nation or family or society where medicine or people or these living beings that are revered were destroyed or done damage to or just taken without explanation. Imagine the grieving family who returned to the gravesite that the army officer had looted, finding their loved one without a head—what a nightmare. This is the basis for collecting.

Some of it is just so much in the American psyche that people don't even think they're doing anything wrong. It's so much a part of the American legend that Native people's "stuff" is up for grabs—whether it's gold or land or water or culture . . . as though it is the divine right, the manifest destiny of the non-Native to end up with it. So grave-robbing and cultural appropriation down to images and words are not at all a leap.

There was an interesting return of people and things at the Slack Farm in Kentucky several decades ago that had been looted. People were just taking things from this area where Native people were buried. There was this cemetery on the Slack Farm. And Native people went there including the Haudenosaunee [Iroquois Confederacy] *tadadaho* [head chief] at the time, Leon Shenandoah, and used public communication and also door-to-door discussion to ask the people to return these people and things. And a lot of them did. They walked back or drove back and returned arm bones and heads and jewelry and clothing and said that they were sorry and they didn't realize it was wrong.

So you know, that tells you a lot about how it doesn't even have to be premeditated or intended to disrupt the lives of living Native peoples or to desecrate a grave—it can be just casual and "Well, everyone else was doing it and I was just going along with the crowd."

**JKK:** It really gets at that core logic of settler colonialism because it's about "ultimate possession," the symbols of conquest and genocide. But to actually own, or want to own, the remnants, literally the remains, it says a lot, it's pretty deep. You did ask just a few minutes ago to imagine how a family would feel coming back to a site that had been disrupted, where their loved ones had been put to rest. I'm not sure I really was able to wrap my head around that entirely until I actually heard you read your poetry about this issue. Beyond understanding this issue in a legal and historical way, your poetry is so moving—another way to speak to the hearts of people. I heard you read at School for Research [now the School for Advanced Research] in Santa Fe back in 2004, and want to ask you how you find poetry as a medium to communicate this area of dispossession, as well as reclamation.

**SSH:** Well, what I do is a lot like gardening, and you don't just plant one kind of flower, you plant all kinds. Here are some plants for food, here are some plants for medicine, here are some plants for beauty, and here are some plants for keeping bugs away from everything else. And that's the kind of writing I do as well. Some writing I do includes the phrase "Notwithstanding the provision of any other law" and they're very technical kinds of drafting, other kinds of writing are in the category of "just tell on them." And when you can't do anything else, sometimes you resort to being the witness, or being the camp-crier, or being the person who sends out a cautionary tale.

And also, I commit poetry, and that comes from a different place, poetry comes from and is received as music is. So it's not, it doesn't come from the other side of the brain that produces "Notwithstanding any other provision of law" or that is involved with the construction of a column or an opinion piece. It comes as heart-sounds, it comes as a drumbeat might. And sometimes it's the only way to really get your point across, and when all else fails, sometimes a poem works, whereas people might not respond to anything else, any other kind of information, they might respond to a poem.

**JKK:** Well, if I can switch gears here, in narrating the opening story you really took us through a period in the sixties and mentioned the first act, the National Museum of the American Indian Act in 1989 and then the NAGPRA in 1990. Moving through those decades, was it the evidence that you were able to document that made the difference in getting those two federal laws to pass? What did it take, and what kind of resistance was there?

**SSH:** Well, people didn't believe us. They were saying, "Oh no, that didn't happen." But here's what we didn't know at the time—that some of the people who were telling us that were the very people who had the knowledge at hand, were the very scholars who knew exactly where things were written and how they had covered it up. And were the same bureaucrats who knew exactly how things had happened and didn't have those particular papers ready and were the same people who misfiled the vital information that we needed to make our case.

So we were dealing not only with disbelief but duplicity. And duplicity of a kind that made us go back and reexamine everything and re-interview and have meetings that went over the same thing over and over again. And we knew at some point that we weren't wrong, and that we just had to do more and more in the way of policy-making. And so the first thing we really did was coalesce to gain the American Indian Religious Freedom Act [AIRFA], which applied to Native Hawaiians, Alaskan Natives, and American Indians—1978 is when it was signed into law by President Carter.

And that had been one of his campaign promises. When he was asked in a meeting a week before the election, "Would you sign the American Indian Religious Freedom Act if Congress sends it to you?" And he said, "Yes, and I'll tell you why, because my Bible tells me so." And that was so interesting—it's not true, of course, but he was making the point that the way he interpreted his religious foundational document went to respect, that he was to be a respecter of all religions. And that's why he supported the AIRFA, and I thought that was really quite wonderful, and by the way he was the president who kept every single promise he ever made to Native people, and I'm enormously grateful for that.

And so we were able to get the AIRFA, which goes to museums and sacred objects and all manner of topics that have to do with religious freedom and how Native American religious freedom has been impeded. And so we gained the first real repatriation policy, and repatriation themselves under the auspices of the Religious Freedom Act. And that policy was reported to Congress in 1979 as part of the President's Report to Congress on Native American religious freedom. And those federal agencies involved at the time were the directors of all the military services museums, so the army museums, the navy museums and so forth, and the Smithsonian, although it was dragged kicking and screaming by the defense representatives.

And what they agreed to was a policy returning all cultural patrimony, and by that they meant all patrimony that would include Native human beings, and it would include Native sacred objects and historic objects. So it was everything under that term "cultural patrimony." We changed that in the repatriation laws, which were follow-on laws to that religious freedom policy. And we changed that to "cultural patrimony" to mean those items that are communally owned and can't have been alienated by any one person because they belong to the group as a whole, whether the group is a clan or a society or a nation.

So these policies were policies that we gained through the Religious Freedom Act and then through the commitment to do follow-on laws. And so those repatriation laws, the Museum of the American Indian Act, the Native Languages Act, all of these are follow-on to the American Indian Religious Freedom policy. And the reason that we needed that was that we needed a positive statement that the U.S. declares that it's the policy of the United States to preserve and protect Native American religious freedom. We had to have an affirmative statement because there had been so many federal actions taken under federal policy, really just regulations without even a law originating them during the "Civilization Act" regulations that outlawed the Sun Dance and all other similar ceremonies and outlawed the heathen acts of a conjurer by a so-called "medicine man" and so forth. They were horrible anti-Indian, anti-human-rights regulations that were in place for more than fifty years, from the 1880s to the 1930s. And we're still recovering from those and the religious freedom policy statement is part of that recovery.

**JKK:** Right. Now, you mentioned that time with your mother and Vine Deloria Jr. when you were trying to imagine what it would take to get things in the right hands and how these materials and remains go from a museum and agency or school to the right people. For those unfamiliar with what this process actually looks like on the ground, could you give us an example of a successful repatriation since 1990 when the federal law passed?

**SSH:** Well, the Smithsonian, the army, many other entities have returned people and things that were taken from the massacre at Sand Creek, for example, including a scalp that was just repatriated a couple of weeks ago. So, things and people are being brought forward by those who hold them, and they are being identified through the repatriation process. And sometimes they are things that appear through the Post Office, through the postal service, and people will say, "We think these come from . . ." or "This has been in my family and it came from here or there."

And some things you rely on the federal repatriation laws to coax out. And each of the federal repositories has to do an inventory of their holdings in these areas of sacred objects and cultural patrimony and human remains, funerary items whether associated or not with a particular burial. And these inventories will lead people who are doing repatriation work to interact with the museum or other repository in such a way that they can find other materials or they have written information about companion materials or people. So the repatriations themselves take a very long time and involve people getting ready to receive them in the first instance.

That's sometimes the most difficult thing for people who have no ceremonies for, here's what you do when a museum steals your grandpa and steals his clothes and cuts his head off—and now what? We don't have that kind of ceremony, but, we do now. People are figuring out collectively what's the best way to do these repatriations. In some cases, it's left in the hands of very few people because it's not something that the great number of Native people want to think about or can think about. It's just too much on top of daily life of poverty and all sorts of emergency situations. People just can't deal with this kind of psychic assault.

So in some cases people, the greater number of Native people are just saying "You handle this" to the people who do repatriations. I do repatriation policy, I don't do repatriations. The only thing that I counsel people about when my counsel is sought is to approach it in a very practical, commonsense way because our people have always been very practical people. What would you do if the river overflowed and all the people were floating around? What would you do? You'd put them back immediately, on higher ground or right there when the water receded. You would do what you could to restore the peace and dignity accorded to those people, or what should be accorded those people.

We have models and commonsense ways of approaching cataclysms. And in some ways it's easier to think about these as almost natural occurrences. You know, the high winds came, the high waters came, then to think about it for what it really was, the bad people came and did bad things to us. Or the people came and became bad people because of what they did to us. So there's so many ways to think about this, and it's oftentimes easier to think of it in the simplest way so you can live with the aftermath. You know, the time has passed and we have now a whole growth industry involving repatriation, including repatriation offices in the federal government and the main coordinating one for the national NAGPRA: the national repatriation law is in the National Park Service in the Interior Department. And it has just been responsible for a ruling that sanctioned grave-robbing. It in a really calculated way decided that it was good politics to split the difference between the people and things, so the human remains are now subject because of this rule to repatriation by Native people, even if they can't be completely culturally identified.

And they're in this category called "culturally unidentifiable" human remains. And it doesn't mean they're unidentifiable; it just means they haven't been identified. And one of the main ways that you identity them is by the things they were buried with, but the crass political decision was made to let the museums and agencies keep the things they were buried with, the associated funerary objects. So, we Native people can get Grandma back but not her moccasins, not her shawl. Or maybe a precious item that her grandchildren put in with her as a token of their love for her, so we may not know who that is because we don't have the associated funerary objects. So this is really just an example of how wrongheaded people can be even when they're implementing a federal law, which is designed to bring some small measure of justice for Native people in the modern era.

The repatriation laws are really our human rights laws. And what we're seeing happen is human rights stripped away by just such rulings and it really deserves the attention of everyone, all decent people should look at this and say, "Their graves were already robbed once. Don't let the museums be the fences for the thieves."

**JKK:** This is the 2010 ruling?

**SSH:** Yes. And it's not even unassociated funerary objects, it's associated funerary objects with these people that are being declared as the property of the museums and other entities that hold them today. So if you hold onto stolen goods long enough they're yours—that is the message. And that shouldn't be the message of a human rights law, and that shouldn't be the message of any law.

**JKK:** That's right. And that also means that even if Grandma's entire body comes back whole in terms of the remains, it's still a form of dismemberment.

**SSH:** It is indeed. Because American common law, European common law, everyone's common law is based on the rights of the deceased and the rights of the deceased family. And this is property of the deceased. So it's a desecration of that person's final resting place. It's being assaulted again while we're just now beginning to heal from the wounds of the initial assault.

**JKK:** It also seems, then, to be coming on the long trail of the last two decades where our anthropology and archaeology departments, for example, that didn't want to relinquish their collections, often classified some of these materials as "culturally unidentifiable" as a loophole to hold on to them. And you've just pointed out—if they've been marked "culturally unidentifiable" that just simply means that they haven't yet been identified. And so there are gatekeepers preventing them from being properly identified and therefore reclaimed for a proper burial.

**SSH:** Right. And so again, it's hiding the evidence. You're letting these pawnshops and roadside attractions, even if they're called a "national museum," hide the evidence of their bad faith.

**JKK:** Well, certainly we need some broad-based education so that, as you say, the common person can denounce this ongoing dispossession and desecration. As we're concluding the interview, where does this leave us in terms of the future of NAGPRA?

**SSH:** The future is bright if you look at it as the act is intended, as justice and human rights for Native Americans. If you look at it as a vehicle for loopholes allowing scientists and non-scientists the ability to continue to pillage and to loot and to profit from it, then what's at risk are all the goodwill fair dealings and optimism that have been created by the repatriation laws. And there's a lot of that, there's a lot of education that has taken place. There are a lot of people who understand much more, non-Native people understand much more about Native peoples than they did before the repatriation law as a result of the coming together of the people who care most about these people and these materials. So we can either go forward in a good way or we can revert to the stuff of massacres and nightmares.

# WINONA LaDUKE ON ENVIRONMENTAL ACTIVISM

Winona LaDuke (Anishinaabe) generously gave me a personal interview the afternoon she was at Wesleyan University to deliver a lecture, "Indigenous Thinking about a Post-Carbon, Post-Empire Economy," for the 2008 student welcome inaugurating the new academic year. LaDuke is from the Makwa Dodaem (Bear clan) of the Mississippi band of the White Earth Reservation in northern Minnesota. She is the author of the novel *Last Standing Woman* (1997) and the nonfiction books *All Our Relations: Native Struggles for Land and Life* (1999) and *Recovering the Sacred: The Power of Naming and Claiming* (2005). She is the executive director of Honor the Earth, an organization she cofounded with Indigo Girls in 1993. This Native-led organization's mission is "to create awareness and support for Native environmental issues and to develop needed financial and political resources for the survival of sustainable Native communities. Honor the Earth develops these resources by using music, the arts, the media, and Indigenous wisdom to ask people to recognize our joint dependency on the Earth and be a voice for those not heard."

This interview took place on September 9, 2008.

**J. Kēhaulani Kauanui:** I want to start by asking you if you would speak to your own personal history and trajectory and how you became involved in such multi-leveled activism, community work, and sustainability.

**Winona LaDuke:** First, I have to say that I'm a product of good family and good parenting. My mom is a Russian Jew, she's from New York, and my grandmother was a union member of the Ladies Pocketbook Makers and International Ladies' Garment Workers Union. My mom ran off to Mexico and was an artist, and then she married my father, who was from White Earth. He had left the reservation and was selling wild rice, which is ironic because I am selling wild rice, fifty years later, and that's how he met my mother, selling wild rice. We moved to Los Angeles, and I was born in East LA, where my dad was an extra in the Westerns. My dad was also an organizer in the Native community there, so I have a lot of memories of LA Indian organizing. Then, I was raised in a small town in southern Oregon where my parents were engaged in civil rights work and some anti-racism work. It was also the time of the Vietnam War, and my parents were antiwar activists. Having said that, I come from a long history of Native social- and peace-justice work, so I was raised that you should at least use your First Amendment rights or you're going to lose them.

**JKK:** You went to college at Harvard University, yes?

**WL:** Yes.

**JKK:** And how did you track your way to the reservation to do the work you do now?

**WL:** Right. I was an undergraduate. I went to Harvard, and I entered as the class of '76. There were seven Native students in my class, and they came and found me on the second or third day of school, and it was awesome. I worked for the Boston Indian Council and the Commission on Indian Affairs, and so I began working in the community. Early on, my father had known Slow Turtle or John Peters, and I subsequently went and lived at Wampanoag, and my father had been there before.

Having said that, I was politicized more deeply at college, as many students are. I met Jimmy Durham, who was director of the International Indian Treaty Council. He came to give a lecture one day and he talked about Indian people, Indigenous people, and decolonization, and it reframed the discussion in my head on understanding this as part of a worldwide set of issues that Māori people and Aboriginal people and the Masai and the Sami people are all facing. Breaking out of that isolation and being able to have a broader analysis in understanding the United States as a world power and a world economy that dominates other peoples' economies was very important to me.

I asked him if I could work for him as a researcher, that I was basically a geek, and I still am; I'm proud of it, I like researching, I've done a lot of investigative journals work. I find it interesting, and I was asked by Jimmy to research energy policy in Indian Country.

**JKK:** Oh, what period was this?

**WL:** Oh, '77. I worked for the Treaty Council from 1977 to 1979.

**JKK:** And you're researching energy policy in Indian Country? Could you say more about that?

**WL:** Well, Jimmy knew what I didn't know, but I had a working knowledge. I was on the debate team in high school, and one of the topics was energy policy, so I had kind of a foundation of resolve that the U.S. should have a national energy policy, which is a question we're still debating and the case that you couldn't beat. I don't know if you know anything about debate, but you have a pro and a con, and the case you could never beat was the uranium mining case. They used all Navajo data, so I knew that there was no safe way to mine uranium. Jimmy and I talked about it, and he asked me to write up some report on the state of energy companies negotiating and owning energy resources in Indian Country and what their labor histories were, what their environmental histories were, what their corporate histories were, which countries they've recently been kicked out of for violations as third-world countries nationalized and took over control of their resources, and why they came back to Indian Country, which was largely a result of being thrown out of third-world countries.

I prepared the documents, and then we had the first UN Forum on the Rights of Indigenous People at the UN, which was in 1977, and Jimmy asked me to present some of those documents. I went, when I was eighteen, to the UN, and that politicized me immensely because I had this once-in-a-lifetime opportunity to see 250 political leaders of Indigenous communities. They came from very grassroots and very traditional vantage points, and were there saying that they had a right to exist and that we as Indigenous people should have our right to be recognized. That obviously left a major mark on me and defined a lot of my politics, and I went back to Harvard late for my sophomore year; I was about a week and a half, two weeks late for school because I was in Europe.

I came back and, fortunately, I still passed my classes; I did not do that badly at school, but I asked Jimmy if I could go work in the Navajo reservation. I had never lived on a reservation—I had visited, but I had never lived, and I certainly had no experience of Navajo, although I would travel there with my father. When I went there, I worked for the National Indian Youth Council, and then the New Mexico Indian Environmental Education Project, and my job was basically to take documents that were written in "government-ese" is what I call it—very hard to understand—and to translate them into common, everyday English so that you or I could understand them. Then I handed them to people who translated them into Navajo, because these huge mining companies—Exxon, Mobil and United Nuclear, Conoco—were in the middle of negotiating a set of new agreements and pushing on the Navajos for more uranium.

What I understood by the time I had done the research was, for instance, there wasn't a word for radiation in Navajo, so you couldn't have informed consent. You couldn't explain to people what was going to happen, because they didn't have a way to describe it conceptually. So that really framed a lot of my thinking, this question of how large corporations or large governments get to control the destiny of peoples. Who controls political power, how decisions are made, and a lot of the work that I've done is not only about evening the odds, about feeling like we have the intellectual capital in our communities to have discussions and be at the table, but also more than that. In a lot of our communities, you could say no, we don't want this strip mine, or no, we don't want this power plant, or no, we don't want this, but unless you have something that is going to shore up an Indigenous economy which has been essentially cannibalized by a dominant world economy, you will never. You've got to have some security.

I'm a world-development economist by training. My interest is in self-reliant, healthy, sustainable, rural economies and my primary area of focus is Native communities.

**JKK:** How did you decide to launch the incredible community development projects that you have going?

**WL:** I actually moved back to White Earth. I'm a White Earth tribal member, but I had never lived there. I had visited there as a child, and Vernon Bellecourt, who passed away, would see me at these AIM meetings—and I was raised largely in the cloth of the American Indian Movement as my political education—he'd see me and he'd say, "You should move home, you should move home," and I said, "Okay."

So, I finished Harvard in January 1981 and I took a job as a principal of a high school on the White Earth Reservation, which I was not suited for but it got me back to the reservation. I moved back there in January '81. I packed up from Cambridge, and I have lived there ever since, which would be pretty much my entire adult life. I've lived up in northern Canada for a while, too.

At first, in our work at White Earth, we fought to get our land back, and we fought in the courts and in the legislature, and we lost. And then I asked my board—it was a citizens' movement, it was a public movement, there were thousands of people in the streets and in the council meetings, and I was a part of that movement—but I asked my board of Anishinabek if I could create this other mechanism, because I had seen that the Nature Conservancy and the Trust for Public Lands were purchasing land and that if we couldn't get it back through the systems that they had said we had opened to us, we should try an alternative. And so, my board, Anishinabek, gave me permission to create the White Earth Land Recovery Project, which was created in 1989. Next year is the twentieth anniversary.

**JKK:** Beautiful.

**WL:** It's like having a twenty-year-old child. I think that, as Indigenous people, we have a toolbox. That is to say, you've got to look at where you're trying to go and what you're going to compromise to get there or how it's going to work. On my reservation there's a lot of people that say, "Well, they stole it, they should give it back." And I agree. We support the return of all publicly held lands by government agencies; we think that should be returned to us, which is about a third of our reservation, but in the meantime, you've got second- and third-generation non-Indian landholders who are not going to give up that land, so the question of can you purchase it becomes a very important question.

Sometimes your tool is a 501(c)3 land trust, sometimes it's an LLC—which I had to create to do wind energy development so I could have partnerships— and sometimes your work is through a tribal government, which is an IRA tribal government, and sometimes it's just a question. To me, if we, as Indigenous people are looking at this long-term and we're looking at how we're going to get there, that's what we need to figure out. And we use different tools.

**JKK:** The IRA government, tribal government, refers to the Indian Reorganization Act. Is White Earth Tribal Government an IRA government?

**WL:** Yes. White Earth has a tribal government that's an IRA government, and we're part of the Minnesota Chippewa Tribe.

**JKK:** In terms of the Land Recovery Project, would you tell us more in terms of how you're able to hold those lands, and also how much land has been acquired, and how the reservation community has dealt with some of those transitions?

**WL:** That's an interesting question. We're a nonprofit organization and we're one of the largest in the country, and by and large tribal communities or tribal reservation communities don't have a lot of nonprofit infrastructure. With that, most nonprofits that work in Indian Country are non-Indians like, say, the Save the Children that come and help the Indians, and the tribal government, including on our reservation was largely the main source of employment and the main source of political power. I believe in a multi-sectored base of power, and different people have different ways of expressing that, and I think that we should encourage our people to be nurtured and to grow and to realize our potential, because we're better people and better communities for it.

So I work in this sector. We purchased fourteen hundred acres of land, which is not a lot, but that's good for now. Our most recent purchase was a K–8 elementary school, which is our new offices and is where we're putting our radio station, because we just got an FCC license to operate a radio station. This is about two years down the road and we're putting a wind turbine up there.

**JKK:** Excellent.

**WL:** So, there were some big capital expenditures. I'm probably going to try and purchase another five acres for another wind turbine; that's what my mission is. Our organization works on many levels, but we're organized as a nonprofit— I'm not going to say that we're a land trust, but a part of our mandate is to purchase land.

**JKK:** It sounds like the 501(c)3 gives you more autonomy given the recent rulings against tribes being able to recuperate land and have it held in trust.

**WL:** Right. We probably have about 350 acres that we tried to give to the tribe for almost ten years, but these rulings on the tax-exempt status of those lands and if they can put them in trust are a bit challenging for the tribe, so in the meantime we battle the state every year—and we've won, we're 12–0 or so, 18–0, on our right to hold lands as a nonprofit.

**JKK:** So there have been challenges?

**WL:** The state tax—the counties took us to court and we won.

**JKK:** You mentioned public lands earlier, and I wanted to acknowledge that when you ran for vice-president with Ralph Nader, one of the platforms for your campaign was that you supported the return of all national parks to tribes. Could you say more about that, given that the U.S. government is making noise about selling off national parks?

**WL:** Yes. Last Saturday night I went to the Chumash Heritage Center in the middle of Los Angeles. LA is way too big for me, but I found this place where they had this canyon full of thousands-of-years-old oak trees in their heritage center. They're on their most sacred sites, and it was wedged in between these housing developments, and I just thought what a miracle that this is here and that these people have kept this safe. To me, it's a perfect example of how an Indigenous community does something that nobody else can do.

Whether it's a wildlife refuge or the Itasca State Park or the Chippewa National Forest or the Rice Lake Refuge or the whole Boundary Waters Canoe Area, those are all annexed from our people. And that's our area. Let alone the National Bison Range in the Black Hills of South Dakota and Grand Canyon National Park, Glacier National Park. I can't go into the details of all of them, but I will tell you that a large set of those came from Indigenous people, and I just have to say that my personal fan club is for Gerard Baker, who is the highest Indian in the National Park Service. He's the head superintendent of Mount Rushmore National Park.

He's from the Three Affiliated Tribes—Mandan, Hidatsa, and Arikara—a guy with braids down to his waist and he's in his sixties. He's a great big six-five guy, and I'm the biggest fan. But he upsets a lot of people in the National Park Service and in the conservative white community of South Dakota, because here is a great big proud Native man who is watching over those four presidents and invites a lot of Native people up there. This is a different park right now, and to me he is the example of what it could be like.

**JKK:** In terms of developing a new consciousness?

**WL:** A totally new consciousness.

**JKK:** Or a shift.

**WL:** And you got what a fan I am?

**JKK:** Yes.

**WL:** You should see, I have a picture of me and him on the computer and I'm like, "I can't believe I'm next to Gerard Baker." It's so funny, I mean, other people like rock stars—but, Gerard Baker.

**JKK:** When you met with the students at Wesleyan University, you were asked about a number of things. The students were especially interested in your discussion about environmental sustainability.

**WL:** People want a technological fix, and they are assuming that there is one. We have created the most inefficient economy in the world, and the consequences of that are what we have now. Efficiency is not bad thing—actually, it's the good thing, and it's the responsible thing. It's like growing up—deciding to be grown-ups in the world and having something that makes sense.

We're battling this coal company from North Dakota, because they have a lot of ligneous coal, which is just slightly above burning dirt. But they have the biggest wind potential in the country, so I tell them, "Come on," but they still want to bring all their coal on. And then keep wanting to call it "clean."

I took my eight-year-old to a shareholders meeting for AutoTemp Power—I'm negotiating a power purchase agreement for my wind turbine, but they have these coal plants—so I took my eight-year-old to this meeting because I had a press conference and I thought that I could get in the paper if I had an eight-year-old. He's really cute, has a long ponytail, he's a sweet little guy. He travels with me a lot—I don't want you to think that I sell my children for media, but it was funny because they had released this press advisory, AutoTemp Power had said that there was going to be protesters at their shareholders meeting, and they made it sound kind of like there were threats, so there were a lot of cops. And there were like four people that came to the press conference—including my eight-year-old son and this guy dressed as an otter. So it was like, whoa, those are some scary protesters.

But I had this long conversation with the guy from the power company, and he said, "Well, we have this plant, we've had it for twelve years, and this is a really good plant," and I said, "That's your problem: it's a twelve-year-old plant." That was before all the data came in on climate change, so you can't, you can't sell me a twelve-year plant. Just because it's really well researched twelve years ago doesn't mean it holds anything. Now, I said, "Why don't you just put up a thousand megawatts of wind and we'll call it even, we'll hammer 'em good." But it's right next to this one reservation too.

**JKK:** What about the power of the wind in terms of your work in the rural areas in northern Minnesota?

**WL:** It's very much circumstantial. In general, in order to not bake, we have to put up 185,000 megawatts of renewables in the next ten years. That could be solar, and that could be wind, and we also need to cut our consumption and get more efficient. It turns out the Indian reservations are the windiest place in the country. My reservation has Class IV wind, and we could power a lot, but you've heard my story, which is I'm trying to build the intellectual capacity rather than lease it out. I don't want to lease my wind rights; I want to control it—not me personally, but them, the royal I: we, my community. The thing is that renewable energy is democratized power production, because what we have is centralized power plants now and centralized power in grids, which have political and social implications. They've had tremendous social implications on your generation and my generation, because we just go and switch the light and we don't know where it comes from. We take no responsibility for it, and it's coming from a nuclear power plant right over here. That's what we've conditioned our society to be, is disassociated from the natural world and the larger world. We want food that's prepared and we want to shop at Whole Foods, and we want climate-controlled buildings and climate-controlled cars and we want everything like we live in a bubble or something. Conceptually, that's what's happened to us.

I wrote an energy plan for our tribe and, in one of my geeky moments, after burning through like five consultants who each came in with a plan that we should import garbage and turn it into energy on my reservation, I said, "Why would I want to do that when I have wind power," and he said, "But you could make money by emptying garbage and it's emissions free," and I was like, "Yeah, right." That's why consultants irritate me. Because they're like, "Boy, am I glad I don't work for her." Everybody has their agenda.

Anyway, we wrote this energy plan and we basically said: get efficient. Burn wood in the highly efficient stoves, because we have a lot of wood and we don't have any dinosaurs. You need a mass transit in this country that works, a better trade system. It would be embarrassing to Bulgaria, someone said, I mean, it's a joke. Restructuring our communities—I hate to say that, because people don't like that word, but get real. If you've got people commuting two hours to work, that is not sustainable in a post-peat petroleum economy. Wind is an essential element.

**JKK:** Would you speak to the importance of local food production in relation to environmental sustainability?

**WL:** We have a farm-to-school program on my reservation. I had to hire a prep cook because this is my eight-year-old's school, and they were just reheating portions that arrived from Food Services of America. They had lost this ability to crack eggs—it does take a lot more labor, peeling potatoes instead of undoing that—but I have a federal grant to bring in a prep cook, and then I have an organizer that finds me farmers, and it's working well. The school really likes it and we save them money on their food bill, and it's a cool thing. But it's a process, because there's a lot of institutional momentum built into a certain paradigm—the economies of scale—which has no actual analysis of the cost of economies of scale. It is inaccurate given the amount of energy you put into an industrial food economy versus a local organic one.

**JKK:** Next, will you address the issue of genetically modified organisms and how GMOs are taking over food production, especially in the United States and particularly affecting Native communities?

**WL:** I was out in Hawai'i in January of last year. I was there for the legislative session opening on January 17, which was really nice since I'm from northern Minnesota. I took out a big delegation of Native people because we have a battle—in which we are doing pretty well—to keep our wild rice from getting genetically engineered. We think "wild" should mean something like not genetically engineered—it comes from a lake or river. We have been in this since about 2000 and they have not genetically engineered it anywhere, and I don't think that they will. We've grown some momentum and we did get some legislation passed in the state of Minnesota, which requires a full EIS [environmental impact study] prior to the introduction of any test plots of genetically engineered wild rice. In the meantime, there's no funding.

We heard other communities are facing the same thing; our food supply is increasingly genetically engineered and then radiated, with no long-term health studies, which is problematic to say the least. So, having said that, there's a line that we drew which said, "I got it that those Cheetos are genetically engineered, but you can't touch the rice." I don't know what kind of line that is, but it's like in Hawai'i: one of their most sacred foods is kalo, which is taro. It's a root crop; it's similar to us and our wild rice, which is our most sacred food, and the University of Hawai'i did genetically engineer taro. They patented it and genetically engineered it, and two or three years ago they tore up the patents and gave them to the Native Hawaiians and said "We won't patent it," but there's one researcher who did genetically engineer taro. Now, what the Hawaiians have going for them is that rice is a grass, and grasses are sexually very prolific. Kalo, or taro, has sex largely through transplanting part of the corn; it's not as prolific as a grass, and so the chance of containment is much higher. If I had a genetically engineered type of grass in a field it would contaminate the whole field.

We went out there, and they had been trying for two years to get a hearing. They did get a hearing this year, but the state of Hawai'i is largely beholden to the biotech industry. The University of Hawai'i is heavily a research institution—as most of these universities are, where public education's become private—and Hawai'i has more open-air test plots of genetically engineered crops than any place in the country, largely because of their isolation and their climate. So those guys are up against biotech, and it's very serious.

I went to the island of Molokai, which is kind of like a big Indian reservation.

I used to go there because I had one girlfriend who was a beauty queen from Molokai, so I used to go hang out with her there. They have these test plots right next to their housing projects, and I just thought, "Well, I don't know how much Bt corn [genetically modified maize] I'd want floating in." This is like the health-affected and already at-risk population of pollen from new GMO strains.

It's not right. It's not right, but that's the rage. A lot of these communities don't have the capacity to work on this to the level we'd like to; to try and inform tribal communities about these risks is a big issue. The general community doesn't know. But the line is drawn in a lot of these communities when you take our most sacred relative and you want to genetically engineer them. That gets these guys. I went to the Hawai'i state legislature and I almost cried. I brought my little eight-year-old son—you can imagine, right, he's like my buddy—and my nephew. We came and we walked in with those guys and there was like a thousand Hawaiians walking in and they're all chanting in Hawaiian as we walk into the legislature. Now, of course, the Indians have to walk really far, and you guys had to only walk across the street, which is probably how you could keep all together, but this issue is very significant. The same thing is happening in our area, so it's interesting where your consciousness is at on that.

**JKK:** Shifting gears here, since we're so close to the U.S. national elections, what about your take on the current presidential race?

**WL:** I believe that the system is incredibly flawed. I believe in a multi-party system. I think that this country deserves more than a two-party system, and I don't think we have more in the present structure, so that's why I have run for office and that's why I am generally civically engaged. Voting is good. I put in thirty years working on these issues, and I think if you do thirty years, we'll actually get something done.

Change—that's how change happens, is people dedicate their lives to it. Barack comes from a similar cloth. We came out of community organizing, and my largest funder for many years was the Catholic Church, the Campaign for Human Development, and my program officer was his program officer, so I know where the guy comes from and I know where his analysis comes from. Now, how that is represented and articulated as one tries to appear more conservative is a different arena, and that's what he's trying to do now, and the political terrain is tough.

I support Ralph's right to run. We had to litigate to get on the ballot, and as some of you will remember, Ralph and I were the not allowed into the debates. We actually have a little booklet that said that we weren't allowed in the debates in '96 and 2000, with our little mug shots in it. Ralph got barred by officers as he was on his way to a debate.

Where I'm at, with my community and the constituency I represent, is that

I actually think we could get a good energy policy and good sets of environmental and human rights policies out of Barack Obama, but not absent a social movement, because nobody's going to save us. My perception is that there isn't anybody who is going to save us. Another facet is that I think the intersection between peat, oil, climate change, and the disaster of the Bush administration has put this economy and this country in a pretty tough spot. I think a movement for the greening of the economy and the re-localization of food is something that is increasing in its resonance, exterior to the corporate interests of Washington. I'm going to be voting, and I'm probably going to be driving Indians to the polls, because God only knows most of them don't have a car that works on my reservation. So, we're getting out that vote, but I also know that I don't hold my breath for any politician, because I would have passed out a long time ago.

**JKK:** What about the McCain-Palin ticket? Might Native voters feel an obligation to support McCain given his record in relation to tribal sovereignty?

**WL:** Yes, and I have to do a bit more looking at that. Anybody who comes out of Alaska as a politician is pretty dicey. The Native community has really been impacted up there by the creation of Alaska and the Alaska Native Claims Settlement Act, and pretty much every politician is owned by the oil companies— and that would be the first flag—and then there's Sarah Palin's ardent support for aerial shooting of wolves in the Arctic National Wildlife Refuge. One of the concerns I have is that what appeared to be kind of a bizarre and innocuous choice actually appears to be a lot more dangerous than I had thought. Considering McCain's age and circumstances, I thought, "This is not a good thing."

The Crow Nation gave Obama a name. The Crows are the most conservative Indians in the country, so I'm figuring that if they supported Obama, I don't know what it's like in other communities. I actually think that some of the Native community might support McCain out of some historic loyalty to him on Indian affairs, but by and large, I don't think that's plausible, unless you're seeing something I'm not. There's going to be a few, but by and large I think the Indian policy that would be crafted by an Obama administration would be far better.

**JKK:** What about your approach to economic sustainability and rural development might appeal across racial and Indigenous lines?

**WL:** I have immense privilege in my life. I'm here with you, and I work in my own community, and I work with people whose ancestors hung out with my ancestors, and in America that's pretty darn rare. I've got the same ceremonies, and we have things that are wealth but that can't be measured. Yet, at the same time, I wander this country and I talk at colleges, but I go from reservation to reservation too. I go to a lot of reservations who want me to talk about these issues—and then I get to go inside communities, and my analysis is, you look out over the horizon and want to see that you're not alone, and you're not, because these issues that we're working on in our communities are basic, rural issues. They are basic issues of dignity to me.

Dan Jones from Green for All is working on these issues in urban areas and the question of, Do you want to put everybody in jail, or do you want to give them green jobs? Which is what we're looking at. You don't know how many of our young men on my reservation. My son is seventeen, and when we deal with the police I say "You stay here by your mom," because the reality is that young Native men with long ponytails are probably higher on the profile list—but on my reservation they say that 60 percent of kids between sixteen and twenty were involved in the criminal justice system. Which doesn't mean they're hanging out with judges, you know, it means that they got some misdemeanor. Being a youth is almost criminalized in this country, at this point, and so they're basically telling these kids, "Well, you can go into the military or you can go to jail," so we have a high rate of enlistment.

To me, these young people of color, kids in poverty, we have to have a different choice for them besides those two. These rural communities need to have a place where they can stay and they can have a vital, affirming life. I look at them through my own glasses, obviously, because that's my experience, but what I find is that politics is very personal but you also need a broader analysis to understand that. So I work on my reservation, but I work with a lot of really conservative Norwegian and German Lutherans—this is northern Minnesota—and it's a very interesting dynamic, because historically, a lot of them would say, "those Indians, you people," and there's not only a separation but a lot of prejudice, a lot of racism.

These border towns were built on exploiting Indians. That's the reality. Up in northern Minnesota the towns are built on the Indian dollar, and now you have the third generation of those people who don't want to deal with what white privilege is—that's just the reality of their situation—and who want to make excuses. But then, the other side of that is that you get someone like me who says, "We know what our history is, and what we're trying to do is come up with a future that is good, and that we could all benefit from." We'll have a set of just relations if we work on this. If we keep the present system going it's not going to be just for anybody, but, you know, you're not going to do much better than us in this next round if we put some more coal plants in. You can't fish in those lakes either. I want to see everybody be healthy, because our humanity is improved if we are good to each other.

Our organizing strategy is leading by example, that's what I call it. I could be like Ward Churchill and do analysis for a long time on what's wrong, or I could do something. It turns out that when you put up the first wind turbine, everybody says "How'd you do that?" because we liberated ourselves from the box and we decided that we—as people who are low on the social totem pole—deserved a wind turbine and an espresso coffee shop and wireless Internet. And they say, "How'd you do that?" "You know," I said, "we worked together, we came up with this plan, and we did it." And that in and of itself is something that liberates other rural people, who might not be Native, because they say, "That looks like a good idea. I've got really windy land too." Working in oppressed communities is entirely different than working with people who feel entitled and privileged, and somehow, in these communities—in all communities—you have to figure out how to give yourself permission to get out of your box, whatever your box is. We know what our box is, so it's a question of getting out of it.

**JKK:** I want to ask you about your organizing with the Indigenous Women's Network, and also how you see the global Indigenous movement. In the early nineties, one of the ways I first came across you and your work was through the newsletter of the Indigenous Women's Network, and I'm hoping you would speak to where you see the status of Native women in North America at this particular historical moment, and also how the strength of Native women's resistance has informed what you do.

**WL:** Well, I see a lot of women's leadership. And they're rising. Arguably, it's fair to say that, in general, the colonial process brought a power structure that excluded Native women. And so our whole struggle, it's not the same struggle as white feminists, because it's in the context of our community dealing with colonialism, in terms of patriarchy, as a curse. I have the privilege of working with a lot of really amazing and strong Native women, and I see a lot of nongovernmental organizations. In Minnesota we have a lot of tribal chairs that are women, so we are seeing the rise of that in that arena of political power, as opposed to these others.

When you live in an oppressed area, you still suffer from major oppression. I can't complain, I have a good life, but I think that women have a lot of challenges in terms of dealing with the sexism. How do you deal with the fact that you are the one that is working and doing child care? We have an extended family system, so we're pretty good, but it's challenging, and I think we are not given enough credit.

But, the other side of that is that I know I'm a really good multi-task organizer because I'm a woman, and I've never had the privilege of having some space to write—I've always had this great busy life. I'm encouraged by the state of the movement and the power and beauty of a lot of our young people. I have a mentorship, an internship program, and I generally attract young women. Seeing those young Native women leave and do amazing things—it's very good.

**JKK:** In closing, what do you see are the most pressing issues globally for Indigenous peoples? You mentioned your first trip to the United Nations in

1977. In 2007, thirty years later, the United Nations adopted the Declaration on the Rights of Indigenous Peoples, and I wonder if you might close with some thoughts in terms of global solidarity and issues of environmental sustainability tied to your vision.

**WL:** Yes, that is right. It was thirty years later, and you still had the four opposing countries—the axis of evil, one might call them—the U.S., Canada, Australia, and New Zealand, who didn't sign on. I had the privilege of going to Australia in May, and what I will tell you is that there's a National Sorry Day; they apologize to Aborigines in Australia, as Canada now does too. We haven't had a national sorry day in the U.S., which would be nice, but apologies must be accompanied not by financial compensation, but by justice. I think these issues are core to the gut of where we're going as Indigenous peoples, some kind of reconciliation, preservation of that which makes us Indigenous—whether it is language, food, land, water—are common issues in Indigenous communities. We are faced with the continuing industrialization of world food economies and energy economies in the face of declining oil. That set of discussions is challenging Indigenous communities across the board.

At the same time, corporations move further into communities and return. I didn't think I was going to be around for the second round of uranium mining battles, but it looks like I'm still here. In climate change discussions, some people have been proposing nuclear power as the answer, but we have become addicted to the industrial economy. Most of us don't produce our own food, we don't produce our own energy, we outsource a lot of our intellectual capital, and we send our children off to school in other places. They sometimes come back with some relevant thoughts, but not always. I think that level of dependency is part of what we need to address in our own community.

**JKK:** So again, back to the local.

**WL:** I see the big picture, and then I see the picture of my own community—a snapshot of what there is. Here I am in Connecticut, and I know that there are wealthy tribes here. I know that there's a potential to do good things with that wealth, but I also know that money doesn't buy everything.

# MARIA LaHOOD AND RASHID KHALIDI ON ZIONIST EXCAVATIONS AT THE MAMILLA CEMETERY IN JERUSALEM

This interview with Maria LaHood and Rashid Khalidi focused on a case involving the construction of the Museum of Tolerance by the Simon Wiesenthal Center on top of the oldest Muslim cemetery in Jerusalem. In response to this desecration and violation of human rights, in 2010 the Center for Constitutional Rights (CCR) and other groups filed a petition on behalf of the Palestinian descendants of those buried at the cemetery. The petition, signed by approximately ten thousand individuals, was filed with several international bodies, including UNESCO, and urged Israel to halt construction of the Museum of Tolerance, investigate human rights violations, rebury human remains, and declare the Mamilla cemetery a protected antiquity site. Despite moral outcry, construction of the museum is under way at the time of this writing. Updates can be found on the CCR website.

Maria LaHood is a senior staff attorney at the CCR, where she specializes in international human rights litigation, seeking accountability for war crimes, torture, and extrajudicial killings abroad. The CCR is dedicated to advancing and protecting the rights guaranteed by the U.S. Constitution and the UN's Universal Declaration of Human Rights. Founded in 1966 by attorneys who represented activists in the civil rights movements in the South, the CCR is a nonprofit legal and educational organization committed to the creative use of law as a positive force for social change.

Rashid Khalidi is the Edward Said Professor of Arab Studies at Columbia University. He has taught at the Lebanese University, the American University of Beirut, Georgetown University, and the University of Chicago. He was president of the Middle East Studies Association in 1994. Khalidi is author of numerous books, including *British Policy towards Syria and Palestine, 1906–1914* (1980); *Under Siege: PLO Decisionmaking during the 1982 War* (1986); *Palestinian Identity: The Construction of Modern National Consciousness* (1997); *Resurrecting Empire: Western Footprints and America's Perilous Path in the Middle East* (2004); *The Iron Cage: The Story of the Palestinian Struggle for Statehood* (2006); *Sowing*

*Crisis: The Cold War and American Dominance in the Middle East* (2009); and *Brokers of Deceit: How the U.S. Has Undermined Peace in the Middle East* (2013). He is also the author of over one hundred articles on Middle Eastern history.

This interview took place on August 16, 2011.

**J. Kēhaulani Kauanui:** I'd like to start by asking if you would provide a brief synopsis of this case and how each of you came to be involved.

**Rashid Khalidi:** I was made aware of the desecration of the cemetery—which actually has been ongoing for a very long time—only a few years ago, when the Museum of Tolerance began its efforts to begin excavation for building Simon Wiesenthal's building of this so-called Center for Human Dignity/Museum of Tolerance in the middle of an old cemetery. I had known that the cemetery contained the remains of some my ancestors going back several hundred years. A member of another family which had some of their ancestors there brought this to my attention and said it would really be great if we could do something about this; all legal efforts inside of Israel seem to have come to a dead end. That's how I was drawn into it a couple of years ago.

**JKK:** And Maria, how did the Center for Constitutional Rights get involved?

**Maria LaHood:** We were approached by Rashid and other family members who knew of some our work in human rights and in Palestinian rights, and they came to us seeking legal assistance. What could be done to stop this atrocity?

**JKK:** In different Native American and Indigenous media news sources, when the question of Palestinian human rights is raised, sometimes readers or listeners, depending on the media venue, will ask, "What does this have to do with Indigenous politics? What does this have to do with Indigenous peoples? Isn't this a Middle Eastern issue?" Could you speak to that question of Palestinian people as an Indigenous people subject to settler colonialism and an illegal occupation?

**RK:** Well, that's precisely the way to frame it. This is a case of a burial ground which was in use for, as far as we know, at least a thousand years continuously until 1948 when West Jerusalem was taken over and incorporated into Israel. At that time, the land was simply taken over by the Israeli state or by agencies of the Israeli state. Initially it was not touched, but starting in the early 1960s various agencies of the Israeli state, the municipality of Jerusalem, and others took over portions of the cemetery. At that time, the Palestinian population inside Israel—that is to say, Palestinian citizens of Israel—lived under military rule. So they were not able to protest, they were not able to do very much, although they did at the time attempt to raise their voices against the desecration of what is the oldest and probably the most venerated burial ground in Palestine.

It's known to contain the remains of warriors, of judges, of famous figures going back to the period of the Crusades. In fact, some of the army of Saladin, the forces that finally defeated the Crusaders and retook the Holy City in 1187, are known to have been buried there. So it was a very famous, very venerated, very well known burial site, and there was a great deal of negative reaction to it, but not much could be done at the time.

So I think that there are a lot of parallels between what has been done to Native American burial sites all over North America and this case in Jerusalem.

**JKK:** Yes. Also, too, given the significance and the importance of the cemetery to Muslims, it's my understanding that even prior to the June developments of this year, that the chief archaeologist that was appointed by the Israel Antiquities Authority to excavate the site had concluded after a review of the site that construction should not continue because he acknowledged that it contains tens of thousands of skeletal remains and that to dig would constitute an archaeological crime. How could the Jerusalem Municipal Planning Committee grant final permission for construction of the museum there despite his assessment?

**RK:** Well, the archaeologist, whose name is Sulimani, did in fact report exactly as you said—that in the very small part of the site that he was allowed to excavate or to do quick excavations in before the pressure of development lead to them shutting it down, he discovered a very large number of remains and that it would have been a crime for this to continue. The words he used were "archaeological crime," exactly as you said. They were able to do this simply because this was all suppressed in court. The Israel Antiquities Authority basically did not faithfully transmit what Sulimani himself had put in his report, as he said in a sworn affidavit. They essentially redacted his report to make it appear that there was nothing of significance on the site, that everything had been examined, which was not the case. He had only looked at a tiny fragment of the site that was supposed to be turned into this so-called Museum of Tolerance.

The Israeli Supreme Court, which considered this on two separate occasions, refused to look into—on the second time that it considered it—the fact that they were being deceived and that the Israeli Antiquities Authority was in fact not faithfully reporting what their own archaeologist had discovered.

**JKK:** And now, given the significance of the site, and in light of the cover-up or suppression of this evidence, how are the Israeli government and the Jerusalem Municipality planning committee justifying these acts of desecration?

**ML:** You know, like Rashid said, after the Israeli Antiquities Authority certainly misrepresented what the archaeologist had said—that the area had been released for construction and the museum could be built—the High Court did sort of a balancing and found that the importance of urban development actually outweighed the cultural, historic, and religious value of the Mamilla cemetery to Muslims and found that it could proceed. It placed a couple parameters on the construction, but that was it. And once the court was re-petitioned with Sulimani's affidavit showing that the Israeli Antiquities Author-ity had not represented the truth, the Israeli High Court didn't care. So that was basically its reasoning, to devalue the equal rights and the cultural rights and the religious rights of Muslims.

**JKK:** That's really important—equal rights, cultural rights, and religious rights. I want to ask, Rashid, you've described this as the "so-called Museum of Tolerance." Could you speak to that question of how could they be erecting a museum supposedly devoted to this—and as you mentioned earlier, devoted to dignity—on top of a cemetery? It just seems so perverted.

**RK:** I mean, that's the irony of it. We're talking here about a very sacred burial site. Elsewhere in Jerusalem burial sites are taken care of with inordinate atten-tion, and their dignity is protected. And that's the case of Jewish burial sites, it's the case of Christian burial sites all over the city. Here, what you have is a disre-gard similar to the disregard of the sacred places and the burial sites of Native Americans. It's as if, as Maria said, in this case development needs are simply more important than the dignity one would normally accord to absolutely any other burial site if those involved were not Palestinian-Muslim. So I think that there's an element of discrimination here, which unfortunately makes the names that are given to the structures that are supposed to be built hypocritical to say the least. I mean, a Center for Human Dignity and a Museum of Toler-ance built against the protest of the descendants of the people interred at the cemetery is beyond ironic.

**JKK:** It's very colonial. I want to ask, is the Simon Wiesenthal Center on record about this discrimination and the protests involved by the petitioners such as yourself?

**RK:** They have turned an absolute blind eye to everything. I mean, Maria can give details of how unresponsive, of how callous they've been in their responses.

**ML:** Even worse, at one point they said, "The petitioners can go to the moon for all we care, we're going to build this museum." Regardless of the fact that the museum will actually be a symbol of the opposite of everything it suppos-edly seeks to promote—tolerance, dignity, equality—it actually will be, if it is constructed, a constant reminder of the fact that those values are actually not respected.

**JKK:** That's right. Flagrant disregard.

**ML:** We've reached out, because it was Rabbi Hier, who is the head of the Simon Wiesenthal Center, who said that, and who has come out strongly in opposition to the descendants who want to protect the graves of their ancestors. We actually have sought help from the board of the Simon Wiesenthal Center, the funders, and we have heard from no one. No response whatsoever.

**JKK:** Rashid, given that you're one of the descendants, and you said that you learned of this case through family members, could you speak to the other petitioners? It's my understanding that sixty or so individual descendants from fifteen of Jerusalem's oldest Muslim families have come together to work on a petition and are working on an injunction with the Center for Constitutional Rights. This is a civil volunteer initiative with no particular political persuasion per se, is that right?

**RK:** Absolutely correct, that's exactly right. This is an unusual initiative, because it's not in any way political. And it's unusual that people would get together in this way and this quickly. All the funding was provided by members of these families, of these fifteen families, the sixty individuals, for all of our efforts. What the Center for Constitutional Rights is doing is pro bono, but all the costs of printing up stuff and sending stuff out and so forth have been borne by the families out of a deep concern for the remains of their ancestors.

I have to say, one of the most disturbing things in the Sulimani report is he discovered layer upon layer upon layer of graves going back to the eleventh century. The excavations eventually reached bedrock. Hundreds, thousands—we actually don't know how many thousands—of human remains were removed, and we don't know where they are to this day. We don't know whose remains were removed, we don't know where they were taken to. I mean, the degree of callousness involved—this is a very old cemetery, it's very likely that many of these remains are of course unidentifiable, some like a thousand years old or six or four or three hundred years old might be perfectly unidentifiable, but that's not the point. The point is this was a cemetery that was in use in my lifetime. I was born in 1948. It was used right up until 1948.

So it's not an ancient burial ground that was completely abandoned for centuries. It was being used right up until it was incorporated, the area was incorporated into Israel. And the remains there, right up to very possibly the twentieth century, have just been taken away to a place we don't know, we have not been informed, nobody's been informed! Muslim religious authorities, who are the legal owners of the property—but the Israeli government doesn't recognize that—and all the families who are concerned, including the fifteen families involved in this case, have never been informed of what happened to these remains.

So again, the parallels are a little eerie with what has been done to Native American remains all over the United States at different epochs until finally some kind of sense of justice began to affect that situation and there were some changes.

**JKK:** You're absolutely right. That still continues today all over the place. I recently interviewed some Tongva [Gabrielino] women from what is now known as Southern California. In Los Angeles they're trying to build a Mexican-American Cultural Heritage Museum on top of an Indian burial site that includes Tongva ancestral burials. And in Hawaiʻi there's desecration going on all the time to make room for more hotels and golf courses, including even a Christian church desecrating their own burial site to make way for a recreation room. So I mean lots of really twisted, hypocritical actions. I wanted to ask, too, there's nongovernmental organizations that are also part of this petition claim, is that right?

**RK:** That's correct. A number of Palestinian, Israeli, and other groups signed on to our petition. It was the families who organized this; it's the family group, the ad hoc coalition who put this together with CCR, which has been involved, but a number of NGOs within Palestine and Israel also signed on.

**JKK:** Maria, the Center for Constitutional Rights advocates to protect rights guaranteed by the U.S. Constitution but also the United Nations Universal Declaration on Human Rights. Would you speak to the element of human rights in this case, and international law?

**ML:** Yes. So here, because the High Court of Israel had of course rejected different petitioners' claims, there was nowhere else to turn to, so we decided to go to United Nations bodies to seek protection. First of all, there's the Human Rights Council, which is an intergovernmental body in the UN that's responsible for promoting human rights and making recommendations to address human rights violations. Within that, there are several special mandate holders. There are special rapporteurs tasked with dealing with different themes. We appealed to the special rapporteur on Contemporary Forms of Racism and Racial Discrimination, the special rapporteur on Freedom of Religion and Belief, and the independent expert in the field of cultural rights.

We explained exactly what was happening and how the petitioners' human rights were violated through these actions. Now, their abilities are to basically seek and urge an appeal to Israel. They can also do investigations, they can monitor, they can recommend solutions to the Human Rights Council, and they can actually conduct fact-finding missions and report their findings.

We also sought assistance from the UN High Commissioner for Human Rights, who's really the principal UN office that's mandated to promote human rights and support those special procedures. And then we reached out to UNESCO, the United Nations Educational, Scientific and Cultural Organization, because of their expertise on the issue. We essentially asked for the Museum of Tolerance construction to be stopped, for the whereabouts of the remains to be disclosed—as Rashid said, nobody even knows what they've done with the bodies of the deceased—that those remains be reburied where they were in conjunction with the proper Muslim authorities, and that the entire cemetery be preserved and protected.

The Human Rights Council itself this year and last year has passed resolutions expressing its grave concern at what's been happening, at the excavation of tombs and the removal of remains from the cemetery. One of the special rapporteurs has asked Israel, at least, what is it doing to protect the cultural heritage and freedom of religion in regards to the cemetery. And we know as well that UNESCO has raised the issue with Israel, although that's about it.

So it's a long haul to try to impact Israel in this area. But we know that nothing else can affect it other than international pressure and condemnation. It's also why we're trying to appeal to the Simon Wiesenthal Center. We actually have a public petition, which nearly ten thousand people have signed now. So people can appeal essentially the same appeals as petitioners are making: to protect the cemetery and stop the museum. If people can contact the Simon Wiesenthal Center to tell them what they think about this, I think that's the only way we're going to be able to prevent it from happening.

**JKK:** It seems like an element of public shaming and exposure is what's going to have to come down. I mean, it's clear that Israel has a long history of flagrantly ignoring UN resolutions in general. But, in terms of UNESCO, given that they are charged with really keeping their eye on World Heritage sites, is it true that they said that this in a sense is out of their purview or something like that?

**ML:** Rashid can speak to that a bit more, but they claim that their mandate is focused on the Old City, so that they can't field the mission. But they have urged the protection of Palestinian cultural heritage throughout Jerusalem, which obviously includes Mamilla. They've done fact-finding missions, even as far back as 1986 when Israel assured that holy sites would be safeguarded, including Mamilla. Because, obviously Jerusalem is disputed territory; there needs to be international bodies that are protecting the holy sites there. Since 1947, the regime that was created was intended to provide for the protection of the holy sites of all religions in Jerusalem, and that's clearly not being done.

**JKK:** Right. Rashid, would you like to speak to that as well and how this interfaces with even the formation of Israel at the time?

**RK:** Well as Maria just said, the reason that Jerusalem is not accepted as the capital of Israel and Israel's control over West Jerusalem and the occupied part of East Jerusalem is still not fully accepted de jure by most countries is that the 1947 partition resolution was supposed to establish a special regime for the entire Jerusalem area, which was supposed to be a corpus separatum, a separate body under some kind of international supervision. And, exactly as Maria said, that supervision in particular included protection of holy sites throughout the Jerusalem area, not just the Old City, not just the Haram esh-Sharif Temple

Mount area, not just the Holy Sepulchre and so forth, but as far south as Bethlehem and areas to the east, north, and west of the city.

In other words, it was an area that was much larger than the actual municipality itself that was supposed to fall under this special regime under this 1947 resolution. In consequence of this—and this is the resolution which legitimizes the establishment of the State of Israel, by the way, this is the resolution that called for a Jewish state and an Arab state. It's the same resolution that mandates this in Jerusalem as far as holy sites there are concerned. And this is why all countries in the world have never recognized Jerusalem as Israel's capital and consider that the situation in Jerusalem is unsettled, that it is disputed territory, exactly as Maria said.

We have tried to make these arguments to our own government. Michael Ratner, who's the head of the CCR, and I actually went down to Washington and spent some time at the State Department trying to argue this case. And Michael and I have been in touch with people there ever since, as have some of our colleagues in Jerusalem speaking to the American consulate, members of the family group, trying to urge on them, first of all, that there is this international protection which is supposed to be provided by this 1947 resolution.

There are Security Council resolutions, including one voted for by the United States as late as 1980, which talk about the entire Jerusalem—not just occupied Arab East Jerusalem, the entire Holy City—as being an international responsibility, which talk about things that Israel's doing that are illegitimate. The United States voted for a resolution in the Security Council, which calls on Israel to stop the kinds of things it's doing, had been doing up until that point, and unfortunately continues to do.

And on that basis, we argued that the United States actually had a responsibility to get involved, in addition to which the Simon Wiesenthal Center is American. It's a Los Angeles–based institution. An American institution is involved in the desecration of the oldest Muslim cemetery in Jerusalem in a fashion which exacerbates tensions there and which harms, we would argue, the image of the United States, not just Israel. In other words, this is an Israeli government-supported initiative, but is an initiative by a private, American organization: the Simon Wiesenthal Center. Unfortunately, we haven't had much response to these arguments.

**JKK:** I see. I want to just note, too, because we're independent radio and have to abide by FCC guidelines, of course, we're not allowed to put out a call for action per se, but we can certainly brainstorm what it might take to stop this action. And I want to just point out, during this August break, members of Congress, rather than being at home listening to their constituents talk about concerns going on the ground here, over eighty-one representatives of Congress, nearly 20 percent of the House, are going to be in Israel this month [August 2008] on an all-expenses-paid junket organized by an affiliate of the American Israel

Public Affairs Committee. I wonder about reaching out to those reps who are going there, to educate them and perhaps having the head archaeologist who spoke out maybe attach a letter or something—Sulimani, who, you pointed out, was the chief archaeologist for the Israeli Antiquities Authority.

**RK:** Well, I've just written something where I call this the "Magical Mystery Tour." These people are going to be brainwashed, hoodwinked, shown exactly what the people who are paying for their trip want them to see, and will come back to pass further resolutions and launch further standing ovations next time an Israeli prime minister comes to speak before Congress, as they did when Prime Minister Netanyahu was there a couple months ago.

This is a source of great sadness to me: it is in fact the case that my former representative Jesse Jackson Jr.—I used to live in Chicago in that First Congressional District—will in fact be one of these eighty-one representatives who's being feted and toured and essentially being hoodwinked in my view by their host. I'm sure they won't be shown anything about this case or many, many other striking and egregious elements of the Israeli occupation or the situation in general.

**JKK:** Maria, you said the petition really calls for the reburial of disinterred remains, the relocation of the museum outside the cemetery, and preservation of the cemetery at large as a heritage site.

**ML:** Yes. We should mention too that Jerusalem on more than once occasion actually offered the Simon Wiesenthal Center other sites.

**RK:** The Israeli Municipality, that's correct.

**ML:** They rejected them.

**JKK:** Could you say more about that, and what their rationale was?

**ML:** Well, at one point, I believe, originally Frank Gehry was the architect and had actually drawn out plans for the museum. He subsequently withdrew, but before he did withdraw, at one point they had claimed that the plans were actually designed for that specific property. Of course, his designs were withdrawn, so the Simon Wiesenthal Center had to solicit new designs, new drawings, and they had to do that from Israeli architects. There's no justification that's been given for why they would reject other sites.

Obviously, if they did find another site, then perhaps there would be some chance that the museum could actually exemplify the tolerance that they put forth to promote. But there's no chance that they will do that on the Mamilla cemetery.

**JKK:** Maria, could you provide us with a brief timeline of what's happened since last year, 2010, around the human rights petition up until just last month in July?

**ML:** Well, sure. We submitted our petition in February of 2010. And then several months later, in June, we actually filed an addendum that was in part to provide updates with new evidence because the Simon Wiesenthal Center had come out making misrepresentations about what was happening. They said, "Well, this is just a parking lot. This isn't even part of Mamilla cemetery." Yes, part of the area had a parking lot built on it subsequently, but there were still, as Sulimani said, layers of graves underneath that were being destroyed.

We actually continued to submit updates over the month about the work on the Museum of Tolerance. There was another decision later by Israeli authorities to permit construction of a judicial complex on a separate cemetery. There was bulldozing, as you mentioned, people were trying to refurbish the grave markers now that they could get in—some of the older headstones—and those were bulldozed. Then at the beginning of this year, some folks tried to get an injunction from an Israeli district court. It was actually the Israeli Sharia-appointed caretaker for the cemetery to try to stop the destruction of more grave markers that were renovated. And that was rejected, of course, by the Israeli district court.

We continued to appeal to UNESCO and to the human rights bodies. Finally, in February, we found out that at least the special rapporteur on Freedom of Religion had sought answers from Israel on this issue, and of course Israel hadn't responded. In June there were more bulldozers that came in to what had been a formerly intact part of Mamilla cemetery and disposed of nearly a hundred more grave markers. That was just three weeks after the early June decision by the Jerusalem Municipal Planning Committee, which granted permission for construction to begin within three months.

And then, last month is when the Israeli Interior Ministry approved the plans, essentially providing the final administrative green light for construction to begin immediately. Rashid, I don't know if you want to talk about the letter that was submitted by community leaders.

**RK:** Let me pick up exactly where Maria stopped. In light of July's latest desecration of the only remaining part of the cemetery where there are many visible grave markers, bulldozers came in in the middle of the night working under searchlights, earth-moving equipment, and began to remove large numbers of grave markers and gravestones. They were surprised by local people who came along and alerted the media, who came along with cameras.

As soon as people with cameras started to photograph them, the municipality employees fled like the thieves in the night that they were, they took off.

It's quite remarkable, the descriptions by the various media are quite striking, and the pictures, the nighttime photographs are really quite shocking, to see this large-scale earth-moving equipment working in a cemetery. There are many pictures of the damage. In many cases they are very old gravestones, in some cases they were restored gravestones where new mortar was put around old graves, and in some cases they are one-hundred- and two-hundred-year-old engraved markers that were shattered by this desecration.

In light of this latest horror, forty-five leading personalities from Jerusalem of all faiths from inside Israel—including almost all the Arab members of the Knesset, all the Arab-elected members of the Parliament, and dozens of other important figures, ministers in the Palestinian Authority government, bishops, clerics, academics, forty-five of the most important people in Jerusalem and in the country of different faiths—issued an appeal asking for support in stopping this desecration. It's been forwarded to the United Nations; a letter has just been sent forwarding it to the secretary-general of the United Nations, to the president of the Security Council, and to the president of the General Assembly, and representations are going to be made in Geneva at the UN Human Rights Council and other UN bodies, as well as other ways that this is being brought to the attention of various people who are responsible all over the world. It's been sent to various Arab leaders and so on and so forth.

So here you have an instance of an initiative taken by families who have ancestors which were buried in this cemetery leading to a pretty much unprecedented across the board—I mean we're talking about people from all faiths, we're talking about Muslims and Christians, Palestinians of all faiths, we're talking about people from both sides of the Green Line, people from within Israel and people from the Occupied Territories, people from occupied East Jerusalem, people of all political persuasions, and people who have no political persuasion, academics and distinguished merchants and so on and so forth—in Jerusalem, all unified around the demand that these desecrations be stopped.

**JKK:** Right. Are any rabbis speaking out?

**RK:** We actually had the support in our initial petition of a number of Israeli groups, including Rabbis for Human Rights, who issued a statement calling on the Simon Wiesenthal Center to reconsider, so we have had some support from not only rabbis but various other Israeli groups and other groups outside of Israel, Jewish groups.

**JKK:** And also, in terms of the letter putting pressure on Israel and asking these UN bodies to send a delegation to investigate, Maria, you mentioned that they can go on a fact-finding mission. Have any of them committed to undertaking that work?

**ML:** No, none of them have. And in fact, we were made aware that the head of UNESCO was actually in Jerusalem after having received our petition, and we have no reason to think that the issue was raised.

**RK:** If I could just insert something here. One of the things that we have to remember is that it's not somebody that just floats above politics. It's a body that's eminently political, and the international balance of forces very much affects what the UN can and cannot do. The United Nations secretary-general and the various UN bodies are subject to various pressures, among them the pressure of funding. The biggest funder of the UN is the United States. And as we all know, the power of the U.S. purse is in the hands of Congress. Eighty-one members of Congress are being toured by a group affiliated to the biggest lobby for Israel, so that the people who hold the purse strings for the United Nations are vocal and vociferous in insisting that the United Nations not do anything in Israel.

And that's one of the reasons that the UN in some circumstances is hamstrung, both because our administration puts pressure on it and because Congress can get up on its hind legs and howl about this, that, or the other. They are currently howling about the Palestinian attempts to bring the issue of admission of Palestine before the United Nations in the fall. But this is the kind of thing that makes the heads of UN bodies like UNESCO perhaps reluctant to do what their mandates actually indicate that they should be doing.

**JKK:** That political pressure. Now, that letter that you mentioned, from forty-five distinguished community leaders . . . that was submitted to the UN?

**ML:** Yes.

**JKK:** If one had to summarize the current status of the case, how would it go?

**RK:** Starting in February 2010, we have taken this to as many venues as we can, the family coalition ably supported by our friends and colleagues at the Center for Constitutional Rights. To be fair, it's been picked up by a lot of media, especially in the Arab world, but even some in the Western media. And after this latest desecration, these forty-five community leaders picked it up. We hope that this is not just something that will find an echo in the Arab world, or among Muslims. We hope that this will something that will find an echo as more and more people hear about it among anybody who feels that there should be dignity and respect for the dead, all the dead. People who believe that Indigenous peoples have rights, people who believe that there should be equal treatment of sacred sites, that some sites are not more sacred than others, which is in effect what's being said here.

The Jewish cemeteries on the Mount of Olives, one can visit them today. They're beautifully tended, as they should be. There was some desecration that took place in those cemeteries under Jordanian rule before 1967. A huge fuss was rightly made about that. The idea that some cemeteries deserve that kind of care and attention and others can be simply treated with complete disdain—bulldozers running amok—is something that we hope and we think that people should feel is wrong and should do something about.

Now, there are some ways, we mentioned the website where people can sign the petition, but there are many other ways we hope that people, and ideally government and the media, can take this issue up. We welcome any help we can get.

**JKK:** Right. When I first learned about this case, it was from Laura Raymond at the Center for Constitutional Rights a couple months ago, and she produced a press release that I sent to the World Archaeological Congress. I'm not sure how many people followed up with the suggestions embedded in the press release itself, but I'll tell you that only one person acknowledged that I sent it. And that was in a private message to me, not on the list itself, and that's out of numerous hundreds and hundreds of academics affiliated in any remote way with the field of archaeology. I myself am not an archaeologist.

**RK:** My daughter actually is, and she's in touch with people on the Ethics Committee of the World Archaeological Congress, so we're actually about to move into that realm as well. Part of the issue here is our good friends at the Center for Constitutional Rights are dealing with innumerable pressing issues. And all the people involved with this are not full-time employees, every one of us has a day job, some of us have several day jobs. So this is a volunteer effort. The people in Jerusalem are doing this on top of all the other pressures of occupation that they face. Those of us who are here, in the West, living in the United States are dealing with these issues on top of everything else we have to deal with.

Were we a fully funded NGO—which we're not hoping to be—like the Simon Wiesenthal Center, which has offices in New York, LA, so on and so forth, a huge multimillion-dollar budget and so on, it would be perfectly easy to go into high gear on every level of this. We are hopefully going to reach out to archaeologists. We think that there are various issues that archaeologists should be concerned about that are involved in this. You know we haven't even mentioned this yet, but one of the things Sulimani, the Israeli archaeologist who was mandated by the Israel Antiquities Authority to do this dig, found was an enormous number of valuable artifacts. We don't know what's happened to those artifacts.

Things from the city of Jerusalem going back to the eleventh century were apparently uncovered in this dig from his very preliminary report and his affidavit, what we've been able to see. All these things have just been covered up. Whereas a toothpick going back to the biblical era is trumpeted and cosseted and we get publication about it, the oldest Muslim cemetery in Jerusalem had an archaeological exploratory excavation, the results of which were simply covered up. So on an archaeological level, again I'll quote what Maria said Sulimani said in his affidavit: this is an archaeological crime. It's not just a desecration of a cemetery. I mean, I would be against digging in a cemetery at all, I don't think there should have been an excavation. But given that the Israeli law mandated that, that's what was done. What was then discovered is part of the patrimony of mankind and should not have been, as it has been, covered up. We don't know what they did with it.

We don't know what they found, what gravestones. Muslims do not bury with anything—artifacts or jewelry—on the body. People are wrapped simply in a shroud and laid in the earth in a specific fashion. But gravestones and so forth are a part of Muslim custom. So there would have been, and Sulimani's affidavit indicates that there was, a variety of indications of various levels of occupations in Jerusalem. His report is tantalizing; the affidavit is tantalizing. We have no idea about these things. And this is, I think he aptly described it as an archaeological crime, so hopefully some of our archaeologist friends will be able to take this up.

**JKK:** Right. Well, in terms of the human rights violations, it also seems to be a crime against humanity. In closing, I want to make sure we have the website addresses so that they can go learn more about these cases and decide how they want to act. Maria, would you be able to give those addresses for the campaign as well as the Center for Constitutional Rights site?

**ML:** Yes, the campaign website is mamillacampaign.org. And then CCR's website is CCRjustice.org, and search "Mamilla."

**JKK:** Any closing thoughts as we wrap up the program?

**RK:** Let me just say, I'm really glad that you tied this to issues of Native Americans and Indigenous rights, because I think that's one of the important ways of framing what's happening. This is not just something that is taking place in faraway Jerusalem This is something that relates to concerns worldwide, and I'm very glad you've managed to frame it in that way.

**ML:** Well, my thought is what we're trying do here is protect a historic Muslim cemetery, but I think the larger issue of course is about the status of Jerusalem and about justice and peace in the region. We're hopeful that starting in a place where we feel like most people can agree, if you can build a Museum of Tolerance someplace else in Jerusalem, why in the world would you build it on a historic Muslim cemetery? So that if we can make some headway just in this area, we increase the prospect that human rights can be respected and that justice and peace could actually be achieved in the area.

# JAMES LUNA ON THE (PERFORMANCE) ART OF IRONY

I had the pleasure of interviewing performance and installation artist James Luna (Luiseño) via telephone as he spoke from the La Jolla Reservation in San Diego, California. He passed away on March 4, 2018, in New Orleans, where he was Artist-in-Residence at the Joan Mitchell Center. Luna earned a BFA in studio arts from the University of California Irvine in 1976 and an MS in counseling at San Diego State University in 1983. He has served as an academic counselor at Palomar Community College in San Marcos, California, and has also been a part-time instructor in studio arts at both UC San Diego and UC Irvine. Luna was awarded prestigious fellowships, including the Distinguished Fellow Award in 2007 from the Eiteljorg Museum in Indianapolis. In 2005 he represented the National Museum of the American Indian at the Venice Biennale. His one-man exhibits have been seen at Essex University in Colchester, England; at Santa Clara University; at the Snelgrove Art Gallery at the University of Saskatchewan; at the Tozzer Library at Harvard University; at the University of Wyoming; at the Santa Monica Museum of Art; at the University of California at Santa Cruz; at the Hood Museum at Dartmouth University; and at the Carl Gormon Gallery at UC Davis. He had numerous video productions to his credit, as well as group exhibits and other performances. At the time of the interview Luna had an exhibit, *Emendatio,* at the George Gustav Heye Center in New York City, one of the satellite museums for the National Museum of the American Indian. In 2017 he was awarded a Guggenheim Fellowship.

This interview took place on March 18, 2008.

**J. Kēhaulani Kauanui:** I want to ask you first if you would tell us more about your background, and how you became an artist. I'm also interested in how your grounding as a member of the La Jolla band of Mission Indians has provided a foundation for your artistic vision.

**James Luna:** Okay, well. This is James Luna. I'm a Payómkawichum Indian. We were formerly known as Luiseño Indians, and I'm enrolled and reside on the La Jolla Indian Reservation in North County, San Diego. I'm currently speaking to you from my office at Palomar College, where I hold a full-time position as an academic counselor. That's how I pay for my art habit.

Art has just been something that's been with me for my entire life. I guess maybe the defining moment was when I came to terms with what I had as far as an artist as a special gift, and so that's recognizing something that other people can't do. Or maybe not do as well. And so it's provided a lot of things that are very important to my life. I think it's probably gotten me to live longer, because first of all, I got to express things that maybe were eating at me, and things that are eating at you take their toll. You become less angry when you have a voice.

It just continued from there, and the next defining moment was in college, at the University of California, Irvine, where I began as a painter and then got introduced to performance, and I found my place or my medium to speak to the things that were eating away at me but at a variety of media levels. So that's what I do as a performance and installation artist. I mentioned that I live on the La Jolla Indian Reservation. Living there I think provides me, well, as I said—well, I haven't said, but as I think—a lifetime of subjects to work with, you know, which include myself, my family, the tribe, the situations going on there that provide me with kind of a microcosm of what's happening in other Indian communities both on the reservation and off.

**JKK:** In the period where you were in art school, in terms of issues that were eating at you, I would guess that California Native nations were not as visible as they are in this time period.

**JL:** That's definitely true, but it kind of goes beyond that. When I first started out at the university, there were only six of us. So that told you something. But what I did discover there, because I hadn't gone to Indian school and pretty much had been Indian around my family, when you get to mirror up against another tribal group and find out how similar you are in so many ways, and at the same time, you know, different, you start to see the world, as I did, through a bigger lens. You know, that what we are experiencing in my family and in the tribe wasn't too much different from other tribal groups.

As far as misrepresentation, well, that's an issue that I do use in my work. I've used it all along because I was in art early on, starting maybe as early as grammar school and stepping a few notches up in high school, that you look at what you're taught—and I guess this is just generally speaking, not just about art but about all facets of education—that as a tribal person, you're left out. You get a couple words of mention and then it's business as usual. And then there's just other things that you begin to see as you begin to read and learn about the tribal experience, you know, about dysfunction, where that came from and where it goes. So, you know, we had plenty of that in the family, so as I stepped back and looked at it I thought, "Wow, you know, this is why," and then tried to explain it to myself, and then perhaps to explain it to others.

**JKK:** And, specifically, how did you make your way into doing performance art and installation art?

**JL:** I was painting, and at that time it was hard-edge. I had dropped out for a couple years, and when I went back I was more determined to get my degree and be serious about art, because when I was out in the working world after I had dropped out I saw the short ends of that, without an education about where you could go and, you know, what was I doing in this factory? So, when I came back to school as a much more matured and better student, I dove into my paintings, but what made a difference this time was that I had a theme. I started incorporating Indian motifs into my paintings, which were also hard-edge, and then adding my own version of hard-edge on raw canvas, raw material, mixing up the designs with more organic kind of dripping and stuff. So it became exciting for me. This is something that I could do easily.

But it got to a point where, because we were absorbed in conceptual work in addition to what we were doing with painting, that I needed an outlet for other cultural things that I was experiencing at that time. And in the sixties, at that time—the late sixties, early seventies—it was a great time to be in school as an ethnic person, because things started to come forth and alive. They were recruiting Indians to go to school, along with other ethnic groups, and starting culture clubs and cultural studies. And you felt more akin to what was going on there; of course the antiwar sentiment was strong and I think, like other students, you felt that you could make a change and that you were at the center of all these activities.

But the painting just didn't speak to that. I just probably wasn't that gifted a painter or, I don't know, maybe you can't speak to that kind of complexity of ideas and thoughts in painting. So I started writing on them. And then I got introduced to performance and that was it, because I thought, "Wow, where has this been?" Even though I had been exposed to it through video, it's another thing being exposed to it live and in the classroom along with a great instructor, and my instructor was Basjan Auder. And he really supported me and my work, and it's strange because he's passed on, and in those recent surveys a couple years ago of his work, I saw my work in his work. I saw his influence upon me. I'd never stepped back to look at that. And in performance, I found that you could use words, you could speak them, you could write them. Your body, its movements was another voice. You could use other media. In this movement, it could be, you know, tribal dance. In these other mediums, in what you play, it could be tribal music.

So I just started, you know, looking at all the possibilities and integrating Indian thematic messages—not just thematically but also with addition of other tribal objects and sounds and smells that, you know, it became complete. So, performance for me, being introduced to it first, I also took my structure as a painter so that there was a structure to this performance, it just wasn't catch-as-catch-can. And that I incorporated my writing that I was doing for my paintings, which were performance, became a script. And looking back, when I started doing installation, which reverted back to my writings and paintings on the wall but with objects, it was a smooth transition because I saw them as both stages, you know, literally a stage to expound on these themes. And that, looking back on performance, I think one of the ways that I sort of was able to bypass stage fright and all these other things as far as being in front of a live audience as opposed to doing a painting that's on a wall, was I saw myself as an object, and that was the key to that. But it was also a key for me to slip back and forth between these two mediums, and I don't know, there aren't a whole lot of artists that do that. Now I'm not tooting my own horn here, but I'm very comfortable with it. It just depends on the theme; which way will be the better medium to say what I need to say.

**JKK:** What I really like about it is that Indigenous people are so often pressured by those of the dominant culture to perform for them. I love that you've taken control of that form and you're the one that's dictating the performance. I want to get at how you use humor to expose what I'm seeing as the irrationality of colonialism, and ask you about the use of humor and irony in your work.

**JL:** Well, you know, that's just one of my weapons. I don't want to be labeled as a humorist, but that certainly is a part of the work. Not every piece is humorous, but what I've found in wanting to speak to what Indian culture was about, you know, that had to be a vital part of it because in our ways, which goes contrary to how people see us, you know, I see us as pretty funny people. We always have a laugh, even at the saddest times, you know, that's the way you sort of heal.

I was thinking about that and I started to observe more, and because you're around it you grow up with it. Of course, some people are better than others at it, but any humor I can best describe as witty, there's a lesson to some of the stories. It's fast, it's dry. I don't know of other humor that's quite like it. And also you throw in body language or tribal grunts and words, and it really becomes alive. And how it's used, and where it's used—it's like I tell white people, if you're around us and people start kidding you then you've been accepted, they like you. In Western culture it would have been the negative, but in Native culture you kind of warm up to people and listen to them and then kind of mock them if you like them. And that's just the way it is.

As I mentioned, even at sad times, using humor is part of the healing process. We might be digging graves at the cemetery for someone and there's a whole large group of people, or maybe just a few, but one of the things that happens is people start the stories and the stories come up about the deceased or the family or just each other. And you know what you're doing is serious, but it makes it less sad, and you can get through that. And of course there is sadness at the funeral, but after that everybody kind of eases up and moves on, and that's the whole purpose of post-ceremony or gathering after a funeral, because that's all part of the letting go, you know. In our way, we have a big meal after the funeral as a thank-you, and a lot of times you walk in there and you wouldn't even think it was after something sad like that, I mean there are sad people but for the most part people are feeling relieved—I guess that's the word I was looking for—and you walk away feeling, you know, it's done.

So I started looking at the humor and figuring out how I could use it, and one of the things that I noticed was that if I interjected something humorous, I could bring people in, and then I would hit them over the head with something more serious. But it was a way of hooking them, but it's also a way of relaxing people, getting them to be part of this. In my performances, I've noticed that in the beginning, if it's a predominantly white audience, which it usually is, people are confronted by my humor and they just don't know how to deal with it. You know, they'll be quiet, they'll kind of nod, and I can see them looking at each other like, "Is that supposed to be funny?" Or "What did he mean by that?" There will be one Indian in the audience and they'll laugh, and they'll give permission for everybody else to laugh. It's kind of a phenomenon. Or, it takes a while for everybody to catch on, or I'll just look at the audience and say "Loosen up," and then they begin to understand what I'm doing.

In my scripting, I've been described—or the performances have been described—as a roller coaster. Well, it is, because that's how I script it. If I'm going to use something very painful, something very somber, I'm not going to let it ride, you know, I'll come back to lessen it up. Which may not be like a knee-slapping, humorous thing, but it'll be something in there to give people some relief and either return or go to another place, so it's a vital part of my scripting or performance, but I also use it in my object-oriented installations.

**JKK:** And these performances really compel audience members to confront their own perceptions about Native people. Would you say more in terms of the aims, thinking through the aims when you're preparing a script?

**JL:** Well, each script is individual. I'm touring right now a work, *Water, Movement, Fire, Voices*, and it's twofold. One, it's conceptual. I have a short intermission and then I come out with a rock-and-roll thing. The conceptual part is because I enjoy doing conceptual work, but for this work it's probably the most Indian piece I've done. I mimic animals. And then the second half, it's because I enjoy music and it's another way to get people to listen to these stories that I have that are important for them to know. And so it's not all about stereotypes, but certainly there's enough in there for them to confront these. One of them is, when I enter, I come and I'm in a blanket and I have these feathers in my hair.

And it was just because I had seen these South American Indians and I liked the simplicity of their regalia, so I had these things made with plumes and stuff, and I had my hair up in a knot on top of my head and I just simply stick these things in. But it becomes very tribal, and very elegant. I just didn't want to come out there, and it was also a shift for me using my red hat, which is decorated with some Indian things and some feathers in it so the hat itself becomes a contradiction. You know, wearing a hat, but the hat is red and it's decorated to make it regalia. And then an Indian in a blanket.

The whole Indian in a blanket is of course what people see, but what I wanted them to see in this particular piece was how I saw the blanket used. We use it in our gambling games, when the men sit across from each other over an open fire in between them at night, and they hold a blanket in their mouth, the team that is setting up the play, because beneath the blanket they exchange dice, so to speak. And the other team is trying to guess what hands are in them. And so they'll make a call, and there's songs going on that taunt each other, you know, it's at night, they're making noises, they're singing. It's a beautiful thing; it's not just like playing cards, it goes deeper than that. So I was looking at the blanket, you know, covering up your hands that you have to guess, you know, which one it is. So it's sort of a psychological kind of thing. But I thought, well, isn't that what I do in performance?

And then, last summer, I saw the blanket used where they would hold the blanket up, and this is in Juneau, and one of the Alaskan tribes that presented their dances and costumes, or regalia, would go behind the blanket and they would drop the blanket and the dancer would emerge as an animal. He didn't change—he changed into an animal, he just didn't change his clothes. And that's how I perceived it. And that's how I presented it in the performance, that's how I used the blanket, because I wanted to tell people about the complexity of Native dance, that it isn't that you just put this stuff on and jump around. No, your intent is to become part of that and you can become an animal. And as I practiced, as I rehearsed becoming these animals, what became prominent to me were the prominent things about a certain way an animal would move, or his face.

And so I guess in that way I was breaking stereotypical ideas about what people think of Indians dancing around, you know, wild Indians dancing around a fire. The beauty of the stories and that the stories are not just about the past, but these stories are about the present, these stories are about what happened to me this year and the year before, you know, what I had learned from them and how I had gone to this celebration up in Juneau and brought with me ideas. So even in that way, I'm subtly breaking perceptions, but other times, depending on my mood and what I see and what I feel, it might be a lot more confrontational. I guess what I'm trying to say here is there's a mix of ways to do that. Presenting stereotypical things like dance and regalia doesn't stop there, you know; at the same time, you can teach somebody. When a work is much more in your face, like, take a picture with a real Indian, that's confrontational, but that piece calls for that.

But at the same time, too, there are moments where that's humorous, at the same time, too, you know, it isn't just me because I've got the audience involved with it too. Before I go off, that's one of the reasons that I like both those mediums, because I involve the audience. They become part of the work, they're not just static, sort of standing there looking at a painting, or static there looking at a sculpture; they're actually involved someplace. Because I'll either get them to come up to be onstage with me or I'll go out in the audience. I'm very cognizant of that, I don't want to be an entertainer. What I do is entertaining, but I'm not an entertainer. I'm there to share.

**JKK**: Yeah, I want to go back to that. I did see the video *Take a Picture of a Real Indian,* where you're appearing on a makeshift stage in front of an audience and appeal to them and say, "Come on, take a picture of a real Indian," and in the video clip I saw, a white family takes you up on the offer, and then the video cuts, and I wonder if you could talk about what happens when they go up there. How does it play out once they've had the picture? Do they engage you? Do sometimes they feel duped or hostile after they realize that they've been roped into the performance themselves?

**JL**: That performance is scripted to be strategically experienced. I come out as a bare-boned Indian, so to speak, which is breechcloth and moccasins, but it's enough for people to say "Oh yeah, look at the Indian." And in that setting, in a gallery, you know, you've got to figure who's going to go to a gallery for an opening, you know, to experience this, but a lot of times, or most of the time, people aren't asked to experience. So it does make it different for them, and what I've learned from this piece is that the actual debate that starts when I start to do this performance and people take their picture and then get to stand back and watch other people, you know, they start to see something.

The second character is just me in my street clothes, and people start to get a sense, "Oh yeah, that's the same guy. You know, he doesn't have to wear regalia to be an Indian." And while I'm doing this there's also a monologue going, which a lot of times people just don't listen to, which is, "Take a picture with a real Indian. Take a picture here tonight. Take two, leave one, take one home. America likes to say 'her Indians.' America likes to see us dance for them. America likes our arts and crafts. America likes to name military weapons and airplanes after our peoples. America likes to name their film festival after one of our most sacred ceremonies. America doesn't know me." And then I leave.

So that's kind of interesting to me, after saying that, that anybody would get up there. But it's strategically planned that way because the last Indian that I come up with is in a war dance outfit, so to speak—you know, the one with the colors and the beads and the feathers—and usually an "ooh" goes up and people are really jostling to get their picture with me, which was the whole point of this thing, that if there was anybody for them to not take a picture with, that was probably the guy. But, you know, people forget, and like I said, this was a gallery setting, so it's different. I have done this in public, and it's way different. I did it in a kind of an outside market area in San Francisco, and that audience was very hesitant to get up there with me, kind of curious about what it was. There was a lot more questions about that, and they would talk to the cameramen, "What is this about?" They were a lot more hesitant, and I guess people in the outside world are less trusting in your everyday setting as opposed to coming into a safe gallery environment to see art.

**JKK:** I want to ask you about one of your earlier performances, from over two decades ago, which opened at the Museum of Man in San Diego, California, and showed between 1985 and 1987. In that one, you used your own body to critique the objectification of Native peoples, as well as the use of exhibition by Western museum practices and cultural displays. Listeners who are unfamiliar with this should know that you put your own body on exhibit, as though it was an object, where you laid in a glass museum case wearing only a loincloth. Tell us more about that, and what you'd set out to do. Also, how did the museum visitors responded?

**JL:** Well, that's the artifact piece, which I've only performed twice, and that was more of a—well, that started out as kind of a confrontational piece, you know, dealing with representation of our peoples, at first in museums, but then actually, if you think about it, in all mediums: books, movies, and stuff. Our place, our role, which is usually very minimal. And in the museums, they're always about the past, and what they feed into your head is that we're people of the past, that we'll never live up to our glory again, and, you know, these are the things they used to do and used to use, when in reality, we're the same people, it's just that people won't allow us to grow.

And a lot of those things in the museums don't belong there. A lot of these things in museums we still use; we just incorporate it as part of our lifestyle today. So I feel that the museums and other institutions that have created this aura, a misconception. So I had thought about this piece for a long time and it got accepted to be part of "Art in Public Places," which was the perfect vehicle for that work, and it was Sushi Gallery in San Diego, and we were talking about where to perform it, and I was thinking, in public. And I thought, you know, maybe a post office, but that wouldn't have worked because there would have been a million forms to fill out to do that. I was thinking about a library, but that's also city governments. Just trying to think of someplace and someone said, "Why don't you try the Museum of Man that's here?" And I said, "They'll never go for it," which was untrue, because as soon as I brought up the issue they accepted it. There was very little debate. The only thing that they had asked for was that I make the exhibit museum-quality. And I thought that was a great suggestion, because I wasn't thinking of that, I was just thinking of the whole thing, and hadn't really thought about how I would present it in a final version. And it's essentially an exhibit of a current Indian man—me, lying in that bed of sand on this table was only one portion of it.

There's another display case that houses my personal artifacts, which for a Native person is not out of the ordinary, because it speaks to my eclectic taste in music—you know, we don't sit around listening to flute music. We listen to country-and-western and blues. And so it had my cassettes, that's how old the piece was, and favorite albums and books, and it wasn't about Indian lore, it was about Jack Kerouac and Charles Bukowski. And there were pictures of me and my mom, my grandma, me and my dad, the other side of the family, arrest records, divorce papers—you know, things that, for some reason, I think that the general public doesn't think about when they think about Indians, is that we do just about everything they do, and maybe more, because we can be eclectic, and maybe we have to.

You know that I do like to listen to Indian music, but that's not the only thing I listen to. So we're kind of blessed to have all these cultural things besides American culture, and that's what that case was about, you know, we're a part of it. And then the other case had my medicine objects, which were not labeled. And when I do things in these works, I know that a majority of the people will not get it, but for other people that get it, you know, hopefully they'll share that with someone else. It isn't for me to teach them, spoon-feed them. If that was the case, I'd put up all these things defining what I do, but that's not what I do, that's where I don't go. So these medicine objects were un-labeled, no dates, no "It was made from this," "They used to do this." No, it was unlabeled for people to understand that they were still in use. I had thought about this piece and I had come up with those other elements of it later. Before deciding that I would be an object in this thing, as I started doing this, it then became apparent; these are my objects, these are my things, you know, what's missing here?

Well, the Indian man is missing. Well, you are the Indian man. And iron-ically, when I presented it it was just days from my birthday, so the only date that was on this enclosed table that I was lying on, it said, "James Luna, Luiseño Indian, born February 8th, 1950." And, you know, that's all they needed to know. And, you know, I started saying in the beginning that this was con-frontational; it was, but it was another kind of confrontational, it was almost a passive resistance, presentation, because I just lay motionless for people to look at and for people to think, and for people to understand this, particularly in a museum where we're surrounded by bones, and old things that ancients used to use, and they're confronted by the reality that, oh, here's a real Indian, you know. What do you do with it? So I thought, you know, that this would be a successful piece because it just felt that way, but I didn't realize at the time what it would make for me as far as my career, because that was—I'm trying to re-member the year—'83, so it was like five years later when they asked me to do it in New York, but it had been circulated—this, what I had done, and chosen as one of the works to highlight the decade and be part of this decade show.

And then I went into another kind of gear because I thought, well, it worked in San Diego in a museum on a Saturday afternoon with families, it won't work in New York. And it did, it did, it still held its strength and did much for my career because since then it's been written about internationally as part of text-books and stuff because people see it as an important work on a lot of levels. One is a Native conceptual artist that crossed into mainstream performance installation; the subject matter, which crosses anthropology, art, social scienc-es, you know, and culturally anthropology. So, you know, people are intrigued by that piece, so I guess we all have our work that we can look back to and say okay, and I guess the artifact piece is that piece.

**JKK:** Yes, and for listeners, that was the New York City multi-sited exhibit called *The Decade Show: Frameworks of Identity in the 1980s.* Speaking of which, I want to ask you about the new exhibit that's just opened up at the Gustav Heye Center in New York at the National Museum of the American Indian. This is an exhibit called *Emendatio* and, as I understand it, this was part of the work chosen for the 2005 Biennale in Venice, Italy.

**JL:** Well, the exhibit is, speaking of works and shows that, you know, make a mark. The National Museum of the American Indian, which had opened that previous year, had decided that in addition to the typical—or atypical—way of showing a culture. The museum got both praised and panned for by not being a strictly anthropological museum showing, you know, our objects, that they would go beyond that and talk about the living culture of Indigenous America. That they would also venture out into other areas, like fine art.

**JKK:** Yes.

**JL:** And so with this Venice Biennale coming up, they decided that they would select an artist and present them in a pool to be selected to represent the Unit-ed States at this international art show. Well, it didn't happen, because it was in disarray because this administration, the Bush administration, had pulled funding for it, didn't see art as a priority. And so the museum decided that they would do it independently, and from the selection committee, but yet still be sanctioned by the Biennale committee. So that's what we got, but we were not on the side where the major international countries present their artists. But that was okay, because I felt I was representing *my* country, and, you know, my country may not be the United States, and this was more representative of what I do as an outsider.

So sometimes it's better to be an outsider than to be an insider, but I was tickled because of all the artists to choose from, that I was selected. And, you know, a great honor, so that'll always be with me. But it premiered in Indianapolis at the Eiteljorg Museum this past November, '07, and then it made its New York debut last week. The work was, well, I had gotten asked real late to do this, so I was kind of pushing ideas around trying to come up with some, though I had some stuff on the table, and one of the things that I had on the table was this wonderful story about a Luiseño man on the coast near San Luis Rey Mission that accepted an invitation—and this is the turn of the century, like 1908—to go to Rome to be trained as a missionary. And they actually had an international school of Indigenous people from all over the world in Rome, with the intent of sending them back out to their countries to convert people.

But in reading about Pablo Tac, this is the name of the man, it didn't seem to me that his total intention was to be trained, because there seemed to be some resistance in his writings. And in actuality those writings that he was doing were the only ones done by a Native California man at that time, expressing a Native point of view, which was phenomenal. Second, he was a linguist and put our language into a crude alphabet, started creating a vocabulary of all our words and then also mastered Latin and Spanish, and I thought what a great story, because these are the things that people don't know about us. And for whatever reason this had been buried and stuff, and so it's my quest to bring it to the forefront. You know, as a matter of fact, it's not just my quest. The person that I hooked up with, Lisbeth Haas, who was at the University of California Santa Cruz, a historian, had done some writing about Native California, so I asked her about Pablo and she said, "Oh, he's going to be a chapter in my book." So, you know, I hit paydirt, I hit gold, because now I had someone that could relay to me the story as they saw it, and as an artist, I would use it. And the whole idea about this Pablo Tac thing was, I thought, perfect because I didn't want to go to Rome doing work that people would have to guess about or not make a connection, and here was a connection which was the church.

As I dug further in this, there was also a connection about architecture and, you know, the whole Catholic culture, so I wanted to make a connection so people would understand us better, and what better way than this story about this man. And so the exhibit, the installations, revolve around him and his contribution and other related subjects as I saw them. So the main exhibit there is called the *Chapel for Pablo Tac*, which is a multimedia installation that is a pretty good size; it's supposed to be the size of the inside of a chapel. And in my ensuing research I had found that the missions of California that are presented as a legacy to Western culture, the majority of them are fake, just like everything else in California. And they're a facade, and I thought, well, great, because, you know, I'm going to make a facade. But I want to make it look the look, and so I studied chapels of the Southwest, and came up with a composite of them, the old walls, an altar, seating. But the information in there, it's different. Rather than a cross on the altar, there's a basket with four feathers that I had found or had been led to buy. The altar speaks of people's sense of wealth, so you have your gold chalice, but on the other side there's eagle feathers. Behind the altar is scripture on tapestry in Spanish by Pablo Tac about why Indians dance. On the walls, there's a faux mural painted on canvas, taken from the Palomar Mission not far from where I live, and then there's vitrines that enclose these other statements about similarities and differences about our cultures. The vials for the last sacrament are next to a clay jar of water, because water is perhaps a sacrament or a gift of life, like I say, juxtaposed with the vials of liquids and minerals for the last rites. A church bell and an Indian rattle, you know, used in similar ways to celebrate the beginning of a ceremony. Sage and incense and a formal Catholic gold-plated incense burner where ours is just a simple shell with, you know, sage, but in retrospect uses a very similar way of calling, you know, calling the Creator.

So the whole thing spoke about similarities and differences. It wasn't just, you know, a statement about Pablo, because I felt also—and this is my own artistic imagination—that he and I are very similar. You know, taking our culture out for people to understand who we really are, and doing it in the best way we can. And I think where we veer off is the language, because I use a language of art and Pablo was using the language of the time, which was Spanish and Latin and then our language. But I felt also, in reading the stories and looking at that, perhaps one of the reasons that he got into words and got into language, that all he had to do was look around in San Luis Rey and see the demise of our culture, because it was a very black period for us. Our numbers had dwindled because of disease, we were no longer hunters and gatherers, we were rounded up to be farmers and this and that for the mission, you know, we weren't free to roam like we could. And that perhaps in one way, he saw language as key to preserving our culture.

You know, how I preserve things is I videotape them. So, similarities and differences, you know, in time and place. The other installations call to some things that I have been doing. *Apparitions* is a video projection on veils; the veils are pages of history, layers of history. And the images that are projected on them in video are Indians of the past, juxtaposed with Indians in the same pose, but they're from the present, to break this idea that we're different people. We're the same people but from a different time and place. And it just goes on like that, couples, groups. And then the final one was more of a conceptual piece in itself, was, you know, I have this picture, this black-and-white picture of this woman, she's a Cupeño Indian from the Hupa area, and she's grinding acorns on the ground, and I just wanted to honor her and women for their toil, and took that image and projected it flat on the floor in a bed of sand where she spins. And it just becomes a mesmerizing image, along with this wonderful music that was done by Jorge Arévalo and all this video work done by my friend Eito Otitigbe. So, you know, I just felt it best spoke to what I was going to say, but again not spoon-feeding people, because people will get it, I hope they'll relay what they saw to other people, or people want to know more, and they should go look it up and read. And of course people that won't get it will never get it, that's my inclination.

**JKK:** Well, in wrapping up our interview I'd like to ask what you're currently working on and what our listeners can anticipate from you in terms of future exhibits and performances.

**JL:** Well, I'm currently touring this *Movement, Voices, Water,* and I'm really happy with it because I think it shows the type of work that I am capable of both conceptual and more theatric, not musical. We got a percussionist to sit in with us, Emiliano Valerio in New York, and it was great because Maurice Caldwell Jr., the guitarist, plays with a loop, kind of an electronic loop, so we get a full sound from him. But with the addition of percussion it just added a whole new dimension, so now I'm thinking of, you know, expanding our entourage to include a percussionist. You know, and maybe in the future, well, which I'm doing already, is working with a band, being a band member with a little big band in Seattle, a Native funk performance, pop collaboration. But it's not my band, so I think I would like to have my own band and explore some other areas of music.

I'm working on a conceptual piece right now that I think—well, we'll see how far I get—but I think it'll be done by August, to premier at the University of Illinois, Springfield, and that's a very conceptual piece, I guess because I was inspired by the piece I did for *Emendatio,* the spinning woman piece, and use video and objects to speak to some things that I've been considering, which may or may not be Indian. But I just want to get back and do some sort of simplistic pieces with not a lot of trapping. Believe it or not, after thirty years, I'm going to take time to paint this summer. I just have this urgency to do this and just kind of pick up where I left off, which I'm really feeling good about.

One thing that didn't come up was this past October, my house burned down, along with twenty-nine other homes on the La Jolla Indian Reservation. So, we're coming back and we're coming back strong and I was donated a home by the Palo Indian Reservation, which has a major casino, and for all the members that were uninsured, eleven of us got these modular homes to start over again. Well, fortunately, my studio stood, so I'm going to put it to good use this summer with working on this conceptual piece and painting, you know, really enjoying my time, and it's going to be really great to be back home.

Beyond that, I'm actually looking forward to maybe at some time starting my own performance group, which would be multiracial, multi-tribal, multimedia, to kind of give me an opportunity to paint some more as a director and writer, you know, sitting in the stage directing these actors, but that won't be for a while. But that's my dream project.

# CHIEF MUTÁWI MUTÁHASH (MANY HEARTS) LYNN MALERBA ON MOHEGAN TRIBAL RESILIENCE AND LEADERSHIP

Lynn Malerba (Mohegan) is the eighteenth chief of the Mohegan Tribe and the tribe's first female chief in almost three hundred years. The Mohegan Tribe is a sovereign, federally recognized Indian nation with its own constitution and government. Chief Malerba is one of seven children born to her mother, Loretta Fielding Roberdge. She has spent much of her life in the land around Mohegan Hill—the small district of the town of Montville—that has been the historical center of the tribe and is home to the Mohegan Church. She came to the position of chief from a long history of involvement with the Mohegan Tribe. In 2010 she was selected by the Mohegan Council of Elders to be the first female Mohegan chief in the modern history of the Mohegan Tribe. Prior to becoming chief she served as chairwoman of the tribal council and worked in tribal government as executive director of Health and Human Services. Preceding her work for the Mohegan Tribe, Lynn had a lengthy career as a registered nurse and served as the director of Cardiology and Pulmonary Services at Lawrence Memorial Hospital in Lawrence, Kansas. She holds a master's degree in public administration from the University of Connecticut, an honorary doctorate from the University of St. Joseph in Hartford, and a doctorate in nursing practice from Yale University; she was also named a Jonas Scholar.

This interview took place on March 1, 2011.

**J. Kēhaulani Kauanui:** I'm really excited to be talking with you and to find out what it means to be a traditional chief in the twenty-first century.

**Chief Mutáwi Mutáhash (Many Hearts) Lynn Malerba:** Thank you very much for inviting me, Kēhaulani. Well, I think to be a traditional chief in the twenty-first century you always need to look back. And as always with any Indian tribe, we receive our inspiration as well as our direction from our ancestors, and we also then need to evolve the role, because times change, tribes change, and the needs of your people change. So, I'm not sure that I have been in the role long enough to tell you exactly what it will evolve to, but I do know that I am very fortunate to have known three chiefs in my lifetime, and that I also look for inspiration from my elders, because they are the people have inspired me throughout my life, and they are the people who have truly donated and volunteered their time to keep our tribe very vibrant and to maintain our tribal traditions and to be sure that our tribal family stayed connected.

**JKK:** Yes, and I noticed that in the media coverage for your induction as chief they did note the chiefly lineage that you come from, being a great-grand-daughter of a sachem, and also the work that your mother has done for the tribe. Would you be willing to speak to that lineage?

**LM:** Oh, absolutely. So, my great-grandfather was Chief Matahga. And his name could be interpreted in two ways: one is Faithful Warrior and the other is He Who Dances, because he was really known as someone who practiced and celebrated our tribal culture. And during my installation I was very honored because I was presented with the Wolf Club that he carved. Every chief since him has received the Wolf Club, and it has been passed down. So, as a matter of fact, that is sitting on my desk as a form of inspiration to me. I am just one person in a line of chiefs, and I need to be faithful to all the chiefs that have come before me.

In our tradition, our artifacts and all of those things that we hold dear are intended to give us inspiration, but also tell us a little bit of that person's story. So it is very proudly on my desk right now. In addition to that, my great-grandfather has three living grandchildren, and they were with me at installation. My mother was one, and she has been involved in tribal politics since her early twenties, and she was encouraged by her grandfather to become involved in tribal activities. Part of her initial involvement was being on the burial committee, which she still is to this day.

Our burial grounds are very sacred to us. They've never been disturbed, despite the fact that the state of Connecticut made them into a state park, and we had to repurchase them. They are a place that is very sacred to us, a very peaceful place, and it's where all of our ancestors reside. So she started out her career in tribal politics on the burial committee, but she was on tribal council for thirty years, and it was an act of love. She, I think, followed our medicine woman Gladys Tantaquidgeon's words, in that Gladys always told us we must stand in love for our tribe.

I believe that it was an act of love that my mother was involved continuous-ly, and continues to be involved with the tribe, and volunteers her time and her thoughts and her energies in a way that's very positive. She was on the tribal council long before federal recognition, while we were going through federal recognition, and after, when we were developing the business. She retired in the year 2000. She is a real source of inspiration to me, because she did this while raising seven children. She did this while being employed, locally, as a teacher's aide. Yet, this was so important to her that she knew that this was something that she would spend a great deal of her life doing. And so, I'm very impressed by her as well as all of the other female leaders in the tribe.

During installation, Chief Matahga's three grandchildren escorted me into the circle, and that was really very touching to me and very important. My mother's cousin took Chief Matahga's headdress out of the museum and wore it for that day. It was something that I will never forget, and it was something that was just incredibly powerful to me to have the people that I grew up with and the people who are my links to our ancestors to be with me, and that did bring our ancestors into the circle with us. I was not able to meet my great-grandfather; he died the year before I was born.

**JKK:** Right, and that honoring. Also, within a Hawaiian context, even that Wolf Club would carry the *mana*, would be said to carry the power of your fore-bear. That's beautiful. Speaking of a long line of your mother's inspiration and her work as a woman and the female lineage that you speak of, would you be willing to address the issue—the media was very much noting that you are the first modern female chief and in going back to the early eighteenth century the second known female chief in the tribe's history?

**LM:** Well, Ann Uncas was the chief during a brief period of time, we think around 1723. There was a bit of controversy over who was the rightful chief—either John Uncas or Ben Uncas, so she, I think, was an interim chief until that was resolved. There's not a lot written about it. There's a bit of oral tradition about that, but certainly I think it's wonderful that there was a female chief so long ago. I think it points to the fact that tribes are very egalitarian and always have been and that women have always played an equal role in tribal politics, in tribal leadership. Whether they were actually named to be a female leader and held a formal leadership role or it was an informal leadership role, I do believe that women were very much respected in the Mohegan Tribe tradition. I believe that they were very much listened to by our male councilors and our male chiefs as representing the needs and wishes of the tribal membership.

**JKK:** That's incredible too. The position of chief in the Mohegan Tribe as I understand it is a lifetime appointment, yes?

**LM:** It is.

**JKK:** How does it work?

**LM:** This process was a little bit different because we had a constitutional change in 1996, and, as you know, our late Chief Sturges was in the position even when the constitutional change was made. And he died a little bit over three years ago. The tribe felt very strongly that there should be a long period of mourning, because he was considered such a great chief, and we really miss him to this day, and he certainly is another source of inspiration for us.

When the constitution changed, the difference between this process and the old process was that the elders would gather, and they would decide who they thought would be the chief. And they would put that person up as their nomination for chief, and then the tribe would do an up-or-down vote—a yes-or-no vote—and obviously, once the elders spoke, it would be very unusual for that chief not to be appointed and installed. The most recent constitutional change vests that power with our elected council of elders, and so they are in charge of appointing the chief. When they considered naming a new chief, they actually asked all of the tribal membership to provide their thoughts on the issue. And so, being a very diligent tribal member and exercising my tribal rights, I very quickly wrote a very long, passionate letter about who I thought that should be, never, ever thinking that my name would come up for consideration, because I was quite happily the chairwoman of the tribal council at that time, and I was very busy and going about my duties in the best way that I knew how.

So when the elders called me into their office and asked to speak with me, I really thought it was just about something they wanted to chat about in terms of tribal council versus elder council business. And when they told me that they had thought about it and they had deliberated about it, you could have just knocked me right out of my chair, because it was completely unexpected. And, of course, I thought I was too young. I certainly did not think that it was even a possibility, so it was never anything that entered my mind. It really took me by complete surprise, so my response was I just need to go home and think about this, because it's such an honor. I wanted to be sure that I was equal to the challenge and that I would be the right person for the tribe for this time—because it is a lifetime appointment—and that I would be able to fulfill my duties in a way that would be honorable and bring positive things for our membership.

**JKK:** Well, as you say, that takes the evolving of the role, but that obviously this is coming from a really strong position in terms of history and heritage. So in a sense it's a combo; it's not 100 percent a hereditary position, but that doesn't mean that there's not this ancestral element in terms of lineage of leadership. It seems that there's a hybrid democracy in terms of the practices that bring about the position, given the constitutional change?

**LM:** Yes, I think that's correct, and again, I know that the council of elders very much deliberated this issue in terms of what they expected the role to be. Their sense of the role of chief was that it would evolve, that it is a new day, and because it is a lifetime appointment they wanted someone who could be very actively engaged throughout Indian Country—within our own tribe, but also locally, because they wanted someone who is well known locally, who has a lot of contact with the local community. That's something that is very special about the Mohegan Tribe's relationship to our local community.

That dates right back to Uncas, because it was his understanding and his leadership that determined that we would welcome the English and Dutch settlers, and that we would embrace them because he felt that that would be the key to our survival, that as people immigrated to the United States there would be more and more and more people immigrating. And if we didn't develop a positive relationship then our tribe would be imperiled because of it.

Growing up here on Mohegan Hill, and growing up in Uncasville and working in the local community for a long time, I have received a lot of positive feedback from the local community because they know me and they know my family. And I think that that is a real positive thing for us.

**JKK:** I wonder if any of those local communities around the reservation understand that the role of sachem still persists in the twenty-first century?

**LM:** Yes, and we just had this conversation yesterday with some of our elders, they were having lunch with us. And one of the things that Jayne Fawcett shared with us and has shared with us on multiple occasions is that there is a law on the books in the state of Connecticut that the Mohegan Tribe is not allowed to have a chief. So it's very important to us to continue to have a chief, because it does demonstrate that the state of Connecticut cannot play a patronizing role in our tribal government—that we are a sovereign and that the state of Connecticut cannot choose our leaders, which they did try to do. And they can also not decide how we will manage our government.

It is a very important role that the chief plays in terms of the continuity of our tribal government, but also in making that very positive public statement that we are a sovereign government, we have been a sovereign government, and that we predated the formation of the state of Connecticut.

**JKK:** For those unfamiliar with this very rich history of leadership of Uncas that has been regarded in some ways as controversial given the cooperative element, could you give a bit more background in terms of the role that he played and how those decisions actually mark the role that Mohegan play today in terms of the Mohegan way or that spirit of cooperation, that ethos of cooperating with the outside community?

**LM:** Certainly. So at one point in time, the Mohegan Tribe and the Pequot Tribe were one. We emigrated from Delaware through New York to the eastern bank of the Thames River. And we were known as the invaders as we came through Connecticut—there were many, many tribes in Connecticut during that era, some who are now extinct. There were about twenty-three tribes in Connecticut that completely died out.

And Chief Sassacus and Chief Uncas—well, Chief Sassacus was the chief of the Pequot Tribe, and Uncas was his son-in-law. And they had a very, very differing philosophy on how to address the immigration of people into the state of

Connecticut and the people coming in from Europe. Sassacus thought that we should fight them to the death, and Uncas felt that that would be our demise and that it really would be better to have a spirit of cooperation. So Uncas and his followers eventually settled on the western banks of the Thames River and took the old clan name Mohegan back, which is known as the Wolf people.

We were part of one of three clans of the Delaware, and the Wolf clan was our clan. And so he took the old name Mohegan back and settled this side of the river. And he did extend an olive branch, so to speak, to all of the European settlers and decided that that really would be the key to our survival. We lived within the community here, we embraced the people who came to Connecticut and, I think, sometimes to our detriment. Because certainly I think, if you look at the history of Connecticut, Indians have not been treated fairly and there have been difficulties, as with any other Native tribe.

I think what's different for the eastern tribes—and it's something that people need to remember, is that we lost our lands in the 1600s, we lost numerous tribal members. It's estimated that the New England population of tribes was decimated, not only with skirmishes with the Dutch and the English and also intertribal skirmishes but also with our lack of our immunity to communicable diseases. Smallpox was devastating to our tribal communities. It's estimated that we lost 90 percent of our tribal lands, 90 percent of our populations between the 1600s and the 1700s.

So typically when people think about Indian tribes, they're much more familiar with the losses that the western tribes experienced so much later on in the 1800s and the early 1900s because it was better documented. A lot of our stories were oral histories, were passed down through oral tradition, and there was definitely a sense of all of the settlers trying to write the New England tribes out of existence, so to speak. So there was no culture, they portray the New England Indians as having been long gone, long before they settled these shores, which is obviously not true.

I think that people always need to think about New England Indians in a different way, because we experienced first contact with European settlers. Our stories were very devastating to us, just as the stories in the West were very devastating, but I think that they are less known. And if you think about New England tribes, sometimes people are surprised that we still exist. If that's not their experience and it's not their knowledge of Native America, they forget that we're still here, despite all of the challenges that we faced. And we're very fortunate that our leaders were willing to provide such good leadership that although our numbers diminished we were able to survive.

I think a very interesting statistic for Mohegan is that, in the early 1600s, we controlled about twenty thousand acres of territory. By 1700 that number was down to two thousand acres, and by 1861 it was down to about an eighth of an acre, just the parcel that our church resides on. A lot of those lands obviously were taken illegally from us. We actually sued the colony of Connecticut, went to England twice, sued the colony of Connecticut. Twice, King George of England agreed that our lands had been taken illegally, but twice they were never restored. And one of our chiefs actually died in London and is buried in Southwark Cathedral.

**JKK:** So really a rarely known history, and a rare history. And that is going from survival—basic survival—to resilience. You mentioned earlier the labor of love, the work that your mother has put into the tribe, and also your great-grandfather, and so much of that it seems is about—from my outsider perspective—holding down community, staying, regrouping and surviving as a people long before federal recognition, through the generations. And I think that that is also a misnomer with a lot of tribes that do have casino enterprises. The general population rarely understands the politics of building a tribal economy, often seeing it in a distorted way, and the media fuels that. But talking about the tribes as though they're newcomers. Would you be willing to speak to that long endurance and also in relationship to the Connecticut colony and the state of Connecticut?

**LM:** Oh, absolutely, and I think a great example of that is if you look at our former medicine women, Fidelia Fielding and Emma Baker. In the late 1800s and early 1900s, we actually had two burial grounds. One was Fort Shantok and one was in Norwich, and now we call it Uncas Memorial. But in Norwich it was called the Royal Burial Ground. And we had a very difficult time in the early 1800s because there was a planned Masonic temple to be built on top of our burial ground. And so Emma Baker went to the governor, along with my great-grandfather and a tribal delegation, to ask the governor to please stop this construction. They were unsuccessful, so our bones were dug up and thrown into the river or burned, our headstones were taken out of the ground, and you can see some headstones in the foundations of local buildings in the city of Norwich. And the Masonic temple was built on top of our burial grounds.

It was for lack of resources that we could not fight this. We could not hire an attorney, we did not have the twenty-five dollars that it would take back in that day to hire an attorney to fight this. We beseeched the governor to please stop, and we were unsuccessful in doing that. So when you think about all of the losses that we experienced, the other side of that is that we remained a very vibrant culture. It was considered—and again think about who settled in this area, it was the Puritans—it was considered the work of the devil to speak our language. It was considered the work of the devil to maintain our traditional ways.

But our leaders did anyway, and they did so in a way that was perhaps a little less obvious to the settlers. And our Ladies' Sewing Society is a perfect example of that. Our Ladies' Sewing Society was little bit of a militant organization, and that's where people did speak the language, and that's where people told their stories, and that's where people continued to enjoy the practice of our culture. And the Ladies' Sewing Society was also a very vibrant group of women who bossed the men around a little bit and certainly let them know what they felt that they should be doing in terms of our leaders. I think that that's a long-standing tradition that we're very proud of.

But we continued to practice our culture, and we had our wigwams, we had them at our church. And one thing you need to know about our church was that we were told that we must convert to Christianity or that we would be relocated to Wisconsin. And there were three women in the local community that helped fund-raise to build the church and we said, "Fine, we'll be Christians, that's fine. This is our home, this is our place." And of course there's such an attachment to our land and this place in terms of it being part of our identity. And so that's how we ended up having a church, and that was the last piece of our reservation.

In 1861 the state continued to try to interfere with tribal politics, continued to try to choose our leaders for us. They wanted to choose leaders that would make decisions that would be favorable to the state. And so that's when we decided to abolish our reservation. Because we said, "We do not want to be part of the reservation system." There were overseers that were assigned to Mohegan, to manage our affairs for us, and we knew that this was not going to allow us to be self-determining and self-governing if we continued in that way. And again, I think that that's what's a little bit different about the New England tribes, is that there are reasons why we were landless and had reservations.

So, in 1934, when the Indian Reorganization Act was passed, tribes could go through that process to be what we call "re-recognized," or "reaffirmed," because we knew who we were. And I don't think that there's another society in the United States that has to prove who they are, except for Native Americans. And, it was later on—I want to say it was in the 1980s—that the Indian Gaming Regulatory Act was passed. The reason that was passed is because the federal government knows that they have a trust responsibility to all Native communities in the United State, because we ceded our land and our natural resources and our water rights and our fishing rights to the United States in return for health and human services, for health care and education.

The United States recognizes and realizes that they have not fulfilled their trust responsibility. And they passed the Indian Gaming Regulatory Act to be able to provide tribes with an economic advantage. So people look at casinos and they think that every tribe in the United States has been wildly successful with casinos. But when you look at the statistics, 15 percent of the gaming tribes create 75 percent of the revenues. So even though there are many, many tribes that operate casinos, they don't operate casinos in locations that perhaps are favorable in terms of the economics. We happen to be very fortunate because we are in between Boston and New York; we have a large population base that we can draw from for our business.

But casinos are considered a tribal business in that they are designed to provide governmental services for our tribe. So, it is to fund our government, it is to help us reacquire our indigenous lands that were taken from us, it is to help us provide for elder services, for health care, for education of our youth, just as, say, the state lottery—it's governmental gaming. I think that people get that confused a bit and somehow think it is about individual wealth for individual tribal members. Tribes are communal in nature, and it's about strengthening our tribal community as opposed to providing for individual wealth to our tribal members. I think that that's a very important distinction that people need to think about.

**JKK:** Yes, I'm so glad that you've laid that out, because there are so many misunderstandings and misperceptions. And politicians and media alike seem happy to perpetuate those myths.

**LM:** Oh, absolutely. When I pick up the newspaper—and sometimes I have to read the blogs, which I should never do—when I pick up the newspaper and I see people saying, "Those tribes, they don't pay any taxes," well, that's not actually true. When you think about our casino, Mohegan Sun, our tribal members pay individual taxes because we don't live on a reservation, and the only people that live on a reservation right now are a small handful of people that live on tribal land. Our elder retirement community is on tribal lands, and we're very proud of our retirement community. We take good care of our elders, and we know that that's job one for us is to make sure that our elders are well cared for.

When you think about the fact that our compact with the state provides 25 percent of our slot revenues to go back to the state, when every other corporation in the state pays 7 percent corporate tax and/or gets tax rebates or tax incentives, it's a bit of a misnomer. When you think about the fact that we employ approximately eight thousand people, and all of those people live in our communities, participate in the local economy, and pay taxes in the state of Connecticut, that's very important. And the other piece of our tribal economy is that we purchase hundreds of millions of dollars in goods and services from about two thousand companies in the state of Connecticut. So our business is good for everyone—and again, being part of this community, part of what we do with our revenues are charitable donations and supporting not-for-profit organizations, because we believe that much has been given to us and it is our responsibility to give back to our local community, as well as to our tribal community.

**JKK:** So within even a cultural logic of reciprocity?

**LM:** Yes.

**JKK:** That's incredible, too, because that is the sort of cultural persistence and continuity that seems to remain invisible because people don't really know what they're looking at. I mean, your example of the Ladies' Sewing Society and the church—so many people in the dominant culture would point to that and think that that is just assimilation, not knowing that that actually can become the cover for cultural persistence.

**LM:** Absolutely, and I think that the other things we've done with our tribal revenues are very important to us. We've refurbished our church, we've refurbished our museum, and made sure that it's climate-controlled and that all of our artifacts are protected. And we've refurbished both of our burial grounds. We were actually successful in working with the city of Norwich and the state of Connecticut to take the Masonic temple back down and to restore the burial ground to a peaceful place. And we've re-interred some of the bones that were taken from that burial ground. Those are things that are very, very important to us. And they are things that we would not have been able to do without having the economy to do that.

If you go to our museum—and I would invite you to come visit our museum, it's a very small museum. It was built by Gladys Tantaquidgeon's father and her brother. Her brother was the chief during his time, and Gladys was our long-esteemed medicine woman. She lived to be 106, and she's somebody who's an icon in our tribal community. Our museum has artifacts from all the tribal families, and so they are parts of our history—living, breathing parts of our history. So you'll see bow-and-arrows there, you'll see clubs there, you'll see baskets that our tribal members made. It's just chock full of small, modest stone and wooden building, but when you walk in, the feeling that you get is immediate. You feel that you are at home, you feel you are in commune with people that perhaps you never met. And there are photographs of people that perhaps you did know growing up as a child, and it's just a very, very special place.

**JKK:** That's wonderful. I just want to reiterate—the issue for tribes reinvesting in their communities then takes place in all these realms, it seems, from protecting burial sites to the health care of a community, and also certainly the broader community that's non-tribal benefits from this economic reinvestment. And indeed, the casino in that part of the state has revitalized not only that region of the state, but it's clear that the state of Connecticut is actually dependent on tribal revenues from gaming enterprises.

**LM:** Absolutely, and one of the things that the tribe has done to be proactive is to work with the state to make sure that the revenues come back to those local communities. We obviously do not control what the state does with the revenues that we provide to them, but we wanted to make sure that we were an advocate for our local communities and that whatever funding schemes that the state had decided, the local communities were treated fairly and that they benefited from the community. We also do provide an annual payment to our host community, which is the town of Montville, and our casino is in the Uncasville section of Montville, named after Chief Uncas. So again, it's about the relationships that we've had over time.

**JKK:** Also, regarding that—the relationships with the town and also the economic revitalization of the tribal nation, you've mentioned the land loss over the long haul of the centuries, and you did mention the tribe abolishing their reservation to avoid real surveillance and control by the state. In terms of the contemporary land base and buying back land, what is the acreage of the Mohegan reservation today?

**LM:** I want to say it's approximately four hundred acres. And again, the most important piece of that to us are the burial grounds, and are where our church and museum is, and where our elder housing, our retirement housing is. Where our retirement housing is, is a very special place to us. It's Fort Hill, and it's where Uncas used to hold his council meetings. And so again, we tried to make sure that as we have to repurchase our land—it's not something that we can just take—that we think about it very carefully, and that we think about the parcels of land that we would like to have as being contiguous and so that it would be a meaningful purchase. We are limited by our compact with the state to taking seven hundred acres into trust without paying any taxes on that. Once we reach seven hundred acres, any other land that we purchase will have to be considered "fee simple" land, which means that we would have to pay taxes—local and state taxes on that.

**JKK:** And that would not be allowed to be held in trust by the Department of the Interior then.

**LM:** That's correct.

**JKK:** And for those unfamiliar with the Indian Gaming Regulatory Act, that is a federal act passed during the Reagan administration that actually requires tribes and states to develop a compact of agreement around casino enterprises, and those are only allowed in states that already allow gaming.

**LM:** Well, tribes could also do what they call Class II gaming, which are video and lottery terminals, without having a compact with the state. But if you want to do Class III gaming, which entails real slot machines and table games, then you need to have a compact with the state.

**JKK:** I want to go back—you've mentioned burial sites and ancestral burials starting with when you talked about the work of your mother sitting on the burial committee. You've also acknowledged that your great-grandfather sought to protect the royal burials. And now this ongoing work to restore the burial with pulling down the Masonic temple. Could you speak to why burials are so important? There's so many non-Indigenous listeners who perhaps don't really get that piece in terms of the ancestral link but also the responsibilities that living Native people have towards those burial sites. And I also noticed, looking at the Mohegan's website, that the issue of repatriation is one of the issues the tribe's involved in right now under the Native American Graves Protection and Repatriation Act of 1990, also known as NAGPRA. Could you speak to the role of burial sites head-on and in relation to this effort to repatriate Mohegan remains and sacred objects and items of cultural patrimony?

**LM:** Well, certainly, every burial is considered sacred. And to think that someone's burial would be disturbed is just an anomaly to Native people. People are buried with objects of importance to them, because they're buried with objects that will carry them into the next life. Certainly in the Native American tradition, and in the Mohegan tradition, we believe that we travel from East to West, and that we travel the Great White Way, and that when you die you are really just assuming another life. You are traveling to your ancestors, and they will be greeting you on the other side. And I think that that's very common to all Native people.

NAGPRA was very, very important because people's graves have been disturbed, bones have been taken out, and they've been placed in academic institutions and museums, and no other society would allow that to happen. NAGPRA was a very, very important piece of legislation, and we have received burial objects back from museums, and we have received bones back from museums. And we have re-interred them, because we do believe that our ancestors are not at rest if they have been disturbed. This is a very, very important piece of legislation, and I can't believe that it took so long to pass that legislation. But I think that it was lack of sensitivity to Native peoples, and I think that the dominant culture thought that it was perfectly fine to study our bones and think about tribes in a very academic way, instead of a personal way that these were people who existed and these were people who were important to us.

**JKK:** That's an ongoing campaign we have here at Wesleyan University, actually, is to get the institution compliant with NAGPRA. That's really a push for all museums and educational institutions across the country. I'm so glad to hear that the tribe has taken that up as one of its key issues. What else are the key issues going right now in the Mohegan Tribe?

**LM:** I would think that one of the things we struggle with is just the demographics of our tribe, because we have a very young tribe. When you think about what happened in New England, all of the tribes' numbers dwindled. And then, we had a baby boom as well, during the thirties, forties, and fifties, and we are in the middle of a baby boom again. And so when we think about our tribal community, and when think about our tribal population and what our wishes are for the next thirteen generations, we need to make sure that we are not solely dependent just on the casino for our economic initiatives, and that we need to diversify in terms of other businesses.

And tribes have been very successful in doing just that. There are tribes that are involved in energy projects, there are tribes that are involved in light manufacturing, and I know one tribe owns a very special chocolate recipe. They bought it from a chocolatier, and they supply a very large chain of department stores with chocolate. When you think about what's going on with our tribe, I think it's very important for us to diversify our portfolio in terms of income so that we can continue to provide those things that are very, very special and make us a tribal community.

One of things that we're very proud about is the fact that our former medicine woman Fidelia Fielding left us six hundred words in a Mohegan-to-English dictionary. And what we're trying to do now, we have a linguist here in the tribe who is working to fill in the blanks to make the language a bit more modern and to help us make it more of a spoken language again. And I think that that's very important to us, because again, when you think about the fact that the dominant culture did not want us to speak our language, the fact that we still have remnants of our language and we can speak our language is very important. It's a bit like Latin in terms of—it's perhaps easier to read than to speak eloquently yet. But we're working on it, and certainly that's something that I've been working on personally is to learn the language.

And I'm remembering phrases from my old English classes, such as verb conjugations that cause me to shudder a bit, but I'm hoping to become more fluent in it. And one of the things that I've done is start to write some Mohegan blessings and some Mohegan prayers for different occasions. One was for my installation ceremony, and it was a little lengthy and it was very difficult for me to learn, but I was very proud that I was able to get through it.

I think the other thing that tribes are still struggling with across the nation is challenges to their sovereignty. I think that's something that is about educating and the states, the local communities, the federal government that tribes are sovereigns and that we were recognized in the United States Constitution, and that recognition provides the authority for the United States to deal directly with tribes. I know that the federal government must consult with us, and that was something that President Clinton wrote into law, that any agency working with an Indian tribe must consult with all of the tribes across the United States whenever there is a policy change anticipated to receive feedback and to make sure that the tribes have the opportunity to weigh in on any legislation and any policy change. So, I think that that's a very, very important piece of legislation. Also, I think it's the duty of all the tribes in the United States to actively engage and actively participate in that process. And I think President Obama has taken that responsibility very seriously as well.

**JKK:** And shifting too from the U.S. national front regarding policy, if we could come back around and talk about the way that the Mohegan Tribe governs itself as a sovereign. You were a tribal chairwoman before being installed as traditional chief. Could you explain how your position interfaces with the council of elders and the tribal council, and the distinction of being a tribal chair and being a tribal chief?

**LM:** Oh, certainly. Being the tribal chair is a fascinating position, and it's one that I enjoyed because you really set policy for the tribal government. You are on the board of directors for the business and you interact with the local and state government, again, in a government-to-government manner. And so it's a great position, it's endlessly fascinating, every day is different, and I think it's something that is a real honor to be elected. And you are elected to that position by your membership, and the tribe has a government that is a representative form of government.

So the nine people on the tribal council, that's their job—to represent their people and to make decisions based on their constituents. And so you serve at the will of the people, and they are very, very comfortable about approaching you if they think that you are doing the right thing or the wrong thing, which is important. I think it's important to get that very up-close-and-personal feedback, and, being a small tribe, you always know exactly where you stand with the membership. I think that that's the way your tribal members exert their will on you. And that's one of the criteria for the Bureau of Indian Affairs, that the leaders exert influence on the membership and the membership also has reciprocal influence on the leaders.

And so, that's a very hands-on, operationally driven position. The council of elders is responsible for all things cultural, including NAGPRA and our cultural department and our annual wigwam, as well as the Constitution. And so they are the constitutional review board, and they are the ones that would submit any proposed constitutional changes to the membership for a vote. The chief, I believe—and again, because it's a new day and we haven't had a chief in three years—I think that the chief's role is more advisory. I think the chief's role is to have the longer look, because it is a lifetime position. I think it's to collaborate with both elected bodies, and I think that it's to reflect the wishes and the desires and the concerns of the membership to both elected bodies, as well.

And so, one of the things that I've been doing is holding talking circles with the membership to understand what their concerns are, and I've held those at the church, because again our church is very important to us, it's where all of our tribal community activities happened. So while it was a house of worship, it also was our social center and our political center. And so in keeping with my ancestors, I've held those meetings at the church. I meet with elders regularly, I meet with the tribal council regularly, as well as informally meet with some of the people who are my elders, who have been leaders during my lifetime.

**JKK:** I see. And does that mean too that the role of chief is also to play a diplomatic role outside of the tribe, or is that left to the tribal chairperson?

**LM:** I think that that can be a shared thing. I'm not sure that we've kind of worked through those things in terms of how that might happen. One of the things that I'm very proud about is the fact that in Indian Country I do represent the eastern tribes at a couple of national level meetings. I am on the Tribal Self-Governance Advisory Council for Indian Health Services, so we meet directly with the director of Indian Health Services, and that's kind of a nod to my health-care background. I also was appointed to the Tribal Nations' Leadership Council for the Department of Justice to advise U.S. Attorney General Holder on issues related to tribes and the Department of Justice.

**JKK:** I see, so when you spoke about Obama really stepping up, you have inside experience in seeing that in operation.

**LM:** Absolutely. I'm thrilled that he's convened tribal leaders now twice, and he has a follow-up meeting coming up soon. I think that that's very important— so he had a town-hall-style meeting with tribal leaders, he followed that up this year and then had a smaller meeting with the twelve regions of the United States represented. And I think that's a really important step for President Obama.

**JKK:** Well, thank you for explaining that too. I want to ask you, what is the population of the tribe? You mentioned being a small tribe and also having that face-to-face relationship with the people and the governing leaders.

**LM:** Right. We have—and the number changes—approximately eighteen hundred tribal members, and of that, perhaps 60 percent are voting members because they're over the age of eighteen. We have a very strong population here in Connecticut, obviously. We have a very strong population within ten to twenty miles of the reservation, but there are tribal members that live in every town in Connecticut. We also have tribal members who live throughout the United States—I believe in all states except for seven, the last time I looked at that. And so, that's a little more of a challenge to do the outreach to those members to make sure that they remain in touch with the tribe and that they know what the issues of the tribe are, but families are good at providing outreach to those members and making sure that they stay informed of all things Mohegan. I think that that's a real strength for our tribal families, that they will always do that outreach and make sure that if there are issues of importance that people are educated about that.

**JKK:** Incredible. Well, in conclusion, I'd like to invite you to leave with any parting thoughts that we might consider.

**LM:** In conclusion, I'd like people to understand that each tribe has a very unique history. It's one that they're very proud of, and while each tribe has experienced many losses, what most tribes are most proud of is that we have survived regardless of all of the challenges that have been placed in our way. And because we were able to survive we have thrived, and we continue to pass on that very rich legacy to each generation. And that's something that we will never lose, and it's something that each tribe is very diligent about passing on— our knowledge, our history—and linking that next generation to the ancestors that came before them.

# AILEEN MORETON-ROBINSON ON WHITENESS AND INDIGENEITY IN AUSTRALIA

Aileen Moreton-Robinson (Quandamooka), professor of Indigenous studies at Queensland University of Technology, is a Geonpul woman from Minjerribah (North Stradbroke Island), Quandamooka First Nation (Moreton Bay), in Queensland, Australia. She has advocated for Indigenous rights at local, state, national, and international levels and has worked for a number of Indigenous organizations. Her scholarly work theorizes settler colonialism and white possession in Australia. She is the author of two monographs, *The White Possessive: Property, Power, and Indigenous Sovereignty* (2015) and *Talkin' Up to the White Woman: Aboriginal Women and Feminism* (1999), and the coeditor of *Critical Indigenous Studies: Engagements in First World Locations* (2016), *Sovereign Subjects: Indigenous Sovereignty Matters* (2007), and *Whitening Race: Essays in Social and Cultural Criticism* (2004). During our interview we discussed contemporary Indigenous politics in Australia, especially in light of Prime Minister Kevin Rudd's apology to Australia's Indigenous peoples and the Australian government's military invasion of the Northern Territory in the name of "protecting" Aboriginal children. The interview was done live in studio at WESU during a visit to Wesleyan University that I organized for her to deliver a public lecture. Although the interview seems to close abruptly, that is far from the case. Interspersed throughout our conversation we were treated to select tracks from her son Adam James's CD that had just been released, *The Country Singer*—and so the episode closed out with Moreton-Robinson introducing one last song, which was about her grandmother.

This interview took place on April 15, 2008.

**J. Kēhaulani Kauanui:** It's wonderful to have you right here in the studio all the way from Australia. I want to start off by asking you to please tell our listeners more about your background.

**Aileen Moreton-Robinson:** Thank you, Kēhaulani. It is indeed a pleasure and a privilege to be here. I'm a Goenpul woman from First Nation people of Quanda-mooka, and for anybody that's been to Brisbane, you actually fly over Moreton Bay as you touch down at the airport. I grew up on Minjerribah [North Strad-broke Island], and that's where basically most of my family lives. We're salt-water people, and we are in the throes of our native title claim at the moment. I'm involved in that at the community level and in terms of my, I suppose, aca-demic trajectory, I came to the academy as a mature-aged student, and I really arrived I guess at the academy with a political activist background. And it was during my time on the ground, in terms of demonstrations and protesting and also doing all the other stuff like the press releases, analyzing legislation, et cetera, et cetera, that I recognized that whatever it was that we did, we always seem to be outmaneuvered by white bureaucrats and lawyers and the govern-ment. And so I began to think about what was it that I really didn't understand, and so that led me to realize that the particular knowledges that I had about white people were based in the experiences that were grounded in the unequal power relations that existed within our communities, but it seemed obvious that experiential knowledge was not sufficient, because I didn't really under-stand how their epistemologies had developed and how their knowledge is produced and how knowledge actually filters out into society. And so I felt that I needed to equip myself with knowledge from the academy in the hope that that would actually assist me to be far more politically effective.

**JKK:** Well, this really sets you apart from so many Indigenous scholars who are more concerned with the study of indigeneity, so I hear you talking about your own training in the study of whiteness as a way to sort of deconstruct the logics of settler colonialism.

**AMR:** Yes, I basically decided that I really needed to understand theory. So in my first year I was offered honors in three disciplines—archaeology, anthropology, and sociology—and I accepted two. I started on a trajectory in anthropology and sociology accepting that most of my coursework would be learning the epistemology of both disciplines. So my training, my grounding has been in theory. However, in my third year I ended up pulling out of anthropology for a number of reasons, basically because I already knew who I was, I didn't really need anthropology to tell me who I was, but I wanted to know about the theory that informed the kind of ethnographies that had been produced about Aborig-inal people and to gain an understanding of the genealogy of that knowledge production. So I was really interested in how anthropology came to be and I was interested in how theories were developed and then applied in the field, and so it was good training, really good training. On the other hand, sociolo-gy for me was really liberating, because in Australia in particular we have this split between sociology and anthropology. Sociology does not concern itself primarily with the study of Aborigines, while anthropology does. Sociology is concerned with the "mainstream." So for me I really love sociology, because I learned about the development of capitalism. I was able to understand more about how imperialism and colonialism functioned, and I was able to gain greater insights into how whiteness operates.

**JKK:** Excellent. Now, from there, what was your entrée into a critical examination of feminism?

**AMR:** I didn't study feminism as an undergrad. What happened was I was awarded First Class Honours at the Australian National University in sociology and then I won, I think I may have been the first Indigenous person to win, an Australian postgraduate scholarship to enroll in a PhD. I started actually looking at citizenship and particularly the formation of citizenship in Australia and Indigenous peoples' status as citizens. And, of course, as life always intervenes, we decided that we would buy a house, so this scholarship wasn't enough to support the mortgage, so I basically had to seek work, but I completed six months of that PhD, but, you know, it was a fantastic time because I learned a lot of theory about the development of citizenship in the West, and I think I was one of the first Indigenous people within the academy to recognize that the 1967 referendum, which is when Australia likes to tell the rest of world it gave Aboriginal people citizenship rights, was actually a whole heap of crap. The referendum that occurred in 1967 only changed one clause in our Constitution and it actually deleted the other, and the one that was deleted was a clause that said we were not to be counted in the census, and the other clause that was changed was that the federal government was now able to make laws on behalf of any race.

**JKK:** Right.

**AMR:** So that was not about Aborigines per se.

**JKK:** And that's not enfranchisement either.

**AMR:** No. Those things had happened incrementally over time, voting rights in the sixties and award wages in the sixties. So the remainder, I guess, of the rights that we gained, the citizenship rights that we gained, occurred through the revoking of discriminatory legislation.

**JKK:** So taking down in a piecemeal fashion things that were in place around legal discrimination?

**AMR:** Yes.

**JKK:** I see. I want to ask you what led to the founding of the Australian Critical Race and Whiteness Studies Association, and how did that emerge from the ongoing work that you have been producing?

**AMR:** My book was probably the first book that was produced on whiteness.

And I hadn't even, you know, read the American literature, this was my theory on whiteness that I was developing. I supposed what has always driven me is Indigenous sovereignty and of course that is just totally lacking in any analysis about Aborigines within anthropology. As you know, they don't make the connection about land tenure in terms of sovereignty. This is just, you know, Indigenous land-tenure systems. So Indigenous sovereignty has always driven me. What I did was come to the American whiteness literature after doing the *Talkin' Up to the White Woman,* and that started me thinking about ways in which I could utilize some of the theory, but I also knew that wasn't sufficient in terms of the whiteness literature in the United States, basically because Indigenous sovereignty and Indigenous people are fundamentally invisible.

**JKK:** Yes.

**AMR:** And so there was a flaw there, but my theorizing is informing the way in which I perceive collective action, so I also knew that in order to be able to create a field of study, you know, to create critical race and whiteness studies as a field of study, I really needed to attract like-minded people to me. So what I did was I actually applied for and received money to hold a number of conferences, and out of those conferences we formed the association. And I knew that part of developing a field meant you had to have publication tied to it, so we had to set up a journal, and a website was really important in terms of allowing for accessibility and also creating membership of the association. And so the whole purpose of it was to construct, to start to build this emerging field and to make Indigenous sovereignty the center of that, so whiteness studies in Australia starts from the epistemological premise of Indigenous sovereignty.

**JKK:** Yes. And on Indigenous sovereignty I want to ask you about your last edited book, *Sovereign Subjects.* This is a first in many ways, and I wonder if you could tell our listeners about this cutting-edge volume and what the state of scholarship on Indigenous sovereignty in Australia looks like.

**AMR:** The book on Indigenous sovereignty came out of a symposium of Indigenous scholars, because what I wanted was to break people out of the discourse of rights, which is very much shaped by the social contract, and also I wanted people to understand that Indigenous sovereignty is not necessarily configured through the discourse of rights that has been the main way of talking about it. And by that I mean it's really the legal, you know, the political and legal framework that has shaped the way in which sovereignty is theorized about within the academy; it is not the same way that we as Indigenous people construct our sovereignty. So I decided that I wanted to actually bring together a number of Indigenous scholars who in their respective ways would write about sovereignty. The book covers things like Indigenous sovereignty and the writing of history, Indigenous sovereignty and Indigenous literature, Indigenous sovereignty and biodiversity, Indigenous sovereignty and welfare reform. So it really was about trying to break open what Foucault would call it the judicio-politico framework in order to demonstrate that it's really the way in which the sovereignty of the state shapes the way in which we talk about Aboriginal sovereignty. So I wanted to kind of open up these various ways. And the book isn't about defining what Indigenous sovereignty is, although it discursively does that, but it was more about like saying there is this scholarship here, there are different ways we can talk about sovereignty, and that the academy needs to take note of this intellectual rigor.

**JKK:** And as I understand it, it's the first book on Aboriginal sovereignty edited by an Indigenous editor?

**AMR:** Yes it is, and I'm very proud of that. And certainly I think that we who have tenure within the academy have a responsibility to use our positions to provide access to publication for our people, and that, you know, was one of the things that I decided to do: I had to get a book contract to get this work out there into mainstream.

**JKK:** And all of the contributors are also Indigenous scholars who have made those contributions. I want to ask you about the book that you're completing now, your sole-authored book on white possession. Can you briefly tell us what it covers in scope and what brought you to this new project?

**AMR:** I been theorizing about white possession for about the last seven years and trying to move my idea of how that's constituted in various ways, so, you know, I've been analyzing the law in terms of what I call the possessive logic of patriarchal white sovereignty and looking at how that shaped decision making in the *Wik Peoples v. Queensland* case, which is the second major case after *Mabo* [*v. Queensland*] in terms of native title. And I'm also looking at it in terms of the construction of national identity, various literatures, so trying to move and push myself to develop a theory which I think I've probably cracked. So that kind of happened in December last year, but it was part of a broader project tied to what I was doing in my postdoctoral work. In my postdoctoral work I really wanted to ask questions of Indigenous people tied to what they thought about white people. So I conducted interviews across three generations—my mom's generation, so those born in the thirties and forties; my own generation, born in the fifties and sixties; and then my children's generation, seventies and eighties—because I wanted to kind of look at how whiteness traveled across those generations. Because you really have three different kinds of generations, like during the thirties and forties, the people whose lives were still fundamentally regulated on a day-to-day basis. And, you know, you had acts which stipulated where you can go, whom you can marry, what you can wear, what you can eat. And then to move into my generation, which is kind of like after the First World War, Second World War, where the discriminatory legislation is still there but you're finding the effects of the Second World War impacting on, you know, globally in terms of races and you have human rights coming out and so, you know, it's a time of shift which we see emerging in the sixties and then ultimately the discourse of rights arriving in the seventies—including gay rights, women's rights, and other civil rights. And so, I wanted to see how whiteness traveled across time and, you know, I also wanted to explain how racism works.

**JKK:** How it functions on an everyday level?

**AMR:** How it functions on an everyday level. What Indigenous people were talking about in terms of white people was their possessiveness. But they didn't say they were possessive in an explicit way. It was the way in which they would say things like, Well, you go into a store and they just look at you as if you've got no right to be in the space. It's like when you move into a room and everybody looks at you and then the room gets loud because there's basically all white people in it and you're just left there, standing usually on your own until some, you know, nice liberal white person comes up to talk to you and then they end up telling you about themselves. So I really started to realize that there was this discourse of possessiveness that was really rich, and so I kind of thought, well, this is, this is kind of like what my people are saying. So how is it that I theorize it? Right? That, of course, is the hard part. And like I said, I had been writing about it for some time, but I really didn't pull it together until December. And what I am really arguing is that Indigenous sovereignty is in a different relationship to the state as opposed to the way in which citizens have a relationship to the state. And that the relationship between citizens and the state is through the racial contract, right, but Indigenous sovereignty is different from that. And what Indigenous people confront is this possessiveness in the everyday. And I'm also arguing that through citizenship, the subjectivity of white people is, at an ontological and epistemological level, possessive. And it emerged historically as an integral part of the new subject, I mean, well, I don't want to bog this interview down with too much gobbledygook, but yes. So it's really a book, I think, that will offer an Indigenous theory of the way in which we experience racism and I think, you know, from the various papers that I've given it resonates with people's everyday experiences. And, you know, at a very fundamental level it just makes sense because everything Indigenous that you try to do, you know, in terms of government or just your neighbors, really involves this tension around Indigenous sovereignty and white possession because the very presence of Indigenous people, I would argue, ontologically disturbs white people because of that history and because of that unfinished business. I mean, you have treaties over here but I would still say there's a lot of unfinished business.

**JKK:** That's right.

**AMR:** And I think that the way in which it is always a fight to get anything Indigenous up, you know, whether it's in the academy, whether it's trying to set up an Indigenous organization within a town, whether it's about trying to get an Indigenous program running, you know, it's always contested.

**JKK:** Yes.

**AMR:** Right, that's the premise from where we start. It's not about, "Oh yes, we love Indigenous people. You are all very welcome into the space, and we are sharing, caring people." No, that's not what happens. It's about, well, you know, "You want to make this claim? Justify it, substantiate it. Why do you wanna be here? Why do you want these resources?" Et cetera.

**JKK:** Now, segueing in talking about some of the current issues going on in Australia right now, I mean one of the things making headlines in this country recently, was the Australian government's apology to Aboriginal people, which I'll ask you about shortly, but first I want to actually go back to something you referenced a little earlier. I want to ask you about the *Mabo* land rights case decided in 1992. For our listeners, I want to let you know this was a dispute between the Meriam people of the Murray Islands in the Torres Strait and the government of Queensland in which several Meriam people, principally Eddie Mabo, contested that they have certain native title rights over the Murray Islands and that the Queensland Coast Islands Declaratory Act of 1985 was intended to retrospectively abolish their native title rights if they existed. Many scholars of Indigenous sovereignty around the globe talk about the *Mabo* decision as a landmark case that recognized native title to the lands in Australia, but your work has shown that there's more to it than that.

**AMR:** The *Mabo* decision is actually a landmark case in the sense that basically never before had the courts ever acknowledged that Indigenous people had proprietary rights. Australia did not have a treaty: the British landed with the military, and no treaties were ever developed. And so *terra nullius* was the concept or legal fiction that prevailed and, I would argue, still prevails.

**JKK:** And I want to make sure that listeners unfamiliar with this concept understand *terra nullius*. Would you mind talking a little but about Captain Cook in terms of that declaration?

**AMR:** *Terra nullius* was one of the forms under which land could be taken in international law like it's conquered, ceded, and *terra nullius,* which meant land belonging to no one, uninhabited land. Right? And we have Captain James Cook to thank for that. And so Captain Cook basically, despite the fact that he does see Indigenous people and, you know, he sees that they've got places to live, that they're hunting and gathering. He basically said that they lived in a state of nature and because they lived in a state of nature, and weren't up for trading, that they were, they had no sense of property. And so he deemed that the land was uninhabited despite the instructions to the contrary both from the admiral and the Royal Society in England, which said he was to take possession of Australia with the consent of the Natives. And it prevails through the *Mabo* decision because the *Mabo* decision did not overturn *terra nullius;* what the *Mabo* decision did was diminish *terra nullius* by recognizing native title rights, but it did so in a way in which it created what I call a hybrid of settlement in that it also acknowledged that the validity, the legitimacy of the state was still intact. Right? So it didn't overturn *terra nullius* and say, "Look, we should start again, we need treaties." Instead, what it said was, "Yes, okay, native title was here. It was incremental, it still exists on vacant ground land and leases, and Indigenous people can claim that land on the basis of the proprietary rights." And so that was a watershed, because it recognized that we had some form of proprietary rights. But after the *Mabo* decision, there was considerable back-lash in the white community, as would be expected, you know, all the usual drama about "Aborigines are going to be taking over your backyards," and this again goes to my theory of white possession in the way in which that had to be constantly asserted in the press that this is a white country, we own it, and we're actually giving Aborigines something special.

**JKK:** That's what's going on here in Connecticut as well.

**AMR:** Yes. And so what happened after the *Mabo* decision was that the Commonwealth government created native title legislation, and within that native title legislation it basically put in the criteria for registering claims. But the native title legislation that came in was negotiated on the basis that Aboriginal people also had to legitimate everything, all legislation and all law that existed prior to 1975, which was when the racial discrimination act came in. And the swap for that was that Indigenous people would have the right to negotiate as part of the package of rights. Now, I really want to point out to your listeners, this bunch of rights is really about the right to hunt and gather; there is no right to residence that's explicit as part of the Native Title Act. You do have to ask yourself, well if the legislation says that it's based on the traditional law and custom of the people, but there's no right of residence, where were they? You know? It's just so totally illogical that a right of residence is not part of it, but it's also indicative of how *terra nullius* is still working discursively within that legislation.

**JKK:** Now, I want to ask you about something that's happened more recently. In June 2007, just to let our listeners know, under the guise of protecting Indigenous children from sexual abuse, the Howard government of Australia declared a so-called national emergency plan to have the military and police take control of dozens of Aboriginal communities throughout the Northern Territory. Recall that I was with you in Brisbane when this action took place and I know that he imposed martial law. I remember that he called on military troops and police to invade over sixty towns and camps . . .

**AMR:** Yes, seventy-three towns and camps.

**JKK:** And he was enforcing a series of draconian measures. Can you please explain more about what went down and where things stand now?

**AMR:** Well, from where I sat basically we were in election mode as well, and one of the key ways in which Howard got elected the first time, or to the term previous to the one that he was running for, was on the basis of the *Tampa* incident in Australia, so the race card very much played a role in Howard's election. And that was also demonstrated by the polls that were taken at the time. The *Tampa* incident was about refugees being on a Norwegian ship and the Australian government refusing to let the ship dock and refusing to accept the refugees into Australia. And what happened was that the refugees had been picked up by the *Tampa*, which was a Norwegian vessel, because it was sinking, and the Australian military were there and they took photos of children in the water. And Howard played the race card: what he did was put the photos up, the press did a wonderful job of doing his bidding, and they were arguing that people were trying to kill their own children by throwing them overboard when in actual fact what was happening was the boat was sinking, so parents were wanting to get their children off and then jumping in the water to, you know, stop them from drowning and to hold them up. But it got played out that these people were even trying to drown their own children, and the Australian public, of course, didn't want those kinds of people in Australia and so after the incident he was, he leapt ahead in the polls. And I think the same could be said for the Northern Territory Intervention, that he attempted to play the race card again in order to get votes, except this time I think it did backfire—although how much the Northern Territory Intervention played in the change of government in Australia has yet to be analyzed. I'd say it did play a part, but I wouldn't say it was actually the catalyst for the change of government, you know. And the Northern Territory Intervention came out of supposedly a report regarding sexual abuse within Indigenous communities, but the report itself did not make the recommendations, which the Howard government ran with in terms of policy. So, for example, as part of this military intervention, they decided there would be health checks for all Indigenous children in seventy-three communities where Indigenous people held title to land, and there was a permanent system that would exclude access by outsiders that was to be revoked. That there would be a ban on alcohol and pornography, and the ban on pornography meant that all community organization computers would be fitted out with a blocking mechanism prohibiting access to pornography.

They also decided that there should be a change of land tenure. Now, in the Northern Territory, Indigenous people who hold land tenure there hold inalienable freehold title, which means it can't be bought or sold. So he advocated that there be a change in land tenure to ninety-nine-year leases and that some of that land would be turned into vacant ground land so that Indigenous people could buy their own homes. Howard also decided to shut down the Community Development Employment Program, which is basically the main labor market, if we can call it that, for Indigenous communities, given that there's roughly 26 percent of the population on Community Development Employment Programs, which are basically work for unemployment benefit schemes, and there's about 32 percent unemployed aside from that. So if you start adding the 26 to the 32, you know, that's what—about 58 percent of Indigenous people—close to 60 percent of Indigenous people are unemployed in our country.

And the other part of it was to quarantine welfare payments so that monies for food, electricity, and clothing would be taken out of those welfare payments. Now, since the new government has come to power, the Labor Party, they have decided that the permit system can stay and that the Community Development Employment Program can stay, but they are still pushing ahead with the other reforms.

August last year was when the actual intervention on the ground happened, and we're yet to have a report on all this sexual abuse that's occurring in our communities. Instead, what's become quite obvious is that the communities are totally under-resourced and the poverty is not because Indigenous people are, you know, these dysfunctional beings; it's because there are just not the resources there to provide for adequate health care, education, food—you know, in some communities you can pay up to twelve dollars for a lettuce.

**JKK:** We'll keep our attention on that issue here from this part of the world. Now, as we're wrapping up the interview, I want to be sure to ask you about this recent apology. The *New York Times* reported that the new Australian government of Prime Minister Kevin Rudd apologized for past mistreatment of Aboriginal peoples, specifically those who make up the "stolen generations." As background for our audience, I want to note that a 1997 report estimated that the Australian government took between one in ten and one in three Aboriginal children from their homes and families throughout the twentieth century before the policy was formally abandoned in '69. Can you please tell us about the politics of this apology?

**AMR:** What happened was we had a Royal Commission into Aboriginal Deaths in Custody in the early nineties after numerous Indigenous people died in custody. And one of the findings of the report of the Royal Commission was that there needed to be reconciliation between Indigenous people and non-Indigenous people in Australia. So the Commonwealth government, which was the Labor government at the time, set up a reconciliation committee. And the committee's brief was to try and set out the terms for reconciliation, formal terms of reconciliation, between Indigenous people and non-Indigenous people in Australia. At the same time, there was advocacy by Indigenous people, and this is in the eighties, for an investigation into the Stolen Generations. And so a commission of inquiry was set up, headed up by Sir Ronald Wilson, a human rights advocate, and Mick Dodson, an Indigenous barrister, and Jackie Huggins, an Indigenous historian—they were the main movers and shakers on the inquiry. And they basically interviewed people who had been taken from their families and put in institutions during the twentieth century. The report that came out of their findings, which was called *Bringing Them Home*, recommended that there should be a national apology to Indigenous people and the reconciliation council called a big *corroboree* in 2001 to put on the table its findings about reconciliation, of which one was a national apology to the Stolen Generations.

John Howard refused to apologize and played it out in public, stating, "We can't apologize, because that would set us up for litigation." And he said, "I have deep personal regret about what happened, but we can't formally apologize." However, as there were Labor governments at the state level, quite a number of state governments ran with it and did apologize in the Parliament to Indigenous people. And one of the first things that Rudd said that he would do if he won the election last year was that he would formally apologize, and he did do that and he invited basically all the prime ministers, ex-prime ministers that are still alive, including John Howard, to attend, and all attended except for John Howard. He still refused to endorse it, and it was a momentous occasion for people of the "stolen generations" in Australia. Very moving. I mean, John Howard may not have been there—and basically that sent a clear message to everyone that this was something very personal to him—it wasn't just about his party politics and that he was driving that. But, Kevin Rudd basically made sure that the apology was screened on television, that radio shows would pick it up. And it was an amazing day for people of the "stolen generations" and for Indigenous people in general, because it was also the first time in our history that the federal Parliament was actually opened with a "welcome to country" ceremony by the traditional owners in Canberra. So on a number of levels, it really touched hearts and minds, I think, of a lot of Indigenous people who felt that in receiving the apology they could move on with their life's journey. And I totally endorsed it and agreed with it, but for me the main concern was that these people should also be compensated for the abuse that they suffered in these institutions and the trauma that they'd carried through their lives. And at first the idea of compensation was rejected, but I've seen in the last two weeks Rudd moved to give the terms to the parliamentary standing committee and the attorney general's department to develop the terms of reference and investigate the possibilities of compensation for the Stolen Generations.

# STEVEN NEWCOMB ON DECODING THE CHRISTIAN DOCTRINE OF DISCOVERY

Steven Newcomb (Shawnee/Lenape), one of the foremost legal scholars on Indigenous issues, is the Indigenous law research coordinator at the Sycuan education department of the Sycuan band of the Kumeyaay Nation in San Diego County, California. He is the author of *Pagans in the Promised Land: Decoding the Doctrine of Christian Discovery* (2008), which provides a provocative challenge to current U.S. federal Indian law and policy. His book draws upon major findings in the theory of the human mind (cognitive theory) as a framework for challenging the presumption that the United States has a legitimate claim to "plenary power" over originally free and independent Native nations. Newcomb argues that U.S. federal Indian law and policy are premised on Old Testament narratives of the Chosen People and the Promised Land, as exemplified in the 1823 U.S. Supreme Court ruling, in *Johnson v. M'Intosh,* that the first "Christian people" to "discover" lands inhabited by "natives, who were heathens," have an ultimate title to dominion over these lands and peoples. Newcomb is the cofounder and codirector of the Indigenous Law Institute, a fellow with the American Indian Policy and Media Initiative at Buffalo State College and a columnist for *Indian Country Today*. In 2014 he coproduced a documentary based on *Pagans in the Promised Land*, titled *The Doctrine of Discovery: Unmasking the Domination Code*, directed by Dakota filmmaker Sheldon Peters Wolfchild.

This interview took place on March 25, 2008.

**J. Kēhaulani Kauanui:** It's wonderful to be able to connect with you about your new book, *Pagans in the Promised Land*. I want to start by acknowledging your incredible intellectual labor here. I found this book very difficult to put down once I started reading it. I pretty much was racing through it. I found it to be a very compelling and persuasive argument that you have, as well as a deeply decolonizing text.

**Steven Newcomb:** Well, thank you very much. It was a long time in coming to fruition, that's for sure.

**JKK:** This book successfully examines the inner workings of the dominant society's collective mind to understand the conceptions the U.S. government has used against Native peoples in the past and currently in the present. You use major findings in the theory of the human mind, also known as cognitive theory, as a framework for challenging the presumption that the United States has any legitimate claim in asserting its power over originally free and independent Native nations. Can you please explain for a general audience what cognitive theory is and how you use it as a tool to explain the dominant cultural assumptions most Americans hold in relation to Native Americans?

**SN:** Well, succinctly put, as you've stated, cognitive theory is the scientific investigation of the human mind through the study of human conceptual systems, the systems of ideas. And one of the findings of that field of research is that some 95 percent of our consciousness is on the unconscious level; we just use all kinds of tasks or underlying patterns in our thinking without being conscious of what we're doing in the process of thinking, reasoning. And so the cognitive science and cognitive theory field of research is an effort to bring that unconscious up to the surface, up to the level of consciousness so we can be aware of the structures of our thought patterns and so forth. And some of those structures of our thought—and by the way, one of the findings of this field also says that all human thought is imaginative—but some of the key findings of that research is that our thought is structured in terms of such phenomena as conceptual metaphors, idealized cognitive models, image schemas, and different terms like that, but basically it's saying that our thinking occurs on the basis of the structure, function, activities, and orientation of the human body. So thinking or thought is embodied, so some of the researchers have referred to it as the "embodied mind." And so in using that particular framework to look at federal Indian law, for example, I was able to begin to see, or maybe put terminology to, many of the patterns I had already been noticing in my research for a couple of decades. And I had been compiling a lot of that, but I didn't have the theoretical framework that would enable me to express it clearly in the way that I have in the book. So that took some time to master that particular theoretical framework. But, for example, in federal Indian law, there's a particular metaphor that's very important, and that is "Having Control Is Up." And so the United States is always conceptualized as being "up" in comparison to Indian nations. And the Indian nations are considered to be "down," because they're considered to be subject to the control of the United States. So that's the up/down, what they call a schema. But it's really talking about how our human body is oriented—when we're standing we're most in control of our situation, when we're sitting down we're less in control, and when we're lying down we're least in control of . . . whatever particular situation we're in. So we reason in terms of these types of structures is the point. And so federal Indian law, one of the baselines of it, is that the United States is always conceptualized by U.S.

government officials as being in the position of supremacy *over* originally free and independent Indian nations.

**JKK:** So up and over, so to speak.

**SN:** Yes, well, up/down, over/under, above/below, that sort of thing. And so, the sovereignty that is considered—that the United States is considered to have is a capital "S" and then the sovereignty that Indian nations are considered to have, from the point of view of the United States . . . a lowercase "s," for example. So you have the status of the United States being regarded as much higher than the Indian nations'.

**JKK:** You're getting into these really deep sort of infrastructural schemas that can help us unlock this dominant paradigm that hasn't even been properly diagnosed up until now.

**SN:** Well, I think that's a very good point, and the dominant paradigm—I explain that pretty clearly in terms of a Latin verb that's not very well known at all even by Latin scholars. I brought this particular verb to the attention of a Latin professor at the University of Oregon years ago when I first found it, he claimed that it never, didn't even exist, which I thought was odd because I had just looked it up in the Latin-English dictionary. But the verb is *domo*, and there are seven basic meanings to that word: to subjugate, which means to put under a yoke; to subdue, which means to put under an obligation of paying obedience and tribute to a lord or to a superior; to put into subservience—and by the way, the prefix "sub" is always "under" and then you have your other words—so subservience is under the obligation of serving a superior or lord; to tame, which is to break the spirit of; to domesticate, which is to place into the domestic realm of the lord; and to cultivate and till—so those are the essential meanings of, particular meanings of *domo*. And then "cultivate" is related to *colere* in Latin, which is the word for "to colonize." *Colere* means "to colonize" and "to design," so that's also the meaning of cultivation. And then you have "to till," which in the book I explain, within the framework of the history, it means to overturn the existing original order of the Indigenous nations and to replace that with a colonizing occupying force or power.

**JKK:** And that really is the dominant modality of settler colonialism.

**SN:** Right, exactly.

**JKK:** Because it's always already about replacing Indigenous peoples.

**SN:** Right, and then *domo* is related to *dominate,* which means "he who subdues" in Sanskrit, and that is the origin of the term in Latin *dominus*: he who subdues, and *domanus*: he who has subdued. Well he who subdues, is, by his very nature, a conqueror; he subdues, it is some generic conqueror. So you look at the different conquerors in history and they follow those patterns, but my point being these are embedded patterns within the English language and are used, unconsciously, for the purposes of the domination framework and thus the term "dominant society."

**JKK:** Dominant society and he who asserts dominion over?

**SN:** Right, exactly. So really "dominion" is a euphemism, a more positive-sounding term for domination that goes back to *domo* and *dominus* and *domanus* and *dominate* and all those terms. And that's related to Genesis 1:28 of the Old Testament, because there you have the admonition to "man" to "go forth and subdue the Earth and exercise dominion over all living things." And so, within the Hebrew terminology, that term in Hebrew for "subdue" is a militaristic term, which in the worst-case scenario means "to rape." It's not a term of stewardship at all, and it's a very negative term. And then, "dominion" is a term in the Hebrew, which means to put your foot on the neck of the one who's been conquered and to step up on like a stool and that sort of conception. So when you have that being the, considered to be the sort of the first commandment of that Old Testament framework, it says something, you know: how you conceive of something predetermines in large part how you will behave toward that thing. So if you conceive of the Earth as being some kind of an inanimate substance or object that you have the right to subdue and exercise domination over, that will predetermine how you behave toward that. You don't understand it as a living being, an existing ecosystem with intricate types of inner-relationships between all forms of life but something that you have the capacity and the means and permission to conquer and subdue.

**JKK:** It's also deeply patriarchal, isn't it?

**SN:** Oh, very much so. And so the sense of paternalistic, of strict father model that goes back to that Old Testament deity within the Western framework. But you see that also in the Roman tradition, I mean it's not necessarily just the Old Testament. But it's very much patriarchal, yes. So therefore, very much subjugating of women and so forth.

**JKK:** Now getting at some of the Christian underpinnings of U.S. federal law and policy, please tell us about the provocative title of your book, *Pagans in the Promised Land: Decoding the Doctrine of Christian Discovery.* Can you explain this in lay terms? I'd like to know how that informs the status quo today in terms of the U.S. government's position that Native nations are subordinate in status in relation to the federal government.

**SN:** The title really comes out of the 1823, or my reading of, the 1823 Supreme Court ruling *Johnson v. M'Intosh*, which was a property law case that really had nothing to do with Indians but it did have to do with—nothing to do with Indians as far as *parties* to the particular legal case—but it had to do with a competition between, or supposed competition, I should say, because it was a faked case, as we have subsequently found out. But on its face it was a dispute between two different claimants, one the group that had received land directly or a land title directly from an Indian nation, and the other one that had received the title to the same lands from the United States. And so the competition for the Court was which of these two parties had the superior title from the point of view of the United States court system. And so the Supreme Court found on behalf of the people, the person rather, William M'Intosh, who had received the title from the United States government.

In the course of handing down this decision, of writing the decision, Chief Justice John Marshall looked back to the colonial charters of England and made a very specific distinction—categorical distinction—between Christian people, as this is the terminology found in most old English charters, and Natives, who are heathens, in Marshall's terminology. And so, for example, the John Cabot Charter gave the Cabots permission to seek out, discover, and find whatsoever isles, countries, regions of the heathen and infidel, which before this time had been unknown to all Christian people. And Marshall took that type of language and extrapolated from that and used that within the *Johnson* ruling. And he actually put italics on the words "Christian people," which I thought was very odd. But when I tried to ask the law professor that I had taken federal Indian law from about this he just thought it was customary . . . and dismissed it, more or less. But what it showed me was that there was this connection. As soon as you start using the term "Christian," then you're connected to the whole Christian framework, the religious framework of Christianity and, of course, the Bible that is the source of that particular religious tradition. So then you have to go back to the Old Testament, which is the start of that story. And then you look at that, that Old Testament story of the Chosen People in the Promised Land and so the story of Abram, who became Abraham.

And I call it a colonial adventure story in the book because it's basically this particular group of people who are taken by a deity to look at a land that they are to go and possess, but the land is already inhabited by the Indigenous peoples of that region. And so this becomes a conceptual pattern for any society that looks at that model—such as the nations or monarchies of Christendom during the so-called "Age of Discovery"—they took it upon themselves to visualize themselves as being, imagining themselves as being in that Old Testament story, and being the new Chosen People who are going to the promised lands and those promised lands were any lands in the world that had not yet been taken over, conquered, subdued, by Christian people.

**JKK:** Right.

**SN:** So that's the pattern that Marshall used in the *Johnson v. M'Intosh* ruling and in my argument in the book, I say that he thereby incorporated these Old

Testament Christian religious patterns into United States federal Indian law or U.S. law, I should say, through a Supreme Court ruling, handed down by the Supreme Court in 1823.

**JKK:** Right. Your analysis of the *Johnson* ruling really differs from the vast majority of legal scholarship on this case, because it really hasn't been critically examined in terms of the religious concepts embedded in the ruling. You're really exposing the hidden biblical background.

**SN:** I'd say that's exactly correct. The one who came closest to that would be Robert Williams in his book *The American Indian in Western Legal Thought*. But the thing is he runs right up to it, looks it right in the face, and then misidentifies it, because at the conclusion of the book he gives a quote from Joseph Story, who was sitting on the Court at the time of the *Johnson* ruling, who later wrote that as infidels, heathens, and savages "they," meaning the American Indians, were not allowed to possess the prerogatives belonging to completely sovereign, independent nations. Well, *infidels, heathens*, and *savages* are basically these—well, certainly *infidels* and *heathens* are—these religious terms that I mentioned already and within that Christian religious framework. But Williams looks at that exact quote and identifies the Doctrine of Discovery, which is really what we're talking about here, as a *secular* principle, which means non-religious principle. My scholarship doesn't lose sight of the distinction between religious and secular frameworks and the fact that the underlying pattern within the *Johnson* ruling, and consequently of all the cases that follow from that ruling within the federal Indian law system, come out of that same religious tradition of conquest and subjugation.

**JKK:** Right, and I want to make sure that our listeners know as background here that regarding the 1823 Supreme Court ruling in *Johnson v. M'Intosh*, that opinion was written by [Chief] Justice Marshall, and this is the first case . . .

**SN:** Right. And so in the second of the trilogy, the second decision of the trilogy, which was *Cherokee Nation v. Georgia*, from 1831, you have Marshall coming up with the, coining the term "domestic dependent nation." Go back to the discussion we had about *domo*, one of those [meanings] being "to tame" and the other one being "to domesticate," and so there you have the use of the framework: domestic dependent nation. And a dependency is a relationship, it's not an identity. And so you have a relationship between the United States and Indian nations, but Marshall uses that and manipulates that in such a way to make it look as if Indian nations, at some point, lost their original free and independent existence without their permission. And what's interesting about that is that that ties directly into the *Johnson* ruling, because in that ruling Marshall said their rights—meaning the Indians' rights—to complete sovereignty as independent nations were "necessarily diminished" "by the original, fundamental principle that discovery gave title to those who made" the discovery. So he's saying that the original independence of Indian nations went away or disappeared or somehow vanished into thin air simply by virtue of the fact that "Christian people" had "discovered" a place that was already well known to the people who were already living there.

**JKK:** Right, and that there's another level of perversity here, which as we know the U.S. didn't even claim to discover, so to speak. That the *Johnson v. M'Intosh* ruling, as I understand it, says that the U.S. inherited the successorship of title after the American Revolution, and inherits this from Britain, right?

**SN:** Yes, exactly. Yes, so that the successor to the state of Christendom or monarchy of Christendom that supposedly had it originally.

**JKK:** So, also, just to make sure our audience knows, the third ruling in the Marshall trilogy is *Worcester v. Georgia*. So it's these three cases that really even—there's not a Native case that goes to the Supreme Court today that doesn't rely on these three rulings.

**SN:** Those three from the early 1800s form the basic outline or framework of federal Indian law as it's understood by the United States government today. The reason why this is important . . . several reasons, and let me back up actually and mention that *Worcester* was in 1832 and that one case had to do with the dispute between Georgia and the Cherokee Nation, and actually there are aspects of it that are very, very positive and appear to completely contradict and perhaps even overturn the *Johnson* ruling. But that isn't how the United States government or the Supreme Court has interpreted it. But I think there is a lot of potential usefulness in that particular decision, when taken out of the context of the *Johnson* ruling. But in any case, those decisions are important because they actually create the framework for understanding the United States' position on the Indian title, or what they call original Indian title. And according to one assistant U.S. attorney who argued before the Supreme Court, in the case *U.S. v. Dann* in the 1980s, he said in an interview that it's simply a title to roam, a title to roam the land, not to own the land. And that it's not a fee title as we ordinarily understand fee title and the common-law understanding of title. An Aboriginal person from Australia commented on a similar attitude on the part of the government of Australia, saying that they were recognized as only having a title to wander. So a title to wander, and a title to roam. And it's only good as against any other Aboriginal or Indigenous people, but not good as against the United States. In other words, it cannot compete with the presumption of fee . . . or fee title or dominion title in the United States.

**JKK:** Because fee title is considered simple title, right? That's the strongest sort of legal case to property.

**SN:** Right, exactly . . . allodial title. Another term for it is radical fee title, meaning the rooted, the most rooted title. Now think about that, the most rooted title is, of course, the title of the existence of the particular Indian nation or Indigenous nation that's been existing in that place for thousands and thousands of years. And then you see the trickery in Marshall's use of language when he refers to the Doctrine of Discovery as the original fundamental principle. Well that's not the original, fundamental principle. It's the Indigenous peoples' existence within their own homeland for thousands and thousands of years. But this is the amazing way in which the English language is used to manipulate reality to the cognitive and social construction of meaning and reality.

**JKK:** It's a complete inversion.

**SN:** Yes.

**JKK:** It's really flipping the script. It's a colonial imposition.

**SN:** Right. And occupation, yes.

**JKK:** That also should clue us in to what happens now when people talk about the Indigenous category, not just being a cultural category, but from a U.S. perspective it's seen as a politically subordinate category in the sense that Native nations are allowed "use" rights and occupancy rights but not sovereign title over the land.

**SN:** Right. I mean it's considered . . . if you go to an Indian reservation, you'll see a sign somewhere that says you're on a federal reservation. It's considered to be federal land, so this is kind of the distortion or schizophrenia of the whole framework that the original title is not considered to be in the Indian nation itself but in the United States by virtue of the—I hate using that term "virtue" but—vis-à-vis the Doctrine of Discovery. The other thing I want to mention about the *Johnson* ruling is that a lot of people have understood it as saying, or Marshall as saying for the Supreme Court, that it was based on a conquest. And I think it's important to acknowledge that he did not say that: he laid out all of these various nuances of rules of conquest and then said that those could not be applied to Indians, so some new and different rule had to be devised. Well, if some new and different rule had been devised before the Supreme Court was writing the ruling, he would have simply gone on to explain what that rule was. But he didn't do that; instead, he said any rule which can be suggested will be met with difficulty. Well, "can be suggested" means it hasn't been yet suggested. So he was about to suggest it, and what he came up with is the pretension of converting the discovery of an inhabited country into conquest. That means pretending to convert discovery into conquest. Or as I put it, pretending that the discovery of heathen—so-called heathen—lands by Christian people results in the immediate conquest of the so-called heathens, just by mere presence of Christians as compared to so-called heathens or non-Christians. So it's a pretend conquest.

**JKK:** And that has to do with the mandates that those who are part of Christendom are citing—

**SN:** Yes.

**JKK:** —to undergird their right to dominate. Right?

**SN:** Exactly, and Christendom, d-o-m, is right back to *domo* and that whole domination framework. And freedom is a very similar kind of term. If freedom meant free, it would just say free, but it says free-dom, d-o-m. So it's referring to the baron, the *Freheit* in German. Free-dom is the baron's estate; the baron is free on the land that he has been granted by the crown within his vast estate, but the serfs or the people that have no land, that have to come to work for the baron as a workforce, are not free. So you see the bumper sticker that says, "Freedom is not free," well, within this explanation I'm providing now, it doesn't even mean "free."

**JKK:** I see.

**SN:** Which is a real twisted logic.

**JKK:** Now, how do you distinguish in the work between Christendom and Christianity, and what is the dominating mentality of Christendom that you flesh out?

**SN:** In the papal bulls from 1493, and there were several of them issued after Cristobal Colon returned to Europe, western Europe, from the Caribbean, you have a number of these Vatican papal documents that refer to the Christian empire. And they say that the king and queen of Spain are authorized to go and to subjugate barbarous nations in order to propagate the Christian religion and—or I should say to spread the Christian religion—and propagate the Christian empire, *Christiani imperii* in the Latin. And you see, later in that document, that it says "We trust in Him," with a capital "H" on "Him," "from whom empires and governments and all good things proceed." Now I mention the English version, but when you go to the Latin version and you look up the word *governments*, it says *dominationes*, dominations, so, from whom empires, dominations, and all good things proceed. So it's as if the empires and dominations are within the category all good things that proceed out of this deity: that's the domination or Christendom framework. So to the extent that the United States behaves in that tradition, in keeping with the legacy of that tradition, by dominating and dispossessing Indian nations and disregarding their treaties and interpreting their treaties within this domination paradigm that I'm mentioning, then that is distinguished from what a lot of people have as an understanding of Christianity that is a very beneficial type of religious tradition, that, you know, says "Do unto others as you'd have them do unto you" and the Golden Rule and those types of things. So, to avoid that confusion, my friend Peter d'Errico, who wrote the foreword to the book, made that distinction between people's ordinary understanding of Christianity and Christendom.

**JKK:** Right, and he talks about that as the complex between the church and the state.

**SN:** Yes, but there's no separation of church and state when you have the state using religious dogma and religious doctrine as a means of subjugation, as a means of dispossession and theft of Native lands and resources.

**JKK:** That's right. One of the other things that I found very provocative about the book is that you've argued that since the U.S. claims the right of Christian discovery, it is always already violating the presumed separation of church and state, in terms of its own U.S. Indian law and policy.

**SN:** Right, exactly. And you see that throughout the whole—if you go and look up what Indian commissioners have written back in the nineteenth century and all the way through it—you see that same kind of attitude. Not the type of Christianity that's beneficial, but the Christendom that is very destructive. That's why you have Indian languages on the verge of extinction today, because of the policies, generations of U.S. policy, to put Indian children in indoctrination centers that they call schools, to tear them away from their families and communities and traditions, their ceremonial life, and then beat them or abuse them and cases such as up in Oregon where elders told me that when they were children their tongues were put on dry ice to peel the top layer of skin off their tongue simply for speaking their own language. That kind of abuse, you know, horrible, and many other worse types of examples. So after generations of that, then all of a sudden you see, you know, fewer and fewer people passing the language on and then you get to the point where there are, you know, that languages are in danger of being lost altogether. And you don't see the United States coming forth to put as much time, effort, energy, or money into revitalizing those languages as they put into destroying them.

**JKK:** Well, and that's part of what you theorized as part of the conqueror model.

**SN:** Right.

**JKK:** Now, getting to this, the undoing of the Chosen People/Promised Land model and the undoing of the conqueror model, which I think really is the task of decolonization, your work has really exposed this as the embedded patterns in terms of the dominant culture's human imagination and your example of the suppression of indigenous languages is a perfect example of how this manifested in terms of the day-to-day workings of U.S. federal Indian policy. What would you say to someone who reads the book and says, well, you know, they take it out of context, and say, okay, so this is the unconscious behavior of Americans; what do you mean by using the human imagination? For many people it might be seen as too abstract, but you're really bringing this into how it actually manifests itself. Could you say more?

**SN:** Yes. Let me give you an example of, you know, the consequences on the ground. The case of the Western Shoshone people is the most telling example right now, the Western Shoshone Nation. They have a treaty with the United States that goes back to 1863, the Treaty of Ruby Valley, that is an immense country that they have as a result of that treaty. The treaties are said to be, according to case law, interpreted as the Indian people understood them at the time that they were made or signed. That would mean within the tradition, the language traditions, the spiritual understandings of their relationship to the land, within their culture. Okay? That would be the correct way to interpret it, in keeping with their understand at the time it was made. Instead, the United States has specifically said to the Committee on the Elimination of Racial Discrimination at the United Nations, in 2001, when asked how they interpret the Ruby Valley Treaty, the response was *Johnson v. M'Intosh*. So right there you have the interpretation of their treaty as being merely a title to roam and that some thirty billion, with a "b," thirty billion dollars in gold has been taken out of their land with tremendous amount of ecological devastation of the water and the land and so forth as a result and not one penny of that money going to the Western Shoshone people, and not one acknowledgment on the part of the United States that the Western Shoshone had any right to the land whatsoever. So, you know, that's how it affects . . . and now they're talking about, they actually, they have the Cortez Mine, interestingly named for a Spanish conquistador . . .

**JKK:** The mine itself is called Cortez?

**SN:** Yes, it's the Cortez Mining Company. And then they have another one called the Columbus Mining Company, and their logo on their website shows little ships, you know.

**JKK:** So just blatant.

**SN:** Oh, totally blatant. And then they are talking about now tearing down, doing great destruction to Mount Tenabo which is a very significant cultural and spiritual location for the Western Shoshone people, but they've found that there's, you know, billions of dollars in gold in that land so they want to tear it down or, you know, tear big amounts of it down and pull the gold out of there. So, that's, yes, we can say it's abstract, it's imagination and all that, but we're only talking about how people think and conceive which means that that predetermines how they behave. And so, in terms of a reform, it's very challenging because you're really talking about the need to reform the culture that exists, away from a paradigm of domination, to something more in keeping with Indigenous understandings of the sacred nature of the Earth, the inter-relationship of all life-forms, the delicate balance within all ecosystems and how those have to be sustained or they will not enable us to live. And so if you destroy the very basis of your life, you have no life.

Pretty simple understanding. But that's an understanding of certain types of limits, and in a consumptive society that believes in no real limits and wants no limits for economic purposes, the consumer society, then you have that competition there, and contradiction. So I think that there's some real fundamental change that needs to occur, and how that's going to come about is anybody's guess.

**JKK:** Yes, well, and also just that ongoing work of trying to dislodge these common conceptions and to really expose how absurd they are. One of the best examples at the beginning of the book is to look at, you question, you know, why aren't Indian nations as truly sovereign nations, able to hold their own land in trust for themselves? And you use the Vatican as an example . . .

**SN:** You know, the United States is said to have a trust relationship with Indian nations, something that they've very much used against the Western Shoshone by saying that the United States as trustee could take money from one account and put money in a different account, thereby paying itself, the government paying itself on behalf of the wards, meaning the Western Shoshones, and say that they've been paid even though they haven't received one cent and the Supreme Court went ahead with that form of logic, if you can call it logic. But in any case, that trust relationship is the basis upon which Indian lands are considered to be federal lands, held in trust, for any particular federally recognized Indian tribe. And my point is that if our nations are truly sovereign nations, then they should be able to hold the lands in trust for themselves and it would be, you know, absurd to think that the lands of the United States would be held in trust by some other country or the lands of the Vatican would be held in trust by Italy within the boundaries of which the Vatican city-state lies, you know. So I just think that that's one of these contradictions that is the direct result of the framework I lay out in the book.

**JKK:** Now, in terms of reform, I want to go back to something you said about the necessity of reforming the culture. We know that to be true as well in relation to the law, that just changing the law alone doesn't necessarily change the sentiment of the people. How can something like *Johnson v. M'Intosh* be struck down as bad law?

**SN:** Well that's the $64,000 question, I mean, you know, how do you get a case to the Supreme Court that would even have the same elements in it for the Court to be able to strike that down? I think that that's a real challenge. It's sort of like, well, if you have it embedded in there and there's no way to revisit that case or the elements of that case, then they'll just consider it to stand on the basis of precedent, and Peter d'Errico alludes to that, somewhat. And we have to remember that law is not distinct from the culture; it's an outgrowth of the culture. And so, *Johnson v. M'Intosh* comes out of a much earlier time when these things were pretty normative, these attitudes and ideas were pretty much normative within the elite circles of the United States where these decisions had importance and they were more likely to be accepted by the larger society. The effort of my book is to call this into question and bring it up to the surface where people can actually see that it even exists. As long as it stays hidden from view, no one can challenge it. And so hopefully there would be a big even societal shift where we could figure out how to revise the way in which Indian nations are categorized within the law, and the original free and independent existence of those nations is something that should be and must be acknowledged by the United States. And of course they're going to resist that indefinitely, so it's going to continue to be a challenge and a struggle to decolonize not just our own minds but those of the masses within the dominating society.

**JKK:** And also I want to acknowledge for people who might not be familiar that there are activists around the world calling for the papal bulls to be revoked.

**SN:** Well, yes. We chose one back in 1992, the *Inter caetera* papal bull of May 4, 1493, that called for the subjugation of barbarous nations, or Indigenous nations as they're now referred to. And we called for Pope John Paul to revoke that particular papal document, and we've maintained that call by resuming that with the new pope, Benedict—is it the sixteenth? I can't remember. We've renewed that call with Pope Benedict, the current pope, and so we have actually had some meetings with the representative from the Holy See to the United Nations, and so we're moving forward with that dialogue.

**JKK:** Yes, and that's really extraordinary in another way, that to even raise that as a campaign is really about reeducating the public and raising critical consciousness about what the papal bulls are and how they still really are operative.

**SN:** Well that's really important, and the Internet, of course, has been amazing in that effort. I'm always astonished to see how much the papal bull has circulated throughout the Internet. It's been picked up by people in Africa, people in India, who are also impacted by these documents and by the tradition of Christendom, and other peoples in the world. And so it's something that really is a point of unification, that we're all opposed to that type of mentality, I would hope. And those of us that want to see a shift, a paradigm shift, away from the culture of domination and so forth, and exploitation, subjugation, and greed, to something that is more in keeping with the Indigenous patterns of values of, you know, respect the Earth as our mother and have a sacred regard for all living things.

**JKK:** Yes, our existence relies on that, as does the existence of all humans.

**SN:** That's right.

**JKK:** Now, as we're wrapping up our interview, I'd like to ask if you would like to add anything about the Declaration on the Rights of Indigenous Peoples.

**SN:** I will say that the Human Rights of Indigenous Peoples Fact Sheet #9, issued by the United Nations some years ago, actually defines Indigenous peoples as being the original people of a particular place when a secondary settler population came in and established dominance over them. And the thing that's troubling about that is that it accepts the condition of dominance as a given and doesn't suggest for a moment that that dominance be lifted or removed in order for the human rights of the Indigenous peoples to be upheld or to be promoted or whatever term you want to use. So, you know, this again seems to me that the dominance is a given, and then whatever human rights you can imagine to eke out within that system of dominance is going to be okay within that framework. And so the United States has formally adopted that position by saying self-determination within or from the perspective of the United States means only internal self-determination, subject to the authority of the nation-state within which the Indigenous peoples are located. And that was not the basis upon which Indian leaders went into the international arena to begin with to assert their nationhood and to remind people of the original free and independent existence of all of our respective nations and peoples.

# JEAN M. O'BRIEN ON TRACING THE ORIGINS OF THE PERSISTENT MYTH OF THE "VANISHING INDIAN"

My interview with Jean M. O'Brien (enrolled citizen of the White Earth Ojibwe Nation) took place shortly after the release of her book *Firsting and Lasting: Writing Indians out of Existence in New England* (2010), during her visit to Wesleyan University, where she delivered a public lecture I organized. O'Brien is a professor in the history department at the University of Minnesota, where she is also affiliated with the departments of American studies and American Indian studies. She received her PhD from the University of Chicago in 1990. O'Brien is also the author of *Dispossession by Degrees: Indian Land and Identity in Natick, Massachusetts, 1650–1790* (1997). We worked together as cofounders of the Native American and Indigenous Studies Association, and at the time of this interview she was serving as its president. Since then she has coedited a book with Amy E. Den Ouden, *Recognition, Sovereignty Struggles, and Indigenous Rights in the United States: A Sourcebook* (2013). Her forthcoming book, with Lisa M. Blee, is *Monumental Mobility: The Memory Work of Massasoit* (2018).

This interview took place on September 21, 2010.

**J. Kēhaulani Kauanui:** I would like to ask how you came to be a scholar working in Native American history.

**Jean M. O'Brien:** Well, I guess, as it is for so many of us who are Native, I come to this work through my personal history. I'm a citizen of the White Earth Ojibwe Nation in Minnesota, and I'm one of the many people from my reservation that actually didn't grow up on the reservation. My mother did, though, and my grandmother was there and had a home until her death, although she lived with us for the last years of her life. So I spent a lot of time not living there but connected to the community. We spent summers there and we were immersed in the identity of being Ojibwe and being in Minnesota and having a love for our place. I just was always interested in our history and I had actually two parents who were interested in history and the history of our family, and so I always wanted to know more and do more. I actually never really imagined that I was going to be a historian, but that's how things panned out—that was just something that happened along the way, I guess.

**JKK:** And many people would assume that any Native American scholar would be researching and writing about their own tribe, so to speak. Your first book, *Dispossession by Degrees*, is about Indian dispossession in Natick, Massachusetts. What led you to that project, and were you ever pressured by your advisers or mentors or even your community or family to stick to "your own" history?

**JMO:** Well, that's a really great question, and you know it's a question that people ask me frequently. And I guess it has a sort of interesting time-based answer, because I went to graduate school in the 1980s from northern Minnesota to the University of Chicago, where I was surprised to be admitted, frankly. And I arrived there, and it was my aspiration to do Ojibwe history at that time, but I was going to graduate school at a time when I didn't know if I was going to be able to do Indian history at all. And so, I got to Chicago and I was fortunate enough to be able to find advisers there who were very open to doing Indian history even though they didn't specialize in it. They didn't have a single historian there down to this day that specializes in American Indian history.

And so, it's interesting, when I arrived—as I had done my entire life—I got into the classroom and there would be projects you would have to do and I always looked for projects that had to do with Indians. So I found myself in my first graduate seminar and it was on community histories in early America, and so I searched and searched and I found this place in Natick, Massachusetts, that was an Indian town and I thought, "Oh, here we go, I can do this, I can do this project." And so I did this seminar paper on Natick and I realized that every single narrative that I found about what had happened to Natick people didn't make any sense to me. I mean at this time, really, the prevailing notion in New England and everywhere else was that New England Indians had become extinct. And it made no sense to me when I went and looked at the records. All of this was all supposed to have happened right around King Philip's War in the 1600s—1676 to 1677 was when this terrible battle was waged. So I picked up the vital records of Natick and I found all these births, marriages, deaths being recorded in the eighteenth century. And I got obsessed with this story. So I ended up deciding to pursue it as my doctoral dissertation because I wanted to know what happened here and I wanted to understand this narrative that people had disappeared.

**JKK:** So you immediately saw the contradiction between the records you were looking at versus what the general population was claiming about the place and the people?

**JMO:** Absolutely, and I just wanted to know. And in fact, it's just one of those happy accidents, I guess, that the methodologies that people were pushing at that time lent themselves for me to be able to reconstruct this history of Natick in the 1700s, through the 1700s really. But as I write in my acknowledgments in that book, one of the things I discovered along the way is so many parallels between that story of Natick and my own reservation community of White Earth. And even though it's a different period of time, there's a very similar story of dispossession that happens under allotment policy in the late 1800s and early 1900s in White Earth. I think we find so many commonalities across the Indigenous world, and that ended up being one that all made sense to me. It was part of the stories I grew up with.

**JKK:** Can you say more about allotment being one of the major ways that many Native nations had their lands stolen from them?

**JMO:** How it worked was the idea—especially in the late nineteenth century, but there are precursors—that Indian peoples, in spite of all the efforts of all the policy makers in the past, were simply not becoming assimilated into U.S. society and culture. And that was the objective that had always underlaid the policy in one way or another. And so, the idea was to speed up that process through dividing up reservation homelands into individual parcels to convey the idea of capitalism and the market and to just immerse Indian people by force into the capitalist economy. And the idea was that they would learn more that way.

And so what ended up happening—my community of White Earth is the classic example of fraud. I mean it's just unbelievable—even though there were allegedly or supposedly protections built in for people to hold onto their lands while they learned all of these new things, in fact, through lots of fraudulent practices land loss started almost immediately and resulted in about 95 percent of the reservation base being lost within a couple decades.

And you know, people at White Earth have been trying to get the land back ever since. It's really similar to what ended up happening in Natick and other places in the 1600s, 1700s, and 1800s.

**JKK:** The other thing you mentioned is King Philip's War, which marks the tilt in power with the settlers over the tribes, since before that tribes held the bulk of power. King Philip was known as Metacomet, his Indigenous name. Given that very few Americans even know about that war, can you lay out some of this history for the international reader?

**JMO:** King Philip's War, Metacomet's War—of course it's named by non-Indians, right? What happens here is after more than five, almost six decades of the English incursion into New England there's—well, there are all kinds of really complicated things that accompany that with epidemics, with warfare, with missionization and all that. But what ends up happening with King Philip's

War is, in the 1670s, he's the leader from the Wampanoag, and he just decides enough is enough. And he mounts this pan-Indian resistance basically to try to get rid of the English. And what's interesting about people knowing or not knowing about King Philip's War is to this day if you look at the percentages and the numbers—it's the most deadly warfare in what you might think of as U.S. history. And it really was; it almost tipped the balance back to Indians. It resulted in the destruction of many towns throughout New England. In the end it's catastrophic, it's death and slavery for many Native peoples in southern New England.

**JKK:** This gets to the concept of colonialism that all of your work addresses. I've heard you speak in different contexts where you note that in the field of American history there's still this persistent notion that colonialism ended with the American Revolution. Could you could speak to that notion of colonialism experienced by Native nations and that idea that the only colonialism was constituted by the British colonies?

**JMO:** Right. I think this is just such an interesting construct, and scholars I don't think have grappled with this adequately at all. There's this idea that there's something called "colonial history" for the U.S. and that that ends with the American Revolution. And you know, for Native peoples that's simply not true. Colonialism for Native peoples, Indigenous peoples in the United States and elsewhere, I would argue continues to this day. And Indigenous peoples are still coping with the effects of invasion, conquest, and everything else. So, no independence for Native peoples with the independence movement of the British colonies. The only independence that happens there has to do with this imperial relationship between Britain and its colonies.

**JKK:** *Dispossession by Degrees* certainly relates to your newest book, *Firsting and Lasting: Writing Indians out of Existence in New England*, which traces the origins of the persistent myth—another myth!—this the one of the "vanishing Indian." Could you address that ideology, that myth, that's so pervasive in U.S. society, even now in the twenty-first century? You really trace the genealogy of that in New England that then comes to really seep into the American national consciousness, the U.S. national imaginary. Could you explain that?

**JMO:** Maybe a good way to start is to talk about why I did this project, this book. It's just a logical outgrowth of the first book, where I think I argue pretty persuasively that Indian people did not disappear through the 1700s in Natick and elsewhere in New England. But that led to another series of questions, and those questions were really about, "Well, why did people think so?" And so what I did, I used some of the sources from the first book, especially local histories, which is what I concentrate on in the second project. And I saw in these local histories in Natick and elsewhere stories about Indians vanishing or being declared extinct. And I wanted to look at this whole process to see what was going on in local histories throughout this region that I was guessing helped create this ideology of the "vanishing Indian."

And you know, there's a huge literature on Indian extinction and the "vanishing Indian" that happens in literature, representation and so forth. I wanted to get at what the whole process of history-writing was doing at the time, because I suspected that that's where most people were getting their ideas of Indians. And I really wanted to pin it down at the local level to talk about a history that I knew pretty well and to just look at how these nineteenth-century histories looked back on the Indian history of the past and simultaneously argued that Indians had become extinct, that they'd vanished. And they do it in really precise ways. Its most extreme form is talking about "the last" Indian person, last—as they cast it—full-blooded Indian that lives in the particular town. And they have a name, they have stories attached to them, and so that makes it much more tangible and real to people. While at the same time, clearly, Indians really are not vanishing, and so I wanted to get at, "Well, what convinces them that they have?" So that's the basic idea of the project.

**JKK:** It is such an excellent work—one that really gets at the mind-set of ordinary non-Indians based on your critical study of six hundred local histories that were written between 1820 and 1880. Please share more about the archive and which parts of New England you focused your attention on.

**JMO:** If people read my books they might realize I'm pretty obsessive. So what I did was I wanted to focus on southern New England more generally and not northern New England, because that would entail another massive body of work and I wanted it to be contained and to be in an area that I thought I knew pretty well. And so I decided on Massachusetts, Connecticut, and Rhode Island, because they do operate in some ways as a region. And I decided 1820 because that's a period in time when the U.S. is trying to forge its own nationalism; it's attempting to create a culture that's distinct from Europe to match its independence. And then by 1880 something really different is going on both in the region and nationally. This time urbanization, industrialization are really making things different in terms of publication and everything else, so that's how I bound it by time.

And so of course I decided that I had to read every single thing that was written of these places, which took a while to track down. So I did a lot of reading. And in the end there were a few things that I wasn't able to locate, but I wanted to do it that way because you never know what you're going to miss—the "golden nugget." And I found a lot of "golden nuggets" that I might have overlooked if I hadn't tried to sample.

And I came along the way to think about this as a project of vernacular history, that a great deal of the way that people are getting their historical knowledge, I think, in this period of time is even through sitting through lectures, basically historical orations is what they would call them at the time. Fourth of July, celebrations of the bicentennial of the incorporation of the town, they're these massive gatherings of people who aren't necessarily sitting around studying history but they're hearing historical accounts of their places and about Indians. Indians are almost always a part of these orations. This is where I think they're getting their ideas about who Indians are, what an Indian is, and the idea that Indians, if they aren't already gone, are going to be gone soon.

**JKK:** In relation to vernacular history, please explain what makes the local so important here, since you document hundreds of local histories that altogether produce a grand narrative.

**JMO:** Right. So, there's just a huge spectrum, probably has always been, of people who get interested in pursuing history as an avocation or a profession. I mean there was effectively the emergence of a professional-historical scholarly approach in the nineteenth century. But there's also the local minister, devoting an hour a night to reading about the locality and writing that history. And so you get this huge range of local histories, from multivolume, thick, dense histories to little, tiny pamphlets really. Or in fact just the publication of a historical oration that came out of a historical commemoration. And it seems to me that's where most people are figuring out what they think about their history and about the racial formation of their place.

**JKK:** You also looked at censuses and actual monuments as well as accounts of historical pageants and commemorations. Tell us about community attendance at these events.

**JMO:** I think one of the things that I think would surprise a lot of people today is these commemorations—I don't think it would surprise people that commemorations of settlement are things that were popular, I mean think of Fourth of July celebrations—people get together and they have a good time. But I think what people would find surprising is that the centerpiece of these commemorations was the historical oration, which, you know, if you look at the length of these—and I have—people must have been sitting for a couple of hours listening to history for fun. I know that strikes many people as preposterous, but there you have it. So, this is part of what people are doing, and they're learning about who they are, who they think they are, where they are, and why they are where they are through these orations I think.

   And monuments that people encounter as they traverse the landscape where they live that are about commemorating people like Miles Standish, the captain and military commander of the Pilgrims in the early 1600s. And leaders like Miantonomo, and Uncas and Massasoit who were what I call these famous "first Indians" who enter into diplomacy with the English and authorize the English presence—in these accounts, I might add.

**JKK:** And in the title there's an argument. Can you say more about the "Firsting and Lasting"?

**JMO:** So, these are clearly, well, at least the word "firsting" is made up—I made it up. And "lasting" is a word I play on, and I coupled them because I noticed a really important pattern in the texts as I consumed them, basically. And I approached the project with an idea about the last full-blooded Indian that you see accounts of in many of these histories. I thought I was going to find a lot more of those stories than I did, but I found a lot of versions of trying to put Indian peoples in the past by using this motif of "the last of."

But as I read I was noticing that alongside this what you're getting are claims by non-Indians about them being the first people to bring institutions that are worthy of notice into the New World as they think about it. So they in very subtle ways by telling what I think of as really mundane stories about the first birth of the first white child, the first house that was built here, where it was located, the first church, and all of these things are a way of putting Indian history in the past, making it a preface, making it an inauthentic beginning of history of these places. So these notions I think are coupled, whereas what ends up happening, putting Indians in the past, what non-Indians are doing is they're subtly seizing indigeneity for themselves by claiming to be the first peoples who are creating these institutions that are about making modernity. That's the way I argue it in the book.

**JKK:** Yes, and how these histories became a primary means by which white Americans asserted their own modernity while denying it to Indian peoples. Like you said, "putting Indians in the past," where Indians always are relegated to the ancient, while there is also a degradation of their past by saying that they don't have a history, or that they didn't have a history at that particular time when these histories were being written by white settlers.

**JMO:** Right, and I even have a few passages where they out-and-out say that— that Indians had no history, they built no institutions, they had no books to contain their feats, and all these things. They really believed this, so you get this idea that Indians can't possibly have been making history. And it's all a part of a construct where—you talked about degradation, degeneration—but that's a central motif in all this. And it all gets tied up into the idea of blood and purity. So they create narratives about Indians where intermarriage becomes a way for Indians to become inauthentic as Indians, and it's coupled with this idea that Indian cultures never change. And if there's culture change that happens such as language loss, which is a really important issue in New England and many other places, that somehow those peoples are degenerate and not fully and authentically Indian. So it's this construct that makes that whole process of "lasting" happen, as well as the "firsting."

**JKK:** The contemporary denial of Indigenous modernity is startling—the persistent discourse of a civilizing project and coming into the modern age. Even today, I hear Indigenous students complain, "People expect me to look a certain way, dress a certain way, live in a wigwam or tepee," and I point out, "Well, we don't ask if white students still churn their own butter, make their own soap or ride in stagecoaches." So how is it that some people get to progress or become modern and again Indigenous peoples seen as primitive still are always just seen as stuck and if they move they're not seen as real?

**JMO:** I think it really comes out of the developing racial ideology of the era of, well, especially the era I'm looking at—the classic, golden era of scientific racism whereby there's an idea of race, which at least most of us recognize as not having much analytical purchase anymore. But the idea that there are separate races and they have particular traits, and that's what they look like, that's what they do. And failure to comply with those ideas messes up people's thinking. But it's a dynamic that's used to deny the Indianness of New England Indians.

And the idea that Indians have never changed of course is preposterous, because Indians had always changed and embraced change to make their way in a changing world; that's just what people do. And as you say, I have this thing with my students—we have to talk about how this is an expectation, and frankly it is an expectation that remains today in the minds of many. And so I look to good examples; I use similar kinds of strategies to get people to think about it. But I also—and I'm sure you do too—talk about the fact that you can imagine taking up English for Native peoples as a strategy, it's a weapon. They embrace English and use it in literacy, in writing, in all these things, that's just what you do.

**JKK:** And language is so important because even if someone says, "Oh, that's an exaggeration, we don't expect people to live in wigwams, in tepees and huts," there are other expectations. "Do you practice your traditional rituals? Do you know your indigenous language?" And religion and language are two of the areas that U.S. policy set out to destroy.

**JMO:** Absolutely, and it came on the heels of what the English were doing in New England and elsewhere. It was really, really an aggressive campaign to force Indians to change and to comply with these ideas about civilization. And you know Indians selectively did, but they did it in their own ways, and so this is how Indians remain Indians in New England and elsewhere.

**JKK:** And continue to resist! Let's discuss the concepts of race and degradation in relation to scientific racism and the concept of degeneration that is in your book. Why the fixation on the so-called "last full-blooded Indian," and why the denial that Indigenous people who were supposedly unmixed had descendants and that their racially mixed descendants didn't count? Why the fixation on the full-blood Indian, whereas these different Europeans were mixing with each other? Why are some people allowed to mix and not others?

**JMO:** I actually wish I could fully answer that question; I'm still not sure except to talk about ideology. And you know, the idea of degeneration is really central in making this whole myth of extinction work. I think it's an essential rubric whereby it works. And so, I talk about different configurations of what you can think about as a one-drop rule. And the idea of blood purity for Indian peoples is on the one hand a part of the whole ideology of who the races are. On the other hand it's quite convenient for non-Indians to imagine that Indians are disappearing—after all, this is a colonial situation in which they're claiming a landscape and they're wanting to claim it as rightfully theirs. And part of what makes that go is to say, "Well, see, these Indians can't possibly survive in civilization. We've tried so hard and it just hasn't taken, hasn't worked."

And so there's a process of claiming a landscape that goes along with this, but along the way I came to think about it—well, lots of people have talked about the relationship between Indians and African Americans in the idea of blood. And it kind of works like this, well, one drop of blood for an African American is a "pollution narrative." If you can make a claim that a person possesses even one drop of African blood then they're subjected to slavery depending on the moment in time, or racial discrimination. Whereas for Indian people, you have to demonstrate how many drops of blood you have. There's this idea of "blood quantum" and qualifying for Indianness based on this idea of race with the metaphor of blood coming through and making it work.

Whereas I discovered along the way, which I find almost amusing, is that so-called "Puritans" have this much more expansive definition for themselves as being part of what they think of as a New England race descended from the Puritan fathers and all that, where any kind of association that you can make to the people and places of New England qualifies you for this racial category—I think of as a racial category. A "New English" race and the privileges of whiteness, of claiming place comes through this. And so I juxtapose these ideas of blood and race in trying to think about the racial terrain of New England at the time and actually into the future in many ways.

**JKK:** And then, that also means that there's again the erasure of the descendants who are marrying people of African ancestry and European descent. Again this, trying to map the "last of" in terms of different local histories, this came out in your book and of course your lecture the other day, of doing portraits of the last so-called Indian of this tribe and that tribe. And noting that it's not just Ishi "the last Yahi" out in California. But you saw this with Nantucket, with Pautuxet, also with the Narragansett.

**JMO:** And you know, I think a lot of people are familiar with the famous James Fenimore Cooper novel *The Last of the Mohicans*. Well, of course, this was on my mind as I was doing this research. Well, I found one "last Indian," or claimed "last Indian," that predated that novel from 1821 in Massachusetts. But I found lots of last Indians which I play with a little in the book because the people who are writing about last Indians end up being confused, sometimes in a single volume they've got more than one and they can't keep their story straight.

But I have one anecdote, it's apocryphal, it may not even be the case, but I'm told by a friend of mine who works on New England Indian history, in anthropology, that there's a portrait, or at least there was, in the Nantucket Historical Society that depicted a last Indian. And I'm guessing that if it's there, it's a woman by the name of Dorcas Honorable, who claimed to be the last Indian of Nantucket. And the caption says, "Dorcas Honorable: The Last of the Nantucket." And underneath that it says, "Donated by Her Daughter." So you get massive confusion. What's going on there? I mean, I think the only thing that can explain something like that is these ideas about qualifying for being a full-blooded Indian, being a full-blooded Native of the land.

**JKK:** And Indigenous individuals being asked to measure up, show the card, name the blood quantum, as in "What's your fraction?"

**JMO:** Exactly. We're familiar with this whole discourse, and it comes out of this, I think.

**JKK:** I want to go back to that issue of land rights. You point out in *Firsting and Lasting* that the erasure and then the memorialization of Indian peoples also served the pragmatic colonial goal to refute Indian claims to land and rights. In terms of the consolidation, you examine these land deeds and how they get fetishized in terms of who are the "first Indians" who are supposedly authorizing these sales. Please say more about that.

**JMO:** Well, I tried to think about what the major themes are in these narratives. And I kind of knew what some of them were going to be in advance. But I think the most important theme is land and the claims that these histories make about the rightful transfer of Native land to non-Indian peoples. What you get—it's really interesting—in some of these books are full chapters on how it is their ancestors purchased these lands from Indian people, and they'll even reproduce these deeds. I mean they'll produce facsimiles of the actual deed on which they rest their claim to this land lawfully. So they're really trying to clarify for the general public and themselves that nothing untoward happened here, there was no fraud involved, that we did our best and we attended to Native rights, we didn't seize this land.

And they're doing this in part just in relation to thinking about other parts of the country. They're trying to claim a moral superiority to other places where in the nineteenth century, obviously throughout the 1800s there's wars, there's the policy of removal that translates into not just *the* Trail of Tears but many trails of tears for Native people as they're removed in advance of, or not always in advance of, non-Indian peoples coming to claim their land. This is really a part of claiming these places and proving—you know, there's one illustration that I showed the other day that is a map illustrative of the Indian purchase of ancient Windsor. Well, what this map is supposed to show is that every square inch of Native homeland can be accounted for by purchase.

**JKK:** Well, what about the average person who might be saying, "Well, so what if it was done legitimately through a deed of sale. What's the issue with that?"

**JMO:** Well, I mean of course it's not clear what's going on with these deeds, and in fact there are plenty of instances where people are frustrated because they can't find the deed. There are all kinds of other explanations that people have for getting the land like "right of conquest." I mean there's this whole ideology that comes from this colonial period that builds, and they interact—"there's the land grant from the King," all these things. There's lots of different ways of saying this land came into our hands through really respectable means is I guess one way of thinking about it.

**JKK:** It's an attempt to legitimate theft. Here I'm recalling a photograph from your research with the signatures of the individual Indians that supposedly signed away those lands. We know from other research and also from the persistent communities today that individuals could rarely sign away land, or alienate land and in many ways thought they were signing off use rights so that English settlers could actually have access to fishing and hunting grounds but not forever and not to alienate it from the tribe. But what really stuck out was one with symbols that people used to sign their own names, which shows that even written literacy at the time was different. So we can't assume that a 1650 deed was understood by the person signing it, which gets at this issue of informed consent.

**JMO:** Absolutely it does, I mean, we can't know from these deeds what was being represented to those who left their marks on those documents. And as you said, this is a clash of land systems that are completely different. It's not about individual land ownership; it's the group that possesses the land, and there are complicated systems whereby people are accorded use of particular parcels of land, but not forever. It always resides in the group. So there's a huge contradiction and clash that's happening here, and of course it changes over time. But in the seventeenth century, where not until the 1650s, and then with only a small percentage of Native people even acquiring literacy in either language—because it happens both ways—what can these possibly mean?

**JKK:** Here I might use a personal story to illustrate. I moved to Middletown, Connecticut, from Santa Cruz, California, in 2000. It was summertime, and the city of Middletown was celebrating its founding, its 350th year. And I saw in the paper that they were going to have "parade and pageantry," and I called city council and asked if the Indian tribe whose homeland we're on—and I didn't know at the time that it was the Wangunk, and that's one of the reasons why I also introduce the show by acknowledging the people of this place. When I called city council and said, "Will there be any of the Native groups of this land in that ceremony?" And they said, "Well of course, people whose families have been here for 350 years, the natives will be here." And I said, "No, no, I don't mean white people as natives, I'm talking about American Indians, and what's the name of the tribe?" Well, they didn't even actually know what I was asking or what I was after. There was deep confusion and irritation on the line. I got put on hold, and somebody brought a supervisor on the phone: "Ma'am, what's the problem here?" I said, "I'm just trying to figure out two things: the name of the tribe of the place now called Middletown, whose land we are on, and if they will be taking part in this 350th commemoration." He replied, "They're extinct," so I asked, "Well, who are they?" His answer: "Well, I don't know, maybe you should call somebody at Foxwood's Casino and ask!" I was incensed. "You want me to call a casino an hour away and ask the Mashantucket Pequot tribe if they know who the tribe of Middletown is?"

You know, I found out in a very different way, I didn't even get an easy answer when I telephoned the Connecticut Historical Society. But eventually I did find out through a local scholar, Paul Grant Costa, who was then completing his doctorate in history at Yale University. But in Middletown today that history is included in one sentence on the town green. And there's also some information on a plaque at the gates of the cemetery called "Indian Hill," where it actually names the Wangunk Indians. And yet the official doctrine is still that they're extinct, and yet in my twelve years at Wesleyan University I have had students interviewing Wangunk descendants. So right there we see the contradiction, the erasure, the invisibility.

**JMO:** Well, yes, I think this is how successful this narrative was in the nineteenth century, because I too have—I mean I think it's less so now, I hope, maybe not—I've had many students, graduate students who come from New England. And I'd be talking about this research that I'd be working on, and they'd say, "That's what I was taught when I was growing up in Connecticut. I was taught that the Indians of New England were extinct." And so as recently— well, I don't know, is it still going on, maybe in a lot of places? I wouldn't be surprised. It's just, it's incredible the power of this ideology, and it's appealing to many people.

**JKK:** And that links to the ongoing and raging debates in this region over U.S.

federal recognition. Let's discuss the edited volume you and Amy Den Ouden are collaborating on—*Recognition, Sovereignty Struggles, and Indigenous Rights in the United States*—all about Indigenous battles for and over that you're working on about federal recognition. I am happy to have an essay about the Hawaiian case included in the book. So much of your work resonates for people studying what's going on in this current moment over battles of federal recognition—saying that they don't exist anymore, they're not real, why should they have these collective rights, collective claims to land? And of course New England is a hot spot for that, especially Connecticut. We've had an attorney general who has been so hostile to the state-recognized tribes in Connecticut getting federal recognition. And yet as Amy Den Ouden has pointed out, Connecticut has perhaps the longest continuously occupied reservations in all of North America, maybe next to Virginia as the only exception. The Connecticut colony recognized these tribes before the state of Connecticut was even formed. Your historical work provides a critical genealogy for these contemporary struggles. How does the early American period inform struggles today regarding the federal recognition process?

**JMO:** On the most basic level, the federal relationship of treaty-making with the tribes has long, or had long, defined recognition, and whether a tribal nation was accorded sovereignty by the United States in that nation-to-nation relationship that was evident through treaty-making, which becomes the basis of everything that Native peoples as separate tribal nations exercise in terms of rights, and struggle with, I should say.

But colonialism in New England and in most of the so-called original thirteen—with the exception New York and a few other places—conquest had preceded the existence of the United States. And so there aren't federal treaties, there aren't national treaties with tribes through much of New England and other places. But that doesn't mean that tribal peoples were not recognized as separate political entities; they were. Straight through, well until the middle to the end of the 1800s, when in connection with, basically, the Civil War, and abolition of slavery, and the extension of citizenship to African Americans becomes a problem for people who had agitated on behalf of abolition especially in New England, that tribes, tribal citizens, tribal members were not citizens necessarily of the states in which they resided. And so, what happens in each of these places in the 1800s in connection with the Civil War is there's the extension of citizenship and the movement toward "detribalization," to try to eradicate the political status in tribal nations, in New England.

And I want to be really clear here, what's being eradicated is the recognition of those states and commonwealths of the political status of tribal nations there by fiat, saying "We no longer recognize you." I mean it's a complicated and contested set of struggles that I'm not doing justice to here, but it would take a long time to do justice to . . . And so that creates a situation where—it doesn't mean that the tribal nations disappear once again. It's something that operates on the political level. So it creates the situation we have today of struggles over reasserting a relationship, a political relationship of recognition of the tribal sovereignty of Native peoples who have been here all along.

**JKK:** Now, what about your next book monograph, *Children's Literature and Colonialism in Nineteenth-Century New England*?

**JMO:** I think all of us who are educators at whatever level, we have this ongoing conversation about what is going on with what kids are getting taught about Indians, and frustration over standards and textbooks and all these kinds of things. And over the years it's got me thinking about historical education for kids. I don't even have any, I just teach them all the time, so that's where this emanates from, right? Well, actually it's part of this book that I just published. I collected children's literature and schoolbooks because I was thinking, "Well, if you want to talk about how people know what they think they know about Indians or anything else, you should go and see what the curriculum looks like—look at the books, see what they're reading and how they're reading and what they're learning this way."

And I found really a lot of rich things there, but they didn't quite fit into this book, so I decided maybe this is just another separate project. And I'm just at the beginning stages of trying to formulate it so I don't know what it will look like. But it does, I mean I guess it also is the logical successor to this book so I have this progression of books that I kind of unfold because they raise these successive questions for me. So we'll see where it goes. I may in fact—I have this theory that's completely unsubstantiated that in the nineteenth century there's a lot of Indian history in schoolbooks about history, in geography actually. And I suspect that in the twentieth century that drops out, until maybe the sixties and seventies. And we, and you of course are a major part of this, are in a major reclamation project of a history that has been—well, what do you call it, I don't even know—ignored, swept under the carpet, not acknowledged as worthy as such. And we're all working hard to convince people otherwise. So that's where this project comes from, and we'll see what I can make of it.

**JKK:** And why geography in those books where children are getting taught? What do you think that's about?

**JMO:** Well, because it's about place, right? And so, I've only looked at a few of those so far, and there aren't as many, as there are many, many history books. But geographies will talk about place-names, you know, they'll talk about these are the people who used to live here. So you get that kind of narrative. And right now I'm puzzling over how broad to get, because it occurs to me, I could be thinking about "How is Indian history broadly speaking being taught in the U.S.?" So I'm trying to figure out how to contain that question. Because I really do want to keep it focused locally, because I think that that's for me my comfort level and I feel like I can gain more purchase at that scale.

But I have to have something to bounce it off of, right, and one of the things that surprised me is how much world history is getting taught in the 1800s. That surprised me. So, again, I think that's one of the things that disappeared in the twentieth century and has been resurrected and or was totally recast in just the last three decades.

**JKK:** Before we wrap up, I want to acknowledge your 2011 presidency for the Native American and Indigenous Studies Association [NAISA] and our collaborative work on a six-person steering committee from 2005 to found NAISA in 2008. What is your take on the state of Native studies in relation to what you called earlier a massive reclamation project, fighting against this historical erasure?

**JMO:** Well, it's twin love of yours and mine, right, this association that we've worked so long and hard at. I think it's safe to say that we were very surprised at the incredible need—I mean we knew there was a need out there, but we were surprised at the incredible response. And that I was hoping that this would be the case from your involvement, how it was instantly global. And we drew people from Australia and New Zealand and elsewhere, from eleven countries at the very first meeting we called to inquire on the desire to have such an association. And it's grown from there, we're so big, I mean we're struggling with making sure we're actually managing to run our affairs. We're working on that, and what I think has been so especially energizing for me is, I don't think it's safe to say what Indigenous studies is at this point in time, because we're now beginning sustained conversations across all kinds of borders that are yielding more questions than answers. We're just learning so much from each other, and so I hesitate to say what the state is because I think we're in a discovery moment, and one that's really rich and very exciting.

**JKK:** And so you're really pointing at the scoping out beyond American Indian studies, and not just Native American studies but in terms of what happens when you're bringing a Chamorro studies from Guam in conversation with Indigenous studies from Mexico with American studies in the U.S. with First Nation studies from Canada and so on.

**JMO:** That is part of the struggle over the name of our association, which I think most of us will go ahead and admit seems kind of clunky, but you need to have a lot of words to describe something that we don't have a single label for at this point. We probably should have thrown some other words in there, but people seemed more or less satisfied that this would be open enough to the various conversations we might not even know yet we'll be having.

**JKK:** Right. And I would think that you have a particular perspective coming out of the University of Minnesota, which has the very first American Indian studies program in the country

**JMO:** Yes, the first full-scale department with tenure lines and majors and minors. And we teach three years of two languages, and yes, it's a really fabulous place to be. And Minneapolis has a long history of activism: birthplace of the American Indian movement, hotbed of Indian activities, community-centered organizations, the American Indian Center as one of many places where Natives come together, political organizing, and the arts. One of my favorite places is Birchbark Books, owned by the incredible Ojibwe novelist Louise Erdrich.

**JKK:** Any parting thoughts?

**JMO:** There are great histories out there to be unearthed, discovered, and connections to be made.

# JONATHAN KAMAKAWIWOʻOLE OSORIO ON A HAWAIIAN LAND CASE BEFORE THE U.S. SUPREME COURT

I interviewed Jonathan Kay Kamakawiwoʻole Osorio (Kanaka Maoli) just a week before a major Hawaiian land case went before the U.S. Supreme Court on February 25, 2009. The Court heard oral arguments in the case of *State of Hawaii v. Office of Hawaiian Affairs, et al.,* since the State of Hawaiʻi has asked the Court to rule on whether or not the state has the authority to sell, exchange, or transfer 1.2 million acres of land formerly held by the Hawaiian monarchy as Crown and Government Lands. This land base constitutes 29 percent of the total land area of what is now known as the State of Hawaiʻi and almost all the land claimed by the state as "public lands." Prior to the state's appeal to the U.S. Supreme Court, the Hawaiʻi Supreme Court unanimously ruled that the state should keep the land trust intact until Native Hawaiian claims to these lands are settled, and prohibited the state from selling or otherwise disposing of the properties to private parties. It did so based on the 1993 Apology Resolution, in which Congress acknowledged and apologized for the United States' role and affirmed that "the indigenous Hawaiian people never directly relinquished their claims to their inherent sovereignty as a people or over their national lands to the United States, either through their monarchy or through a plebiscite or referendum." Osorio was an original plaintiff in the suit to prevent the sale of these lands and was a defendant in the appeal to the U.S. Supreme Court. In our interview we discussed the complex issues raised by the case, including the origins of the lawsuit, land title (based on Keanu Sai's understanding of the Māhale), the politics of the Apology Resolution, and the Hawaiian nation's claim to these lands under international law. Osorio is an associate professor at the Kamakakūokalani Center for Hawaiian Studies at the University of Hawaiʻi at Mānoa and is the author of *Dismembering Lāhui: A History of the Hawaiian Nation to 1887* (2002). He is also a composer and singer and has been a Hawaiian music recording artist since 1975.

This interview took place on February 17, 2009.

**J. Kēhaulani Kauanui:** Aloha. To start, can you offer an account of the origins of this case dating back to 1994 and how you became an original plaintiff who has now become defendant?

**Jonathan Kamakawiwoʻole Osorio:** I became an original plaintiff in the case, which started soon after the Congress of the United States passed Apology Resolution 103-150. It became really clear to residents of the state of Hawaiʻi that the United States was taking seriously the claims of Native Hawaiians and descendants of the Hawaiian Kingdom that a terrible wrong had been done—and, in fact, 103-150 details the horrors and America's responsibility for it. As an assistant professor at the Center for Hawaiian Studies, I was doing research on the Hawaiian Kingdom and especially in the creation of nation land titles through law, through the Hawaiian Kingdom law and constitutional land statue law, and was really concerned that the United States really had no title to the Crown and Government Lands of the Kingdom, which were essentially ceased at the time of the overthrow that the United States was apologizing for and then given to the United States in 1898. So, as a plaintiff, what I was really looking at were two things: one was the restoration of these lands to the Hawaiian people, to the Hawaiian nation, and two was respecting law, because the notion that you can have basically all of the lands of the people that are lawfully theirs, not just morally or historically or ancestrally, but lawfully theirs, that these could be taken by a government that purports to respect law, I found intolerable.

**JKK:** And now you were joined by three other Kanaka Maoli men in the original lawsuit, right? Before the Office of Hawaiian Affairs joined you?

**JKO:** That's true. We all came into this separately, and I was acquainted with only one of the other plaintiffs at the time—over the course of time I think we've only met each other once or twice.

**JKK:** Now, the question being presented to the Court is whether or not that Apology Resolution strips the State of Hawaiʻi of its authority to sell lands ceded to it by the federal government in 1898 when the United States of America unilaterally annexed Hawaiʻi. Now, with your research on the Hawaiian Kingdom, knowing full well that these lands are actually the Hawaiian Kingdom Crown and Government Lands, it is interesting to me that the issue of title is not at all being discussed by, say, the Office of Hawaiian Affairs, that there's been no challenge, especially in the media accounts, about whether the state—or the United States—even has title to these lands. And the other thing is that the Apology Resolution itself says that the Native Hawaiian people never relinquished title to these national lands. Could you speak to that?

**JKO:** That's correct. In the first place, there are basically two sets of plaintiffs here. For all I know there may be actually six different plaintiffs. Although I tend to think that the four plaintiffs share some things in common, I am not really sure of that.

**JKK:** Do you mean the individual Kanaka Maoli plaintiffs?

**JKO:** Yeah, the individual Kanaka Maoli plaintiffs. But the Office of Hawaiian Affairs has been *really* clear about its place in this suit. It wants to prevent the sale, the state sale of ceded lands, because the Office of Hawaiian Affairs actually draws revenues from leasing them. The state supreme court in 1978 determined that the Office of Hawaiian Affairs revenues, or the Hawaiian people's revenues, should be a 20 percent *pro rata* share of the use of these lands, and the Office of Hawaiian Affairs wants to make sure that the state does not simply sell off those so-called trust lands and basically leave the agency and the Hawaiian people they represent bereft. Okay, so that's their approach to this.

Now, as a plaintiff, I argue that the United States has absolutely no title over these lands and that it is wrong, it was wrong and illegal, not just morally wrong but illegal, for them to take those lands in 1898. But having done this, they really have no legal foundation for being able to transfer these lands to the State of Hawaiʻi, whether a 20 percent *pro rata* share is there for the Office of Hawaiian Affairs or not. We have very different approaches. I absolutely believe that if you respect the law, if you respect law as an institution, you have to respect it completely, and that means that even if it's uncomfortable or inconvenient, for the United States and for the State of Hawaiʻi, we have to recognize that the only entity that has title of these so-called "ceded lands"—the Crown and Government Lands—is the Hawaiian nation. Now the fact that our side— the respondents—is not presenting that argument before the [U.S.] Supreme Court on February 25 [2009] is not through lack of trying on my part. I did offer these arguments up to our attorney, who assured me that it was important for the case and for making this case clear to the Supreme Court justices that title was not on the table for discussion, what was on the table for decision was simply the question of states' rights and whether or not the state attorney general was making a true and accurate argument before the Supreme Court. I looked at this, you know, and I agonized over whether I should remain a party in this case, and I decided, ultimately, that I should because we really cannot afford to lose this case. The state should not be given some kind of authority to sell Crown and Government Lands of our people just because we make a tactical mistake, now.

**JKK:** Right, and it is the Hawaiʻi Supreme Court ruling that's being challenged by the executive branch of the state government, because the Hawaiʻi Supreme Court held that in light of the ongoing reconciliation process it would constitute a breach of fiduciary duty under state law for the state to sell these lands.

**JKO:** Right.

**JKK:** Now, as you know, one branch of the state cannot just simply go and sue another branch of the state and take it to the U.S. Supreme Court, so what's at present now? What's being presented to the U.S. Supreme Court is whether or not that Apology Resolution stripped the state of its authority to sell these lands. Doesn't it seem, then, that it is really the Apology Resolution that's on trial here?

**JKO:** This is what many of us fear, and by many of us I'm not just talking about activists and nationalists in Hawaiʻi; I'm talking about the whole public. You know, in a recent panel former governor John Waiheʻe actually talks about how the state really has sort of managed its legal and moral obligations toward Hawaiians. Not perfectly, you know, certainly, but how it's managed those obligations and tried to do basically the right thing. And what you have here is the possibility that, you know, here we have the United States in 1993 finally acknowledging what we already knew here. We knew this, we were publishing this—it was becoming more and more evident publicly in scholarship and in all sorts of ways—the United States finally acknowledges this, and as far as we were concerned, the language of apology law clearly commits the U.S. to some kind of reconciliation. The Supreme Court of the State of Hawaiʻi says: given this, given the need for pursuing reconciliation, because of this law, we have to take the most cautious approach there is when it comes to the management of these trust lands. This is all they've done, and in fact our attorney is basically arguing that the Hawaiʻi Supreme Court never brings up the issue of title. They don't talk about the apology law clouding title; only the attorney general is saying it. So, frankly, I do not believe that apology law clouds title—federal or state title—to the Kingdom's Crown and Government Lands. I believe *law* clouds title. You know what I mean?

**JKK:** Yes, because those lands were unlawfully acquired.

**JKO:** Because they were unlawfully taken, but they were also, and this is the most important thing for the audiences to understand, is that those lands were lawfully constituted by Hawaiian Kingdom law. This was not make-believe, it was not pretend, it was not some kind of mimicking of some kind of foreign system; this was intentional, and it was rational. The creation of those lands was intentional and rational, and it was intended to protect the nation and its resources. It really would be absolutely outrageous for the United States to continue to insist otherwise, as this becomes more and more known to the public. The United States has used its own laws and its treaties with Native Americans to appropriate Native American lands. We know that this is what they've done. And they've justified it by saying we have done this is a lawful manner. They cannot make that claim here.

**JKK:** Because there are no treaties of cession regarding Hawaiʻi, for one thing.

**JKO:** There is no treaty of annexation. There is no conquest. And if there was, if the United States invaded a friendly country, you know, that's an issue. But what has happened is the United States has simply assumed control of lands that are legally the property of the Hawaiian nation.

**JKK:** Yes, and also just to go back to your earlier point about how these were enshrined under Kingdom law. That was under Kamehameha III's rule—

**JKO:** That's correct.

**JKK:** —during the land division of 1848, known as the Māhele.

**JKO:** That's correct.

**JKK:** So, even the U.S. in the Apology Resolution did not refer to these as "native lands"; they referred to them as national lands.

**JKO:** That's correct.

**JKK:** And so it would seem that the proper point of reference in terms of a legal framework would be international law, not U.S. domestic law.

**JKO:** That's also correct. The solution to this, basically, is for an international body to intercede. Or for the United States to, on its own, recognize that it does not have—it does not own and could not transfer the Crown and Government Lands of a nation-state. And once it does this, I mean, where this goes and where this ends up is difficult to tell, but there's no way around it.

**JKK:** I wonder then if the Court will just avoid deciding this question because they might say it is a political question given that there is this federal legislation looming in the background of this U.S. Supreme Court—also known as the Akaka Bill.

**JKO:** It was just reintroduced.

**JKK:** Just since Obama was inaugurated, this legislation has been reintroduced to Congress and is called the Native Hawaiian Reorganization Act of 2009. And this is known as the Akaka Bill, after Senator Akaka, which has been a political football for the past nine years since neoconservatives have opposed it. Now what is to me so twisted in terms of this U.S. Supreme Court case is that you have both the Office of Hawaiian Affairs and Governor Lingle's state administration in Hawaiʻi supporting this federal legislation that I have always understood to be an attempt to quash Hawaiian title to these same lands. So, could you speak to this Akaka Bill proposal looming in the background of this court case?

**JKO:** It's interesting to see that the media here is really focusing on the lack of banning of gambling as a really big issue. Even at its best, even if the federal recognition bill, if the Akaka Bill—which used to be the Akaka-Stevens Bill— was operating with the largest interests of Native Hawaiians in mind, then it would certainly have, at different points, guaranteed the right of the Natives to claim their native or national lands. It makes no allowances for the Hawaiian people, people who are of Hawaiian ancestry, to make the claim for these lands. And this is a huge problem for any emerging Hawaiian governing entity. Where would the resources come from? What we are talking about is, potentially, a small little bureau or office someplace that will still be dependent on somebody giving it money.

Now, that's only the smallest part of the problem. The biggest problem is that you're still messing around, you're still basically assuming that the United States has the right to withhold the national lands of the Hawaiian nation. This is one of the reasons why I've consistently opposed federal recognition. Because, frankly, if our people really didn't want to separate from the United States entirely and wanted a "nation within a nation" status, if really all of our people really wanted that, I wouldn't argue it. You know, cultures change, and people change. But the fact of the matter is, one still has to deal with the illegality of the U.S. possession of our national lands, and none of the federal recognition bills from 1994 on dealt with that question, and as far as I'm concerned, it's a very easy argument for people who think law matters to make. Fix that. Fix the issue of title first. If Hawaiian people want to be connected to the United States, want to remain part of the United States, that's one thing, but somebody had better figure out how to fix the fact that the U.S. has no right to these lands and really had no right to the sovereignty of the Hawaiian people in the first place.

**JKK:** Yes! And even if Hawaiians all wanted federal recognition, and our land title was recognized first, we'd have to give up title to become federally recognized, because under U.S. law, a Native governing entity can only assert jurisdiction over their lands if they are held under federal supervision.

**JKO:** That's right. We'd basically come under the plenary power of the Congress of the United States.

**JKK:** It's a paradox.

**JKO:** I mean I think that's actually germane to all of this discussion about the ceded lands. I'm a plaintiff insisting that the state should not have the right to sell ceded lands, not because the state has a fiduciary responsibility to the Hawaiian people but because I know those lands to belong to the Hawaiian nation. Until that problem is discussed and addressed, we need to do that. But it's really clear to me. Federal recognition threatens native title, it absolutely does. It will eliminate it, and this is another reason why we really should not, we really cannot, go down that road.

**JKK:** Well, in concluding our interview I want to invite you to leave us with any last thoughts on this case.

**JKO:** I think Americans should be really concerned about what the Supreme Court does in this case. If respect for law matters, and it should, we have seen in the last eight years what the kind of ignoring of national law, international law, have really basically done to undermine the United States' presence and safety in the world. Americans really ought to cherish an approach to law that is rigorous and unflinching. The Kingdom of Hawaiʻi was created in order to protect resources, and the people of this nation had every right to exist; we were a good nation, and the taking of that nation is something that is regretted not just by Hawaiians but by many people of Hawaiʻi because we did things lawfully.

# STEVEN SALAITA ON COLONIZATION AND ETHNIC CLEANSING IN NORTH AMERICA AND PALESTINE

My interview with Steven Salaita was included in the first part of a two-part segment on the politics of Israeli occupation and settler colonialism with a specific focus on the Boycott, Divestment, Sanctions movement. At the time of the interview (2009), Salaita was an assistant professor of English at Virginia Tech (he secured tenure there in 2011). In the interview, he addressed issues of settler colonialism in Palestine and how they compare to the colonization of Native North America.

In his books, Salaita addresses a range of issues relating to literature and cultural politics. His published books include *Anti-Arab Racism in the USA: Where It Comes from and What It Means for Politics* (2006), winner of the 2007 Gustavus Myers Center for the Study of Bigotry and Human Rights' "Outstanding Book" Award; *The Holy Land in Transit: Colonialism and the Quest for Canaan* (2006); *Arab American Literary Fictions, Cultures, and Politics* (2007); *The Uncultured Wars: Arabs, Muslims, and the Poverty of Liberal Thought* (2008); *Modern Arab American Fiction: A Reader's Guide* (2011); *Israel's Dead Soul* (2011); *Uncivil Rites: Palestine and the Limits of Academic Freedom* (2015); and *Inter/Nationalism: Decolonizing Native America and Palestine* (2016).

In 2014, after being hired by the administration at the University of Illinois at Urbana–Champaign but prior to assuming his position there, he was fired after tweeting criticisms of the Israeli government's bombing in Gaza that summer. In response, the Center for Constitutional Rights supported Salaita in filing a civil rights suit against the university, claiming that his First Amendment right to free speech had been violated. As a result of this controversy, the university was censured by the American Association of University Professors and finally awarded Salaita in excess of $800,000 in a settlement. From 2015 to 2017 he held a position as Edward W. Said Chair of American Studies at the American University of Beirut.

This interview took place on May 12, 2009.

**J. Kēhaulani Kauanui:** I want to start by asking about your own personal and professional trajectory, and how you got involved in issues relating to Palestine.

**Steven Salaita:** I was born here in the United States. My father is from Jordan and my mother is Nicaraguan of Palestinian origin, so I've always had a sense of interest in the Middle East and a sense of the importance of the issue of Palestinian nationhood from an early age. And so I started reading when I was a teenager and never stopped.

When I was getting my master's degree, I took a course in Native American studies and really became interested in it, and so I started thinking about the two parts of the world—North America and Palestine—in common and ended up finding lots of interesting connections between the two, so that's what I'm working at. I'm mostly interested in examining Palestine in the context of Indigenous studies, rather than just as something that's examined in Middle East studies.

**JKK:** Yes. Your book, *The Holy Land in Transit,* speaks to colonization both in North America and Palestine. Could you talk about settler colonialism as you examine it in both of these places and different periods?

**SS:** I would love to, sure. There are probably more differences in the way that both parts of the world were colonized than anybody could accommodate, but at the same time, there are more than a few interesting similarities. Even "similarities" is kind of a weak word to use to base a comparative study; there are actually some dialectical interchanges between the two.

Settlers in North America—particularly in New England—had a sense of chosenness and an idea of destiny that comes straight out of the Old Testament, particularly the part where Joshua crosses the river Jordan and he's told by God to exterminate all of the natives—the Canaanites, the Amalekites, the Jebusites, and others—in other words, the indigenous populations, which were tribal and polytheistic at the time. This story plays a central role in an American sense of destiny. You can read it in the writings of Cotton Mather, and you could even see the discourse being put to use in a lot of current geopolitics: again, a sense of exporting modernity, making the world a better and safer place for people who are civilized. The decrying of Native and Indigenous cultural practices that are premodern.

If you go back to Palestine, the correlation is pretty obvious. Zionism started in earnest in the second half of the nineteenth century, and there was always a sense that the United States should and could be central to the completion or the success of the Zionist project. Not only is the United States Israel's strongest and most ardent supporter right now—that's a connection right there—but more than that, a lot of the early Zionist leaders, including David Ben-Gurion, who is sort of considered the father of Israel in the same way that George

Washington is in the United States, actually turned toward the dispossession of North American Indigenous peoples as a source of inspiration. He's quoted as saying something along the lines of, "Look what the Americans did, they took this land that was filled with savages and filled with swamps and they displaced the savages and drained the swamps and they ended up building this great civilization and that's what we're trying to do." So there's a very strong interchange between the United States and Israel, not just in terms of geopolitical interests, but there's also a very strong interchange in terms of how each nation plays into the imagination of the other one.

**JKK:** Yes. In terms of what we call Manifest Destiny here, right?

**SS:** Exactly.

**JKK:** One of my past guests on the show was Steven Newcomb, who has written a book I think you're familiar with, *Pagans in the Promised Land: Decoding the Doctrine of Christian Discovery.*

**SS:** I love that book.

**JKK:** You've mentioned the term "savages." Could you speak to the correlation between American exceptionalism and Israeli exceptionalism and how this is linked to discourses of the so-called savage? In the contemporary media reports, even in this last onslaught in Gaza, I'm very struck by the way the media continues to portray Palestinians, in many respects, as twenty-first-century savages. Could you speak to that and perhaps explain exceptionalism as a concept?

**SS:** The idea of American exceptionalism is tied into Manifest Destiny, of course, and it's the idea that America is exceptional in the world—but as a force of good, not bad, so it's an exceptional force of good. Because to be exceptional doesn't necessarily connote anything positive, but there's a positive context for that sort of claim.

I think Israel's sense of exceptionalism is quite similar to the one in the United States. They don't use the term Manifest Destiny, but the concept is very much at play. They are affecting modernity in Palestine the same way the United States did. In other words, they're taking "pre-civilized" societies and they're either removing them and clearing a space for civilization, or they're undergoing a process of civilizing them and bringing them into modernity.

The language is different, though. In some early Zionist literature, particularly in the first half of the twentieth century, you get a lot of discussion of Palestinians as uncivilized and barbaric and savage, the same type of language that American settlers used and a lot of Americans continue to use regarding North America's Indigenous peoples. But now I think the term *terrorist* or *terrorism* seems to be the adequate stand-in for the notion that the Palestinians are uncivilized. Instead of calling them savages, they tend to refer to them in a blanket way as terrorists. Every form of Palestinian resistance gets deemed an act of terrorism, and that locks them into the same type of perceived premodern space that the word *savage* would have locked—and continues to lock—a lot of natives into.

**JKK:** Could you speak to the concept and process of ethnic cleansing?

**SS:** Yes.

**JKK:** I know that in the context of the academic and cultural boycott and the broad-based campaign to boycott Israel there's a lot of resistance to acknowledging the ethnic cleansing of Palestinians. Could you speak to that and especially draw out some of the comparisons around how this has been used as a method to settle settler-colonial states?

**SS:** The term "ethnic cleansing" is central to the conversation of boycott, and you're right, it's a term that many of Israel's supporters—all the way from the hard right to a lot of progressive Zionists—feel very uncomfortable about.

It simply means, at its most basic, that a particular community and its attendant culture are being removed in the service of replacing it with another community and another culture. There are all kinds of state-sponsored programs in Israel to supposedly Judaize Palestine and to de-Arabize it, and these are the central key words of ethnic cleansing. It's the idea that Palestinian people and their culture either need to be extirpated or appropriated. So there's the process of doing both, much in the same way as it happened and continues to happen in North America. The Pacific Island cultures that are engaged with the United States have dealt with a remarkable amount of appropriation, and American Indians have dealt with a remarkable amount of appropriation, like Philip Deloria discusses in *Playing Indian*.

You see the same some sort of thing in Palestine. They're taking the parts of Palestinian culture that will supplement their credibility as stewards of the land, while at the same time cleansing the land of the dimensions of Palestinian culture that are not only unsatisfying to them, but that are an impediment to the realization of a Judeo-centric state. That's what they're going for. And in the laws of Israel itself, Israeli citizenship is not based on location or genealogy; it's based exclusively on ethnicity. A Jew who was born in the United States can claim Israeli citizenship even if that person has never been in a synagogue or been to the Middle East, even if that person's genealogy doesn't come from the Middle East, whereas the indigenous Palestinians who have been removed don't have that same right. In fact, people can convert to Judaism and then they can claim access to an Israeli citizenship. The very idea of Israel itself as a Jewish state lends itself to ethnic cleansing.

To connect it back to North America, it's not an accident that it wasn't until 1924 that Indians were given American citizenship. There was always a sense that America would have to come into existence and realize its sense of destiny as a land of milk and honey, and realizing its duty to effect modernity under the dictates of God—not in conjunction with the presence of natives, but right through the process of eliminating their presence culturally or, in some cases, physically.

**JKK:** Given the ongoing occupation issues and the violations of UN resolutions and international law in many respects, can you tell us where you stand on the issue of the Boycott, Divestment, Sanctions campaign focused on Israel—that is, the BDS movement?

**SS:** I stand firmly behind it.

**JKK:** And does that include, for you, an academic and cultural boycott?

**SS:** Absolutely it does.

**JKK:** As an academic here in the United States, how would you respond to those who would say, "Steven, how can you alienate your colleagues in Israel? Aren't you building more walls between potential allies and critics in Israel?"

**SS:** I would say that, no, that's not what I'm doing. First of all, I don't have as much of a sense of responsibility toward those Israeli academics who are supposedly going to be affected as much as I have a sense of responsibility toward those Palestinians who are continually having their rights taken away from them—the Palestinian academics. Second of all, the academic and cultural boycott of Israeli institutions does not preclude in any way a sense of community, a sense of shared politics, and a sense of interaction between individual Israelis. In fact, a lot of people involved in the Boycott, Divestment, Sanctions movement are Jewish-Israeli citizens, and you can create a sense of solidarity across ethnic lines. It's based not only politics but on a mutual sense of justice and the notion that we can't allow Israel to keep behaving the way it's been behaving, that serious pressure needs to be exerted on Israel. If we continue to humor Israel and its academics, most of whom are remarkably and directly complicit in violations of human rights, then Israel will have no incentive to quit mistreating and dispossessing and slaughtering the Palestinians.

**JKK:** Do you think we're at a tipping point for the broad-based boycott movement to take hold in the U.S. regarding Israel?

**SS:** I think it's doing pretty well. You have Stanley Fish writing about it in the *New York Times*—sort of screeching about it, actually—and misrepresenting it, but yes, it's becoming an issue. The boycott movement has tons of institutional and individual endorsers, and those academics and activists that identify themselves as Zionists really seem to be in a bit of a fervor about it, which is always a good bellwether for how much our movement is succeeding.

**JKK:** Any closing thoughts you'd like to leave us with?

**SS:** Just the suggestion to check out the boycott movement, to think about assisting in a movement on local campuses or in communities to compel institutions and companies to divest whatever investments they have from companies that do business with Israel. It was, in the end, the wonderful international pressure that helped play a central role in bringing down apartheid in South Africa, and the same thing needs to happen to Israel on behalf of the Palestinians.

# PAUL CHAAT SMITH ON THE POLITICS OF REPRESENTATION

Paul Chaat Smith (Comanche) was a guest on the program to discuss his then newly released book, *Everything You Know about Indians Is Wrong* (2009), a collection of essays written from 1992 to 2008 that chronicles the evolution of his views on the politics of being a Native American, from his involvement as an activist within the American Indian Movement to his present employment at the Smithsonian Institution. In 2001 Smith joined the National Museum of the American Indian, where he currently serves as associate curator. His projects include the permanent history gallery, performance artist James Luna's *Emendatio* at the 2005 Venice Biennale, and *Fritz Scholder: Indian/Not Indian*. Back in 1977, Smith was the founding editor of the American Indian Movement's *Treaty Council News*, and in 1996, with Robert Warrior, he coauthored *Like a Hurricane: The Indian Movement from Alcatraz to Wounded Knee*.

This interview took place on August 25, 2009.

**J. Kēhaulani Kauanui:** I want to first tell you how much I enjoyed reading this book, and that I appreciate the range of topics you cover; everything from activism, art, the politics of museums, Native identity and authenticity debates, as well as a diverse spectrum of popular culture, thinking of everything from *Dances with Wolves* to *Life* magazine. I also just wanted to say, before I launch into my questions, that I find your writing to be both elegant and biting—a rare combination. This collection of essays is certainly very provocative.

**Paul Chaat Smith:** Did you find any of it funny?

**JKK:** I did, in fact. I was laughing a lot through parts of the book, while other parts were painful to read. The chapter on irony made me laugh the most; although it is challenging, it's my favorite chapter.

**PCS:** Sometimes people think they're insulting me if they say the book is funny.

**JKK:** Oh, no.

**PCS:** It's meant to be funny, actually; it was intentional.

**JKK:** Would you tell us some about your personal background and how you came to be a cultural critic and curator?

**PCS:** I think because I wasn't good at very much else, that's probably the simplest way to explain it. I'm somebody who first got into political activism through the American Indian Movement, but found that limiting in many ways. I was always interested in broader issues of culture and history, so I guess partly I ended up writing to figure out what I think about things. Over time, that changed from being narrowly about Indian movement issues to broader, cultural changes—the art world, things like that. I never found a place in a particular career growing up, and I didn't necessarily think of becoming a curator or cultural critic, so it ended up being writing about things that interested me and finding an audience for that.

**JKK:** In the book you identify yourself as a "suburban Indian," which I found refreshing only because one rarely hears Native people cop to suburban backgrounds, even though it's very common. I also appreciate how it messes with the dichotomy between urban and reservation dwelling. Could you speak to that, and where you came from in that respect?

**PCS:** Yes, that was one of the alternative titles for the book at one point: *The Suburban Comanche Way of Knowledge*. I don't know why we didn't go with that.

You talk about a dichotomy, and I think that—as is common for many people—it's often not so simple. I was raised in the city; I was raised in the reservation. In my case, it's sort of hard to shorthand that, but most of the time growing up, I lived in a suburb of Washington, D.C., so it wasn't an urban background either. I was connected to Oklahoma; we went there at least a few times a year. My grandparents on both sides and my relatives are from Oklahoma, so that was a strong influence, but I wasn't actually living there.

The suburban thing was something that, you know, when you're coming of age and looking in the discourse—which I didn't know to call a discourse back then—there's the urban Indian story, which is very romantic and appealing in its own way. And then, of course, the reservation story, which is the center of authenticity and validation. And then suburban, where does that fit in? What does that do?

I think in some cases I wanted to write about that because it was difficult to address. Certainly, in terms of somebody who was questioning my own authenticity for a lot of years in my life, it's not something you really want to advertise. But do you want to go around pretending you're somebody that you're not? Eventually, it gets really boring to do that, so I quit doing it.

**JKK:** It could get exhausting, right?

**PCS:** Yes!

**JKK:** Well, shifting to the urban part of your own story, I really enjoyed reading your reflection on the American Indian Movement and your own political activism, especially after having read the book you coauthored, *Like a Hurricane: The Indian Movement from Alcatraz to Wounded Knee*. Would you speak to that, and also what led you out of the suburbs into the American Indian Movement?

**PCS:** Yes. My introduction to all of that came about as somebody who followed the events on television—which didn't happen very often—and through hearing about it. The event which struck much closer to home was the Trail of Broken Treaties Caravan that came into Washington, D.C., in 1972, just before Nixon was reelected as president. That was literally six miles from my home, and I remember—I didn't take part in it, but I do remember—seeing the encampment on the grounds of the Bureau of Indian Affairs, following the breaking news. It was a very big story in Washington; it never was anywhere else, really, it was eclipsed by other events—Paris peace talks about Vietnam and the election, of course—but that was something that I was very drawn to. I was still in high school at the time. I think braver people than myself would've certainly signed on. I certainly didn't do that, but I was fascinated by it, by this movement.

I went to college a year later and signed up for an internship that was at the Wounded Knee Legal Defense/Offense Committee; this was a year after the occupation of Wounded Knee in 1973. I saw the opportunity to join this legal committee in South Dakota, and I said, "Boy, I bet this would be interesting." So that's how I ended up at the movement, and what I observed there was this amazing energy from folks from cities. Some of the senior leaders—Russell Means, Dennis Banks, the Bellecourt Brothers—really came out of an urban Indian experience, alongside folks from the Pine Ridge Indian Reservation, where the takeover took place. So it was seeing how both of those things were essential. The kind of sophistication that people like Russ Means and Dennis Banks had were beyond the reach of people who had spent their entire lives at Pine Ridge, and I was able to see sort of those two things coming together. Again, these dichotomies that end up not really telling you a very accurate or interesting story began to be exploded.

**JKK:** I want to come back around to some of those questions, in terms of that kind of complication and what it takes when these things are actually happening on the ground. But first, in relation to your own work as a cultural critic coming out of this activist experience and history, what do you see as the role of an Indian intellectual vis-à-vis Native communities and the dominant society? I'm thinking about one of your essays, called "On Romanticism," where you talk about the responsibility to speak out about poachers when you're talking about films and Native appropriation.

**PCS:** I think my ideas about that and my role has changed over the years. Immediately following my work at the Wounded Knee Committee, up until 1979, I really was somebody who was officially part of the movement. I was writing then as a partisan—"propaganda" sounds like a harsh word; I don't mean to say it was a dishonest venture—but it was as somebody trying to advocate for a political line. I was part of the movement in fulfilling that role.

**JKK:** Generating reports from the front?

**PCS:** Yes, and advocating for a position. I was the first editor of the *Treaty Council News*, which was part of the international division of the American Indian Movement. That work raised questions that I've dealt with since then; but again, it was in support of an organizational objective. I found that limiting and, conveniently, the Indian movement fell apart, so I didn't have that gig anymore.

What I found is that there became this way of writing about the Indian world, and about Indian politics and culture, in which there was this self-appointed spokesperson-voice—which a lot of us know—in which, by virtue of whoever you are, magically, at some point, you suddenly feel appointed to speak for Indians in a very general sense. Not necessarily from your own education or scholarship or experience, but in the sense that we can all talk about the treaties and the struggle and all of that.

I began questioning how useful that was, but then I also felt like I wanted to talk. I was interested in debates within the Indian world, and I didn't want to be in this position of talking about the white man and history in the kind of lecturing tone we developed to a fine art beginning in those days. I was interested in talking about issues within the Indian world—not excluding any other audience, but that was more interesting to me than trying to talk in very general terms about our oppression and our struggle. So that's where my work gradually shifted to thinking about questions and working them out through writing and finding other people who were interested in those same questions.

**JKK:** I see, and you said that the Wounded Knee Legal Defense/Offense Committee work that you did emerged from an internship when you were in college, right?

**PCS:** Yes.

**JKK:** Now, did you go back to school after that, or is that what propelled you to go further into the activist world, and what took you to San Francisco?

**PCS:** I went to this interesting college in Ohio that no longer exists called Antioch [it closed in 2008 but reopened in 2011], which was in Yellow Springs, Ohio. I was interested in it because they had a pass/fail system and I wasn't a very good student in school; in fact, I barely graduated from high school. It was also a radical, alternative kind of place, so I liked that about it. It wasn't a good place for me to get an education, because it really relied on the individual to create their own plan for college and be self-motivated, and I was with people that were a lot more skilled in that than I was.

I think, regardless, I probably would've been seduced by the Indian movement anyway. It was pretty exciting for several years. I did go back and forth to college a few times, returned to school a few times, but I did not graduate. Most of what I did in the mid-seventies was basically movement-related.

**JKK:** I see, and you do mention in your book that going to a place without that kind of structure maybe wasn't the best thing.

**PCS:** Not for me. A lot of the students were people who had gone to extremely good high schools, that were much better than the average high school, and who really focused on what they were doing. So, it wasn't the best thing for me, but it got me to the Indian movement, so that was good.

**JKK:** When you left the movement, or when you departed that work in 1979, you went to New York City, right?

**PCS:** Yes.

**JKK:** Could you tell us a little about the eighties for you?

**PCS:** Well, once again, I didn't really know what I was doing. I think I wrote in the book that I ended up in New York because it was the city of choice for political exiles all over the world and I felt like a political exile. I cut my hair—I had very long hair—I cut my hair and I liked passing for someone of Latino descent. New York is a great place when you're in your late twenties and thirties, and that's where I was for about the next eleven years. I knew people; I had friends there. The attraction of New York was that it was kind of a new start, and those felt like good reasons at the time.

**JKK:** Moving to your book, tell us about the title that you chose, *Everything You Know about Indians Is Wrong*, and also about the image that appears on the cover of the book.

**PCS:** I didn't have a strong idea for a title. I thought one would develop; I was sort of playing with ideas like *American Amnesia*, but nothing I felt absolutely clicked. The joke I said was that *Chinese Democracy* should be the title, because it had been so long since my first book that I sort of created this competition with Axl Rose from Guns N' Roses as to who could do their follow-up project sooner. I think I won by a few months; I think I did beat out Guns N' Roses' effort. So *Chinese Democracy*—I always thought it was a great title, but we didn't go with that.

Anyway, the publisher decided to make this their lead title for the spring 2009 catalog, and they really supported the book and called me and said, "Well, here's what we wanted to do with the title: *Everything You Know about Indians Is Wrong.*" I instantly disliked it, and for about a week and a half I felt sure this was the wrong title. Even though before, these people had said how much they loved my writing in the book and everything else, all of a sudden they had bad taste. My wife finally convinced me, she said, "You know what? This is a really *really* good title." And when I asked them, "Where did it come from?" the University of Minnesota Press said, "Well, Paul, it came from your writing. It's in the book itself." That kind of undercut my argument that it was a Beavis and Butt-Head title, and I'm a really smart, sophisticated guy and blah, blah, blah. So anyway, officially, the title was my idea the whole time, and the reaction has been quite good. People are busy these days; they don't have a whole lot of time, so having some mysterious, vague title probably doesn't make the most sense.

The image you ask about—the book is dealing with these issues of romanticism, identity, specific histories, contemporary art, and it's very hard to get those things in an image. So I was very pleased with what they came up with. This image is actually based on a photograph of a diorama at the Natural History Museum in California, and the museum label says it shows Indians gathering something or other for their hide. That clicked with me right away. I thought it really conveyed these ideas of what the book was trying to do, which was to question what people know about Indians and how they know it.

**JKK:** I noticed in your essay titled "Americans without Tears" that you talk about the theory that you have about white people who are interested in Indians. Will you say more? It seems like that's almost a framing device for the whole book.

**PCS:** Yes. The essay was written for a show that included Indian contemporary artists and non-Indian contemporary artists, which is, sadly enough, still somewhat unusual—there tend to be these big group shows of Indian artists that often do not get the attention they deserve. It's sort of a new, innovative thing to include Indian contemporary artists and non-Indian artists in a theme that relates to Indian history and culture. That's the context in which I was writing the essay, and think it's sort of an argument that's at the heart of the book: I feel inarguably that the Indian experience, contact in 1492, created the world we live in today. It was the biggest, most profound event in known human history, yet Indians are marginalized in this amazing way. So, it's like thinking about all the libraries and scholarships that don't exist about Indians in a serious way— what's the reason for that? What is the reason that Indians are ubiquitous, you know? Cities and states and sports teams and rivers and mountains are named after Indians. Indians are everywhere and nowhere at the same time.

Over the years, I had come to the conclusion that really smart white Americans learned at an early age to not take Indian stuff seriously. They're smart, they realize, "Well, what is the real history of the country? What is this thing with Indians? There must be more to it than this." And I think there's almost this self-protection: somebody could look around and say, "You know what, there's probably not a lot of point in really understanding this too deeply, because the whole world is built on not looking at it deeply, not taking it seriously." If you think about who are the white American scholars that really write about Indians—and you and I both know that in the field we have absolutely, stellar, amazing colleagues that are not Indian who have been mentors to me, and I honor them more for this—but generally speaking, the field of history, for example, these questions don't attract the brightest lights. And how could they not? This is core to American history, right?

In a sense, you could say that in other eras the African American experience was put to the side—the Civil War, yes, but the African American experience has never really been central to American history. It was always much more important than we are, though, where there's this end date of relevance of Indians—1890 at the latest. How could that be, given what the country is? Given how the world came to be the way it is? I think it's that really smart people know to stay away.

**JKK:** In the essay "Americans without Tears" you say that Indians are at the center of everything that happened in the Western Hemisphere over the past five centuries, so that experience is at the heart of the history of everyone who lives here. What really strikes me about that is you are demanding that we all reconsider indigeneity as central to the formation of the modern world. In other words, this isn't just simply you calling for inclusion of Indians, right—it's about a major shift in our thinking in terms of our epistemological grounding?

**PCS:** Exactly. And when I worked at the permanent history exhibition at the National Museum of the American Indian [NMAI], one of the things we would do is collect quotes from some of the most conservative scholars and historians—politically conservative—who would say exactly what we were saying: this was the most profound event that happened, this was the greatest transfer of wealth, this is what created, you know, Spain as a superpower. The particular arguments that support this premise—that the Indian experience in central to how the world came to be—is not really debated. It's asserted and then it's clear, then it becomes very specialized, but it's never actually in the world as a powerful idea. As soon as we enter the picture, we're like victims, and it's an anthropological story or a cultural story—it's not about the major questions of history that are still relevant today.

**JKK:** You do get to that, too, in the early essays in the collection, where you discuss Indigenous dispossession on this continent. It seems you do so only in order to make a contemporary story intelligible, which takes me back to what you were saying about the role of Indian intellectuals and coming out of movement politics, where there was a lecturing tone on the meta-history. Would you speak more to your strategy about how you account for that dispossession and your insistence on not using it in that way to instill guilt?

**PCS:** Yes, I was trying to understand the particularities in the way that Indians are perceived in the U.S. in the twentieth century.

Looking at that, it's a bit complicated. You have this absolutely vicious racism toward Indians that exists today and will certainly exist for a long time in areas where Indians live, a sort of very specific kind of colonial violence that happens. But in the part of the country where there aren't visible Indians— where people think there aren't Indians, but of course there are—we're thought to be extinct and/or we're romanticized. So I thought that particular aspect of it was something that I wanted to understand better. How is it that, statistically, Indians in the U.S. are, up until recently, overwhelmingly the poorest folks in the country? And there are examples of vicious racism toward Indians, yet we're seen in sort of a flattering way—a patronizing way, but a flattering way— of being environmentalists, and being spiritual, and all those things. To me, those things seem to work together.

So the guilt, when you're asking about the guilt trip part of it, the victim part of it, this idea that the country owes us something and that we have been treated badly and we're seeking redress, it plays into those stereotypes in a way that it felt hard to see where that advanced anything. I mean, it would deal with things short-term, and the Indian movement was brilliant at using some of these things, but it didn't actually empower us very much and it asked white Americans who tended to be more open-minded, liberal folks who should be strong allies to feel personally responsible or guilty for things that they directly weren't responsible for. I think, also, it made *us* feel important. I remember when I would say those kinds of things, I felt important. I felt like I had been victimized—it had nothing to do with the Fort Laramie Treaty of 1868, but I could sort of take that on, make myself more important, make my life more important in a way, but what does that actually accomplish for the Ogalas who actually have something at stake with that treaty?

Deconstructing what racism toward Indians looks like in the U.S. means you really have to take a hard look at romanticism and how it operates. The difficult questions a lot of my work has tried to take on is how much we, as Indians, believe that, how much we actually believe these New Age ideas about us. It supports a whole discourse about Indians that is disempowering, that doesn't make us smarter, that doesn't make us more strategic. And all of that helps marginalize our situation.

**JKK:** I do recall when you talked about romanticism as a distinctive type of racism that confronts Indians and the sort of demand from the dominant society of wanting the myth over real human struggles. That reminds me, too, you ask in several of the essays the haunting question to dominant society, "Are Indian people allowed to change?" Whereas, you suggest that the real question for Native people is, "How will we live?"

**PCS:** I think the romanticism paradigm sets up a situation where we're Indian as long as we don't change—or that we can change in certain ways, but we still have to have this connection to Indian culture as it has been defined in this discourse, or we're not Indian anymore. I think that idea is based on a whole number of lies that say we were, generally speaking, the same in contact when we were vastly different—that we had similar ideas about culture and the environment and all of that, which is not really true—and that our whole point since contact is to survive and not change. I think it's possible to look at the last five centuries and see that Indian folks—again we're speaking in generalities— have survived because we changed, and we're always about change, like humans generally are.

I think the tag on us is that, of course, we're against technology, we're against the modern world, we're against new ideas, and we have this sort of perfect kind of culture that goes back to the beginning of time or something, that we're the caretakers of.

**JKK:** That leads me to the expression that you address in your book, called "walking in two worlds." You address the problems with it with regard to the ongoing struggles over Native identity, both within and outside of Native communities. How about that stereotype or cliché?

**PCS:** Yes. I think that's something else that a lot of us believe. I mean, a lot of these things that I take on are important ideas that I've held that were very important growing up—some of the books and movies—*Touch the Earth,* for example, this book of wonderful little Indian quotations. These are really important cultural touchstones for Indians of a certain generation in the U.S., walking in two worlds. Like a lot of clichés, there's some truth to it, there's some utility in looking at it that way, but most humans today walk in a lot of different worlds and have complex backgrounds shaped by gender, sexual orientation, personal history, all kinds of things. I think the idea that Indians can be re- duced to the idea of two worlds that we negotiated is sadly hollow.

**JKK:** It's a very static notion about culture, too.

**PCS:** Yes, and it reduces either one of these worlds to something that somehow would suggest, "Well, that's all knowable and understandable and has certain rules and conventions," and it's a lot more complicated than that.

**JKK:** That then feeds into the whole phenomenon of not seeing Indigenous agency and respecting Indian authorship. I remember in your essay "On Romanticism" you note, "We are witnessing a new age in the objectification of American Indian history and culture—one that doesn't even need Indians except as endorsers." What's the alternative?

**PCS:** I think it's a lot about Indian folks settling—in movies, for example, for being the actors. Being an actor is certainly an honorable thing to be, but to not think that has a legitimacy and an authenticity versus who wrote the script, who directed the film, who green-lighted the project—all of the other things that actually make it an important cultural artifact. I certainly noticed there was an anti-intellectual part of our accepting of this colonized notion of what it means to be Indian, that Indians don't write or that an Indian could act but an Indian couldn't direct.

I think there's this trend that was happening certainly in the seventies and eighties with some books and movies where they could be provably false, and the solution was usually to come up with an Indian who would say, "Well, it may not be exactly accurate, but I believe it," or "This reflects what I know the Indian experience," or "This supports a certain story." I think it's a lack of ambition from us, but I guess it's kind of fun to perform that way, too.

**JKK:** Right. Well, I want to use that thread of performance and visibility, if you will, to launch into a discussion about the art world. In several essays you take issue with the Indian Arts and Crafts Act. Would you explain what it is for a general audience and what you see as its problems?

**PCS:** Yes. It goes back to the issue of how Indian identity is understood and defined in the U.S., and the many different ways this is done. The legislation really had as its goal to support Indian artisans who were making work but couldn't sell jewelry, blankets, things like that because they were undercut by products from elsewhere, China, for example. Jewelry would have the word "Zuni" on it, and that would somehow be legal because that part was made in Zuni or something like that. So, anyway, there's the effort of this law that would seem to be admirable in supporting Indian folks making work and from these counterfeits. But it also extended to the art world, and part of it required that there be evidence, that someone at a gallery who was saying they were Indian had to prove that they were Indian.

That got into the complexities of how that's done, and it's not simple. The government does not have a rule that says all Indians must be a certain degree; it doesn't work like that. Basically, it ended up trying to police identity in the arts, which I think never works. It's complicated because there are writers and artists who say they're Indian and they're not, and it ends up being exposed, but then they have this career. So the question is, What do you do about that? I don't know. I'm not sure that you can ever define a system or legislation that's going to solve that problem. The issue of what makes somebody an Indian is a monster, and I don't see a way that the complexities of that are going to go away or be easily solved.

**JKK:** What is the policy for the NMAI in terms of representing Native artists?

**PCS:** That would be hard to characterize exactly. We have a modern and contemporary art program that exhibits American Indian artists, but we also have these festivals in which people, in some cases, are selling work and are performing in other cases. The procedure for all of that changes depending on what kind of event it is, so it's hard to generalize it. The museum is trying to be thoughtful about all of these issues and to recognize the complexity—and we're hemispheric, so we're not even just the U.S.—so how all these issues play out changes radically. It's even different in significant ways in Canada, but it's very different in Latin America, Hawai'i, and other cases as to how that works.

**JKK:** That's right. We don't have enrollment for Native Hawaiians, yet Native Hawaiians are included in the mandate for the museum. So it's interesting in that respect too, in terms of dealing with that diversity, but also across these nation-state borders.

On the issue of the museum itself—I was there at the groundbreaking ceremony as well as the opening events for the Native Nations procession, and I want to ask you: you say in several of the essays you talk about the problematics and politics of the museum, and in the afterword you say, "The NMAI always struck me as a bad idea, but a bad idea whose time had come." Would you explain what you mean, and also the paradox of the entire project?

**PCS:** I think the paradox was built in and is actually a great strength of the museum. To me, it's this tightly compressed Haiku of contradictions. It's part of the Smithsonian, a national museum of American Indians, and it's also hemispheric; it also only exists because of a collection from this one investment banker and Indian hobbyist collector, and it's on the main street of the U.S., the National Mall.

I always want us to lighten up and appreciate all those contradictions. I think the museum came together as a project when we were in what I call our "Dances with Wolves," triumphalist, Columbus-quincentenary phase, which was very much "We talk, you listen, and this is the way it's going to be." And it was also a political project, in the best sense of the word. It came out of this obsession that museums have. What other minority group has such a thing about museums? You don't see African Americans worrying a great deal about museums, and yet we—because of the way anthropology worked and the ways these museums actually owned not just a lot of our stuff but, in some cases, our ancestors—it's an intense interest for Indians in the U.S.

You factor all that in, and that it's part of the federal government, and what you get is what we were calling for a while, "museum different." It's always going to be mostly about the U.S.-Indian world, that's just a reality, and it's always going to have these stakeholders who feel very strongly how things should be, and it's always going to be a process of negotiation. My constituency is different than a lot of my colleagues' who curate contemporary art, because my constituency is made up of all kinds of folks who wouldn't necessarily go to a contemporary art museum.

I think of us as a big shopping mall. You have your Macy's at one end, and that might be traditional historic objects; you have a little boutique, some of my projects, perhaps—and I think that's appropriate because the Indian world is complex and disputatious. I think that's good, I think we're always trying to be like a chamber of commerce and make it all polite and respectful and interesting, but all that makes kind of for a boring museum experience.

**JKK:** You reference the modern and contemporary art program at the museum, and I want to ask what you think the role of museums is in developing contemporary Indian art? Also, there's a really provocative section from your book where you say: "I believe making Indian art is a vocation fraught with danger." Could you speak to those two things?

**PCS:** Well, I think a lot of folks would say there really is no need for Indian contemporary art, because what we're good at is making blankets and pots and all that. Of course, the blankets and pots were like inventions that were made often out of market forces and complex political situations, but that's how we're identified. So, when you have artists that do work that isn't familiar, that's challenging.

I think that supports one of the main goals of the museum, which is to say "Look, we're still here, we're still alive." It's kind of pathetic we have to say that, but a lot of visitors that come to Washington are actually fuzzy about whether Indians still exist or not. To show artists that are making work that is challenging to people's preconceived ideas about Indians can be very powerful. I think it has its place in the museum. I've always said that a museum's most important objective has to be to reframe and retell history, that that's always the most important goal. I think the art program that we've developed supports that and does things that a conventional history exhibition could never do.

**JKK:** You also seem drawn to artwork that is political but not didactic, and you discuss the work of James Luna, Erica Lord, and Faye HeavyShield, just to name a few. Could you tell us who you've got your eye on now, and also about this artist, Brian Jungen, who you will be curating really shortly for an October [2009] exhibit?

**PCS:** I've been interested in artists whose work can't be immediately understood as addressing a particular audience or answering a certain question. I'm very interested in artists that do work that raises questions and is more open-ended and can also simultaneously speak to Indian audiences and non-Indian audiences. So James Luna, his famous work from the 1980s—the artifact piece was him lying in a museum, the Museum of Man in San Diego, in a case so that people came by and didn't realize that was an actual person in there. I guess what draws me to a work like that is that he is speaking to an Indian audience, and at the same time he's critiquing a natural history museum. He's interested in a discussion within the Indian world, within his community. And I think that's the most powerful kind of work; and again, it isn't as simple as a political narrative, where it's a right or wrong, or victimization, or stereotypes, and somebody can look and "Oh yeah, I get it and I'm on the right side." I think most of his work makes everyone uncomfortable to some degree, or raises questions. So that's the work that I've focused on.

Brian Jungen, who you ask about, is an artist from British Columbia who makes these amazing sculptures out of ordinary objects. His most famous series, called *Prototypes for New Understanding*, were made from Nike Air Jordan shoes and were fashioned to look like Northwest Coast masks. It comments on how objects become fetishized, collected; as people might recall, when the Air Jordans came out, killings took place because they were so coveted. They were very expensive. Interestingly enough, Brian isn't from the Northwest Coast; he's from British Columbia, but from the interior, hundreds of miles to the north and the east, so he's not making a comment about his own identity or cultural beliefs. He's talking about the wallpapering of that imagery in a place like Vancouver, where it's everywhere. I think it's work that addresses a lot of issues people are thinking about, and is really amazingly accessible. Our show with him opens in October 2009 in Washington, and for people not familiar with his work, I think it's going to be a revelation.

**JKK:** Excellent. We talked earlier about your essay "A Place Called Irony." One of my own concerns is how colonialism gets mistaken for irony. You also talk about irony in the essay as a male figure, almost as a person, yet your title of the piece is irony as a place. I want to ask you about that, as well as your suggestion that knowing how to read the signs of irony is part of what you call "basic fluency all Indians must have to make sense in this empire of the senseless."

**PCS:** I came across a quote, I can't remember who it's from, but it talked about how Indians often talk about our experience, especially historically, in terms of irony or romantic transcendence. I thought that was really interesting, how much we're attracted to the device of humor and being ironic about our experience, so I was trying to investigate that. In the essay, irony dies, and at that moment when I was writing it, I wanted us to get past irony as this tool that is no longer useful. But, I don't know, we love irony. The downside is that it becomes a discourse in itself, that is, a way to not engage with difficult issues because it's all funny.

**JKK:** Well, in conclusion, I want to ask if there's anything in particular you want to leave us with.

**PCS:** The book is priced to sell, it doesn't have a lot of big words, it's not that long, and it makes a great Christmas gift.

# CIRCE STURM ON CHEROKEE IDENTITY POLITICS AND THE PHENOMENON OF RACIAL SHIFTING

Circe Sturm (Mississippi Choctaw descendant) granted me an interview to discuss her book *Becoming Indian: The Struggle over Cherokee Identity in the Twenty-First Century* (2011), which examines Cherokee identity politics and the phenomenon of racial shifting. The work explores the social and cultural values that lie behind this phenomenon and delves into the motivations of these individuals who find deep personal and collective meaning in reclaiming (or simply claiming) Indianness. Sturm teaches at the University of Texas at Austin, where she is an associate professor of anthropology and codirector of the Native American and Indigenous studies program. Her first book, *Blood Politics: Race, Culture and Identity in the Cherokee Nation of Oklahoma* (2002), explores issues of race, culture, nation, and citizenship in Cherokee Country, particularly as they are expressed through the idiom of "blood." I first met Sturm in 2003 when she was writing the book I interviewed her about, while we were both in-residence fellows at the School of American Research (now the School for Advanced Research). There she was a National Endowment for the Humanities Resident Scholar.

This interview took place on September 20, 2011.

**J. Kēhaulani Kauanui:** I want to start by asking if you could tell us some about your personal and academic background and how you came to do research on Cherokees.

**Circe Sturm:** Well, I was trained at the University of California at Davis, where I studied cultural anthropology as well as Native American studies. It was one of the few places at the time, in the mid-nineties, where you could do work in both programs and get a degree, where you had social science training as well as interdisciplinary training from Native American studies.

My personal background is that I am a Mississippi Choctaw descendant on my father's side, and I became interested in questions about blood and belonging that were sort of personal. Of course they were personal, but then I started getting more interested in why the kinds of questions that I had personally were not being addressed in the academic arena and not in terms of their broader political implications. At the time in the early nineties, there was still not much work being done on the intersections between race and citizenship and these narratives of blood and belonging. So, I started my first work really examining that topic with my first book, *Blood Politics*.

I ended up working in Cherokee Country because that context is much more like my personal context in the sense that there is much more diverse tribal citizenship than there is with Mississippi Choctaw. In the context of Mississippi Choctaw, there is a half-blood-quantum requirement for citizenship, whereas in the Cherokee Nation there is a descendancy requirement. Because of that, you have much more diversity and these issues are much more in the forefront in the Cherokee Nation than they are in a community like the Mississippi Choctaw.

**JKK:** For those who are not familiar with these categories, when you say the Mississippi Choctaw tribal nation has a half-blood requirement, you're talking about a blood-quantum rule of 50 percent. Can you just break down blood quantum as a concept for those who may be new to this? And how blood is at play in Native America?

**CS:** I think it depends on the tribal context. There are places where blood—the idea of blood—dovetails with traditional forms of belief systems about blood, where it may have to do with religious beliefs or clan belonging. It's a descendant tie, but it is also caught up with other metaphysical spiritual beliefs. So, that can preexist and be a part of the tribal community already. But then there's also the broader American U.S.A. nation-state trajectory about kinship beliefs, where there is this notion about blood relationships being quantifiable—that you can measure distance from your kin. And so, because of that, there's this sense that if you have a parent, then you are half whatever that is; you have a 50 percent blood inheritance. If you have a grandparent, then you're 25 percent of whatever that grandparent is. Then, you are measured by that quantifiable blood relationship.

**JKK:** And it always presumes a full-blood Indian ancestor, right? I mean that's the measurement, starting from the so-called full-blood.

**CS:** Right. It doesn't matter if that grandparent was a speaker and a traditionalist and happened to be half. They're going to measure blood belonging back to the full-blood and not to the person fully accepted within the community.

**JKK:** And that's a Euro-American way of measuring Indigenous identity.

**CS:** Exactly.

**JKK:** And now you just contrasted, too, the Mississippi Choctaw Tribe, which has the 50 percent blood-quantum rule, with the Cherokee Nation, which has a descendancy rule. For a general audience, explain please, what's the difference?

**CS:** So, with descendant it's about lineal descent, so it's sort of saying that as long as you have an ancestor you qualify. And in some tribal communities it has to be through the father's line or the mother's line that you have an ancestor on the father's side or mother's side, and that's specified in the citizenship requirement. But in the case of the Cherokee Nation they will accept any ancestor. So, it's basically an ancestry requirement, but there also is an assumption that through that ancestor there is a blood descendancy of some sort. But it doesn't matter what the amount is. It's not about a quantifiable relationship; it's just about a qualitative relationship of having had kin.

**JKK:** If you could speak to the title of your new book, *Becoming Indian: The Struggle over Cherokee Identity in the Twenty-First Century,* how did you choose it? And also, we know there are lots of battles going on at Cherokee around identity, and some of them are really volatile issues and a lot of them are centered on race and also the legacy of slavery. Could you say more?

**CS:** The title was basically trying to convey information to the general audience. If I had used some of the terms I actually employ in the book, I felt like people would be—if I had time to carefully explain—a little bit confused. So, this was a way in which I could signal what the book was about for the broadest possible audience. Basically, the book is dealing with people who are reclaiming or claiming, depending on the context, an Indigenous identity, in this case a Cherokee identity.

The reason why I talk about Indianness is because I also wanted to signal that part of this is largely about—it's about Indigenous politics and the rights to an Indigenous identity—but as you would see in the book, that definition of "Cherokeeness" and indigeneity gets very caught up with a more specifically racialized version of what an Indigenous identity is and idea of Indianness period. And so, it's largely about the shifts in the United States in racial value and how that kind of broader context of shifting racial values is encouraging and providing a context in which people would want to reclaim and reconnect and re-identify.

**JKK:** And now when you say claiming or reclaiming, can you break down the difference? And you're talking about shifting in your book dealing primarily with people who have self-identified as white and then coming to claim a Cherokee identity. What is the difference between claiming and reclaiming? Or claiming versus reclamation? And why Cherokee?

**CS:** So, I should say first off almost everyone who is involved in this process sees it themselves as reclaiming. They do not see themselves as making a new claim. So from their perspective, they are seeing if these are the people who are actually involved in the process, people who I term "racial shifters." I use that term because I'm starting with a census data, where vast numbers of people who identified as white. Probably about 93 percent of them were people who first identified as white who have been shifted to classify themselves as Indian and then to write in Cherokee. If you look at the 1970s to 2000s the Cherokee population grows at a rate of a 1,006 percent. It's an astronomical number. So, it is people who in that context are shifting their racial classification. So, from their perspective they all see this as a process of reclamation. The book also looks at how what I term "citizen Cherokee"—citizens of the three federally recognized Cherokee tribes: Cherokee Nation, Eastern Band of Cherokee Indians, and the United Keetoowah Band of Cherokee Indians—are also responding to this. For many of them, they view this as a process of claiming—claiming a connection where there isn't one or has not been one for a long time. That's why I say both, because I'm trying to acknowledge there are several different perspectives here on the nature of this process.

**JKK:** And I noticed the book is organized into two parts. The first part is on "racial shifters," and the second part is on "citizen Cherokees." You just mentioned the three federally recognized Cherokee governing entities: Cherokee Nation, Eastern Band, and United Keetoowah Band. You've identified—separate from those three, and federal recognition of course means tribal acknowledgment from the federal government that enables tribes to exercise certain elements of their sovereignty, so the government acknowledges sovereignty is inherent, but tribes are limited in terms of how they can exercise that sovereignty, depending on whether they have that federal recognition piece or not—238 self-identified Cherokee organizations, many of whom, if not most, are claiming they are tribes, and some of them are even going after federal recognition. A lot of them have state recognition. Could you speak to that in terms of how that plays a role in how the members of the three federally recognized tribes view these groups?

**CS:** So, just to clarify, there are 238—and that number is always in flux—self-identified Cherokee communities. That means it's not an individual asserting their rights to identify as a descendant in that context; it's people who have come together as a group and a community and seen themselves and named themselves as a Cherokee community. Sometimes they name themselves the Cherokee Band or Cherokee Nation or a different kind of name. In addition to that, there is an additional group of state-recognized Cherokee communities. If you look at state-recognized and self-identified Cherokee groups, there are 235 in addition to the three federally recognized tribes. So, this is a number that the vast majority of almost all of them have come into being in the last thirty years.

For many of the federally recognized Cherokee, this sense of proliferation of communities feels like they're being encroached upon and that it is muddying the waters in terms of their ability to make decisions about their own citizenship issues, about their perception of who they are in the larger public eye and their ability to control access to economic resources or cultural resources. There was some confusion in the early years. There is this feeling that this proliferation is undermining their ability to control how they are perceived by the larger public.

**JKK:** Can you give some examples to illustrate individuals who have shifted their racial identity and claimed or reclaimed? Please tell us more about their narrations of how they see themselves. Also, maybe a couple examples of these self-identified Cherokee organizations or bands and how they operate as a collective, as an entity.

**CS:** There are a lot of variations. There are people who have had this long family narrative of being Indian. Then they start to name that Indianness as Cherokee. Sometimes they actually have some records of sorts—vital records that show that a relative was classified as Indian. They may even have a Cherokee ancestor that was on a different Cherokee roll, such as the 1880 roll, which is not the roll that is used for the base of tribal citizenship by any the three federally recognized tribes. There are people who have documentation of various sorts. Other people, and I would say the majority of them, are a little bit less clear. Not their documentation, but they are going more from the basis of oral history. Having grown up largely in the South, but also in other places with southern roots, and having this narrative of being an American Indian descendant and that gets named as Cherokee, usually by their relatives. Usually, it's their older relatives that are telling them they are Cherokee descendants. Grandma was Cherokee.

What happens is that there's a process by which that narrative of descent, which is common in U.S. society, but that narrative of Indian descent, specifically, Cherokee descent, starts to take on greater significance in their life for a variety of reasons. Oftentimes it's because they come into contact with people who are already members of these groups, who invite them in and bring them in. Or, they tell them things they may not even know that is being named as Cherokee.

They talk about even being Black Dutch. They use this language and these other members of these communities say, "Black Dutch, don't you know that means Cherokee? You need to look into that." Then they start this process of trying to figure out what their genealogy is to the best that they can.

There are a number of common elements that happen discursively in terms of how people talk about this process, but it is largely a social process. You don't have people who have independently created a community. They have to be brought into the community through a narrative of Indian descent that largely becomes specifically marked Cherokee.

**JKK:** You mentioned that so many of these groups are in the South, and your own places of research—you have four specific sites—are all in the South: Oklahoma, Alabama, Arkansas, and Texas. Could you explain why you chose those four sites and how they are similar?

**CS:** One of the places was Alabama. The reason why I chose Alabama was because there was a large thirty-thousand-member state-recognized Cherokee community that was well organized, working on buying land together, where people have moved next door to each other. They're very active in creating a sense of community, nurturing that sense of community, reaching out to the larger surrounding state communities and seeking forms of political recognition. So, I was really interested in what a more established state-recognized Cherokee community looked like and what was going on there.

The other place that I worked was Texas. The reason why I chose Texas was that this is one of the communities where there had been things that I had heard from Cherokee citizens in Oklahoma that were cultural connections that were intriguing to me. So, I had seen published material coming out of this community and spoken with their principal chief in Texas Cherokee. They had things that were written in Cherokee, had some people who still spoke some of the language, and there had been some visitations between some members of the ceremonial community and this community. They were trying to do a stomp dance. There were cultural connections that were intriguing to me that I wanted to follow up on. There was also this fact, in this region where they're located in the northeastern part of Texas, there had historically been Cherokee migration and Cherokee occupation at a point in time. So that was also interesting to me.

The other place I looked at was Arkansas, where in Arkansas and Missouri both, again there were historical reasons for this. There was an earlier wave of westward migration of Cherokees into the Arkansas area before the Trail of Tears and several years before families moved out there. So what's interesting in Arkansas is that it's kind of a hotbed of a lot of this activity. There are a number of these Cherokee groups coming into being and kind of stayed away and then reorganized, and it's always political. They have some minor forms of state recognition, where they have proclamations and things like that, but not like the state recognition that's in Alabama. So, I wanted to know more with what was happening in that state context.

And then another place I was interested in was a community in Oklahoma that was just south of a town where both the Cherokee Nation and the United Keetoowah Band are. This community was claiming descent and rights as the Southern Cherokee Nation to a particular treaty and to a particular identity as Cherokee people from a point in history—a treaty that the Cherokee Nation claims as well. I was interested in what was happening with them being right in the backyard of these two federally recognized nations. What is going on in this context, where they are all vying for the same treaties, same territory, and, to an extent, the same claims of identification.

**JKK:** When we're referring to the three federally recognized tribes—Eastern Band, Cherokee Nation, and United Keetoowah Band—I wanted to just signal that Cherokee Nation is the legal name of a federally recognized tribe. The other historical episode you mentioned was the Trail of Tears. Could you give us a History 101 for people who are not familiar with this deadly removal?

**CS:** Basically, with the passage of the Indian Removal Act in 1830, you have tribes in the Southeast whose homelands were in parts of what is now known as the southeastern United States. Therefore, forcefully removed them from their lands. Very few people had a safe time of this. For many people, it's a very genocidal moment, where people are rounded up into stockades and held there, where there were lots of illness and sickness. Then, forced to march—in the Cherokee's case in 1838—through snow in the winter from Georgia and North Carolina to Oklahoma. The estimate is approximately one-quarter of the tribal population died on the trial. So, for many people, it was such a horrific moment in history that is still very much a part of people's sense of who they are today, as there is a sense of being a survivor. People still tell stories that are very specific to their families about the trail. These stories really do live on.

**JKK:** How do these stories about the Trail of Tears live on for the people reclaiming or claiming Cherokee identity? This is a central part for a lot of people in terms of how they make sense of saying they really are Cherokee, even if their families have identified as white for generations. Could you speak to that?

**CS:** It is interesting, because the Trail of Tears is such a powerful metaphor that even people who remain in the Southeast—I should mention that these 235 communities are really scattered throughout the United States. They concentrate in the Southeast, but you can find a number of them in California and even in Alaska. They really are all over the country, though they do tend to be concentrated primarily in the Southeast. For example, Georgia is the state with the most of these communities, and that's where the original homeland was for the Cherokee people, and that's forty-three of these communities. I wanted to give people a sense of the social geography.

For people who still remained in the Southeast, who were not actually removed on the Trail of Tears, their narrative is that the Trail of Tears still figures into their family history because they hid out. So, their narrative is about hiding, staying attached to the homeland, resisting removal and going underground, so to speak, so that they could stay. It's a painful narrative, and an interesting narrative in ways because to some extent it seems to imply they were able to resist or that they cared more about the homeland than people who were not able to do that. Sometimes that creates resentment for federally recognized Cherokee tribes, who are like, "We directly bore the brunt of this.

Why are you claiming it in this way?" and "Are you trying to suggest that you're better than us somehow?"

**JKK:** So, if I'm not mistaken, in many ways, even these groups that may actually have descendancy, for many of the people in the federally recognized tribes, they may see them as simply claiming a new identity or they see them as having been disconnected for many generations. There's that issue, then, that the forebears of the people who are reclaiming that identity left the tribe at some point, right?

**CS:** Yeah, they're detribalized.

**JKK:** Can you speak to that in particular?

**CS:** I think there is a sense of resentment. Not uniformly, but among many of the sentiments of the federally recognized tribes that this is kind of like, "When the going went tough, your people chose to de-tribalize." Therefore, in that process, they lost right to the nation. So, the idea is this kind of Johnny-come-lately phenomenon, where it is now better to be Cherokee, and better to be Indian, and the tribes have more resources. People are coming to make claims. There is resentment over that issue in particular, but if you talk to the people on the other side of this, who see themselves as reclaimers, they are usually not after economic resources. It is a part of it, but it is much more emotional and it is much more about spiritual connection, community connection, a symbolic value they attribute to this claim, a sense of belonging. It has a different kind of valence than "I am after this for the money" or "I am after this for how it will benefit me."

**JKK:** In the book you document how many of them talk about it as "coming out of the closet" to reclaim it. I want to ask about that and go back to that question about the spiritual or emotional components. A lot of the interviews that you did people say that what moved them to reclaim is a "spiritual awakening." Could you speak to that?

**CS:** The metaphor of the closet is one that permeates our society, but there is this sense that again ties back to the notion of resisting removal and the pressures of assimilation they understand having existed for their family. So, there is this idea of a hidden history of having to hide away who they really are. Sometimes it is something they do not fully understand, so at first they just feel like it is not quite right in the world; they feel alienated. They feel like they don't fit in or they don't belong. There's something amiss. What happens is that over time, they come to understand that sense of alienation and disconnection as being tied to that process of having their Cherokee identities suppressed, hidden away, or forcibly assimilated, depending on how they narrate it. What they talk about in that process of coming to recognize that disconnect and to reclaim, they view it as a spiritual awakening, and in many ways, talk about life before or how it felt to be white versus how empty and alienated and disconnected it felt and this life after as Cherokee, where they feel a sense of fulfillment that is social and largely social, cultural, and spiritual in nature.

**JKK:** You've mentioned the term "belonging" many times in this interview, and you also found it in the interviews with the people who are reclaiming. This issue of belonging and blood belonging—what's going on there?

**CS:** I think it varies for a variety of reasons. They feel disconnected. It is interesting because lots of people do. If you look at U.S. society now, many people are talking about experiencing the same alienation, being forced by economic conditions to move from their communities of origin. There are all kinds of ways in which you can argue that it permeates modern U.S. society. For these people, the narrative of blood belonging becomes incredibly powerful, and it helps to provide a kind of resolution for that problem. Blood stands in for kinship, tribe, culture. It is seen as a thing that bears culture, so that they're not behaving in ways that are appropriately Cherokee or they don't know enough Cherokee culture that they're going to be feeling a sort of disconnect. That's how they understand that, so if you are essentially via blood a certain kind of being, there needs to be a connection between that being and what you actually do every day.

**JKK:** Could you address how you dealt with this ethically as an anthropologist? You don't weigh in on determining if you think they're claiming or reclaiming. You point out that the vast majority within the federally recognized tribes seem to regard them as simply claiming something that's not really theirs. Yet the people who you interviewed really insist it's a reclamation. You don't adjudicate their identities as individuals; you're theorizing and trying to make sense of the phenomenon. You're documenting this social process and different milieu that produce this formation, but in the face of the three federally recognized tribes, their official line, as I understand it, is that they consider these people and groups "wannabes." But as an ethnographer, the role is to listen to the individuals being interviewed and what's going on and the cultural logics of any particular community or organization or group. How did you negotiate or navigate that terrain, since you worked so closely with one of the three federally recognized tribes—especially Cherokee Nation—and doing this work with these individuals?

**CS:** I will say it was hard. It caused me a lot of pain as I tried to negotiate what I was really working with. People were antagonistic to one another. What I tried to do was cover the complexity—because I felt like if I just showed one side of this, then I would not be looking at the larger social landscape, because they are in dialogue with each other and they are reacting to each other and how they perceived one another. One of the things I tried to do was put them side by side, so that the reader could put them in conversation with each other and actually see them in conversation with each other. The book is divided into this kind of race shifters and Cherokee parts. Within these parts, they are speaking to each other.

I also try to show the diversity of all sides. There are some people who pulled out records and showed them to me. I cannot adjudicate their claims, because I cannot possibly do the kinds of research for each individual, where I can come to a consensus and say you are who you say you are or you are not. I don't want to be in that role of authenticating their claims. I don't think that's appropriate, but what I can do is say there are a variety of claims that have a lot of meaning that are having political repercussions. I think what I do say is that this larger antagonism and social world that is happening out there is having political repercussions not only in Cherokee Country but in Indian Country. We need to have different kinds of conversations and different kinds of ways of talking about this than we have had before. For instance, to just dismiss these claims as "wannabes" who are after money really fails to recognize what the deeper motivations might be, and also because it gives it such short shrift, it doesn't empower people to respond in a way, where they have the knowledge they need to adequately respond.

My hope was to listen and portray both sides of this. I do think that I take some stance around state recognition in saying not that state recognition as a whole is problematic but that it is adding another element to the federal Indian model that we have not fully worked out and is complicating questions of sovereignty. That's something where I make an assertion, where we need to have more work in this area and understand what the repercussions of this are. We need to know what the rights of state-recognized tribes versus federally recognized tribes are, so that can be adjudicated appropriately.

It was difficult, but I also felt that everybody was talking about this, but no one was doing systematic, sustained work on it. There had only been short, little pieces, here and there. There needed to be something to put it all together and in one place.

**JKK:** It is definitely high-risk work, politically speaking. I think you did an excellent job in navigating this. It is incredible research, but also the nuance and sensitivity you bring to the theorizing and the links you bring to social broader trends going on in the United States. This isn't a story outside of other questions of race, ethnicity, and nationhood.

I wanted to go back to something. The three federally recognized tribes, for the most part, are hostile to the state-recognition process and state-recognized tribal entities, right?

**CS:** They have now been in communication with one another, and it used to be that it was primarily Cherokee Nation and Eastern Band who were the most concerned about these groups; and it used to be the UKB [United Keetoowah Band] as a kind of an outlier. Now, the UKB seems to have taken a stance along with the other two nations in this regard. Even though the Eastern Band and Cherokee Nation are the two most in conversation about this, the UKB does now also seem to use the same rhetoric. The official tribal government stand from these governments is that they want a moratorium on the recognition of these groups at the federal level. They see them as threatening and they are very concerned about it. Now, that is different from what individuals say. If you talk to individual Cherokee citizens, there are a variety of response. Some people are more open to this process. They have a sort of read of the situation, but the majority are concerned and confused. Part of the difficulty of doing this project is that there is so much variation on all sides. I don't want to monolithically characterize all the federally recognized Cherokee citizens of having an antagonistic perspective.

**JKK:** And that's important to acknowledge around all kinds of policies, including the very contentious debate over the Freedmen issue, which I want to ask you a little bit about, but also to let the people know, when we're talking about this, I'm trying to get at the official governmental stance for these particular tribes, one that is certainly not fully representative of the tribal members.

You've recently come back from Tahlequah, Cherokee Nation, for the national holidays and also there are some really high-profile legal battles going on with Cherokee Nation, in particular, with regard to the Freedmen. This book doesn't zone in on that, but your first book talks about that history. It is an ongoing battle, but it has certainly been in the media more recently. What's going on at Cherokee right now?

**CS:** It's a really troubling time. People are very worried within the Cherokee Nation. To back up for people who may not know—in 2006 the Cherokee Nation Supreme Court decided Freedmen were tribal citizens based on Cherokee law and Cherokee precedent, and then, in 2007, there was an special election where there was a constitutional referendum by Cherokee citizens who voted to require all citizens of the nation be descended from the Cherokee by Blood Rolls, rather than any of the Dawes Rolls, which were also Cherokee Freedmen. So, they switched to that requirement; it ended up ousting the citizens who had been listed on the Cherokee Freedmen Rolls. Now, just this year in January, a Cherokee district court judge said that the constitutional amendment was illegal and reinstated the Cherokee Freedmen so they could vote in the election that was held in May. Then, that decision was finally reconsidered in the Cherokee Supreme Court just this late August. The [Cherokee] Supreme Court had the final say and decided that they could not override, regardless of what the previous law had been, the people's will and a constitutional referendum. And, that is what stood.

So, now, as a result of that, the HUD [Housing and Urban Development] has cut and is refusing to release $33 million of funding to the Cherokee Nation until the question of the Freedmen rights to citizenship can be determined in federal courts. What's unfortunate about this is that the Freedmen no longer have any tribal recourse within tribal court systems. So, they already filed several years ago to the federal court, but now that case is likely to be heard because the tribal court's remedies have been exhausted.

**JKK:** It is unfortunate as I understand it because then it invites the federal government to start to have a say in terms of tribal enrollment and citizenship, which has been one of the main areas where tribes have been able to completely exercise their sovereignty, whereas the U.S. government has infringed in so many other areas of tribal governance.

**CS:** In that regard, I think it is very scary because it goes to the [U.S.] Supreme Court. With the Supreme Court, they can reverse previous decisions. It is almost an unprecedented case, as it provides an opportunity for the Court to really make decisions to fundamentally undermine everyone's sovereignty. I think it is a very scary moment, and I wish things had been handled differently within the Cherokee court system than they were.

**JKK:** When you say it could affect everyone's tribal sovereignty, that means all tribes, not just the Cherokee Nation's, because then that sets a legal precedent.

Are you going to be doing more work on the Freedmen case for your next project? Where are you going with your research?

**CS:** I am working on an article right now. I'm also paying careful attention to what is happening right now because there is this fundamental tension between rights to tribal sovereignty and civil rights that are playing out, which I think say a lot about how our broader race relations, Indigenous relations, and politics in this country. It is an unusual case, so it is very likely I will continue to do work on the topic. I don't know if I will do book-length treatment. I'm on the fence about that.

**JKK:** I want to invite you to leave us with something you want us to consider in relation to these questions you've brought out in your book and the political topics we've been discussing today.

**CS:** I think that moving forward in terms of these issues requires compassion; and I think compassion for people who are feeling embattled on both sides. I would encourage people to not come into this completely closed-minded. Absolutely, people should be protecting their political rights, but I think that there has been a tendency to mischaracterize people on either side of these tensions as being, you know, this is the stand or the way of seeing it or the motivation and to be very reductive in these kinds of arguments. I don't think reductive arguments flying in either direction are really helping us to move forward anyway.

# MARGO TAMEZ ON INDIGENOUS RESISTANCE TO THE U.S.–MEXICO BORDER WALL

## First Interview

Margo Tamez (Ndé Konitsaaiigokiyaa'en) cofounded Lipan Apache Women Defense/Strength, an Indigenous People's Organization of the United Nations Permanent Forum on Indigenous Issues that was formed to protect sacred sites, burial grounds, archaeological resources, ecological biodiversity, and way of life of the Indigenous people of the Lower Rio Grande, North America. She and her mother, Eloisa G. Tamez, founded the group in response to the attempt by the U.S. Department of Homeland Security (DHS) to force their surrender of hereditary lands in El Calaboz, Texas, for the U.S.–Mexico border wall. The DHS had voided more than thirty-five federal laws, including environmental laws and laws protecting American Indian cultural and burial places. However, South Texas Apache women took the lead, in December 2007, in organizing the most persistent, and to date most successful, constitutional law case against the U.S. Army, the U.S. Customs Border Patrol, and the DHS. On October 22, 2008, Tamez delivered testimony in Washington, D.C., before the Organization of American States (OAS) Inter-American Commission on Human Rights, which examines and monitors compliance by member states of the OAS, including the United States, with human rights obligations established in international law. In this, the first of two interviews (a second, from July 4, 2009, follows), Tamez explains how this crisis came about and how she is working to protect the lands of her people from being divided in a way that would result in relocation—a forced Indian removal that would constitute a twenty-first-century genocide. This interview took place while she was a graduate student in American studies at Washington State University. Tamez is an associate professor in the Department of Community, Culture and Global Studies at the University of British Columbia, Okanagan. She is the author of *Raven Eye* (2007) and *Naked Wanting* (2003).

This interview took place on October 28, 2008.

**J. Kēhaulani Kauanui:** Wonderful to speak with you from your home in Washington State. I want to start by asking you how the construction of the U.S.–Mexico border wall began to impact you in terms of directly implicating your own family.

**Margo Tamez:** Well, back in 2006 we started hearing about it in the newspapers and radio, but every once in a while we'd hear reports about a border wall being built along the U.S.–Mexico border. In California, of course, construction began back in the nineties and then, after, with the various different operations of the United States, the southern wall was constructed across Arizona beginning in 2006, I believe. Then, we did start to hear reports that the Department of Homeland Security [DHS] was planning to construct a wall in various different sectors of the Texas–Mexico border as well. And originally, when our communities started to hear those stories, nobody really took them very seriously. Just by physical terrain and the fact that Texas and Mexico already have a natural partition, you could say, between them—which is the Rio Grande River, a very wide, very deep and in some places quite turbulent river. So the concept of trying to wall off Texas, the idea that there was a necessity, was sort of ludicrous in a lot of people's minds.

By 2007 our community members started to receive letters in the mail. I should step back a little bit, actually; prior to letters they received numerous phone calls. Most of the people in the last seventy miles of the Texas–Mexico border—which would be Stark County, Hidalgo County, and Cameron County—did not really understand what these phone calls were about. Again, a lot of the people are bilingual, but a good number of the elderly are not and only speak Spanish. For a long time, people were not really talking to each other very much about these phone calls, or if they were, it was really just within families, so we didn't really understand the greater dimensions of how systematic the phone calls had been and how thorough the U.S. government had been in tracking all of the different property owners along the river. It was at that time, then, that finally my mother and a few other community members down in La Encantada—a different ranchería—then Los Ebanos, then in El Calaboz and La Paloma—these are all different rancherías and older hereditary communities—started talking to each other through the usual networks, at church or at different community meetings or at work, various places where people encounter each other in their daily life. For the most part, I think people were still very afraid and worried. They didn't feel that they had access to, for example, who to call if the United States is saying that they want to take your land and that you needed to surrender it.

It wasn't until my mother and a few other community leaders from the different rancherías started becoming more vocal and talking to the press that more people began to understand that there were a lot of people being called and down the road, which meant that it was a much bigger problem than people had originally thought. When more attention was given to the problem through the indie media, reporters were coming in from various parts of the United States wanting to find out more about what was happening on the ground. Then, people started to understand that there was a really serious problem here, and not only were people not being listened to, but the people themselves didn't feel like they had the power to have any attention brought to the problem either. So, by the summer of 2007 my mother called me and she was very upset, very worried, very frustrated and angry, but there was a certain amount of fear in her voice too. She told me that she had received phone calls from the Department of Homeland Security at her workplace, and that this was a problem for her because she was immediately concerned that they had tapped her line or that they had been following her—it's a private line at the university that she works from, so only a few people know the number. She started to feel this enclosing feeling, not only because they were demanding that she surrender her land over the phone during her work hours, but she had this incredible sinking feeling that she was being surrounded by invisible spores. That is the power of the Department of Homeland Security, to invade your private lines, to perhaps be watching where you go. That very moment is when the whole process changed radically and in a very different direction.

**JKK:** So that recognition of raw state power then in her face, so to speak.

**MT:** Absolutely.

**JKK:** I want to ask you, for context, I understand that this land in particular, that the U.S. Department of Homeland Security was telling your mother she would have to give up, has been in your family—in terms of even recognized by western title—since the early 1700s. Is that right?

**MT:** That's correct. I am Lipan Apache on my mother's side, and I'm also descended from Basque indentured laborers who were brought into the area with the José Escandón conquistador project, the colonial project of Spain's northern provinces in the area of the continent, which was called Nuevo Santander—New Santander. Santander was, and still is today, one of the heartlands of the Basque movement and of the Basque people, so this area is traditionally the hereditary site and sacred site of the Lipan Apache. It is recognized by other tribes as well, but the northern state to the south of us is Tamaulipas, which is sort of a Hispanicization of an older Indigenous language. It meant "the place where the Lipan prayed," Ta ma ho lipam, in the Indigenous Huastecan language. So, many tribes also recognized the sovereign [spiritual beingness and belongingness] space of Apaches [Ndé peoples and Ndé-ness].

I'm also Lipan Apache and Jumano Apache on my father's side, so this area of the continent—South Texas—is a place that Apache people came to. In our oral tradition, we came from places much further to the north—what people think of today as Canada and the Arctic Circle. Over many thousands of years, we've always stayed close to mountains; we're mountain people. Around A.D. 1000 or so the people and the buffalo hunters came down to this area [Texas, Chihuahua, and Coahuila] and made it our place, as Native people do. They adapted and really took to the place. So we have a long history prior to 1767 in this place, but in about 1767, when José Escandón came with many Spanish settlers, they encountered the Lipan Apache. He came with approximately eight hundred soldiers to overcome and to—what they call in Spanish—reduce, to reduce and to pacify the Lipan Apache people. Spain did make certain agreements, not only with its own settlers but with many Native communities as well, and Mexico followed in that direction too, so many Indigenous peoples have land grants in Texas and also other coastal states. Cherokee, I believe, and Choctaw and other tribes had prior relations with Spain.

This is 1767, and this relationship is long established. The Spaniards and the Apaches and other tribes, such as the Comanches, were intermarried in communities which had land grants to secure parts of their ancestral lands from being overtaken and appropriated illegally by powerful interest groups of the state, church, and the quite diverse Spanish colonial settler society. Those land grants are still held in customary law, in international law, and are recognized by the state of Texas.

Texas has a land law office, in which it affirmed legislatively a good number of the Spanish and the Mexican land grants that were given to both European settlers and Natives during those days of the 1700s and 1800s. In Texas law, our land grants are legal, and we're number 336 in the Texas land office. Given also that the majority of current-day landownership in South Texas arose through land grants, not only the impoverished Indian people but also extremely wealthy people, who have thousands and hundreds of thousands and millions of acres in land grants, are also in the same sort of affirmation [by Texas]. A different land-tenure system preexisted U.S. claim to sovereignty and continues to exist.

**JKK:** I want to go back to your mother and also how you came to cofound the Lipan Apache Women Defense/Strength, and why your focus is on the women.

**MT:** That's a good question. Well, my mother called me, and for many years she has supported me and my social and environmental justice and human rights work, and she was actually my inspiration. She raised me to be very concerned with people, our people, poverty, and illness. We lived in a household where social justice was very much part of our life, and the injustices that we lived through and were surviving were often openly discussed. I think that at the time this was happening, I had been keeping some parts of my life separate from my relationship with my mother, mostly out of respect for her, because she was one of the leaders of our family and I didn't want to burden her with the work I did.

So I kept a lot of my organizing work in a separate sphere, but I remember very clearly that by about November 2007 we had received a lot of support from independent communities, Indigenous communities, Native communities, and global communities. I said to my mom, "It's really important. I want you to always understand everything that's happening. You need to be very informed and have every possible piece of information because, ultimately, this is about you and it's about your stories that you haven't been able to tell." I told her that if she wanted me to, I would put every possible means behind this, every apparatus I know, every network I have, every contact that I've ever made, every person, every organization. I will blast this out to the world and I will put the means behind it. I said, "I need you to understand that because once we do that, your life will change forever. And I want you to understand what that means; it will completely change. You will have hardly any privacy and you will be pulled into something so huge, because people have been waiting for you for a long time." And she took a few moments and she said, "Let's go."

There were many moments like that, but it was a gradual process of gaining her permission, gaining her consent, giving her as much information as possible to make decisions, because she was making them for a lot of people with their consent. I don't really have access to the elders that she deals with, so I wanted her to be really clear so that she had the right information to give to people, because ultimately, her face and her message would be attached to this and the media would construct it in a certain way. We needed to be very careful and recognize that we could look into the future and say, "We need to be very accountable for everything we do and everything we say so no harm comes to our people and no harm comes to her." So we made a partnership in that way, and then by the time December 7 came around, which was the deadline that the government had given to all the property owners in South Texas to surrender their lands for the border-wall construction, we had quite a large network and quite a large structure around this. We consented together to create a more formal partnership so that we would have a platform that was manageable and that would allow the press—sort of like a portal, it's not just an idea, it's very much based in material realities—but dealing with the press and dealing with lots of different communities who don't know who we are, we needed to provide a structure so that they could understand it and have something concrete to attach to, like the Lipan Apache Women Defense.

So that really resonated with a lot of different groups, and we really wanted to honor the fact that this—from the perspective of El Calaboz, I cannot speak for any of the other communities, but from El Calaboz, which is my mom's birth ranchería—is very much a traditional matrilineal community, where property and resources are resourced through women. And through women to women's living spaces—their houses, their huts, their corrals, their livestock—

all those things are organized in a very traditional matrilineal formation. We decided that this particular part of the border-wall resistance was innovated by women, and it came from women's prayers; it came from women's visions, it came from my mother's vision that she had which told her that she was supposed to march into and go to the people on December 12, which is a day of the holy recognition of one of the Holy Mothers. So all along she has had this history in El Calaboz, of being empowered by elders from the time she was about five years old when she was first given the Lightning Ceremony. The Lightning Ceremony is connected to her directly through a very ancient cultural practice that many people had thought was gone, that it didn't exist anymore. That we had become completely assimilated to the Spanish and to Mexico and to Texas and to the U.S. culture, but actually, here she is living and breathing certain ways of life and belief systems. She's one of the last people who had this ceremony, and it's always been a very strong element of her life, so as we had to continue to explain and educate lawyers and human rights groups and other groups who wanted to advocate on this issue, we had to always bring it back to that, because they always want to know, of course, well, how are you Indigenous, how are you Indian?

**JKK:** Very typical.

**MT:** So we would say, you have to understand that people in these communities long ago were disallowed, they had to surrender their Indigenous clothing, their Indigenous language, their Indigenous religion, to be alive. So we don't trust people that you might think are Indian, say maybe on a magazine cover wearing feathers and beads and that sort of thing. We have a very distinct culture and we have our own way. It's hard to see, because we live in a modern world. We all dress contemporary, but we have a culture. So it was always a process of taking everyone into a process and journey to understand Indigenous resistances through 425 years, so that they could see us and hear us and manage ideas. So Mom and I decided that it needed to be centered in Indigenous women and Ndé-ness [to reflect the diversity of inter-societal kinship among Lower Rio Grande River peoples], which works with our restoring hereditary title through women, and restoring Indigenous women to their rightful place in our culture. This is really an act of resistance to the colonization of women and of our culture, which has been very damaging to us.

**JKK:** What is so profound here is that you have really been proactive in terms of directing the media, and so active in asserting your own agency in that representation. This movement has effectively stopped the border wall, and the South Texas Apache women have been the most persistent and successful in their constitutional law case and have effectively, thus far, fought against the U.S. Army, the U.S. Customs Border Patrol, and the U.S. Department of Homeland Security. I also understand that your mother, Eloisa Tamez, was recently [in October 2008] awarded a civil rights award, the Henry B. González, by the Texas Civil Rights Project, in part because she was the first landowner to stand up to the U.S. when they threatened to coerce her to sell it. So I want to acknowledge that.

I want to ask you, though, about the numerous tribal nations that have communities living on both sides of the border, and how the border wall would cut through their traditional territories and have an effect on religious ceremonies and practices. The endurance that you've told us has been maintained over these hundreds of years, the maintenance of kinship ties and other kinds of other cultural continuities. Can you tell us more about the bisecting of these Native nations, and also how you understand this attempt at Indian removal as an example of twenty-first-century genocide?

**MT:** Yes, that's all very important. I want to just quickly try to help people understand that prior to me, the placement, I'll say, the U.S.–Mexico border—the international boundary between the two nations—was officiated and instituted in 1848. That's always the date that is associated with that border and the Treaty of Guadalupe Hidalgo. Since then, there have been eleven treaties and covenants and minutes to reestablish that border between the two nations, all the way up to the mid- to late twentieth century. There's still dispute about it, but in the midst of that there are between twelve and twenty tribal groups and Native American groups—federally recognized, non-status groups—that are on both sides of the border that have historical ties to each other. These are the ones I'm aware of, but I'm sure there are many, many more. They have blood ties, kinship ties, cultural ties, and so forth.

Specifically, I want to bring to attention some of the groups that we work with directly, in an organization called the Alianza Indígena sin Fronteras, the Indigenous Alliance without Borders. This is sort of an umbrella group that addresses the human rights and Indigenous rights issues of a collective of tribes, a collective of groups, not representing official tribal governments or councils but really giving a space for marginalized groups within those communities that feel that they are not able to get representation through either their tribal government, their traditional government, the United States or Mexico, or the state where they reside, where they're at on the ground. So this other space gives numerous groups and individuals and families a place to speak, a place to be heard, a place to advance human rights abuses. . . . So, these communities on the border, that those in the interior of the U.S. may hear about, are rising up against the border wall, which is splitting their communities. It's not just that the border wall is splitting their communities again, right now, it's that the border itself split their communities in 1848 without their consultation and without their free and prior informed consent. As Native nations—as Indigenous nations—they are political groups, because they have sovereign rights as Indigenous nations in international law. Therefore, they are treaty-based groups, or other covenant- or charter- or agreement-based nations, and that's a key difference for Indigenous peoples.

So the border wall, then, is just one more violation of international rights. The United States should be held to abide by international law and should be held to Native groups who have specific complaints; they have the right to speak up and to get remedies. When we think about remedies, it's really challenging for Indigenous groups and other citizens of the United States and Mexico to get remedies for the real, physical containment, separation, restrictive structural problems of the wall—which divides families, divides individual and collective family subsistence farms, grazing areas, riparian zones, shepherding traditions, and denies Indigenous peoples who never subjugated their ancestral Native sovereignty to occupier nations and states. In other words, there is no federal recognition of Indigenous peoples of or from our region, and a major reason is that Indigenous peoples here never signed treaties of cession and subjugated sovereignty. If my neighbor here in Pullman puts a wall next to my house, and that wall causes structural damage—floods, plumbing, electrical problems—on my property, there are immediate remedies for that. That's why there are laws, and there's all kinds of rules that we have to follow so that we don't damage each other. But the difference here is that you have Native nations who have many different kinds of rights, and then you have citizens who are not Native who then are also saying that they want to be included in protecting environmental rights—the rights of the wildlife, the rights to protect clean air, clean water, clean soils, riparian pathways—and so the United States took a critical step in removing rights of all groups. They tried to equalize them in that way and to neutralize all groups by voiding out thirty-five federal laws, which provided no remedies for any group, and that's what the logic was.

What we discovered in Texas—which was not teased out in Arizona in litigation by Defenders of Wildlife and Sierra Club and other NGO groups, nonprofit groups, and citizen-based groups—was that there were differential treatments of some groups as opposed to all citizens. There were exclusions for specific groups in Texas that were being teased out in a different way than all citizens. So, in Texas we discovered that there are three different properties—Cameron County, Hidalgo County, and Stark County—which were excluded and set apart as a different group that would not need to have a border wall put across their land. These were all private property owners who had direct ties to the administration. One is the Hunt family, and the Hunt family is one of the most successful, wealthiest, corporate-based families in the United States—the family donated more than three million dollars to George [W.] Bush's presidential library upon his retirement from the presidency. The Moody family also has long-established ties to the administration and to the River Bend Resort. So we discovered that there were holes in the wall. This is a Fifth Amendment, equal protection issue at the federal level, and it is also a human rights issue at the federal, at the local, and at the international levels.

**JKK:** That's right. You're talking about demographic disparities on the basis of race. It sounds like white, wealthy golf resorts and landowners and even farmers are getting spared from getting their lands confiscated?

**MT:** I'm not sure about Arizona. I'll just say that Melissa del Bosque is the journalist who broke that story after in-depth interviews with family members in South Texas, including my mother. In the Arizona lawsuit, it's not clear. I haven't seen any reports or any incisive analysis of if there were any landowners who were excluded.

However, in South Texas it was very clear. Because of the intense amount of focus on our case, and then the cases of the families in Granjeno and Los Ebanos, there were resources and there was attention put toward really examining those disparities, to do it in a very systematic, scholarly, scientific, research-based way that was conducted by professors and scholars and a network from the University of Texas. We did discover that the only groups that were excluded in the seventy miles designated for a wall—a cement and steel wall—were the River Bend Resort, the Moody family ranch, and the Hunt family ranch.

**JKK:** I understand that the University of Texas's Rapoport Center for Human Rights and Justice has also been working in conjunction with an immigration clinic at the school of law there, and they have generated quite a bit of documentation and analysis. I want to ask you, in terms of the human rights violations and speaking to those that might be sitting at home saying, "Well, what about stopping immigration and national security?" Can you tell us what this looks like, on an everyday basis, in terms of the military buildup? I understand that there are currently eighteen thousand U.S. soldiers occupying the border, as well as almost ten thousand Mexican soldiers.

**MT:** In 2006 and in 2007, it was the height of the fear and the hysteria that was circulating in South Texas about the eminent domain and the forced signing of waivers. "Waivers" is a very tricky word; on the one hand, the government can give waivers to certain groups to not have a wall, and on the other hand they've forced groups to sign waivers, which forces the group to surrender their land to the government, so I'm really cautious about that word.

We have to understand the violations of human rights that we're talking about. Oftentimes when that phrase is used, we might think right away of a group being lined up and machine-gunned down. You know, we think about the Holocaust, the images of the Holocaust, but there are specific rights that all groups have, that human beings have.

There are three that I want to make really clear that qualify as human rights violations in South Texas. The first is violation of the right to property and equal protection guaranteed under international human rights law. The government failed to meet the governmental goal of controlling the border and the construction of the border wall. And that failure is singling out specific groups, and the University of Texas has documented thoroughly the racial demographics of the border wall—across the U.S.–Mexico complete border as well as in South Texas—and there are very noticeable disparities. So that's a violation of international human rights law and the Convention on Human Rights, which the United States is a signatory of.

The other is the severe degradation of the environment and violations of the government's obligation to evaluate and take into account harm to the environment when undertaking any public project, because Indigenous people and the environment and nature are very closely interlocking and related. Nature, for those who go hiking, may feel like a religious experience or feel inspiring. However, for Indigenous people nature is religion, nature is an integral part of our subsistence, of our health, of our philosophy of our religious identity, of our everyday way of life, of being Indigenous.

So, violations of the rights of Indigenous communities protected under international human rights law. The law directly impacts the lands of Apache, Kickapoo, Tigua Isleta, and numerous other tribes on the border. One example, say in El Calaboz, is designated to go right through our farmlands and our grazing lands, and just a couple of miles down the road, River Bend Resort has been excluded from having any wall put through their golf course and their deck, which is a place where they have social parties and events.

We feel very strongly that our elders may have cows or bulls or livestock, and for our subsistence farmers their whole livelihood depends on their abilities to produce from the land. This is a way of life that for many hundreds of years was guaranteed to us through sovereign relationships with Spain. So we feel very strongly that to have the wall go through our farmlands in El Calaboz deprives us of not only our subsistence and our way of life, our livelihood, our economic livelihood, and our right to practice in the environment to which we are connected as Indigenous people, but at the same time it doesn't account for the fact that Cameron County is the number one county in the United States for more than ten indicators of poverty. It is the poorest county in the United States, and most of our people live in a state of disparity already, in comparison to other counties in Texas in the north, as well as other counties throughout the United States. They're already a deprived group, and this puts extra burdens on our people and it puts extra burden on our elders, who are not mobile all the time. They would have to take their cows, their livestock, three miles down the road to Garza Road, which is where DHS says the new entry to our lands will be. They would have to go through a militarized checkpoint, what my mother calls "Charlie Checkpoint." My mother is a lieutenant colonel, and when she found out the architecture plans of that checkpoint she said, "Oh, okay, that's Charlie Checkpoint. I've seen that before." She knows that infrastructure, and we would have to show IDs or a passport on United States soil to go through the checkpoint, to go to our land, and then again three miles back to check on our stock every day. That is a sure way to destroy the last vestiges of a culture.

**JKK:** Yes.

**MT:** That is one very important way. So, for those of you who are farmers out there, those of you who are ranchers, for those of you who know people who make their living very simply on the land and have cherished that way of life— and it's not something that just Indigenous people do, it's something that is very dear to human beings all over the world—think about that and try to understand that this is not just a situation where you can go get an apartment or go buy a house somewhere else, that the government's going to pay you some money. This is not a culture that can survive by assimilating even further.

**JKK:** I understand that the federal government has not been forthcoming in terms of honoring the Freedom of Information Act, and that there's not only been a lack of information but also an inadequate process of consultation from the get-go. Could you speak to this issue of freedom of investigation and expression in terms of there being no due diligence here?

**MT:** Yes. I do understand from some of the working group members from the University of Texas that they did apply under the Freedom of Information Act to receive information about what the United States' process is—its research process, its demographics, its own sort of internal analysis of these lands and the property owners who were being designated as targets for the wall. There were many obstacles put in front of the working group to receive that information from the government. There were numerous roadblocks, and the price for that, I believe, was set between twenty and thirty thousand dollars for the University of Texas working group to receive that. They do not know if this is an arbitrary price that was set at that particular moment from the political perspective of an administration that is a very much under a lot of scrutiny in many areas, but certainly this is an area that we're going to pursue even more with the new administration.

This is not going to stop at this point. These things are very much in motion. So consultation on that issue alone from the very beginning has been unavailable actually, which is one of the issues that we fought for and that the omnibus bill that was tagged on to the border security project allowed, in Texas, but did not allow retroactively to the rest of the border. So one of the gains that we made by mobilizing on the issues and structuring a large team of pro bono attorneys and different human rights organizations, NGOs, a lot of different activists from all over the world, and media to come and analyze together with us, was that we were very quickly able to see the lack of consultation, all across the border, and the lack of remedies because thirty-five federal laws were waived.

Say if a scholar or a researcher is working for an agency that usually would be involved in doing environmental assessments, or at archaeological sites, doing surveys for a group that's going to be impacted. Suddenly, because a major law that deals with cultural sites and sacred sites is waived, there's no funding for that person to come and do his or her job. So that's one of the things that happened on the ground, that effect of freezing—from the top all the way down to the bottom for communities such as ours, who'd been targeted to have the wall. The judge in our case, was saying, "Well then, okay, you need to bring forth evidence showing how you're going to be impacted through archaeological, cultural, and environmental resources," and disallowed us to be able to get the public agents or the public civil servants to actually come and do that job, because they're being disallowed to do it.

**JKK:** To do an assessment, a real assessment.

**MT:** Yes. So then we had to depend again on pro bono professors who have that as their expertise, or other groups and other nonprofit organizations who maybe had already done that kind of research and would loan it out to us. You know, you just have to go further and make those different kinds of relationships again. The Lipan Apache Women Defense had done a lot of innovation early on in deciding that it's going to be Indigenous-based and Indigenous-centered, and at the same time, we knew we would not be able to get very far unless we opened it up to inviting a lot of nontraditional allies to come and to work with us, and to educate and to continue to do that education to our new allies and new partners about what this is about.

**JKK:** Right, and I think that you do have such an expansive network of allies who have been working in coalition with people literally globally. I think that is what has been so inspiring for me personally, but also so effective in stopping the border wall to date.

In conclusion, I want to invite you to leave with any parting thoughts.

**MT:** Well, I just want to say thank you to everyone, and thank you to all your listeners. I'm very grateful to you, Kēhaulani, because you've been a great inspiration to me, and the work that you're doing there on independent radio is so important because it's one of the most important pathways of connecting. That's where this all began, was with a voice. A voice that someone could hear online and on radios—it started just like that. And it's very simple, and we ought to all access this a lot more. So I just want to say thank you and bless all of you who are out there, whether you agree with the wall or you want the wall, or you have no concern about it whatsoever. I just want to say thank you to everybody out there.

### Second Interview: The Gendered Effects of Militarization

My second interview with Margo Tamez was part of an episode focused on the gendered effects of militarization on Indigenous women. The guest who preceded her was Vivian Newdick, cofounder of the Comité Pro-Reparaciones para las Hermanas González de Chiapas. Here, Tamez returned to give us an update on the border-wall situation since Obama took office. Tamez is Lipan Apache and Jumano Apache from two Texas–Mexico border communities. This issue remains unresolved and pressing—especially under the Trump administration. Tamez—with the Apache Ndé Nneé Working Group—circulated a petition in the spring of 2017 requesting that the UN Committee on the Elimination of Racial Discrimination (CERD) write to the U.S. government for response to CERD concerning the allegations, submissions, and evidence that the U.S.–Mexico border wall and the recent U.S. Executive Order to expand the border wall are in violation of Indigenous rights, including the rights to Free, Prior and Informed Consent (FPIC) and genuine consultation. The CERD agreed and in the letter also addressed concern that "the discriminatory effect of the previously constructed wall has not been remedied" and the need for protection of sacred sites in light of a variety of violating U.S. exploitations and interests. The United States was asked to reply to the CERD by July 17, 2017. As of March 2018 there had been no response.

This interview took place on July 4, 2009.

**J. Kēhaulani Kauanui:** I want to start by asking you what's changed with the situation down at El Caloboz ranchería since the Obama administration has been put into place. I remember in December of 2008 you sent an open letter to the Obama transition team about the situation along the border, which was co-signed by dozens of organizations and key individuals. Has the Obama administration ever responded?

**Margo Tamez:** No, the Obama administration has not responded formally to us or informally through any other functionaries of the United States government. So we have not heard back from his administration.

**JKK:** I see, so not even someone from the Department of the Interior. No response.

**MT:** No, none at all. And when we did that action, we specifically copied all of these materials and documents—the actual letters, the cover letter with all of the signatories—and sent context materials to show our previous work on this matter in terms of attempting to reach consultation agreements. We were attempting to have consultation and transparency with all other levels of government, from the local level in South Texas along the border through the state level, and congressional levels, as well as agency levels and the transition team, directly to the administration. We really wanted to show that we had been working very assertively and in a good way toward trying to have consultations. And we have not heard back from him or the other people who we copied the letter to in the Department of the Interior—the secretary and his staff, as well as the border congresspersons.

There are four congressmen on the Texas–Mexico border, which is the district to which their staffs are responsible. We copied it to signatories on Congressman [Raul M.] Grijalva's effort regarding the border—congresspeople, congressmen and congresswomen from California, Arizona, and Texas who have been working with him to pressure the Obama administration to come back to the table, to negotiate and consult with local communities, and to reverse the laws that were waived of the 2008 Section 102, an additional legislative tool instituted by U.S. DHS director Michael Chertoff, which waived thirty-six laws, thus facilitating the largest en masse appropriation of lands in U.S. history.

So a lot of work was done in that regard to communicate to numerous officials that we were clearly wanting to have any face-to-face conversation. We felt that the elders of our community, all of our supporters, our family members, and people from the Texas border who were impacted had earned that.

**JKK:** Absolutely. Well, I would hope that the Obama administration would take a careful look at this.

**MT:** Although they are making some attempts to work with Indigenous communities in North America and among the federally recognized Native American nations and tribal groups, we are not really seeing that the Obama administration is going to be very different at all in terms of their work with the Indigenous communities in the United States and Indigenous peoples in the hemisphere and globally.

**JKK:** In April 2009 a federal judge in the Fifth Circuit Court ruled against your mother, Eloisa Garcia Tamez, by affirming the federal government's right to take your family lands at El Calaboz ranchería to complete the wall. Can you tell us more about the ruling and if you and your family will appeal it? You and your mother—on behalf of Lipan Apache Women Defense—are represented by the Center for Constitutional Rights, right?

**MT:** Well, my mother is the plaintiff. She's also the respondent. She's the respondent in the United States government suit against landowners along the Texas–Mexico border, specifically in the last seventy miles of the Texas–Mexico border, who held out the longest. She is named specifically, as well as relatives and other people in our community.

To counteract that, we filed a class-action suit against the state. So she is named along with a member of the Benavidez family of El Calaboz who joined the suit in our community. Lipan Apache Women Defense is an organization my mother and I cofounded in order to do research and to do documentation and education that was required to support the federal case and all of its needs—all of the needs of the teams of attorneys and their associates and staff people, as well as all the other groups who worked with us to build the case. Lipan Apache Women Defense also started working toward restoring historical memory and historical archives of community members. So it's sort of a process that has blossomed out into a much larger understanding of what is defense in this particular space among Apache people and with the Apache women.

**JKK:** Can you clarify—she filed the class-action suit after the federal ruling?

**MT:** Originally, back in 2007, the government sued us. My mother and the other landowners who were refusing to sign the waivers that the government was imposing on the communities through armed force were sued.

At that time, within a month of receiving the notification that the government was going to pursue legal action, my mother and I and a group of people worked with Peter Schey and the attorneys at the Center for Human Rights and Constitutional Law, and we put together a class-action suit against the government. So *Eloisa Tamez v. The United States Department of Homeland Security, The United States Army, and the United States Custom Border Patrol* is the case that the center also represents. This is an international issue in terms of the United States and the Secure Fence Act, being that it is an international boundary region.

If we go back to Bush's original speech, right after the 9/11 destruction of the Twin Towers, that was very much where we started to see, at least from my perspective, the clear direction of how security was going to be framed in the ongoing War on Terror, the War on Drugs, and the war on immigration against specific groups.

In the Americas and in the United States at the U.S.–Mexico border, the Secure Fence Act allowed the United States to bundle up Indigenous communities and other communities on its political borders within the framework of the War on Terror and, through homogenization as "border peoples," Indigenous peoples who've never surrendered through treaties of cession are designated as legally violable and a sacrifice, *homo sacer*, "others" with no legal juridical personality in the space of abjection it creates to spatialize impunity. The issue became an international case, not only because we are literally on the international border—that's very important—but also because the legalization of wall megastructures and militarization benefiting corporations is an act that is intended to "protect" the United States against international threats.

That's how it's always been framed. So we have an international case, as well.

**JKK:** Could you tell us how the communities are faring right now, since the ruling?

**MT:** Yes. From my understanding, at this point the United States constructed the wall in many of the places in which the Department of Homeland Security stated and reported. I wouldn't say it's clear whether they have done all that they had originally intended to build. There's many different reports, and it's very difficult to know, and that's been one of the biggest problems. There's no transparency. Also, the United States failed to comply with the Freedom of Information Act.

Another suit has since been launched by Denise Gilman at the University of Texas, which is a group that also runs our international case. They also recently went ahead and filed another lawsuit against the government for failure to comply. So it's very difficult to know precisely. However, in terms of the Indigenous people, broadly we know that thirty-six federal laws were waived in order for the wall to be constructed. Many of those laws are incredibly important; they're absolutely crucial to the protection of Indigenous people's rights. So, if we're talking about environmental protection, protection of wildlife, water rights, mineral rights, rights to religion, rights to culture, rights to protect resources and economic development—all of these specific rights, for tribes as well as citizens, are very complicated.

It's a disturbing matter, because the Obama administration has had every opportunity and has been pressured by many organizations—Indigenous and non-Indigenous and international groups—as well as congressmen to restore constitutional law, to officially restore the thirty-six laws that were waived. We're left hanging, as it has clearly indicated that it does not intend to restore those laws. This administration intends to pursue construction of the walls and potentially continue another plan for construction of walls throughout other places on the U.S. political borders. We're talking about along the west coast, along the northern border with Canada, and along the east coast all the way back around the Gulf.

That needs to be really clearly understood by Indigenous people along the Mexico–U.S. border. Indigenous people should be very troubled by Obama's refusal to restore those laws, because they allow for the government, the state, to not pick up those particular rights in the interior. And that is happening all over the place, where Indigenous people within the state itself are seeing their rights, their resources, their economies, their self-determined development, and their right to their religion continually eroded and threatened and not upheld by any court in the United States—not the local, state, federal, or Supreme courts. They're being knocked down one by one. That's where we're seeing that those particular rights are not really being upheld, and that they're being actually shrunken.

**JKK:** So this case should concern many different constituents for many different reasons across the board. You're talking about everything from civil rights to human rights to the protection of tribal sovereignty. The ACLU has analyzed this struggle at the U.S.–Mexico border and called this development a no-constitution zone, which should worry everybody who claims to be a U.S. citizen, in terms of the guarantees of the U.S. Constitution.

I know that you recently gave testimony before the United Nations Permanent Forum on Indigenous Issues. How was your report received?

**MT:** Well, it's another very important training for Indigenous people in the United States. Native American groups are doing much more to educate and inform their own communities and other communities that they're enmeshed with.

I submitted my paper to the Permanent Forum of the United Nations, but they're not a mechanism that I'm aware of where you are ever informed of whether the forum is actually going to look at your paper.

We have over eighty-four individuals who each signed the roster to speak for three minutes during the very short period that they assign for the special rapporteur on Indigenous people's rights. Many Indigenous people from groups and organizations all over the world who made trips from thousands and thousands of miles to be able to speak, even just for three minutes, and to work in that mechanism were not heard, because the forum, to my knowledge, did not get beyond maybe number twenty-six or twenty-seven. I think I was number forty-four on the list. So, that was very frustrating and there's no report back to Indigenous organizations about where your paper is at in their process or about if the forum members actually reviewed or if it just gets shredded. So, that's a problem. It's a very cumbersome process for Indigenous people to work within the state and within the United Nations structure.

**JKK:** Yes. I'm sorry to hear that. I hope that [Special Rapporteur] James Anaya responds swiftly. I saw in the testimony you submitted that you recommended that the Permanent Forum request that he schedule site visits.

**MT:** When he spoke to the forum members, or to the delegates, he did instruct us to. One of the other forum members instructed a large group of us to follow the mechanisms in the UN. In other words, the rapporteur's office itself has its own regulations about how to get access to him, how to file a letter to him and request assistance, and how you receive a response. The kind of assistance that his office can give is very limited in establishing a case. It reverts you back to the individual, rather than the collective, complaint—or, I would say, an injury type of legal framework. I think that itself is very frustrating for Indigenous groups, who, for example, might have written a paper for the rights for unrecognized people, and I participated on the paper and signed on.

I think this issue should be a front-runner. My observation is that spending this time at the Permanent Forum taught me about something I had intuited, and now I saw it and heard it, I witnessed it myself. It's very clear to me that the majority of the world's Indigenous peoples are unrecognized by the states in which they live, and generally, globally, are unrecognized by states that they do not live in. So my deeper impression was that the federally recognized tribes and nations in the United States and Canada are absolutely the minority, in terms of the delegates at the Permanent Forum. So the paper that was written for the rights of unrecognized people to be put forward was a priority issue for the special rapporteur and for the Permanent Forum.

For the most part, the response to the requests of this group for the special rapporteur to specifically take this issue up and to do work with this newly convened body of Indigenous delegates was again responded to in the format stipulated by the United Nations, which is contained. That generally is, "Well, you would have to have a specific claim to a human rights obstruction, and it would have to be from a very specific group." So, again, it reverts it back to an individual rather than a collective, and allows the collective to sort of take it out of those containers and start challenging and getting the rapporteur to work to loosen up those constraints within his own office and within his job description. So, you know, it's a lot of work and there is a lot of work to be done. Women, again, are leading that very valiantly. That was very a women-driven and women-led action that was, I think, one of the most powerful actions that I witnessed.

**JKK:** Well, as we're wrapping up the interview I want to just ask you if you could tell us where to now, in terms of the priorities for the Lipan Apache Women Defense?

**MT:** Well, our priorities are, again, focusing more on human rights, education documentation, and research to benefit our cases and to benefit the individuals who look now to our web page, to the work that we do as a model. We have learned that in an international community there are not very many groups doing this kind of documentation and research on the Texas–Mexico border and across the whole U.S.–Mexico border. So we were really shocked, and also we learned a lot by getting feedback from people at the UN that have been learning from what we're doing. We are very much appreciated for the work we're doing.

So we know we want to continue to pursue research and documentation and to continue to develop alternative models and paradigms for Indigenous peoples to document their processes in these issues and concerns. That's a priority. Human rights monitoring is a major priority for us in 2010, so we're going to be focusing on setting up two human rights monitoring stations, working with international groups who want to support this work, who want to see more of our work and documentation and help us to train other groups and other peoples in our region and elsewhere. There are a lot of people asking us to help them and to help train them, from South Dakota, from Canada, and from Mexico, and we've received invitations from folks in South America to do reciprocal training. So we see that our role is really growing in our region and we're very happy about the response from Indigenous peoples in our homes, in our homelands.

Our people at home want me to come home, so I'm going to be going home, hopefully in May or June of 2010. And at that point, I think, we're anticipating a lot of growth and a lot of deeper alliance building. My mother and I are starting an institute of Indigenous people's documentation and research projects in our region. So we see a lot of good things coming.

At the same time, the wall is now built. The elders cannot get to the south side of the road. So we are taking action. This summer we are going to be doing two human rights actions in our community: one to access our cemeteries on the south side of the wall, a little bit further up the road, and another to access our non-grazed, natural riparian areas on the other side of the wall. We're gathering ancestral food and medicine plants right now for revitalizing and transmitting this knowledge to our youth. My mother has not been to the south side of her land since the wall went through, because she has hip issues and it's a pretty rough walk. In Texas, South Texas, there's the heat. It's just not a healthy situation for our elders.

So we're pursuing an appeal. We still have a court jury trial coming up in October 2009. And the last time my mother was in U.S. District Court, Judge Andrew Hanen specifically stated that our case would go to the top of the docket during the jury trials, because he felt that we had documented the Native Indigenous history and cultural, ancestral, continuous connectivity to our lands. He stated that our case had significantly changed the compensation issues in his view, so we're anticipating that we're going to have a very dynamic jury trial. And then, after that, technically until the jury trial is complete, we cannot go forward to the Fifth Circuit. So we are appealing.

# CHIEF RICHARD VELKY ON THE SCHAGHTICOKE STRUGGLE FOR FEDERAL RECOGNITION

**First Interview**

Richard Velky (Schaghticoke) is chief of the Schaghticoke Tribal Nation (STN), based in Kent, Connecticut. During the interview he discussed the tribe's legal battle in response to the Bureau of Indian Affairs' reversal of the tribe's federal acknowledgment following the intervention of state officials. The STN has approximately three hundred members and was historically constituted by people from the Mahican, Potatuck, Tunxis, and Podunk tribes who joined together due to the encroachment of white settlers on their ancestral lands. The STN has been continuously recognized from historic times by both the Colony and State of Connecticut. In 1736 the General Assembly of the Colony of Connecticut created a reservation for them in the town of Kent, which is part of Litchfield County.

Making headlines across the United States, at least in Indigenous media, the Schaghticoke have suffered from having their federal recognition reversed. After nearly two decades of waiting, they had received federal recognition from the Bureau of Indian Affairs (BIA) in January 2004. In making its decision the BIA reviewed roughly thirty thousand documents that traced the tribe's existence back to the 1700s. However, in response, Connecticut state officials appealed the federal decision. Connecticut Attorney General Richard Blumenthal argued that the BIA illegally relied on state recognition to probe the tribe's evidence of continuous community and political authority. He and other state officials have argued that without state recognition, the tribes could not prove their existence because of leadership gaps of three years or more. U.S. congressman Christopher Shays, a Republican, argued that the state recognized reservations but not people. Despite these attacks, and in keeping with the tribe's traditional and historical approach to its neighbors and to the outside world, the STN has consistently stated all future tribal activities would be conducted with respect for the land and its neighbors, while beneficial to the surrounding communities and the state of Connecticut. For the Schaghticoke, the next step was to appeal to the federal courts. A follow-up interview that I conducted with Velky later that same year, on October 16, 2007, follows this one.

Chief Velky has been the leader of the Schaghticoke Tribal Nation since 1987. He was born in 1950 at St. Vincent's Hospital in Bridgeport, Connecticut. He comes from a family of leaders—the latest being his uncle Irving Harris, who served as chief from 1967 to 1979. Chief Harris assisted in establishing the Connecticut Indian Affairs Council and helped move the state's oversight of Connecticut tribes from the Department of Welfare to the Department of Environmental Protection. Chief Velky aided Chief Harris in both of these efforts. Chief Velky served in the U.S. Navy from 1968 to 1971, when he was honorably discharged. He began his political leadership with the tribe by serving as chairman of its Housing Authority Committee in 1975. He later served on the tribal council and then as vice-chairman. In 1987 he was elected chief by the voting tribal members, and today he continues to serve the tribe in that capacity.

This interview took place on February 12, 2007.

**J. Kēhaulani Kauanui:** Gale Courey Toensing reported in *Indian Country Today* that your attorneys filed a motion last month to challenge the authority of James Cason when he reversed your federal recognition while he was associate deputy secretary of the Department of the Interior [which houses the Bureau of Indian Affairs]. Please tell us about the nature of your claim and any updates on that appeals case.

**Richard Velky:** Well, it seems clear to us that Mr. Cason did not have the legal authority to overturn our federal recognition. The laws that govern this situation are very clear, and if he didn't have the authority, then the decision he made is not proper and it must be set aside. I'd like to also add that his former boss at the Interior [Department], Gale Norton, the former secretary of the interior, stands behind the original decision that recognized our tribe in January of 2004. She says our petition is one of the best the department has ever seen.

**JKK:** And she's on record? Is that filed with part of your legal brief?

**RV:** Yes, she is.

**JKK:** Can you explain, when you say he didn't have the legal authority, on what grounds? Could you explain the details there?

**RV:** Yes, it's our understanding of course that he needs to be appointed by the president of the United States, or through the act of Congress, and needs to be voted in. Mr. James Cason was not brought in to sit as the assistant secretary in either one of these forums, therefore making the decisions that he's rendered un-credible.

**JKK:** I see. Now, that would mean that the president never appointed him nor was he confirmed by the Senate?

**RV:** That's correct.

**JKK:** And wasn't he up for a position earlier where he was denied confirmation by the Senate?

**RV:** Yes, he was. I believe sometime back in 2002, twenty-seven or twenty-nine other individuals needed to be confirmed. It's my understanding that three of them were not confirmed, him being one of them.

**JKK:** The Connecticut Alliance against Casino Expansion argues that "the state of Connecticut is at risk" if your tribe gains federal recognition, and yet we know that the state takes in over $500 million a year from gaming revenues produced by the Mashantucket Pequots and the Mohegans. As some of our listeners may know, the Indian Gaming Regulatory Act of 1988 set the standards for gaming on Indian lands, as it requires tribal nations and states to come to a compact agreement. What do you make of Jeff Benedict's work? I know he is the author of *Without Reservation: The Making of America's Most Powerful Indian Tribe and Foxwoods the World's Largest Casino*, and now he has formed the Connecticut Alliance against Casino Expansion and is president of that organization. Do you have any ideas as to what his broader political aims may be as well as his immediate political aims in trying to stop your federal recognition?

**RV:** I can say this: Connecticut now is about to experience 100 percent growth in the casino gaming, but amazingly, with all the opponents of the casino gaming, they just seem to disappear now, they're gone. Jeff Benedict has been awfully quiet, in fact, all of them have. Maybe the fight wasn't about gaming at all. Okay, after all, the former secretary of the interior, Norton, still says we should have been recognized. Maybe the fight was really about trying to finish the Schaghticoke people off by stopping our tribe from being recognized. I can tell you this: they will never finish us off and they will never take our land.

**JKK:** Well, you are definitely a nation of survivors. I'd like to ask you, in terms of those who in the past have narrowly focus on the supposed social ills of gaming at the expense of addressing the history of Native dispossession and this long history of trying to do in the tribe, how do you approach this question where people conflate the issue of social justice and recognition with the tribe's prerogative to develop their political economy?

**RV:** People get confused with recognition and the gaming aspects. Our opponents play on the confusion, and to deny the Native Americans control over the remains of the reservation from the 1700s it is a lot easier for them to muddy the water by saying our efforts are about gaming. We feel our recognition by our letter of intent from 1981 was long before gaming was even thought about; however, the state and our opposition would have everyone believing that of course we knew what was going to happen, seven years before it did. The fact is, the Schaghticoke nation is focused on our recognition. It's about keeping our land, and it is about ensuring our tribe isn't to be terminated by people who think we don't fit into their definition of Native Americans.

**JKK:** Right, and with that sort of the challenge of their definitions, we're talking really about dominant, white American perceptions about what makes a person an Indigenous person, right?

**RV:** That's correct.

**JKK:** And this narrative of being diluted or racially mixed has certainly been used against the recognition of Indigenous peoples; that's definitely been the case in Hawai'i.

**RV:** And it continues to be so here.

**JKK:** What about some of the historical ironies at play? How is it that the state could say, you can't use the state history of recognizing the tribe to say that the tribe is really a tribe?

**RV:** Well, that's one we haven't really figured out ourselves yet. For over three hundred years the state has been the overseer of our land. Our land that was outlined to us by the Connecticut General Assembly in 1736, this land was somewhere in the vicinity of 2,500 acres. And through the years this land has been taken from us, as the state officials were the overseers, they have kept records, journals, of individuals, throughout the centuries. And yet, when it comes time, through the federal recognition process, where the state can stand up and be heard, they choose to look the other way and just disown a people, a people that was one of the first citizens of the state of Connecticut. They just look the other way on us. This should be something that Congress should definitely take a serious look at.

**JKK:** Yes, and maybe with the shift in Capitol Hill that's something that can actually happen in the 110th Congress.

**RV:** Hopefully it could be, yes.

**JKK:** Now, beyond Connecticut, I know that Attorney General Richard Blumenthal along with Larry Long [attorney general of South Dakota] are leading a movement of state AGs across the U.S.A. who are filing briefs to cut back tribal jurisdiction. With nearly twenty attorney generals unified, they now argue that parts of the Indian Reorganization Act of 1934 are unconstitutional. How do you see Blumenthal's role in having your tribe's recognition reversed as part of his broader political intentions? And also, isn't it the case that he is breaking his obligation and duty as a public servant, because as I understand, the state attorney general is supposed to serve as a guardian for state recognized tribes.

**RV:** That is correct, and he has the duty and we are citizens of the state of Connecticut, but he seems to look the other way, and it's difficult to watch

Mr. Blumenthal assault us on tribal rights, in the name of stopping gaming, when in Connecticut he has done nothing to stop the multibillion-dollar expansion efforts that are under way. It is awful difficult to watch him as he takes millions of dollars from the people of Connecticut and uses it against the people, including our tribe, who seek nothing more than the right to continue our existence. That is not what the people of our state here want. We've come to learn that Mr. Blumenthal doesn't have 20/20 vision. And on the issues of fairness and due process, he wears blinders when he looks at our tribe and recognition efforts. The fact that the judge once said that Blumenthal's actions threatened to subvert a process for our petition tells the whole story about the position of fairness hearings for us. And for some other tribes to come yet.

**JKK:** Is the threat of broadening the land claims of the tribe at issue here? Is the attorney general threatened by potential land claims that the Schaghticoke might be able to make after federal recognition? Is that one of the issues that's a factor [if we put gaming aside]? What role does land reclamation play?

**RV:** Well, I'm certain it does play a role. Our land reservation is located in Kent, Connecticut. It's in the northwestern part of the state and it's among a very well-to-do group of people today. But years ago, that was an isolated area. That's why we were left so quietly to live our lives, because nobody wanted that part of the state. And we do have a claim issue today, which was from land that was taken from us from the 1736 Connecticut General Assembly. This land was taken away improperly according to the U.S. Nonintercourse Act of 1790. We are in pursuit of retrieving our land to have our homeland restored to the tribe once again. Our land had been flooded by the Housatonic River when they built a dam in 1903. Our burial grounds are still underwater because of the building of this dam. They stopped us from assembling on our reservation during the twentieth century; they burned our homes down so that we wouldn't come back. So yes, he does have contention when it comes to the land, and it's something that we'll fight diligently to restore back to us rightfully.

**JKK:** I want to ask you more about supporting that struggle, but I want to back up for a minute and ask: What role have Senators Dodd and Lieberman played in the state being a factor in the reversal of your recognition?

**RV:** There should be a history book on that one, and our efforts are still being written. However, I will say in 2002 Senator Dodd and Senator Lieberman had tried to pass a bill and it was voted down, 85 to 15, and it dealt with the recognition efforts. Schaghticoke Tribal Nation supported the bill, however, and we supported it except for one clause that they had in there: they wanted another moratorium on any further recognition efforts, so when it came to that, Schaghticoke did have a problem. We felt that after twenty-five years, that was enough of a moratorium. But there's still time for the state political leaders to ensure that the decision made by the United States government was improperly influenced by any lobbyist and a handful of hyper-wealthy individuals who use Connecticut as their vacation home, meaning Kent. No matter how cynical it may become, it is hard to believe the elected leaders here would turn their backs on fundamental fairness.

**JKK:** I appreciate the open-ended nature of your stance that there is still time to do the right thing and that it is a social justice issue. I want to ask you, given that state representatives oppose your tribal nation in the name of state residents, where does that leave Connecticut residents who are not citizens of your tribe who may or may not belong to other nations—they might be white American, Chinese Americans, African Americans. What can residents of Connecticut do to support your struggle? Especially since the opposition to your tribe which many of us might absolutely be against that opposition, and in support of you—what can we do to stop what's being done in our name? Do we need a counter-TASK [Town Action to Save Kent] force?

**RV:** Could be. You know, our recognition has implications for every Connecticut resident. A lawful, thoughtful, and correct decision was reversed by a handful of wealthy influential individuals who bought access into Washington, D.C., to advance their selfish interests. Maybe I should not have this faith in how our government should function, but it is supposed to be fair. Again, the Schaghticoke people were one of Connecticut's first families. If they can get away with doing this to our tribe, the fairness necessary throughout our democracy is threatened, and every citizen should be concerned.

**JKK:** Yes. Thank you for that answer. I want to ask you a question of another, more sensitive nature. Is your tribe being supported—morally, politically, or otherwise—by either the Mashantucket Pequot Tribal Nation or the Mohegans?

**RV:** You know, perhaps they're the best suited to answer that question. But I will say, that while we once were together on the state Indian Affairs Commission, that relationship no longer exists. It saddens me to say that the Mashantucket Pequot Tribe and the Mohegan Tribal Nation have not supported the Schaghticoke Tribal Nation, in any way. I'm concerned that if they had said to the state—I'm certain rather that if they had said to the state—What the heck is going on here? You need to have the tribe be acknowledged, just like we were. For the other Connecticut people to go through the same process, for these tribes to go through the same process that Mashantucket and Mohegan did—to do anything other than to go through a process similar to them which no longer exists today is asking other Indigenous groups in the state of Connecticut to go beyond what others had to do to be federally recognized. Mashantuckets were recognized by an act of Congress, the Mohegan tribe was recognized in the same way that we were. They were given a negative preliminary decision, which reversed into a positive final determination based upon new evidence that they submitted. Well, the Schaghticoke Tribal Nation did the same. However, when Mohegan did it there wasn't a fight. There was a fight once Schaghticoke did it. I would ask our brothers and sisters on the eastern part of this here state that they look once again to all the struggles that the Indigenous tribes have gone through and to put their support behind their people once again.

**JKK:** Chief Velky, is there anything else you'd like to share with us?

**RV:** Yes, I'd just like to remind everybody that the federal recognition process isn't an easy process. It wasn't set up to be easy, and they didn't make it easy, and it continues to be very tough. However, I don't believe that it was supposed to be a "gotcha" system, and that's what we're in today. A tribe has seven criteria they need to achieve to be federally recognized. The Schaghticoke successfully achieved all seven of these criteria, and then it turned into the "gotcha game." Our history is deep, our history is here in Connecticut. . . . Our relationship with the state goes back three hundred years, it will continue for another three hundred years, and we ask the state of Connecticut to finally do the right thing and to acknowledge us and stand behind us so the federal government does.

## Second Interview: Schaghticoke Tribal Nation Appeals

My follow-up interview with Chief Velky details the tribe's appeal of the BIA's unprecedented decision to strip the Schaghticoke Tribal Nation of its federal acknowledgment. The tribe had just filed a motion for summary judgment in the U.S. District Court in New Haven, Connecticut, for its claim that the loss of its federal status resulted from unlawful political influence by powerful politicians and a White House–connected lobbyist who violated federal laws, agency regulations, congressional ethics rules, and court orders to have the BIA decision reversed. Despite the fact that the tribe had painstakingly followed the process and achieved recognition on their petition's merits, political opponents launched a public-relations campaign accusing the tribe of politically manipulating the process to gain federal recognition, and then launched their own secret campaign to politically manipulate the process to reverse that decision. The lobbyist group—Barbour, Griffith and Rogers [BGR]—is named in the tribe's lawsuit, where they are charged with harmful and unlawful interference with the tribe's recognition. BGR's communications regarding the STN reached to the governor of Connecticut, White House staff, Interior Department officials, the anti-Indian group One Nation United, and even former secretary of state Henry Kissinger, who is a resident of Kent, Connecticut

This interview took place on October 16, 2007.

**J. Kēhaulani Kauanui:** Chief Velky, I want to ask you about the state's resistance to your tribe's federal recognition case. Clearly, the state is opposed to any federal recognition of tribes that would lead to more casinos, yet on the other hand the state seems happy to take in more than $422 million annually from Foxwoods and the Mohegan Sun, the two existing Indian casinos that have been driving the state's economy since they opened. In other words, from my perspective the state politicians seem to alternately use the tribes and then bash them. What do you think is at the center of the state's opposition to your tribe's quest for federal recognition?

**Richard Velky:** Well, I can't speak to why the Connecticut officials broke the law and stole our rightful recognition, but I do know what they did. What took the Schaghticokes nearly twenty-five years to document was destroyed in months by backdoor dealings of politicians and highly paid power brokers with ties to the Bush White House. Now despite the fact that the tribe has painstakingly followed the process and achieved recognition on our petition merits, political opponents launched a public-relations campaign accusing the tribe of politically manipulating the process to gain our federal recognition. Then they cynically launched their own secret campaign to politically manipulate the process to reverse that decision. By law and the specific direction of Judge Dorsey, the administrative process *must* be free from political pressure and lobbying. In new information that has surfaced, through the depositions and freedom of information requests, it is clear that there was a comprehensive and massive effort, unprecedented in scope, to apply political pressure and improperly influence the Department of the Interior to take our recognition away.

**JKK:** So how is it that the state always manages to somehow succeed in mischaracterizing the Connecticut tribes as the ones who are exploiting the system, when it was historically the colony and now the state that is dispossessing and exploiting the process, and dispossessing the tribe?

**RV:** Yes, well, in the beginning the state of Connecticut was content in simply stealing the tribe's land. Now they teamed up with the Bush White House and perverted the rule of law. To do what never has been done before, and that's to take back a federal recognition. Our motion for summary judgment before Judge Dorsey is about the truth and fairness. While we can never expect a politician in Connecticut to tell the truth, I still have hope that the court stands for justice. Now, the fact is, our tribe has been here since before there was a Connecticut, and we're not going anywhere today either.

**JKK:** Well, when you say "ties to the Bush White House," it seems to me that this case has many deep links to corrupt behavior on the part of the state and the federal government. It's clear to me from having followed the case that the Schaghticoke Tribal Nation's petition was impeccable. How is it that the Hartford media has persisted to portray this as a case of chicanery on the part of the tribe instead of investigating the underlying political machinations? I read in a September 25 piece by Rick Green in the *Hartford Courant*—even in that he reduced the issue to one of simple cronyism, and his piece to me read more like an editorial than a news report. Can you tell our listeners of the tribe's struggle to get fair media representation and investigative journalism in the state on your case?

**RV:** Well, I can tell you this: the media is starting to understand what happened to our tribe, that elected officials acted illegally and improperly to steal our recognition. Now this is about fairness and the rule of law, nothing more. What people are realizing is that if you are opposed to a particular issue on social or moral grounds, you simply cannot do whatever you want to advance your cause. It's one of the earliest lessons most people learn; it's not okay to break the rules or the law.

**JKK:** Yes. Well, it just seems that when this gets released I would hope that it would be on the front page of the *New York Times* and the *Wall Street Journal* for that matter. Now in the spring of 2007, I understand that your tribe followed the lawsuit in Washington, D.C., against TASK [Town Action to Save Kent], and it was put on hold, pending the resolution of your legal claims in the U.S. District Court of New Haven, until Judge Dorsey rules in your appeal. Can you tell us more about this second lawsuit? Why was it filed in D.C., and why do you think it has been put on hold?

**RV:** Well, again, we now have a clear picture of what Connecticut officials did, illegally behind the scenes in Washington to steal our recognition. We know that they worked with the Bush White House insiders, we know they involved officials from other states, we know that they used political pressure illegally to overturn our recognition. The D.C. lawsuit is simply another avenue for us to pursue our rights. And it's on hold right now, pending the outcome of the federal court right here in Connecticut.

**JKK:** Now, is part of that because Barbour, Griffith and Rogers is a lobbyist group based in Washington, D.C.? Is that part of it?

**RV:** Well, that plays into it without a doubt, yes it does.

**JKK:** You mentioned that state officials got other states' officials involved. Would you tell us more about that?

**RV:** Well, it just didn't stop with the Connecticut attorney general, you know; it went to the governor, to our congressional leaders, and to our senators. It trickled down to selectmen and other people in the town to get organizations to fight the tribe in our pursuit for federal recognition.

**JKK:** Wasn't there a governor from another state or some politicians from Virginia that were involved in that?

**RV:** Yes, there was. There was Congressman Wolfe, who got together with Congressman Shays of Connecticut's Fourth District and supported the state in the fight to take the recognition away from us.

**JKK:** I should note that the Virginia case is also extremely loaded, because here we see the anniversary celebrations of the settlement of colonial Williamsburg, and the Virginia tribes are really trying to fight for federal recognition as well. So there's a heavy backlash in the state of Virginia.

Now, Connecticut Attorney General Richard Blumenthal divulged the contents of two sealed motions, one of which was filed by the tribe in May 2007. As I understand it, your motion sought the court's permission to take testimony from former principal deputy assistant director for Indian affairs Martin, who had been willing to testify about the mistreatment of the tribe's petition, the mistreatment that it received.

I read in Gale Courey Toensing's report from *Indian Country Today* that U.S. District Court judge Dorsey, whom you mentioned, denied your tribe's request for ruling of contempt and sanctions against Blumenthal and also denied your request to interview Martin. What factors do you think were at play in his decision?

**RV:** I can't speak for the judge in our case, but I can tell you that our tribe has faith that justice will prevail on our case. We've carefully documented what politicians like Richard Blumenthal, the state attorney general, did to our tribe. Our case rests with the federal courts now. We're hopeful that justice and the rule of law will prevail here. The attorney general's action that exposed the contents of our sealed motion—I think that I would say shame on him for not following the letter of the law. I think Connecticut deserves better and expects more out of our attorney general than what Mr. Blumenthal is giving us.

**JKK:** Yes, especially when he's always ranting about following the rule of law.

**RV:** Absolutely.

**JKK:** Now, the lobbyist group Barbour, Griffith and Rogers is named in your tribe's lawsuit. . . . How instrumental do you think they were as the politicians' proxy?

**RV:** Well, you know, our motion for summary judgment describes in great detail how Barbour, Griffith and Rogers were at the center [of an effort] to steal our federal recognition. The deposition reveals senior Connecticut officials and their minions, including lobbyists from the firm. You know, they met secretly with White House officials, they threatened the secretary of the interior, Gale Norton, with the loss of her job if the recognition was not overturned and cautioned each other to keep their activities hidden and be careful with what they were writing. You know, they recruited powerful third parties from outside Connecticut to pressure the White House and in turn the Department of the

Interior into reversing the final determination on Schaghticoke. In the end our recognition was reversed because of the political pressure, not the merits. We have to have faith that justice will prevail now and we will be awarded a fair opportunity here.

**JKK:** Yes. Well, do you think in some other form Judge Dorsey might be able to subpoena the interview with Martin?

**RV:** If there's nothing else I've learned throughout this long, agonizing system of going through federal recognition and the courts, it's that the judge can order just about anything that he wants as long as it's fair and within the process, and that's all we ever asked for here.

**JKK:** Now, for those who aren't familiar with this process who would say, Well, wait a minute, the town didn't want the tribe to be recognized, they hired a lobbying campaign who went and did what they needed to do to try and stop it—what's wrong with that? You know, what if they say this is corporate democracy at work here?

**RV:** Well, if we were just going through the system itself, that being the recognition process, there probably wouldn't be anything wrong with it, but we were underneath the federal court judge's orders that specifically said, do not circumvent the system, and stay within the process, and nobody was to deal with the Department of the Interior without notifying the other party. They violated that by asking these other groups to circumvent the judge's order. So that would be the difference. We didn't just go through a normal process; we went through a normal process plus the court order.

**JKK:** Yes, since the politicians were not allowed or supposed to be able to use any kind of proxy.

**RV:** Absolutely not, and neither were we, and we didn't. We followed the rules and the law.

**JKK:** Well, I'd like to just note that for a future program, I'm definitely going to be investigating this anti-Indian group One Nation United. They've been mobilizing against Native Hawaiians as well, and they seem to be part of the ongoing backlash against Indigenous rights in this country. I'd also be curious to see what role former secretary of state Henry Kissinger might have played in this, because he's still such a powerful man. . . .

**RV:** Well, I welcome you to do that informal investigation, if you will, and look into this and let Indian Country know, because this is a powerful force fighting tribes and their recognition.

**JKK:** Yes. Now, speaking of Kent, what is the profile of Kent as an affluent town, and what do you think is at stake in terms of land claims and changing the landscape? I mean, when I talk to students at Wesleyan and people in the neighborhood, family members, a lot of them say, you know, Look, how much of this has to do with wealthy white landowners in Kent and their fear with a quaint woodsy town being transformed by a casino?

**RV:** Well, you know, Kent is becoming a super-wealthy highway for New Yorkers, not for Connecticut people. And the Kent of yesterday was a quaint woodsy town. I can tell you that because tribal members have lived, have died, and have been buried on our reservation for nearly three centuries—so we're attuned to what's going on there. Recognition of our tribe won't change our reservation character. If anything, it will help us to protect it. You know, the only thing that will change is our ability to own and manage our land for the first time since early colonial days. As for the land claims, you know, they were filed to ensure we protect what's left of our reservation in Kent and to ensure the area's real character is preserved. Not carved into McMansions, if you will.

**JKK:** Speaking of that, can you tell us about some of the ways that federal recognition would help the Schaghticoke to protect that rural landscape?

**RV:** Well, it would give us the right to go back and exercise our values again as a tribal nation, it would bring our people closer together and back to our homelands, and this is something that we've been striving for since 1976. You know, this was something we started long before our [quest for] federal recognition— well, at least five years before we started that. . . . So we always had the intentions of getting back to our homeland and uniting again as a tribe. It would help us, you know, with our elders and our young ones for future generations.

**JKK:** Yes, and it just seems, similar to the reversal of events, when you talked about the state politicians accusing the tribes of chicanery, yet it's the state politicians that went out and did the backdoor dealing. Similarly, with this issue of Kent as an affluent town, it's as though the residents make out the tribe to be the ones who are going to change everything, when it's settler colonialism that changed everything. And I think what's so profound here is that what the settlers have done historically is what their descendants are accusing the tribe of trying to do to them—as though they're the victims

**RV:** You hit the nail right on the head there!

**JKK:** Now, besides white property rights there seem to be also issues of class tension and the public's perception regarding what they think the tribe's authenticity is, or is not. What would you say in response to those who oppose the tribe's claims based on their own racial prejudices, say, or class prejudices, or how they think an "Indian" should "look"?

**RV:** Yes, I appreciate that question, but there is one important thing to know: there is no question about the legitimacy of Schaghticoke Tribal Nation. The state of Connecticut has recognized our tribe since the early eighteenth centu-ry, and according to the Bureau of Indian Affairs the Schaghticoke petition was the most comprehensive ever presented to them. Every tribal member on our rolls has proved that they are a descendant from those listed in the eighteenth-century records. So they can put that to rest.

**JKK:** Yes, and I like your point because you get right to the heart of it, and that the rest is irrelevant, isn't it, in terms of looks, it shouldn't be about what some-body looks like, and just for our listeners, this is a point that I'm often encour-aging people to think about: the conflation of race and indigeneity. From my perspective, having lived in New England for the past seven and a half years, when I go back out West I hear people say, Well, you know, the tribes there "look black" or "look white." And I think, wait a minute, that's about intermix-ing with the surrounding population to survive; it doesn't mean that they're not their own tribe as well and that that's something distinct, that indigeneity is distinct regardless of the racial mixing.

**RV:** Absolutely, and it's not in the looks; it's in the blood and genealogy, and like I said, it has been proven that our membership is 100 percent solid recognized back to the eighteenth-century list of tribal members. There's no question here for us.

**JKK:** Yes, and just to remind people that racial appearance is not on the list of seven criteria that your tribe met before the recognition was reversed and stolen.

Now, you mentioned earlier something about the pending land claims, and I want to return to that. I understand that those land claims are on hold. Can you please tell us about these claims? Is it two thousand acres of land, and what about it in terms of this land being currently claimed by the town, the Kent school, Connecticut Light and Power, and the state government?

**RV:** Well, every acre of land involved in our land claims was once part of our historical reservation. Over the years it was stolen or sold without our permis-sion. The land claims are really more about our protection of what we have left. We kept most of our land claims to undeveloped land. We're trying to encour-age a dialogue with our neighbors who hold undeveloped pieces of our reser-vation, you know, such as the Kent school up there. And we have always made use of our land and its resources—including how we farmed it, we hunted it, we fished it—similar to our neighbors' on the other side of the river. We would like that to continue. We're willing to work with our neighbors, as we always have been. We believe we share the same interests and we want to preserve our reservation lands in their natural state also.

**JKK:** And are those two thousand acres contiguous with the four-hundred-acre reservation?

**RV:** Yes, they are. And as I indicated, they are undeveloped lands.

**JKK:** I really appreciate how you pointed out that TASK is made of up a lot of New Yorkers too. I mean, I hadn't really thought of it in that respect, because the TASK folks always talk about themselves as Connecticut citizens, and they work so closely with the state government that it hadn't really struck me that these are people with second and third homes up there that are coming up from Manhattan.

**RV:** That's correct, and one important giveaway really is when they have an important town meeting, it's always on a Friday evening so they can get back from New York to vote, so there's the giveaway.

**JKK:** Oh my goodness! Now I want to go to something that is a little bit more sensitive that isn't about the Kent people per se. I understand that there are six individuals who have organized under the name of the "Schaghticoke Indian Tribe"—not your tribal nation, the Schaghticoke Tribal Nation, but Schaghticoke Indian Tribe, led by Alan Russell—and that these individuals have requested standing in the STN's appeal of the BIA reversal of your federal judgment, and they have also filed a petition with the BIA for their own federal recognition. Can you please shed some light on who they are and what their splinter group is about? Do they have any legitimate claim, or are they simply a faction trying to exploit an internal power struggle?

**RV:** Well, first let me start by noting that Alan Russell is my cousin. In 1997, Alan started his own group, it was called the gathering of the tribe, and in that time around seventy individuals were listed in his group. Now, most of these people cannot pass the seven criteria in the Bureau of Indian Affairs to begin with to be listed as a tribal member, and the individuals that could, they signed up with Schaghticoke Tribal Nation. Today a few people still stand with him, but most of them are his immediate family. I do believe, however, that Alan, just like all of our tribal members, shares the same ongoing concern, which is to protect our reservation and afford our people the rights that they all deserve. I really hope that someday Alan will sign back onto the STN list where he and his family have always been recognized. It would only make sense for all of us to continue forward and to stand united with our efforts by accomplishing our goal, and that's federal recognition.

**JKK:** And hopefully come back into the fold and strengthen the claim?

**RV:** It would, too, it would make it all that much stronger, so the door is always there, it's always open too.

**JKK:** I went to a community meeting last month and I also met some elders that identified themselves as New England Coastal Schaghticokes. Are they part of Alan Russell's Schaghticoke Indian Tribe, or is that another group?

**RV:** That's yet another group. I believe there's another group too, they're calling themselves Schaghticoke, so. There's nothing in the state of Connecticut that doesn't allow them to do it, there's nothing in the [federal] government that doesn't allow them to do it, and the unfortunate thing is, the closer you come to federal recognition, you get the splinter groups. It's not just with our tribe, it's throughout Indian Country, and you know, it's just like Democrats and Republicans—everybody has their own views and wants to take it in a different direction. So, we respect their views also.

**JKK:** Thank you for clarifying that. I've noticed that throughout Indian Country, and that certainly is the case in Native Hawaiian struggles.

**RV:** Yes, I bet, I know it is too.

**JKK:** We have many, many groups, and the name of each usually translates into something that means the "Hawaiian nation" or a variation, and I always have to remind people—they think it's just a simple personality issue—and I point out that what's at stake is what kind of government people want to form. So you know, I can't reduce it to something that's trivial like personality differences. These are pretty serious different political questions, and these are our kin too. Like you said, Alan Russell is your cousin; we're talking about kin here.

**RV:** Yes, we're entitled to have our difference of opinions because we are.

**JKK:** Yes, that's good, because it also reminds us that American Indians and other Indigenous peoples are often held to some other kind of standard—and that's the double standard, as though we're not humans that have our own tensions and different visions for our future.

I know there was a solidarity petition going around for the last year. What can people do to support, to learn more, and what are things that we should keep in mind as this case unfolds in the federal court?

**RV:** Well, their support and prayers are always the first thing I ask for. And the fairness that our tribe has been seeking since we filed our petition in 1994—things were taken away from this tribe for centuries, and who would think that in the twenty-first century something this meaningful for a tribe can be taken away and people could turn their backs to and not ask politicians to explain themselves. We're thankful that we are in federal court today, because if we weren't, I'm afraid that Schaghticoke identity could be stolen from us like they've tried already, but we've been able to persist and prevail and hopefully we'll continue to do so. We do have the petition online, so if anybody wants to get on there and print off a copy I encourage them to and get a list of names and send it back to our tribal office—there is an e-mail listed for our tribal office—so any support, all the prayers that we can get, and that justice be done here.

The federal recognition process should be weighed on merits, not on influence. We appealed an investigation by the inspector general in 2004 because our politicians here in the state said that we had a political influence. After an investigation they said that we didn't do anything but follow the rules and regulations. That's all this tribe ever did, and it took us a great number of years to accomplish our goal to be recognized as a federal tribe, and stand among our brothers and sisters that are federally recognized, and we ask that we get that standing back again.

**JKK:** I also noticed on the website that there's a digest of media coverage for people who want to catch up on the case. If you go the Schaghticoke Tribal Nation's website there seems to be an archive digest, if you will, of different articles. I just also wanted to mention to you and remind our listeners that on a previous program we heard a lecture by esteemed Schaghticoke elder Trudie Lamb Richmond, and she was talking about the Kent town of white settlers coming down on Schaghticoke in the 1700s. She was looking at oral histories of some of what they were doing and she said, "See, TASK has been around for a very long time!"

**RV:** Yes, we have to bring some humor regardless of what we're faced with, and I'm glad you pointed that out. That was nice of her to acknowledge.

**JKK:** And I will definitely give you the last word, but I also just want to remind our listeners when you had mentioned that it's time for us to ask politicians to explain themselves, I think that is very important, and also with Dodd especially with all his campaigning, I mean now more than ever I think is the time for people who are out there listening to actually step up to the plate and ask these politicians—ask Blumenthal, ask Lieberman, Rell, Dodd, Shays, you know, even Rosa DeLauro I saw was at one of those meetings—we need to ask these politicians, what are you doing, and to remind them that they do not speak for all of us, they might speak for a few wealthy landowners, but they don't speak for me. That's for sure.

**RV:** Well, I can say this, that if all these politicians don't have any problem whatsoever in doing this to one of Connecticut's first families, where will they stand when it comes their turn to face the politicians? It takes strong will, because that's what we are faced with. A recognized tribe here in the state, our boundaries outlined by the state assembly since 1736, and for your state representatives to say now that it was about land and not about the people, it's outrageous.

**JKK:** Yes, thank you explaining this to us and unpacking some of these complicated legal issues.

**RV:** I hope that we were able to uncover some of them and again, I look for everybody's support and prayers to get this accomplished. We are a federally recognized tribe that was stripped of our rights, once again—and we will continue to fight to get them restored.

# ROBERT WARRIOR ON INTELLECTUAL SOVEREIGNTY AND THE WORK OF THE PUBLIC INTELLECTUAL

I interviewed Robert Warrior (enrolled member of the Osage Nation) when he was director of American Indian studies at the University of Illinois at Urbana-Champaign. It was also during his term as the first president of the Native American and Indigenous Studies Association (NAISA), an association we cofounded with four other colleagues. Warrior is the author of several books, including *The People and the Word: Reading Native Nonfiction* (2005); *American Indian Literary Nationalism,* with Craig S. Womack and Jace Weaver (2006); *Like a Hurricane: The Indian Movement from Alcatraz to Wounded Knee,* with Paul Chaat Smith (1997); and *Tribal Secrets: Recovering American Indian Intellectual Traditions* (1994). Here we discuss his concept of "intellectual sovereignty," the Osage National Editorial Board and the free press, his endorsement of the U.S. Campaign for the Academic and Cultural Boycott of Israel, Palestine and Edward Said, American Indian activism, the founding of NAISA, and the 2010 conference in Arizona held in the immediate wake of that state's passage of Senate Bill 1070 (authorizing police to racially profile the general population for undocumented people) and House Bill 2281 (banning ethnic studies). Warrior is currently the Hall Distinguished Professor of American Literature and Culture at the University of Kansas.

This interview took place on May 18, 2010.

**J. Kēhaulani Kauanui:** I wanted to start by asking you if you would share some of your personal background to give us a sense of your trajectory and how you came to be a scholar and public intellectual.

**Robert Warrior:** I was born in a really small county in Kansas. When I was born my dad, who is Osage, was a basketball coach. As Osages, we're a people who come from that region, so I was born right there in our homelands, although other people live there now. My mom is non-Native, from Kansas, from a farm family. The Osages were a buffalo-hunting people on the plains and lived there for a really long time, unlike some of the other buffalo-hunting people, who came to the plains later. We also came from the stars, which is an important way we think of ourselves. Now, when we came from the stars we ended up in what are now the Ozark hills in Missouri. We had a combination lifestyle, doing horticulture in villages in the Ozarks during part of the year and then going out on the plains to hunt bison. Now, we live on a reservation in Oklahoma, and I think that our story is really probably in certain ways dominated by the fact that our reservation is on top of the fourth-largest oil field in North America. That brought a lot of resources into our collective group—what became our tribal nation. It's now been 114 years since oil was discovered on our reservation, and it's perhaps the most dominant aspect of our modern history, the part that shapes the possibilities of who we are and who we can be. I should say, though, that at least as important as oil is the fact that we adopted a written constitution as a people, in 1881, and for me that's a really important part of who we are as well.

**JKK:** Yes, I notice that in your book *The People and the Word: Reading Native Nonfiction,* you identify yourself as an Osage constitutionalist. I wanted to ask you more about your work with the Osage Nation, and especially with your work on the Osage Nation Editorial Board that is organized or appointed by the Congress of the Osage Nation. Could you tell us about the role and the editorial board and some of the issues that arise in maintaining the independence of the Osage press?

**RW:** Sure, and let me start by saying that it's a new board. It's the first time I've ever accepted a government appointment. I had to be confirmed by our congress, which created the board. I'm excited about it because I think that it's one of the things that our government, that our Osage government has done that's really progressive. What we're doing now as a board is trying to act in ways that support the idea of a free press among our people. The three of us who are on the board have oversight over the Osage press. Until the creation of our board, the government had that oversight role, which continues to be true in many U.S. Indigenous nations. Ours is an independent board. If it wasn't independent I wouldn't have accepted the position. That independence has been contested by a lot of people, so much so that the legislation creating our board had to go to the Osage Supreme Court. In fact, it was the first case our Supreme Court issued a decision on. Because the free and autonomous exchange of ideas is so important to the development of democratic institutions, my hope is to be able to look back at our work with pride. Some of the things we've already done in support of the staff of the *Osage News,* have been very exciting. Our upcoming elections, coming up in a couple of weeks, will be our first in which there's been a free press, and our staff have really responded in wonderful ways. For instance, the *Osage News* put on a debate between the candidates. One idea

I threw into the mix was to suggest inviting the League of Women Voters in to help out. The editor of the *Osage News* got in touch with the league, and they were eager to help out. They had podiums, microphones, timers, and other equipment, and they also had their protocols for handling debates in fair ways. The debates came across as very serious, and the pictures published later show the intensity the candidates experienced on stage.

Another thing the *Osage News* has done this election cycle is a weekly news roundup featuring short statements by candidates on specific issues. This has worked well, because one of the things you find out in a reservation community is if you're not an incumbent it's hard to make the news. The editor poses a question on Monday, and then on Friday they publish the answers that the politicians provide. I have found it to be an ingenious way of providing a forum for the candidates, and it has been really informative. What does that candidate say about pressing issues—the tribal government taking over our Indian Health Service medical facility, whether or not our government should be investing in business opportunities, et cetera. Usually in Osage politics, you just have to guess what Geoffrey Standing Bear or Cecilia Tall Chief thinks about issues. Thanks to the ingenuity of the *Osage News* editors, we know what they think— or at least what they'll put on the record, and that's a really valuable kind of thing to find out what candidates are willing to say about the issues in front of us as Osage voters.

**JKK:** Yes. And you mention that this is the first election with a free press. Could you just give us a sense of the contrast, and do you think that independent presses are unusual for tribal nations?

**RW:** Freedom of the press is unusual among American Indian peoples. I've been a member of the Native American Journalists Association off and on since 1989. I think it's really a valuable organization, because part of what it's committed to is promoting press freedoms in American Indian communities. This is often a point of contention, with a lot of the papers out there in the American Indian world being owned and operated by tribal councils. So these government-owned papers—I mean you've got to read them with that in mind as far as I'm concerned. People can read them however they want, of course, but it's important to me as I read some of these like *Indian Country Today* or some of the other ones that I say, well, you know, that's one that's owned by a government, so there's a government standing behind it paying for somebody to say what's being said here, or not saying something that one of the people that's there wants to say.

**JKK:** That self-identification as an Osage constitutionalist is something that you mention in your book. Could you speak to that and why you identify yourself in this way?

**RW:** Right, that came out of a crisis—really out of a political crisis—that was going on, and it started back in 1900 when the U.S. government overturned —it's hard to find the exact terms, but they basically announced that the U.S. would no longer recognize our constitutional government we adopted back in 1881. The U.S. government pulled the rug out from under our government, which was all part of a larger policy that the U.S. had in place at that time, and then in 1906 the Congress passed the Osage Allotment Act. That act instituted a number of things, and of course now the U.S. government was telling us how we could be, how we could be a people, and this was always a problem with the U.S. government, its insistence on dictating to you how, why, and what form your peoplehood will take. That's hard to take for a people who had already decided on democracy for ourselves under our own constitution. So, the crisis really had its beginnings there.

By 1994 there was a successful federal lawsuit seeking redress for what the U.S. did to our constitutional government nearly a century before. The judge decided that the way to solve this ongoing problem was to mandate a referendum in which we as Osages could decide for ourselves the shape of our own destiny. That referendum led to the creation of a reformed Osage government, and many of us experienced that new government as a genuine rebirth of our political culture, even though we knew the ruling it was based on had some inherent weaknesses. Sure enough, just two years later, another judge stepped in and ruled that the previous ruling was not valid. That moment of political crisis became for me a galvanizing process in which I had to come to a depth of self-understanding, both as an Osage and as a scholar, that I was and am a constitutionalist and that as such I was open to whatever form a self-determined Osage constitution would take as long as I got to vote on it, but that what I wanted most was to honor the wisdom and foresight of our Osage ancestors who over a century previously had already adopted one for us. What frustrates me about the current Osage constitution is its reliance at crucial moments on U.S. authority rather than our inherent sovereignty. That compromise shows up especially in the enabling legislation that recognizes our reformed government, in which the U.S. Congress disingenuously "reaffirmed" their commitment to our sovereignty as reflected in the 1906 Osage Allotment Act. Affirming Osage sovereignty is the opposite of what the 1906 Osage Allotment Act achieved. It was instead an imposition of coercive U.S. power that foreclosed Osage sovereignty. So, from a strict constitutionalist view that was the price of the new 2008 constitution—acceptance of assertions like this one that our sovereignty is subject to U.S. intervention. So, that's the constitution under which our congress was created, and that's the congress that appointed me to this editorial board.

Interestingly enough, I voted against the constitution when it was put to a vote by all of our people. I was against the constitution. I'm a constitutionalist, so my opposition was not against constitutions per se—I'm not against consti-tutions, but I was against this particular constitution—so I voted against it. I got voted down by other Osages, so I'm willing to live with that result. I was re-ally concerned at that point with the process. I thought that we needed to stop and take a breath and say, what do we really want out of this constitution, how do we make it reflect our values, how do we make it actually the most effective form of constituting ourselves as a people? I was against the process because— it wasn't just that it was too fast, it's never an excuse to say hey you know we just did this too fast—but I thought there were some deep flaws that would be difficult to overcome. It's way too hard, for instance, to amend our new consti-tution, it takes too many people to amend it. It gives the executive branch too much power—and I should note that I'm not criticizing the actual people at this point, except historically, because I'm actually not allowed to. That is, I am not allowed to engage in a discussion of Osage politics in my capacity as an edi-torial board member. Anyway, obviously, it's very complex.

**JKK:** It is. And I'm glad that you're breaking it down for us. It also might be new for many listeners to understand that tribal nations, such as the Osage Nation, have their own congress, so that you're dealing with—you've dealt with in the past—your nation, the U.S. Congress, and now you're talking about the Osage Congress.

**RW:** Right, absolutely.

**JKK:** Also, within the Osage Nation, I understand that you are a founding vice-chair of the Friends of the Osage Language. Can you tell us about this cultural revitalization work?

**RW:** Yes, though when I took my job here in Illinois, I actually had to leave that work behind. My relative Larry Sellers—whom a lot of people might know from his a role as Cloud Dancing on *Dr. Quinn, Medicine Woman* or from *Wayne's World 2*—and I were both students in the Osage Nation lan-guage program a couple of years after it started. He wanted to do something to support our language program that would be independent of the Osage tribal government, so he started a not-for-profit and I helped him, in all the ways that I could. He filed all the papers, which is very complex, and he did a lot of this just on his own, and so he asked me to be on the board of it, and then he asked me to help in the leadership. I did that, and then not long after it actually got going I moved to Illinois, and he had to ask me to step down because I wasn't close enough there to do it. The effort that we were really trying to support is, of course, a really important one.

   All Native-language revitalization programs face some really tough times, because they're trying to do something that is so difficult, and in our case the Osage language has a really tiny number, but it's enough for a people that grew up in homes where they spoke Osage. But they don't really use it that much, I mean they don't have opportunities to use it—they haven't lost it, but they don't have very many opportunities to use it, and of course we're losing them really quickly.

That's hard, but a man named Mogri Lookout has worked for decades on this language program, and just before it was a program he was working on it just day in and day out trying to just keep the language alive, which is so hard, and looking for people to help him, and he wasn't the only one. It's really important to say—there were other people as well, but he was the one that was able to finally able to launch this program with the support of the previous form of our tribal government. Whenever I go to town, I'm always stopping in to see people, but I started taking classes about a year after they started offering them, and for me that meant driving from my house in Norman, Oklahoma, about three hours one night a week to take the class. There are other people in that town without nearly as good a job as mine, and people who didn't even live in that town but who would also drive from two or three hours away, once or twice a week.

And it's really hard. What was so profound to me about becoming part of that community of language learners within our larger Osage community was the camaraderie we had with each other, and these were mainly people who came from the more traditional families as we tend to think of ourselves. The program was open to anyone who wanted to come and learn the Osage language, and so you'd see people on the less traditional side, people who engaged very early on in our reservation era in American forms of government and more American ways of living. There were people that were never a part of this, too, and when you're sitting around the table trying to learn the language, you really learn to appreciate a lot of the differences we have when you're actually on the same kind of task. Night in and night out, you're working on a project that is important.

The one thing I always took away from that experience, Kēhaulani, was that I'd always say to myself as I was driving home to Norman—and I'd get home about midnight or sometimes a little after—I would always say, you know, what I love about this work so much is that it's the one thing I do where I never feel as though I've wasted a single moment of time doing it. Not a single moment of time was wasted, not a single resource that I expended in order to be there, like the Sharpies that I bought to make the flash cards.

I have a little funny story about driving. There was this thing that showed me some of the problems that come when you try to have these programs. I had this one flash card, and I could not remember this one sentence. The program used a sentence-based pedagogy or way of learning, so I would use these flash cards, and I would work on them in the car. There was this one I just couldn't get, so I'd be driving and then I would just say it ten times, then I would say it twenty times, then I'd say it fifty times. And the sentence I couldn't learn was, "You don't know how to drive."

I love that work, and I missed it so much not being there. We have our dances coming up in a couple of weeks, so I'll be back on our reservation, back at Grayhorse dancing, and one of the things that's really neat is that the people that are a part of that language community—I'm not really in it in the same way I was—but as long as I can remember some of the things, I can still participate. But out there under the arbor, when we're dancing and we see each other at those dances, we try to speak Osage to each other, and it really makes me feel so connected to something that you can't really connect with in that kind of study unless you're doing it in the language.

It's not my mother tongue. The language my mother grew up speaking was English, and that's the language of our home. But I started calling it my birthright language. Osage, Wazhazhe ie, is my birthright language. And I never worked out everything that that means, but it seemed really kind of powerful to me at the time.

**JKK:** It is powerful, and that's a beautiful story. Thank you. That actually leads me to ask you about these concepts that you've coined, the term *intellectual sovereignty* in your early work, your first book, *Tribal Secrets: Recovering American Indian Intellectual Traditions*. In that work you argue that a process-centered understanding of sovereignty provides a way of envisioning the work of Native scholars. Can you tell us more about what you mean and how you see that today?

**RW:** When I was working through a lot of those ideas back in the late eighties and early nineties, I wrote the dissertation that became that book. I wrote the first draft of it on our reservation. "Sovereignty" was, as it is now, a really important term. It's a term that some people don't like and it's a term that other people really like, but regardless, it's a term that is with us and it's a really important term.

When I had the idea of intellectual sovereignty, I wanted to be able to make a closer association between what was happening with the idea of sovereignty within tribal nations—at least in the U.S., and that's part of my context, but there's a similar kind of thing in Canada. There are issues of autonomy in Indigenous communities throughout the Americas, and the issues of sovereignty come up in Australia and Aotearoa/New Zealand. For me, I thought, well, what am I doing as a scholar? And the thing that I could do is engage in a form of thinking through what it means to be a scholar who is committed to sovereignty by saying, well, I want to practice intellectual sovereignty and then I want to find out what that means.

I don't know what it means; I was a pretty young scholar back then—and I like to think that I'm still young in some ways now—but I was really trying to figure out, how do I get myself on the path to becoming a mature scholar? That was actually a really deep, a deep Osage concept. A big part of who we are and what we do in our traditional ways of thinking as I understand them is, philosophically, the movement.

And I talk about that in my book, in *Tribal Secrets*; I talk about that movement, from what we call the Hunka to the Tsi-zhu. And again, I mean, I've never been able to dedicate myself to spending the time it takes to be somebody that could ever say I'm an Osage philosopher and really work through these things. There are people like that, and it really takes living there to be able to access a lot of that wisdom. The wisdom that comes out of that, I think, is that what we're trying to do in that old style; we're trying to make that movement between the Hunka, which is really the immature, to the Tsi-zhu, which is the mature.

I thought, that's what I'm trying to do in my life, that's what I'm trying to do in my work. I've always had a family, so I guess I could say now that I have a family in my house, I see that in my kids. I live in one with kids around, and moving toward maturity is really an important thing for me. I think that's important to say about the idea of sovereignty as well.

Sometimes, when we argue about whether or not we have the right term, we're actually not having as productive a discussion as we might have if we would have a different discussion. Maybe it was an immature form of sovereignty that we were talking about in the 1980s and the 1990s, and maybe what we're actually looking for is not a new term, but a more mature version both of the term itself and also of the discussion. So anyway, that's where it's moving. It was an idea, and it's been deployed in various ways. It's really gratifying when a people start picking up your ideas, and it's really humbling especially when you're younger, as I was when I first deployed it and people would take off with it in various ways.

There was a conference back in the late 1990s that took place both in Mexico and in the U.S., in California, and they used Indigenous intellectual sovereignty as a theme. There was also a conference in Canada as well. Those conferences, I really need to point out, were not about me at all. I didn't go to the one in Canada, but I went to the ones in California and Mexico, and they were about the idea. And it's exciting when you're somebody who thought of something and kind of deployed it, and people take it and they further it. I always appreciate being credited for it, but it's taken off in ways that I think are really important. For example, saying, "Well, what are filmmakers doing when they make a film?" Let's talk about visual sovereignty and how it might be that somebody is able to express themselves as an artist or as a scholar, and be doing that in a way that reflects the ongoing discussion why sovereignty is so important.

**JKK:** Definitely. Actually, that leads me to something else I want to ask you about in thinking about the term *intellectual sovereignty* and the concepts of nationalism and the role of a Native critic. In your coauthored book *American Indian Literary Nationalism*, I read your chapter "Native Critics in the World: Edward Said and Nationalism," where you recount your engagement with Edward Said's work while you were a graduate student enrolled in two of his courses. For those who might be unfamiliar with Said, he was a Palestinian American literary theorist and advocate for Palestinian rights who was a professor at Columbia University, as well as a founding figure in postcolonialism. Now, Robert, how has Said's work influenced your understanding of not only the Palestinian movement for justice but also your take on the role of Native critic in nationalism?

**RW:** I don't think anything has influenced me more than Said's work, which was already influencing me by the time I had decided to go to New York. He was part of the reason I decided to pursue my PhD and my doctoral studies in New York at Union Theological Seminary, on the chance that I would be able to take classes with him.

I knew that would be a possibility, because Union Theological Seminary had an arrangement with Columbia University, where Said taught, and so that was part of the reason why I went. I already knew his work pretty well, and I think that a lot of the reasons for why I wanted to pursue that is because I admired his ideas tremendously. I was so struck by the way he was able to do two things as a scholar: he was able to engage the world through his political work, through his engagement in politics, and he was also able to be a scholar who, when people would say that they didn't like his ideas, he would go on and say, okay, you don't like my ideas, but let's talk about why you don't like them. That was his scholarly life, and he actually made a separation between them.

When I wrote the chapter that you're talking about, on nationalism, I wanted to highlight the relationship I had with his ideas, and also with him. I didn't know him well, but I did know him; we would see each other on the street, and he was this wonderfully grand presence on the Upper West Side, you know. I would stop him on the street, and we would talk, and I would remind him of who I was, or I would make an appointment and go to his office to ask him questions, and I would have my fifteen minutes to talk to him. I try to treasure those memories, because he's such a giant intellectual figure. And not everybody knows who he is, but then in my world he's a really considerable presence. I think what he helped me to really work through was this idea of what nationalism was. For me, the title on that book is not a commitment to the idea that somehow we can do literary nationalism. That's the position I take in that coauthored book, that I'm in fact not a literary nationalist, but I think that these are actually important things.

I'm an Osage nationalist, and I'm really happy to say that in the same way that Edward Said was really willing to say he was a Palestinian nationalist. The scholarly form of that I'm not into, because I think that it starts to equate my scholarship with my nationalism, and I have so many problems with nationalism. I mean, nationalism is, in fact, a really big factor in a lot of the enormous problems of the world, and so I can't endorse the idea of nationalism as a scholar. I'm willing to engage in it as an Osage, within the Osage world, because I think that it's one of the most powerful forms available for us as Osages to be able to advance our own aims of making our Osage world better for Osages. So that's why I'm committed to Osage nationalism.

I'm an enormous critic of American nationalism; I think that American nationalism has been disastrous in so many cases. I think that it stands behind so many problems in the world right now. American nationalism is an enormous problem, as are other forms of nationalism around the world, and so when I pick up the mantle of Osage nationalism, it's only within that limited world. I mean, just to be clear, that's 15,000 people or so—maybe it's 17,000 people now, but it's less than 20,000 people—and I think that we're still small enough that we can. Hey, nationalism creates problems for Osages as well. The problem with nationalism is it tends to bring out the worst in us. It often leads to chauvinism; it often leads to men thinking of themselves as the leaders. The way I think about nationalism is that it brings all of us into the discussion and that it helps us to create a forum in which we can be inclusive, so that we can address some of the problems that we have in our community. And those problems are many, but I think some would be solved if we had a healthier discussion about things like sexism and how it affects our communities.

I think there's a problem in the American Indian world—there's a problem in the Osage world—with homophobia.

We use our attitudes and our beliefs, and we bring those beliefs into a public forum and end up leaving some people out. That's the last thing people want to do, is leave people out. And I think that for American Indian people and Indigenous people around the world, one of our fundamental experiences is knowing what it's like to be left out. So this has been something I've also tried to reflect in my work; that's a real fundamental part of who we are. We need to make ourselves aware of who we're leaving out.

I work all the time on trying to make sure that I'm including people. I need to include the disabled—I've been disabled, I've had a disabled placard that lets me park closer to things, and I really appreciated the State of Illinois for issuing that to me, because it made my life easier. So, as a scholar I take into account people who are disabled, as I was. Almost everybody in the American Indian world knows somebody who's disabled, and that's why I want to have a discussion about what health means to those of us who are working around ideas, because it's really important. I think a lot of the disabled American Indian people themselves can help us understand their viewpoint. If we listen more to those people, those gay, lesbian, bisexual, transgender American Indian people who are out there, they can really teach us a lot. They can really tell about what it's like to live in some of our communities and to also be a gay and lesbian person, or a bisexual person, or transgender person, or a queer person—what that's like, to live on a reservation, to be queer.

**JKK:** Yes, well, that leads right into to what I was going to ask you. Revisiting your other coauthored book, *Like a Hurricane: The Indian Movement from Alcatraz to Wounded Knee*, you and Paul Chaat Smith critically examine the period of American Indian political history during that time, and I wondered about your thoughts on American Indian activism today as it differs and some of the most pressing issues affecting Indian Country.

**RW:** That was a really gratifying book to write. A story to tell. And I grew up during that movement; there were kids who were actually participating in all of those things, and that particular social movement was a profound watershed moment in the United States. There were other forms of it in Australia, and in the Indigenous world throughout the Americas and Canada very important-ly. But our book was focused on what happened in the U.S., because in many ways what Paul and I really committed ourselves to doing was telling a story that would help people to understand more about what happened. We noticed that things were just getting lost over time about what had actually happened. Paul joined the movement; he left college and joined the movement. So, it was a really great collaboration between somebody coming from his position, as a person who had been in the movement but who had a lot of questions about it, and me, as somebody who had just finished my PhD.

Paul is a terrific writer and a really wonderful intellect, and I think that one of the things we wanted to do was to leave something for people who wanted to understand their own political history. To me, that was the achievement of it. And we always knew we wanted as many people to read it as possible; we wanted it to be available when people went to Barnes and Noble, or Borders, or Amazon.com. We wanted regular American Indian people to be able to find the book so that they could find the story that we had written. That's been a really gratifying part of the response to it: the main audience of it. And it's done pretty well. It was never a Michael Crichton bestseller or anything like that, but it's done pretty well. We knew that the main audience would be college students, and I hear from college students every year, saying they read *Like a Hurricane.* And that's exactly what we wanted.

The very last paragraph—which we worked on for weeks and weeks, send-ing it back and forth rewriting it—I finally said to Paul, "Let's think about the fifteen-year-old American Indian kid or Indigenous kid maybe somewhere else, who's trying to understand her or his own political history, Let's write the last paragraph for them." And that's who we wrote that last paragraph for. I'm still really happy with that book, so thanks for asking about it.

**JKK:** Are you talking about the last paragraph of the epilogue?

**RW:** No, I'm talking about the last paragraph of the last chapter. This is the last paragraph of the last chapter of *Like a Hurricane*. For Indian people, the movement's grand entry had raised dizzying hopes of respect for treaties and sacred lands, but also of a new kind of person, a new kind of democracy, and a new kind of Indian future. Those hopes lived on even as the memory of the seventy-one-day siege faded. The season of occupations may have ended in the siege at Wounded Knee, but with those occupations a door had been opened and, with it, a world of new possibilities.

**JKK:** Thank you so much for that. Also, you mentioned Paul Chaat Smith and his intellectual contributions and activist work. I also had him on the show, speaking to his book, *Everything Thing You Know about Indians Is Wrong*.

I want to ask you about the Native American Indigenous Studies Association. But before I do that, I want to go back to something else about Edward Said and the movement for Palestinian justice.

**RW:** Okay.

**JKK:** Outside of this interview, you and I have spoken at length about our respective endorsement for the U.S. Campaign for the Academic and Cultural Boycott of Israel, for which I serve as an advisory board member. Can you talk about your perspective on this boycott and issues of Palestinian human rights?

**RW:** Yes. I really got to know those issues well in two trips that I made to Israel, to work as a volunteer for the Israeli government doing archaeology two summers back in the 1980s—in 1985 and 1986. Obviously, I would not say "I'm boycotting the Israeli government," and those academic programs are exactly the things that I now think people should. I'm committed to boycotting, but when I did that I was actually able to go to a lot of Palestinian communities, and I was just so overwhelmed by the way that I was greeted in those communities because I was an American Indian person there. I started by being on the ground there; I got to know a lot of the young people and the things that they were up against in trying to make their own world better. It's just heartbreaking to me. And it's also heartbreaking to me that you have all of the wonderful things about Israel that are within that society—wonderful things about the economy, the way they've been able to develop their nation out of a response to one of the greatest human tragedies ever—and so I really understand the profundity of the existence of Israel. Yet, at the same time, I really do think that ignoring what's going on the other side of that wall, on the other side of that line, I just couldn't take it.

The boycott was so well organized and so well done, with clear aims coming from people there in Gaza and the West Bank. Scholars like me were trying to confront this, and they issued their call, and then when you put it all together—

the American response, the U.S. response to it—I find for those reasons it really made me feel like I was doing something, to try to use my position as a scholar to address and end something.

**JKK:** Now, Robert, I want to shift to discuss the cofounding of the Native American and Indigenous Studies Association. I'm recalling that in 2005, you and Jean O'Brien approached me at the American Studies Association conference in Washington, D.C., to ask if I would work with you on this project, which was your brainchild. How did you come to decide to undertake this work, and why?

**RW:** It came out of a long-standing need for there to be something like the Native American and Indigenous Studies Association: something that would really support the professional needs of those of us who are scholars in institutions like the one that I teach at—the University of Illinois—like the one that you're at—Wesleyan. All over the world, Indigenous scholars are within these institutions, and most of our colleagues on these college campuses, like the one that I'm on, have associations that support their work. That was the primary purpose of this new association as it unfolded. As we talked about it, I didn't have a fully formed idea; it was just an idea that then turned into something else. And, certainly, along the way I've been voted down a number of times on any number of things, and that's totally cool with me. It's got to be a collective effort.

I've seen it go from that to what it's become, with over seven hundred members now, coming into its second annual meeting. To see it develop so quickly into something that matters to people—it matters to seven hundred people that we exist. We don't go knocking on doors saying please join the Native American and Indigenous Studies Association. It was a response to the needs, especially of younger scholars. For younger scholars, who are just entering the institution like this one, there's quite a vulnerability that's a part of that. You and I have tenure, and that means that it's really difficult to get rid of us from the campus, but before you go through that process you really need some help. I only bring it up because getting over that particular line really is fundamental to who we are as scholars. So, I think a really important part of the new association is that it provides that professional help to people.

**JKK:** Yes, absolutely. Now, later this month we're holding the second annual Native American and Indigenous Studies Association conference in Tucson, Arizona. Some may have read about this in *Indian Country Today* or perhaps the *Chronicle of Higher Education*, that we're meeting there, and certainly through all media venues people should know that the state legislature in Arizona recently passed both Senate Bill 1070, which authorizes police to racially profile the general population for undocumented people, as well as House Bill 2281, which targets ethnic studies programs. Now, Robert, given these two new laws, there have been calls for an economic boycott of Arizona—calls that we in the Native American and Indigenous Studies Association have had to respond to as a council, and you and I both know that the council decided unanimously to still hold the conference of the association there. Could you speak to this, and go on record with regard to the calls for a boycott and this decision?

**RW:** Sure, because it was a big decision for us, and it's a controversial one within the association. There were those who wanted us to cancel our meeting. We made a decision in the leadership to go ahead with the meeting based on three reasons. One of those was financial. We really did risk bankruptcy in this relatively new—couple-of-year-old—association if we canceled the hotel contract. These are big, multinational corporations, and so when they put a contract in front of you and you sign it, you know they expect to be paid on it. We are, as a young association, more vulnerable than older associations that *are* in fact in a position to be able to negotiate out of contracts. But coming so close to our meeting, I got a lot of advice and heard from the hotel itself, that this in fact would be an unlikely scenario for us. So, it's part of what we have to face as a young association.

But, I think we also have to do something. We've decided to have really strong relationships with local people, with hosts. We really considered ourselves to be hosted in Arizona, and there is this really terrific group of people at the University of Arizona that has asked us to come. One of my Indigenous values is to try to keep my commitments around issues like this, when somebody asks me to come. We decided to go there, and so it would have been really tricky to not go, especially on that point.

The third reason is that we don't have some of the things in place yet to respond in the way that some of our members did. I think we will have those things in place, but we don't have those in place yet, and I think that it's really important to meet in that regard so that we can talk. That's an important reason we started the association in the first place: getting together to talk, and being able to be face-to-face to do the business of the association.

The primary thing that we do at meetings is share our research and share our work, and my goodness, we really need those opportunities. That's maybe the most gratifying thing about this whole Native American and Indigenous Studies Association, the opportunity to share our work with each other, to see the excitement that that creates among other people who do this work and to share in that as part of this meeting. People feel giddy sometimes. They get to meet people that they've been reading for years, they get to interact, and they get to talk. I love just walking the hallways, especially during sessions. Anybody who's ever been to a conference knows that a lot of the really important stuff doesn't happen in the rooms; it happens in the hallways. You know, you walk around our hallways at our meetings and they're relatively empty during the sessions, and the reason for that is people are inside listening to ideas, and man, that gets me really jazzed every time that I see it.

**JKK:** Yes, I've experienced it that way myself. It certainly has been a challenging time for the first elected council and of course for you as the first elected president of the new association.

**RW:** Yes, and I think that one of the values that I've had as president, that I think has been reflected in our council as well, has been this idea of tenure and academic freedom, which is not something that's ever been really promoted within the Indigenous world. I think it's an important next step toward our own maturity, and I hope our association reflects that. I think that mature forms of Indigenous higher education are really going to have to grapple with what that academic freedom means. We've committed ourselves to it in the association. I think now we have to figure out what it means now that we've committed ourselves to that.

**JKK:** Yes, that's right.

**RW:** It is so important that things like your show exist, and things like our website exist, and that we're all out there trying to so hard to communicate with each other. Things like this provide ways of doing so, and it means a lot to me that they're out there and that they provide new opportunities. I think, in fact, we're actually achieving some of the things that were made possible by those people that came before us. Not just in the 1970s, but back in the 1880s, back in the 1700s and before. And that's exciting. It's hard sometimes, but it's exciting.

# PATRICK WOLFE ON SETTLER COLONIALISM

I interviewed Patrick Wolfe (1949–2016), one of the premier scholars of settler colonialism, in 2010, shortly after we first met in Boston. At the time, he was a Charles Warren Fellow in U.S. history at Harvard University. Prior to that, he was a Charles La Trobe Research Fellow in the history program at La Trobe University in Australia. Wolfe was the author of a pathbreaking book, *Settler Colonialism and the Transformation of Anthropology* (1999). In 2008 he was appointed to the Organization of American Historians' Distinguished Lectureship Program. At that time he was working on a comparative history of settler-colonial regimes in Australia, the United States, Brazil, and Israel-Palestine. That book, *Traces of History: Elementary Structures of Race* (2016), was released shortly before his death in 2016, as was his edited volume, *The Settler Complex: Recuperating Binarism in Colonial Studies.*

This interview took place on July 13, 2010.

**J. Kēhaulani Kauanui:** Aloha. Before we dive in, I want to ask if you'd be willing to share a bit about your personal and professional background.

**Patrick Wolfe:** Yes, certainly. I'm a professional working academic, I'm afraid. I set up the teaching of Koori history—that's Indigenous southeast Australian history—at the University of Melbourne and introduced elders being paid proper money to give lectures. I gave up after a few years because I'm a "Gubbah"—a white guy—and it seemed wrong to me that a white guy should be teaching Aboriginal history when there weren't any Aboriginal people also teaching it. I don't mind white guys teaching it so long as they're not the only ones.

So I left that, and I'm glad to say that the University of Melbourne Aboriginal history section subsequently thrived quite well. I've since written about a lot of comparative Indigenous issues, partly because of the experience of teaching Koori history in Melbourne—there's a lot of American students there because exchange students tend to look for something they can't do at home. The University of Melbourne offers very few things you can't do in California. Koori history—that's one thing you can't do even in San Francisco. So I used to get a disproportionately large number of U.S. students, and when I'd say to them "Why are you doing this course? Where is your interest in Aboriginal history coming from?" 95 percent of them, even the Black ones, would say, "Well, I'm interested in civil rights and maybe doing some kind of work with Black groups and I wanted to come and do some work with Black groups in Australia."

To which I would say, "Yeah, but how about Indigenous people? How about Native Americans? That's the parallel. Just because Aboriginal Australians are called Black, that's just some kind of shared name, misleadingly bracketing them together on the basis of skin color. The real parallel is dispossessed Indigenous people; you know about them? Where's your interest there?" And their eyes would glaze over and they'd say, "Well, I don't think I ever met one," to which I'd say, "Well, probably not knowingly, but I bet you have." And it would go from there.

So that led me to think that there's more to this—when I say "just," I don't mean in a belittling way—there's more to this than just Indigenous history in southeast Australia. There's a whole thing going on here around Indigenous politics and the consequences of invasion and dispossession and genocide, and it's not limited to Australia. I wanted to see what we can say that's universal about Indigenous dispossession everywhere and what's particular to local situations.

**JKK:** "Black" is a term used to describe Indigenous peoples in Australia, and that comes out of a British colonial history, right?

**PW:** I wouldn't like to say it only comes out of a British colonial history, because Indigenous people in Australia very happily call themselves Black. If you go to a party—on occasions I've been to a party where I've been the only non-Indigenous, Gubbah person—they call it a "Black Out." Kooris call themselves Blackfellas, and we're Whitefellas. No doubt it also came out of some kind of colonial background, but it's been taken over and made their own by Indigenous people for their own ends and for their own identity purposes.

**JKK:** I know from time that I've spent in graduate school in Aotearoa/New Zealand, at the University of Auckland, Maori also now self-identify, or did more strongly in an earlier period in the seventies and eighties, as Blacks. And you mention "Gubbah" or Whitefella. In terms of your self-identifying that way, that is really unusual for a lot of white men. Could you speak a little bit more to that in terms of that self-identification and that acknowledgment, especially in the midst of Indigenous peoples?

**PW:** I am an Australian settler. That doesn't mean that I have voluntarily dispossessed anybody, it doesn't mean that I've stolen anybody's child, it doesn't mean that I've participated in any massacres—it's not about my individual consciousness and free will. In terms of my individual free will, I'm a reluctant settler. I would rather not be existing on somebody else's stolen land. But the fact of the matter is that I wouldn't have had a university job if Indigenous people hadn't had their land stolen from them in Australia.

So, in a structural sense, in terms of the history that has put me where I am and Indigenous people where they are, my individual consciousness, my personal attitude has got nothing to do with this. I am a beneficiary and a legatee of the dispossession and the continuing elimination of Aboriginal people in Australia. As such, whatever my personal consciousness, I am a settler, which is to say "Gubbah" in Indigenous terminology, so I am happy to accept that terminology.

**JKK:** In Hawai'i there is some debate about theorists of what is being termed "Asian settler colonialism" that deals with the contentious history of Asian immigrants coming in as plantation labor under coercive or exploitative conditions. Here I am referring mainly, but not exclusively, to the edited volume by Candace Fujikane and Jonathan Okamura titled *Asian Settler Colonialism: From Local Governance to the Habits of Everyday Life in Hawaii*. It prompts questions as to whether or not we should discern different kinds of settlers, and it begs the question of whether all settlers are colonialists. This leads me to ask where you see race fitting into your analysis of what constitutes settler colonialism, especially whiteness.

**PW:** Okay, that's a really tricky and interesting one, as you know. When I'm in Hawai'i, I'm a haole, obviously. I may only be a haole for three days visiting, but I'm a haole. Yes, of course, Japanese indentured people, Filipinos, a whole lot of other non-U.S., nonwhite people from the Pacific were put to work in horrific conditions on pineapple and other plantations in Hawai'i two or three generations ago, so those people have endured colonial exploitation, there's no question about it whatsoever.

I think a parallel there would be, for instance, enslaved Africans in the U.S. Now, looked at from their point of view, they have experienced a colonial history, and it is therefore not right to lump them together with the colonizers, the white folks who brought them there under oppressive and coercive conditions in the first place. Now of course I accept that degrees exist within the population that dispossessed and replaced Native peoples, of course I accept that. But can we just bracket that off for a moment and come back to it?

**JKK:** Yes, but I want to point out that Chinese, Japanese, and Filipinos were drawn to the continental U.S. for agricultural labor—and with the Filipinos, they came as colonial subjects—so wouldn't that be the parallel in the U.S. and not enslaved Africans? Isn't the question of chattel slavery different here?

**PW:** From the Native point of view, when it's a zero-sum contest—you or me, for land, for livelihood, for the places that are special, sacred to you that keep your society alive, culturally, spiritually and every other way as well your economic subsistence, just putting food on your table—it doesn't matter if the people are enslaved or coerced or co-opted. They are still taking your food. They are still part of the invasive society that is taking your land over and driving you off. They may be an unwilling part, just as I said to you I'm a reluctant settler. They may be a lot more reluctant than I am insofar as they may be forced—I chose to go to Australia, after all.

But nonetheless, structurally, in the terms I was talking about before, like it or not, whether or not they collaborate with Indigenous people, they remain part of the settler project. *Asian Settler Colonialism* is edited by a couple of Japanese-descended settlers who have had the courage to come out and say, "We have come through the colonial plantation experience, our people have suffered, but nonetheless, vis-à-vis Natives, vis-à-vis Kanaka Maoli, we are settlers. Which is to say, structurally, we are part of the social process of dispossession." That doesn't mean that they haven't suffered; that doesn't mean they're bad guys. Willingly or not, enslaved or not, at the point of a gun or not, they arrived as part of the settler-colonial project. That doesn't make them settlers in the same sense as the colonizers who coerced them to participate— of course not—but it does make them perforce part of the settler-colonial process of dispossession and elimination. I can't stress strongly enough that it's *not* a matter of volition on their part, and certainly not of culpability. It's just a structural fact.

**JKK:** Also, I want to note that what I think is really important about what they are doing—and you've just mentioned it, in terms of the social process of dispossession—they do talk about settler *practices*. And that's of course part of the subtitle: "The Habits of Everyday Life." I think that that's what's so striking about your work, is that you insist that settler colonialism is a practice.

**PW:** Okay, well, why don't we go back to something I've already said, which is the number of U.S. students that would come to Australia and say that they saw a comparison between the politics of Indigenous people in Australia and the politics of African Americans, of Black people in the United States, the descendants of African slaves. I found myself thinking, "Well, what *is* the difference?" And, of course, the difference is that, in order to establish the European colonial society, two entirely different contributions were extracted from these separate populations. So far as enslaved people, or you may say convicts to Australia, or indentured people—South Asians going to Guyana or Fiji, wherever it may be—the coerced, subordinated labor that is brought in by the Europeans to work the land in the place of the Natives, they're there for their labor. It's their bodies that are colonized in the case of enslaved people who are subject to being bought and sold, that's what they provide. Indigenous people, by contrast, provide the land. Indigenous people's historical role in settler colonialism is to disappear so far as the Europeans go, to get out of the way, to be eliminated, in order that the Europeans can bring in their subordinated, coerced labor, mix that labor with the soil, which is to say set it to work on the expropriated land and produce a surplus profit for the colonizer.

So there are three points to this triangle. There is the colonizer—and I won't just say European, because, for example, in the case of the Japanese, the same kind of thing has applied. I'm a European colonizer, though, so let's talk about European colonialism, which in any event is the bigger global phenomenon. So we'll say Europeans in that sense. The European applies coerced and/or enslaved labor to the land which has been expropriated, which has been taken away, which has been stolen from Indigenous people. So at first you can say: invasion generally is a violent process because nobody gives up their land voluntarily. Whatever the Europeans say about Natives rolling up their blankets and fading away, like the Israelis say about the Palestinians, dissolving into the night—that doesn't happen. People do not give up places where their old people are buried, where they have been born and bred for generations, where they've lived, where their gods are. They do not give that up easily, so it's invariably a violent process.

Europeans usually win, helped by alien diseases and cannons and all the rest of it. Europeans usually win in that violent confrontation. Let's call that the frontier, though the frontier is a very misleading term because it suggests a nice clear black-and-white line with Natives on one side, Europeans on the other. It doesn't work that way. The frontier, it seemed to me the more I thought about it, isn't just a line in space, albeit a misleading line in space—there are all sorts of transitions going on backward and forward across it so it's not a hard and fast line—but it's also a line in time. What happens once the Natives have been violently suppressed—assuming they have been pacified, depending on whose terminology you use—there are still some left around.

Now, the colonizers have to establish a colonial society in their place, on their land. To do that, you have to have a system of laws and regulations; the playing field has got to look level. You're bringing migrants in. They can be unruly; they can want rights that they're often not given first off. A rule of law has to be applied and applied consistently, otherwise the incoming settler society would get out of order. Therefore, the Natives who have survived the initial catastrophe of invasion and violent dispossession, you can't just carry on shooting them on sight. It doesn't work for the settler rule of law that has to appear to be conducted fairly and legitimately.

Therefore, the way in which remaining Natives are eliminated shifts. It becomes more legal and more genteel. It looks better. It is necessary for settlers to continue eliminating Natives for all sorts of reasons, but one is a very important political one. If you're a settler, theoretically at least, you've come with a social contract, you've done all those European things involving subjecting yourself to the rule of the sovereign and you've consented, the whole deal. Natives never did that; their rule of law was prior to colonial rule, independent of it. It springs from a separate source. The colonizers' legal system simply can't deal with that. It can't deal with something that originates outside of itself. So, even on a political level, quite apart from the economic competition, all traces of Native alternatives need to be suppressed or contained or in some way eliminated. This continues after the so-called frontier era but, as I said, in all sorts of genteel ways. Territorially, Natives tend to get banged up on reservations or stations or missions or whatever it is. Now, they may be still alive, and the rhetoric might well shift so that, instead of being marauding savages who are going to rape the white man's women and all this sort of stuff, which is the justification for killing them on the frontier, instead of that they become a kind of romantic dying race and it's the job of the missionary to smooth the pillow of their passing. The rhetoric shifts radically, but the outcome remains consistent with elimination.

When you gather people together and contain them in a fixed locale, you are still the colonizer; you are still vacating their erstwhile territory and rendering it available for colonization, whether it's farming or pastoralism or plantations, whatever it is. They're not on the land anymore. They're confined to a mission. So, even though the missions or stations or reservations are held out as a process of civilizing—"We are giving them the boons, the benefits of this superior culture that we have historically invented"—even though the rhetoric shifts, just by confining them, you continue to eliminate them, to clear their territory to make way for colonial settlement.

You go further down the track, and assimilation begins to kick in, whether it's in the U.S. or Australia—and, I think, in Hawai'i. Native identity gets compromised—as you've shown in the Hawaiian case in your wonderful book *Hawaiian Blood*, and in other cases as well—with blood quantum regulations. Blood quantum eliminates Natives from the reckoning of authentic Natives who count. Of course, in the colonial situation, any Native person is liable to have non-Native relatives somewhere in their ancestry. That's a routine outcome of being invaded. It's used as another way of excluding Natives or eliminating them.

**JKK:** Yes, the contemporary legal definition of "Native Hawaiian" as a "descendant with at least one-half blood quantum of individuals inhabiting the Hawaiian Islands prior to 1778" originated in the Hawaiian Homes Commission Act of 1921 [HHCA] in which the U.S. Congress allotted approximately 200,000 acres of land in small areas across the main islands to be leased for residential, pastoral, and agricultural purposes by eligible "Native Hawaiians." Many Kānaka Maoli—Indigenous Hawaiians—contest the federal and state definition of "Native Hawaiian" at 50 percent not only because it is so exclusionary but because it undercuts indigenous Hawaiian epistemologies that define identity on the basis of one's kinship and genealogy. Thus, I emphasize the strategic, socially embedded, and political aspects of these Indigenous practices.

The blood quantum rule operates through a genocidal logic in both cultural and legal contexts and undermines identity claims based on genealogy that are expansive. In the blood quantum and legal debates about property during the debates that led to the passage of the HHCA, issues of where the Chinese and Japanese stood in Hawaiʻi—in relation both to whites and Hawaiians—were prominent. Eventually, I realized that in many ways, some subtle, others crude, the racialization of Hawaiians was coconstructed in relation to Chinese and Japanese presence in the islands. As I detail in the book, both elite whites and Hawaiians framed the post-overthrow push to rehabilitate Kānaka Maoli in anti-Asian terms by contrasting Kānaka Maoli as U.S. citizens and the Chinese, and especially Japanese, as "aliens." During the early twentieth century, the whiteness of American citizenship was sustained by a series of Asian exclusions, and this racialization of Asians as perpetual "outsiders" would play a key role in the outcome of Hawaiian blood quantum debates.

In Hawaiʻi at this time, Asian groups occupied a racial place somewhat similar to African Americans in their structural relationship to whites during Reconstruction in that they were considered an economic and political threat. The emancipation of black slaves motivated southern whites to search for new systems of racial and economic control, and by the 1890s they passed Jim Crow segregation laws to isolate and intimidate African Americans. In Hawaiʻi, like the U.S. continent, white Americans perceived the Japanese as a distinct danger as both a source of labor competition and a nationalist threat in the emerging world order. Their presence in Hawaiʻi was seen as antithetical to the goals of Americanizing the islands, especially after World War I, a concern that only grew by the time of the HHCA debates, when their numbers were increasing in the islands.

So, with that in mind as a particular context, let us turn back to the question of slavery, whiteness, and indigeneity.

**PW:** This, I think, is where you can get the contrast between enslaved people and Indigenous people very clearly, and also how you can get the way that the process of elimination continues. It's a structure. It's an ongoing process, not a one-off event. It continues right through colonial society. And in the case of blood quantum, it comes through very clearly. Let's think of the U.S. example. As I said, the enslaved and their descendants who were bought and sold were used for one purpose, and that purpose was labor, whereas Indigenous people were there for one purpose, that was to disappear, to surrender their land. Given that Africans were valuable property, you wanted as many as you could get. So the offspring of an enslaved person and a white partner—it doesn't matter what their skin color is, how they present phenotypically, how light or dark they are—they remain a slave, they're valuable property. But, of course, if you're out on the western frontier of the United States, the last thing you want is more Indians, so you're murdering them, or you're cooping them up on reservations.

But what happens racially? What happens to the offspring of a Native, usually a woman—ninety-nine times out of a hundred it's a woman, right? The offspring of a Native woman and a colonizer experiences the opposite of what happens to Black people. With Black people, any amount of African blood whatsoever makes you a slave. Initially, this meant that offspring inherited the status of their mothers—though Maryland was an early exception—but as time went by, slavery became the lot of everyone with African ancestry. After Emancipation this situation became racialized, so that anyone with African ancestry was classified as Black, a situation that reached its apogee in the one-drop rule, which continues into the present in an informal, unstated kind of way. You can have blue eyes and blond hair, but if somewhere back in your ancestry there's any Black person—bam, you're a slave or, today, under the one-drop rule, you're a Black person. Compared to that, let's look at what happens to Natives, whose role, as we've said, is to vanish from the land rather than to provide labor. In their case, the opposite applies. The colonial system wants fewer and fewer Natives, and guess what? It seeps through into the way they're racialized, into their very identities, the identities the colonial society tries to impose upon them.

So the Native case is opposite to the one-drop rule, which makes—isn't this fantastic? there's a real irony here—makes Black blood absolutely powerful in relation to white blood. In the case of Native blood, by contrast, any admixture of white blood compromises your indigeneity, makes you a half-blood or a half-caste or whatever racist term serves to eliminate people. So my point is that invasion doesn't stop at the frontier. It carries right on, right through colonial society in these less violent—that's what I meant by more genteel—ways, more thoroughly legal, bureaucratic ways. But the end outcome, which is eliminating the alternative, prior Native presence, is consistent. Is that clear enough?

**JKK:** Yes, it is. And you did mention earlier that settler colonialism is a zero-sum game, and I know that elsewhere you've referred to the dominant feature of its exploitative nature as a winner-take-all project. And that's what you mean by total replacement. So thinking through in terms of the legal disappearance or things that are based on legal mechanisms of civilizing Indigenous peoples, it's precisely through that rather than, say, through massacres that settler-colonial societies can continue to describe their projects as ones based on progress or that they're supposed to be seen as benign or kind to the Native.

**PW:** Absolutely. "We have come bearing you a gift, the gift of civilization and advancement." And assimilation, which ultimately has the effect of destroying Native society, reducing them demographically, is invariably—and I haven't come across a single settler colony where this doesn't happen—invariably, assimilation is held out as giving Natives the same opportunities as the white man. You steal children at the age of three and you put them in boarding schools and you abuse them, often sexually as well as psychologically, for years on end. Very often, except in the case of a few remarkable people, you put people out at the other end of that system who suffer for the rest of their life with appalling social and psychological pathologies. They'll still be prejudiced against, picked on in the street by cops because they look different, and all the rest of it. They won't actually get any of the advantages that they were promised would be the fruits of the civilizing experience. They will rather have been completely messed up, their families and the wider Native society will have suffered as a consequence, and this is held out as a special gift of civilization, giving the Native the same opportunities as the white man.

**JKK:** We have been discussing a couple examples of Anglo-settler societies, Australia and the United States, and can also obviously bring Canada and Aotearoa /New Zealand into the picture more. Yet I would suggest that the average American would probably be reluctant to see the U.S.A. alongside the other three nations, given their ongoing ties to the British monarchy. Can you speak to that in relation to the persistent myth of American exceptionalism, that idea that the formation of the U.S.A. was about liberation, freedom, and equality framed as the opposite of any monarchical society?

**PW:** Right. First, perhaps this illustrates the answer I'm trying to give: when Chief Joseph and the Nez Perce were fleeing California, they were ultimately tracked down, with appalling consequences, by the U.S. Cavalry. But when they made their great trek, where were they headed? The answer is Canada, so they had no doubt as to who was the worse settler colonizer between the republican and democratic U.S. or a monarchy. And they were by no means—this is not in defense of monarchy, by the way—they were by no means the only colonized people who tried to escape across the Canadian border. African people did too. So, without defending monarchy, let's just say that republican egalitarianism is not a good thing for people who are not part of the club.

The problem with republican citizenship and popular democracy is that those who are outside the realm of this citizenship have no rights. It's a profoundly dehumanizing segregation of the rest of the world from yourself— your citizens, who participate in all these contractual deals to run your society equally and all the rest of it. In terms of what political system is involved, the important question is not whether you speak English, French, or Dutch, not whether you've got a king or a queen or you're republican. The only thing that really counts in regard to settler colonialism is the outcome for the Natives.

I can't imagine a Native confronting a poisoned water hole or a bayonet or whatever instrument of violence they're forced to confront . . . I can't imagine them saying, "Well, at least I'm being killed by a republican rather than a monarchist." I mean, what sort of difference is that going to make? So let's get below the surface of those political distinctions to the real concrete relationships that are applying here. This leads us to the distinction between franchise colonialism and what I call settler colonialism, which refers to a foreign society invading a Native society and trying to take over all of it so as to replace the Natives rather than use them as labor. Settler colonialism brings its own labor. It tries to eliminate the Natives and do something completely new with the land that was theirs.

**JKK:** So, this gets at what makes a settler society different than, say, British relations to India.

**PW:** The situation in India was quite different. There, the colonizers didn't go to get rid of Indians and import English people in their place. Quite the contrary; the colonizers went to sit on top of that society and set it to work for them on their own land. So it's a bit like the relationship of slavery insofar as Natives were valuable. They were indispensable to the project of extracting surplus value through colonialism. The British went to India for mining and to do things like grow jute and opium and tea and cotton and a whole lot of primary products that would then be made up in the metropolis—Manchester cotton mills and so on. The Industrial Revolution, which in most European history books is represented as something that was internal to Europe and proves how superior Europeans are, was a global phenomenon that took raw materials that were made up in these factories from the situation of colonial exploitation, whereupon it used the same colonies as expanding markets for these factories' finished products. Primary production may have been going on in the Deep South in the U.S., it may have been going on in India, it may have been going on in Egypt—to cite three that reference cotton, since I mentioned Manchester. The point is that the Industrial Revolution not only required settler colonialism in order to function. It also required other forms of colonialism, as in the case of the British-Indian colonial regime, which I call franchise colonialism.

Franchise colonialism required a situation where whites oversaw a system in which natives worked for them. Now, that means that the natives remain a large majority, so whites had to have native collaborators to help run the system. They had to have superior access to violence and all the rest of it, better troops. It's always a kind of fragile, vulnerable situation colonizing somewhere like India, or, for that matter, a franchise colony like the Dutch East Indies—today, it's Indonesia—was for the Dutch. When the colonial-nationalist movement gets under way, resists the Europeans, and finally throws them out, the whites turn out not to have been established in the same way that settler colonizers have been established. As I've said, in going to wherever, Australia, settlers didn't go to get Aborigines to work for them, at least not as their first priority. They went to Australia to replace Aborigines and themselves become Australians, so their children would be Australians and Australia would then go on forever.

Europeans in franchise colonies like India, they go to sit on top of native so-ciety. England remains home. They send their children back to boarding school in England. When they turn sixty, they retire back to England before encroach-ing senility can spoil the illusion of their super-humanity. They remain based in England, overseeing the natives in a different kind of colony. Therefore, come the success of the colonial-nationalist movement, when finally, the English get thrown out and they go back to London, they vanish, and the faces on the legis-lative benches change color. Indians take over. They tend, unfortunately, not to alter the system that the British imposed on them too much, because the elites who ran the nationalist movement were educated at Oxford and Cambridge and the British knew who they were handing over to. Basically, they were hand-ing over to brown Englishmen, so they weren't the kind of changes that you'd hope for from a national independence movement. Nonetheless, the fact is that the British had remained a minority dependent upon native labor and therefore native society was ultimately in a position to throw them out. By contrast, the victims of settler genocide, all the programs of elimination that have gone on in settler colonies, those Natives become a minority and can't realistically dream of sending the Whitefellas home.

So it's a different situation. And if I may say at this point, what I mean by settler colonialism is precisely this drive to elimination, this system of winner-take-all. I don't just mean that settler colonies are colonies that happen to have settlers in them. There were tea planters in British India. People go on and on at me about the French in Algeria, and rather like we said earlier, what difference does it make if you're monarchical or republican? In the case of French colo-nialism, the French colonies aren't just places that we rule from outside. They're part of France. In formal political terms, Algeria was meant to be part of main-land France, so the French settlers who went there were seen as somehow dif-ferent from settlers elsewhere. It was a settler society that somehow was more organically wedded to the mother country than somewhere like Hawai'i—at least, prior to statehood—or the United States or Aotearoa/New Zealand. All the same, the fact of the matter is that the French settlers relied on native labor. Come the Algerian independence movement, they get thrown out. Whatev-er the constitutional niceties, whether they're meant to be part of France or not doesn't matter. They're there to be thrown out, because they're a minority dependent on native labor. You can say something similar about South Africa, where whites are something like 15, 16 percent of the population. Yes, they're settlers, yes they stayed there, but it's just a colony that happens to have settlers in it. It's not a settler colony in my sense. Does that make sense?

**JKK:** Most definitely. And also, I am thinking it through in terms of the notion of progress and the notion of the past. One of the most cited passages in your work is that "invasion is a structure and not an event." I would like it if you could speak to the persistent ideological notion that settler colonialism was just an event, that invasion was merely an event, and that that is how they are able to maintain the farce that it's long past, rather than an ongoing process.

**PW:** As an Indigenous person, you're very well aware of these things. These are some of the best-targeted questions I've ever had, so if I could just thank you for that and also acknowledge that, because you're Indigenous, you know what you're talking about in a way that so few scholars do.

So, yes, settler invasion is an ongoing process. That's why I remain a beneficiary and a legatee of the invasion of Australia. That's why I categorize myself as a settler. The prime minister of Australia, the then prime minister John Howard, refused to apologize to Indigenous people for the abduction of the so-called "stolen generations" of Aboriginal people, generally of mixed ancestry, who were taken away by the Australian state. We're not sure how many. It's somewhere around one in five to one in seven Aboriginal children were stolen from their families by the Australian state or by various states within the Commonwealth of Australia throughout the twentieth century.

And a great movement arose to get Mr. Howard to apologize on behalf of the Australian state for what happened. I personally think that movement was a great mistake, because what happened was that the whole issue of Aboriginal rights came to depend on whether or not one man would apologize for the stolen generations—not for the frontier homicides, not for the initial seizure of land or two centuries of systematic destruction, all the rest of it. And also the problem was that an apology would enable them to say, "Okay, now we've apologized, now everyone can go home, forget about it and move on." This is exactly what the subsequent prime minister, Kevin Rudd, did say when he issued his apology. He didn't ask whether or not Aboriginal people would accept his apology. He just unilaterally declared that his apology meant that Australia should now move on. No question of compensation, no question of reparations, nothing like that. In fact, the reverse: the apology provided Rudd with a pretext to rule reparations out, explicitly and deliberately, at the same time. So I think that there are all sorts of problems with the whole apology business.

But nonetheless, to get back to your question, the reason that John Howard refused to apologize—which actually was tactically very stupid, as I said, if he realized he could get away with an apology and have it all over within a week, that would have suited him much better. But anyway, the reason that this bull-necked man refused to apologize was, as he kept saying over and over again, "Yes, bad things went on in the past, but I wasn't there, I didn't do anything wrong, I didn't kill anybody, I didn't steal any children. It's a later time now," failing to recognize that history results from causes and from preconditions, and that the cause and the precondition for contemporary Australian affluence and democracy and all the rest of it is the initial robbery, genocide and continuing elimination of Aboriginal people. Without that happening, as I said, I couldn't have had a job in history at La Trobe University.

So that's the sense in which it's very important to acknowledge that invasion is something that reverberates through continuing history in all sorts of ways. And the Indigenous presence, the Indigenous alternative, needs to be suppressed. Either that or we come to a fair deal. Now, coming to a fair deal doesn't mean finding a bunch of coconuts—brown on the outside and white on the inside—and setting them up in state-designed bureaucracies that just become yet another organ of the settler state. It doesn't mean that. It means handing over to Native sovereignty. How are you going to run your affairs? Who are you going to choose, as opposed to elect? You don't need to go through the Westminster system. Whatever your system of choosing—an elder who will speak for you, or elders who will speak for you, whatever you choose—you go for it, and when you're ready, we'll talk together about what we can agree on. Anything less than that is a state-fabricated charade which is not only running parallel to the real challenge of an open negotiation between an invaded people and their invaders. Actually, these prefabricated, pretending-to-be-Native but actually part of the white colonial system bureaucracies are part of the invasion, because they take away Native initiative. They channel it into areas, into bureaucratic zones, that are always already predominated by being part of the colonial bureaucracy.

**JKK:** And that actually resonates with what you said earlier in the interview, around the colonials themselves really not wanting to acknowledge anything that exists prior to their own system. And that's what Indigenous scholar from Australia, Aileen Moreton-Robinson, who's a premier scholar of whiteness studies there, talks about: the anxiety of settler-colonial societies regarding that persistent Indigenous sovereignty question.

**PW:** That anxiety is crucial and very telling. I think it has huge political potential. Aileen Moreton-Robinson nails it perfectly.

**JKK:** Now, I want to go back to something—you mentioned Palestinians earlier. And we've been talking a bit about American exceptionalism. Certainly there is a question, especially as of late, with the recent attack on the Gaza Freedom Flotilla, about Israeli exceptionalism undergirded by American power. I wonder if you could speak to the question of Israeli-occupied Palestine, perhaps in relation to not only settler colonialism as a process but also the Boycott, Divestment, Sanctions [BDS] movement.

**PW:** Well, first, blinded in ways that one can sympathize with by the Holocaust, people look at Israelis as victims. And, of course, those who died in the Holocaust were victims, as well as their families, and the children who have been subjected to the memories of Auschwitz survivors and so on, and who've had to live with their guilt. Of course those people are victims. But, it's rather like saying the Japanese in Hawai'i suffered terribly in the plantations, but that doesn't stop them being part of the settler-colonial process.

We're not talking about whether individuals are victims or not. We're talking about the fact that, from 1882 on, which is when the first Zionist settlement in Palestine was established, the first so-called *aliya*, which means "uplift," which means "ascent to the Promised Land," European Jews who were suffering pogroms and oppression and all sorts of horrific things in Europe that one should never understate, the Zionist solution to that was, "We are being persecuted, especially within eastern Europe—the so-called Pale of Settlement, the Polish/southwest Russian border, but also traditionally throughout Europe—we are being persecuted because we haven't a got a nation. We haven't got a place that we can call our own, with our own sovereignty and independence. So, like the other peoples around us in nineteenth-century Europe, we need a nation with its own territory."

The only problem is there's no land left in Europe to found a nation in, so initially they were thinking Argentina, then they thought Uganda, at one point the Portuguese offered them Angola, but increasingly it became Palestine—the place, they claimed, that Jews originated from, before being driven out by the Romans in A.D. 70, when the Second Temple was destroyed, this whole mythology. It actually is mythology, in the erroneous sense: there were Jews all over the Diaspora well before A.D. 70. Moreover, not all of those who were in Palestine left, but that's a different story. The point is that some of the European arm of world Jewry who were generally called Ashkenazim, meaning European Jewry—as opposed to Sephardim, who are the Jews who were driven out Iberia, out of Spain and Portugal in the fifteenth century and tended to settle in places like Morocco, as opposed to Yemenis and other Mizrahim who were in places like Iraq and Libya and so on—the point is that some members of the Ashkenazi branch of Jewry decided upon Zionism, though Zionism largely remained a minority tendency until the Nazi era. Zionists decided they would establish a civilized, secular, European colonial nation-state like France or Germany, which had ceased being monarchies and had united themselves and become secular, church-and-state-separated states in the nineteenth century. They were going to have one of those in Palestine. So they set out to establish an autonomous state based on agricultural communities that would be self-sufficient. Of course, having been excluded from agriculture and productive industry in Europe, so that they'd been forced into parasitic occupations like moneylending and condemned as such—this is where the racist image of the Jew as greedy hoarder came from—these people arrive in Palestine quite incompetent as agriculturalists.

Yet they want to exclude the Natives. They want to build a Jewish-only nation-state in somebody else's country, Palestine. That's what settler colonialism is. So they set about first persuading colonial authorities who ruled Palestine, first the Ottoman Empire and then, after World War I, the British Empire under a mandate granted by the League of Nations. The so-called

Yishuv, the Jewish settlers in Palestine, set about first getting the colonial powers to allow more and more Jewish immigration into Palestine from Europe and, second, expanding their contiguous land base so as to build a colonial state-in-waiting there.

So they're different from an ordinary settler colony in that they had to proceed through legal channels. This they did, until they reached the point where they were strong enough to throw out both the colonial authorities, in this case the British mandate authorities, and complete the job of driving Palestinians off their land. This happened in the Nakba—the calamity, the catastrophe as it's called—of 1948, that overtook Palestinians, when something like 65 percent of the Palestinian people were violently driven from their homes, driven to flee outside Mandate Palestine. Their houses were taken from them, either bulldozed or blown up or, more often than not, had Jewish settlers put into them, these people in many cases being Holocaust victims who had been brought from Europe.

So there's tremendous world sympathy. Indeed, the United Nations vote to divide Palestine into Jewish and Palestinian sectors, which took place on November 29, 1947, only happened because the Soviet Union finally came around and cast its votes in favor of Israel. Why did they do that? Because they chose to read Israel as an anti-British colonial movement rather than as a settler-colonial movement. Zionism has these two faces. Now, it is very odd, is it not, that the last European settler colony to be established on Earth—which is Israel, which has displaced Palestinians from their own country and replaced them with Jews, has stolen their country—that the last one on Earth—Tibet isn't a European colony—should have been set up in 1948, after the UN declaration, and at a time when decolonization was the international climate of the moment?

After World War II, the United Nations was all about the British leaving India, the British and French and Portuguese and Spanish leaving Africa, the French and the British leaving southeast Asia, the Dutch leaving the East Indies—that's the mood of the moment. Yet Israel is set up at the same time. A settler colony is established in an anticolonial atmosphere. That is bizarre until one understands that Zionism has two faces: one is it's a resistance to persecution, the Holocaust being the ultimate extreme, but it's a persecution that goes on in Europe. The other is, it's a settler-colonial movement, so it's as if the abused child has grown up to be an abuser—the Zionist response to the persecution of Jews in Europe being to steal somebody else's country outside of Europe.

So, once it's understood in that dual way—as having two faces, I mean—that Zionism is both a response to persecution and a settler-colonial movement, then you're partly back to the situation of Hawaiians in relation to the Japanese, or Native Americans in relation to enslaved Africans. "Yes, these people have suffered but, hullo, they're driving me off my country, they're kill-ing me." They're part of a settler system, regardless of their personal history and their consciousness. Palestinians own that country. They're being driven out of it and being replaced, with the approval, the sanction, and the military and economic support of the West.

We, as Australians, as people from the United States—I distinguish Hawai'i from that, and I distinguish Native Americans from that because you're not part of the system—but people like me, like it or not, and I certainly don't like it, are responsible for the contemporary, current-day Israeli colonization of Pal-estine. Now, in terms of the time scale I talked about previously in places like the U.S. and Australia, that is like going back before the missions and before the assimilation. It's still the frontier era in Israel/Palestine. There's no assim-ilation going on. Palestinians aren't being given land rights in certain places. They're still at the frontier invasion stage, and it's in this day and age, in the twenty-first century.

When genocide was going on in the nineteenth-century United States, international communications were different. There weren't cell phones that you could film with, there wasn't a whole global communications framework whereby what was going on could be seen. I'm not justifying it, but it's pretty different to something going on under the nose of the world, in full view of the world and still being suppressed and successfully lied about, which is what's happening to the settler colonization, the invasion, of Palestine as we speak.

When students or people who've heard my talks ask me: "How did the Eu-ropeans ever get away with the atrocities that they committed on the Australian and American frontiers? How could a Wounded Knee or a Coniston massa-cre go unavenged? How could whole peoples be driven from their ancestral homelands in broad daylight?" When they ask me this question, which they very often do, I have to answer: "Why are you surprised? They didn't even have the Internet or satellite TV in the nineteenth century. We have those things today, we have instant global communication, events relayed live into people's living rooms, but settler-colonial outrages are being perpetrated, nineteenth-century style, under our noses in occupied Palestine every day of the week. So why should the nineteenth century have been any different? There's no reason for surprise."

**JKK:** Yes, that's right, and does that suggest to me that you do support the BDS campaign?

**PW:** Absolutely. I have nothing to do with anything Israeli whatsoever. And anti-Zionist Israeli Jews, they support it too. They're saying, "This is wrong—not in our name, don't help it."

**JKK:** As you know, I serve on the advisory board for the U.S. Campaign for the Academic and Cultural Boycott of Israel as well as the broader boycott move-ment for sure.

**PW:** Again, absolutely, I'm completely in support of it. Actually, in the contemporary U.S. and Australian academy, that does involve a risk. The Zionist lobby—please don't call it the Jewish lobby, by no means all Jews are Zionists and, by the way, not all Zionists are Jewish. We're talking about a political movement: Zionism. Anti-Zionism and anti-Semitism have nothing to do with each other. The Zionist lobby in countries like the U.S. and Australia is so strong. Helen Thomas is a recent example, even though I think her remarks were ill-judged and stupid. Nonetheless, what's happened to her so quickly, this grand old lady of United States journalism, how that day she was suddenly forced to resign—doesn't that show the power and the risk that you take when you speak out in favor of the oppressed, invaded Palestinian nation?

**JKK:** Yes, and when you mention that in Palestine right now it is the frontier era, I mean this for me really highlights the issue. I saw for myself in January 2012, when I traveled there as part of a five-scholar delegation. Obviously, within settler-colonial studies as a field of study for intellectual work in the academy, you know, comparative studies are important, but the settler colonials themselves undertook and still undertake a comparative approach to their own policies, their own military tactics. And I think that Israel modeling its occupation of Palestine in ways similar to what early Americans did to tribal nations throughout the nineteenth century in North America is really key. Speaking to a different comparative angle, could you offer your analysis of analogies between Israel and South Africa?

**PW:** Yes, I don't accept that apartheid and what's going on in Palestine are the same thing, for the reason that the Bantustans, the special Native places that the South African government set up, were set up for the purpose of exploiting Native labor. You were confined to your Bantustan unless you were being domestic labor, or you were working the mines or the farms or the factories of white South Africa, in which case you had to run around with a pass showing you were on your way to or from work, you had permission to be there. But the Bantustans were pools of labor which the workers would be taken out of and used as suited the white authorities, the apartheid authorities.

Palestinians are just being driven out. They're no pool of labor. Sure, they come in handy as cheap and hyper-exploitable labor so long as they're still around, but Israel's primary goal is not to exploit them but to get rid of them. This is why they're energetically and systematically being replaced by anybody but a Palestinian. Bring in a million Russians, call them Jews, it's fine. A significant portion of them are Christians. They end up growing up and getting arrested in Israel running around in Nazi uniforms. Doesn't matter—they're not Palestinian. That's very different from South Africa, where segregation was for the purposes of exploitation for labor. For Palestinians, segregation is being marginalized. Israel is doing everything it can to free itself from any hint of dependence on Palestinian labor because it wants to get rid of them. So

Zionism *is* a form of apartheid in that it's racist, exclusive, and oppressive. Israel's behavior squarely fits the international definition of the crime of apartheid under the 1973 International Convention on the Suppression and Punishment of the Crime of Apartheid and so on. All the same, it's not premised on the same basis as South African apartheid was; it's premised on elimination rather than exploitation. We have to recognize different forms of apartheid. They're all unacceptable.

**JKK:** And that really gets back to the core, which is the Indigenous sovereignty question rather than a color line. I want to ask you something else as we're wrapping up the interview.

Since your book *Settler Colonialism and the Transformation of Anthropology* was published just over a decade ago, the field of settler studies has grown to focus on collaborative and comparative theories of this process. I want to ask you how you see this new field developing.

**PW:** Well, with mixed feelings. As you say, that book came out rather early—embarrassingly early, actually, seeing as I haven't done another book since. As a result, since it was fairly early, and it keeps getting quoted and cited, people quite often ask me, "What do you think?" almost as if they're asking me, "What's happened to your offspring?" which is completely inappropriate. I didn't invent settler-colonial studies. Natives have been experts in the field for centuries.

I have mixed feelings, to be honest. What for me is a political practice—my intellectual practice is an activist practice so far as I'm concerned, which is not to say that I skimp on the facts. It's not to say that I cut corners. It's rather to say that I think the more you look at the facts, the more they stand up. The more rigorously you conduct your research, the more you establish that dispossessed Indigenous people have got the most substantial grounds for complaint and the most substantial claim for reparations and reversal of anyone on Earth. So I'm an activist-intellectual because I think that the truth speaks for itself and I believe you should keep uncovering the truth.

The problem is that I'm not sure that this applies to a mushrooming academic industry which spawns new theories and new buzzwords at the drop of a hat. I have that kind of concern.

**JKK:** Yes. And in conclusion, is there anything in particular with which you would like to close?

**PW:** Yes. There is one thing, and this applies to all settler-colonized peoples, but I want to select the one we've been talking about last, the one that is so central and at the frontier stage as we speak. The last thing I want to say is: Viva Palestine! Long live Palestine! Palestine will be free, from the river to the sea!

# ACKNOWLEDGMENTS

In autumn 2006, I received a call at my office at Wesleyan University from Ken Weiner, then public affairs director at the university's radio station, WESU, who asked if I would be interested in producing a show on Native issues. Without hesitation, I said yes. The timing seemed perfect; I just had submitted my file to go up for tenure a month earlier and would be in a waiting position for several months as my case made its way through the process. I went through the DJ training process that October, practiced on-air skills with a post-punk and contemporary indie music show over the winter, and by February 2007 got on air with a program called *Indigenous Politics: From Native New England and Beyond*.

There are many people to thank for their support in encouraging me to produce this published collection of select interviews from the radio program and for their enthusiasm and sustained engagement during the time the show aired (2007–13).

At WESU, hearty thanks go to Ben Michael (the general manager) and Rick Sinkiewicz (the program manager). I also appreciate the moral support I received early on from DJ "Psychedelic Rick," DJ "Commander Elion," and especially DJ "Dr. Freddy Carroll," as well as numerous board members and community staff at the station.

I had the privilege of presenting talks on my radio work at a few academic gatherings. The first two were at Harvard University: one was a solo lecture I delivered at the Humanities Center and the second was a talk for the symposium "Cultures on the Air! An Initiative on Indigenous Radio." Both were organized and hosted by Luis E. Cárcamo-Huechante. Chaltu may! I also had the pleasure of presenting on my radio work at the University of Illinois at Urbana-Champaign for an Indigenous Media Roundtable event organized by Robert Warrior and Frederick Hoxie as part of the Initiative of the Center for Advanced Study on "Sovereignty and Autonomy in the Western Hemisphere."

At Wesleyan, I especially want to thank those who championed the program from the very start: Jay Hoggard, Joel Pfister, Michael Armstrong Roche, and Gina Ulysse. Thanks also to Wesleyan for awarding me a project grant to cover some of the expenses of the transcriptions. On campus, I have been fortunate to have Information Technology Services support for the audio archive. Thanks especially to Jason Simms for helping me rebuild when my website was hacked, and to Melissa Datre for archiving all of the programs on iTunes U. I want to acknowledge former Wesleyan students Rafael Sturm, Kalia Lydgate, and Amelia Dean Walker for assisting me with sound and production for the first few months of the show as I was getting my bearings.

I thank the following colleagues and friends for their excitement about the program during the years it aired: Joanne Barker, Siobhan Sesnier, David Delgado Shorter, Lucian Gomoll, Bradley Henson, Eve Tuck, Libor Von Schönau, Abe Bobman, Rick Pouliot, LeAnne Howe, Ruth Garby Torres, Amy Den Ouden, Jason Mancini, Kevin McBride, J. Cedric Woods, Lisa Kahaleole Hall, Ju Hui, Judy Han, Philip Havice, John Troutman, and Trudie Lamb Richmond. The late Gale Courey Toensing offered consistent support and encouragement throughout.

Big thanks to those who transcribed the audio recordings of the interviews for this book, some of whom are former students: Taylor McClain, Fiona McLeod, Barbara Yupit-Gomez, Abe Bobman, Corrina Wainwright, and Kent Lebsock. I also extend gratitude to Ireylis Lopez and Fiona McLeod for their assistance with formatting and in helping me organize the interviews.

Early on, I received encouragement from Matthew Graber (producer and host of *Radio against Apartheid* on WPEB) and Tiokasin Ghosthorse (producer and host of *First Voices: Indigenous Radio* on WBAI). I also had the pleasure of linking up with Salma Abu Ayyash (producer of *This Week in Palestine* on WZBC). Mahalo.

In April 2007, WESU became an affiliate station of the independent Pacifica Network. This development enabled the show to be easily accessible by other Pacifica affiliates. During seasons one and two of the program, the show managed to steadily build a broad-based listenership and also garnered modest national attention with an episode called "Reconsidering the Origins of the Thanksgiving," which was featured on the Pacifica homepage and subsequently aired on three of Pacifica's flagship stations: WBAI in New York City, KPFA in Berkeley, and KPFK in Los Angeles. Much appreciation goes out to all of my contacts at the Pacifica syndicate stations that aired the program. The show was first regularly syndicated on a network of stations called "The Detour: The Independent Voice of Appalachia," reaching parts of eastern Tennessee, southwestern Virginia, western Kentucky, all of West Virginia, most of Pennsylvania, southern New York, western Maryland, western North Carolina, western South Carolina, northern Georgia, northern Alabama, and northeastern Mississippi. Other stations that syndicated the program included KUCR in Riverside, California; WAZU, Peoria, Illinois; KRFP, Moscow, Idaho; WETX-LP, Tri-Cities region of Tennessee, Virginia, and North Carolina; WGDR/WGDH, in Plainfield, Vermont; WJSC, Johnson, Vermont; WPCR, Plymouth, New Hampshire;

WBCR-LP, Great Barrington, Massachusetts; WRFN, Nashville, Tennessee; WNJR, out of Washington and Jefferson College Radio in Washington, Pennsylvania; WORT, in Madison, Wisconsin; and WPKN, Bridgeport, Connecticut, and Montauk, New York. These syndication possibilities made for increased visibility and a broad network that bolstered interest in the show—and, in turn, new programming ideas. I especially want to thank Deb Reger (WDGR) and Anthony Fleury (WNJR). And of course I extend a big mahalo to all the listeners who engaged and wrote to me with their reflections, suggestions, and useful feedback.

The episodes have always been available for podcasting and downloading through my own website, www.indigenouspolitics.com, where they are still archived. This has allowed wide access by individuals from all over—community members, activists, and scholars. Notably, a good number of scholars in different regions have written to me to let me know they use the shows as part of their course curricula. For technological support during dire times, I must thank Will Swoffard Cameron. I also want to thank WESU volunteer Michael D'Amico for suggesting I archive the program in the first place and for helping me launch the site. I also appreciate May First/People Link (a member of the Media Action Grassroots Network), an organization that truly redefines the concept of "Internet service provider."

One of the highlights of this period was when I was invited to discuss the program during the eighteenth commemoration of the International Day of the World's Indigenous Peoples at the United Nations on August 9, 2010. The theme for the gathering that year was "Indigenous Media, Empowering Indigenous Voices," and I was one of four invited panelists, the only one on the panel producing *independent* media. Thanks to Sonia Smallacombe, then social affairs officer with the UN Permanent Forum on Indigenous Issues, for nominating me, and to Roberto Múcaro Borrero, then chairperson of the NGO Committee on the International Decade of the World's Indigenous Peoples, and Chandra Roy-Henriksen, then chief of the Secretariat of the UN Permanent Forum on Indigenous Issues. One of the best outcomes of that gathering was getting to meet audience member John Kane (Kahnawake Mohawk), producer of *Let's Talk Native* (on WWKB and WBAI).

I especially appreciate Robert Warrior for encouraging the publication of this book, including it in this series at the University of Minnesota Press, and for his meaningful foreword. Thla-ho!

Many thanks to Rana Barakat and Cynthia Franklin for their critical feedback on the Introduction of this volume when it was in draft stage.

I extend gratitude to Jason Weidemann, Gabriel Levin, and the rest of the team at the University of Minnesota Press for shepherding this project to the finish line.

I especially thank my mother, Carol Lee Gates, who tuned in regularly and offered sustained encouragement, as well as my primary partner, Jason Villani (aka DJ "Lord Lewis"), whom I met at WESU in January 2007 as I was preparing to launch the program. He was a champion of the show and offered unwavering support and sustaining aloha along the way.

Mahalo nui loa to all of the individuals from the Indigenous Nations and communities in the region who welcomed me at different events, enhanced the program, sent ideas for interviews, and offered important critical feedback. Although I could include only a very limited number of the nearly two hundred interviews I want to thank *everyone* who granted me an interview for the show and those who allowed me to tape their public talks for the airwaves.

*Indigenous Politics* was produced on the historic (home)lands of the Wangunk people, who, despite popular assumptions otherwise, endure in the twenty-first century. E ola mau!

# CONTRIBUTORS

**JESSIE LITTLE DOE BAIRD** (Mashpee Wampanoag) is a linguist and cofounder of the Wôpanâak Language Reclamation Project. In 2010 she was awarded a MacArthur Fellowship for her efforts in reviving the Wampanoag language. She also serves as the vice-chairwoman of the Mashpee Wampanoag Indian Tribal Council.

**OMAR BARGHOUTI** is a founding committee member of the Palestinian Campaign for the Academic and Cultural Boycott of Israel and cofounder of the Boycott, Divestment, Sanctions movement. He is author of *Boycott, Divestment, Sanctions: The Global Struggle for Palestinian Rights.*

**LISA BROOKS** (Abenaki) is author of *The Common Pot: The Recovery of Native Space in the Northeast.* Her most recent book is *Our Beloved Kin: A New History of King Philip's War.* She is associate professor of English and American studies at Amherst College.

**KATHLEEN A. BROWN-PÉREZ** (Brothertown Indian Nation) is assistant professor in the Commonwealth College at the University of Massachusetts Amherst and also chairs the Five College Native American and Indian Studies program. She practices federal Indian law in a pro bono role for the Brothertown Indian Nation (Wisconsin).

**MARGARET BRUCHAC** (Abenaki) is assistant professor of anthropology at the University of Pennsylvania and coordinator of the Native American and Indigenous Studies Initiative at Penn. She is author of several books, most recently *Consorting with Savages: Indigenous Informants and American Anthropologists.*

**JESSICA CATTELINO** is author of *High Stakes: Florida Seminole Gaming and Sovereignty,* winner of the Delmos Jones and Jagna Sharff Memorial Book Prize from the Society for the Anthropology of North America. She is writing about the cultural value of water in the Florida Everglades, with focus on the

Seminole Big Cypress Reservation and the nearby agricultural town of Clewiston. She is associate professor of anthropology at the University of California Los Angeles.

**DAVID CORNSILK** (Cherokee Nation) is a recognized tribal genealogist, historian, legal advocate, and civil rights activist. In addition to his long-time activism, he worked in education for a number of years and at the tribal newspaper *Cherokee Observer*.

**SARAH DEER** (Muscogee [Creek] Nation) is author of *The Beginning and End of Rape: Confronting Sexual Violence in Native America* and coauthor of several books, including *Sharing Our Stories of Survival: Native Women Surviving Violence*. In 2014 she was awarded the MacArthur Fellowship. She is professor of women's studies and public policy at the University of Kansas.

**PHILIP J. DELORIA** (Dakota) is professor of history at Harvard University and author of *Playing Indian* and *Indians in Unexpected Places*.

**TONYA GONNELLA FRICHNER** (Onondaga Nation, Snipe clan) (1947–2015) was president and cofounder of the American Indian Law Alliance, a lawyer, and an activist whose academic and professional life was devoted to the pursuit of human rights for Indigenous peoples.

**HONE HARAWIRA** (Ngāpuhi Nui Tonu) is a longtime Māori activist who has played a significant role in Treaty of Waitangi issues, Māori language revitalization, land occupations, and Māori broadcasting. He is a former member of Parliament in New Zealand for the Tai Tokerau region and founder of the Mana Movement.

**SUZAN SHOWN HARJO** (Cheyenne and Hodulgee Muscogee) is a poet, writer, lecturer, curator, and policy advocate. She is president of the Morning Star Institute, a national Native rights organization founded in 1984 for Native people's traditional and cultural advocacy, arts promotion, and research.

**J. KĒHAULANI KAUANUI** (Kanaka Maoli) is professor of American studies and anthropology at Wesleyan University. From 2007 to 2013, she was producer and host of the public affairs radio show *Indigenous Politics* from WESU in Middletown, Connecticut. She is the author of *Hawaiian Blood: Colonialism and the Politics of Sovereignty and Indigeneity* (2008) and *Paradoxes of Hawaiian Sovereignty: Land, Sex, and the Colonial Politics of State Nationalism* (2018). She currently coproduces a radio program on anarchist politics, *Anarchy on Air*.

**RASHID KHALIDI** is Edward Said Professor of Arab Studies at Columbia University. He is author of numerous books, including *The Iron Cage: The Story of the Palestinian Struggle for Statehood*; *Sowing Crisis: The Cold War and American Dominance in the Middle East*; and *Brokers of Deceit: How the U.S. Has Undermined Peace in the Middle East*.

**WINONA LADUKE** (Anishinaabe/White Earth Ojibwe) is author of the novel *Last Standing Woman* and the nonfiction books *All Our Relations: Native Struggles for Land and Life* and *Recovering the Sacred: The Power of Naming and Claiming*. She is executive director of Honor the Earth.

**MARIA LAHOOD** is a deputy legal attorney at the Center for Constitutional Rights, where she specializes in international human rights litigation, seeking accountability for war crimes, torture, and extrajudicial killings abroad. She works closely with Palestine Legal to support students and others whose speech is suppressed for their Palestine advocacy and also works on the Right to Heal initiative with Iraqi civil society and Iraq veterans seeking accountability for the lasting health effects of the Iraq War.

**JAMES LUNA** (Luiseño) (1950–2018) was from the La Jolla reservation in San Diego, California. He was awarded many prestigious fellowships, including the Distinguished Fellow Award in 2007 from the Eiteljorg Museum in Indianapolis. In 2017 he was awarded a Guggenheim Fellowship.

**CHIEF MUTÁWI MUTÁHASH (MANY HEARTS) LYNN MALERBA** (Mohegan) is the eighteenth chief of the Mohegan Tribe. She is chairwoman of the Tribal Self-Governance Advisory Committee of the Federal Indian Health Service, a member of the Justice Department's Tribal Nations Leadership Council, a member of the Tribal Advisory Committee for the National Institute of Health, a member of the Treasury Tribal Advisory Committee, and a technical expert on the Commission for Environmental Cooperation.

**AILEEN MORETON-ROBINSON** (Quandamooka) is professor of Indigenous studies at Queensland University of Technology. She is author of *The White Possessive: Property, Power, and Indigenous Sovereignty* (Minnesota, 2015) and *Talkin' Up to the White Woman: Aboriginal Women and Feminism*.

**STEVEN NEWCOMB** (Shawnee/Lenape) is the Indigenous law research coordinator at the Sycuan education department of the Sycuan band of the Kumeyaay Nation in San Diego County, California; the cofounder and codirector of the Indigenous Law Institute; a fellow with the American Indian Policy and Media Initiative at Buffalo State College; and a columnist for *Indian Country Today*.

He is author of *Pagans in the Promised Land: Decoding the Doctrine of Christian Discovery.*

**JEAN M. O'BRIEN** (White Earth Ojibwe) is author of *Firsting and Lasting: Writing Indians out of Existence in New England* (Minnesota, 2010) and *Dispossession by Degrees: Indian Land and Identity in Natick, Massachusetts, 1650–1790.* She coedited *Recognition, Sovereignty Struggles, and Indigenous Rights in the United States.* Her forthcoming book (with Lisa M. Blee) is *Monumental Mobility: The Memory Work of Massasoit.* She is Distinguished McKnight University Professor of History and American Studies at the University of Minnesota.

**JONATHAN KAMAKAWIWO'OLE OSORIO** (Kanaka Maoli) is associate professor at the Kamakakūokalani Center for Hawaiian Studies, University of Hawai'i at Mānoa, and author of *Dismembering Lāhui: A History of the Hawaiian Nation to 1887.* He is a composer and singer and has been a Hawaiian music recording artist since 1975.

**STEVEN SALAITA** is author of numerous books, including *The Holy Land in Transit: Colonialism and the Quest for Canaan; Israel's Dead Soul; Uncivil Rites: Palestine and the Limits of Academic Freedom;* and *Inter/Nationalism: Decolonizing Native America and Palestine* (Minnesota, 2016). He is an independent scholar who held the position of Edward W. Said Chair of American Studies at the American University of Beirut from 2015 to 2017.

**PAUL CHAAT SMITH** (Comanche) is author of *Everything You Know about Indians Is Wrong* (Minnesota, 2009) and coauthor of *Like a Hurricane: The Indian Movement from Alcatraz to Wounded Knee* (with Robert Warrior). He is associate curator at the National Museum of the American Indian.

**CIRCE STURM** (Mississippi Choctaw descendant) is associate professor of anthropology and codirector of the Native American and Indigenous studies program at the University of Texas at Austin. She is author of *Blood Politics: Race, Culture, and Identity in the Cherokee Nation of Oklahoma* and *Becoming Indian: The Struggle over Cherokee Identity in the Twenty-first Century.*

**MARGO TAMEZ** (Ndé Konitsaaiigokiyaa'en) is cofounder of Lipan Apache Women Defense/Strength. She is associate professor in the Department of Community, Culture, and Global Studies at the University of British Columbia, Okanagan. She is the author of two literary publications, including *Raven Eye.*

**CHIEF RICHARD VELKY** (Schaghticoke) is leader of the Schaghticoke Tribal Nation. In 1987 he was elected chief by the voting tribal members and continues to serve the tribe in that capacity. He served in the U.S. Navy from 1968 to 1971, when he was honorably discharged. He began his political leadership with the tribe by serving as chairman of the tribe's Housing Authority Committee in 1975; he later served on the tribal council and then as vice-chairman.

**ROBERT WARRIOR** (Osage Nation) is author or coauthor of several books, including *The People and the Word: Reading Native Nonfiction* (Minnesota, 2005), *American Indian Literary Nationalism* (with Craig Womack and Jace Weaver); *Like a Hurricane: The Indian Movement from Alcatraz to Wounded Knee* (with Paul Chaat Smith); and *Tribal Secrets: Recovering American Indian Intellectual Traditions* (Minnesota, 1994). He is Hall Distinguished Professor of American Literature and Culture at the University of Kansas.

**PATRICK WOLFE** (1949–2016), one of the premier scholars of settler colonialism, was a Charles La Trobe Research Fellow in the history department at La Trobe University in Australia. His books include *Settler Colonialism and the Transformation of Anthropology* and *Traces of History: Elementary Structures of Race.* He also edited *The Settler Complex: Recuperating Binarism in Colonial Studies.*